Contemporary Issues in Resource Management

Stephen Taylor

Stephen Taylor is Senior Lecturer at Manchester Metropolitan University Business School and the CIPD's chief examiner for the Leading, Managing and Developing People paper.

The Chartered Institute of Personnel and Development is the leading
publisher of books and reports for personnel and training professionals,
students, and all those concerned with the effective management and
development of people at work. For details of all our titles, please contact
the publishing department:
tel: 020 8612 6204
email: publish@cipd.co.uk
The catalogue of all CIPD titles can be viewed on the CIPD website:
www.cipd.co.uk/bookstore

Contemporary Issues in Human Resource Management

Stephen Taylor

Chartered Institute of Personnel and Development

Published by the Chartered Institute of Personnel and Development,
151, The Broadway, London, SW19 1JQ

This edition first published 2011

Typeset by Fakenham Prepress Solutions, Fakenham, Norfolk NR21 8NN

Printed in Malta by Gutenberg Press Ltd.

British Library Cataloguing in Publication Data
A catalogue of this publication is available from the British Library

ISBN 978 1 84398 058 2

The views expressed in this publication are the author's own and may not necessarily reflect those of the CIPD.

The CIPD has made every effort to trace and acknowledge copyright holders. If any source has been overlooked, CIPD Enterprises would be pleased to redress this in future editions.

Chartered Institute of Personnel and Development, CIPD House,
151 The Broadway, London, SW19 1JQ

Tel: 020 8612 6200

Email: cipd@cipd.co.uk

Website: www.cipd.co.uk

Incorporated by Royal Charter

Registered Charity No. 1079797

MIX
Paper from
responsible sources

FSC
www.fsc.org FSC® C022612

The paper used for this book is FSC-certified and totally chlorine-free. FSC (the Forest Stewardship Council) is an international network to promote responsible management of the world's forests.

Contents

LIST OF FIGURES AND TABLES   ix

WALKTHROUGH OF TEXTBOOK FEATURES AND ONLINE RESOURCES   x

Chapter 1   Introduction   1
              Learning outcomes   2
              Contemporary trends: towards a new HR?   3
              Future agendas   10
              Key learning points   13
              Explore further   14
              References   14

Chapter 2   Competition and choice   15
              Introduction   15
              Learning outcomes   15
              Competitive intensity   16
              Financialisation   27
              The impact of increased competitive intensity   29
              Key learning points   30
              Explore further   30
              References   30

Chapter 3   People and skills   32
              Introduction   32
              Learning outcomes   33
              Demand for people   34
              Supply of people   36
              Demand for skills   45
              Supply of skills   49
              The hourglass metaphor   52
              Key learning points   53
              Explore further   54
              References   54

Chapter 4   Regulation and public policy   57
              Introduction   57
              Learning outcomes   58
              A regulatory revolution   58
              Contemporary debates   63
              Likely future developments   68

	The wider public policy agenda	71
	Key learning points	77
	Explore further	77
	References	78
Chapter 5	Social trends	79
	Introduction	79
	Learning outcomes	80
	Affluence and inequality	81
	Individualism	92
	Ethical awareness	102
	Key learning points	107
	Explore further	108
	References	108
Chapter 6	Flexibility and change	112
	Introduction	112
	Learning outcomes	114
	Change management	114
	Managing the consequences of change	124
	Flexible working	127
	Conclusions	133
	Key learning points	134
	Explore further	134
	References	135
Chapter 7	Competing for people	136
	Introduction	136
	Learning outcomes	137
	Reward	137
	Employer branding	147
	Labour market segmentation	152
	Key learning points	155
	Explore further	156
	References	156
Chapter 8	Managing expectations	159
	Introduction	159
	Learning outcomes	159
	Hopes and expectations	160
	Expectancy theory	164
	Equity theory	166
	Psychological contracts	168
	Managing expectations in practice	173
	Are expectations changing?	176

	Key learning points	177
	Explore further	178
	References	178
Chapter 9	**Engaging people**	**181**
	Introduction	181
	Learning outcomes	182
	Defining engagement	182
	Current interest in engagement	184
	Benefits for employees	186
	Benefits for employers	188
	Improving levels of employee engagement	191
	Criticisms of employee engagement initiatives	193
	Line management	195
	Key learning points	200
	Explore further	201
	References	201
Chapter 10	**Managing knowledge and learning**	**203**
	Introduction	203
	Learning outcomes	204
	Human capital	205
	Knowledge management	213
	Learning organisations	219
	Managing knowledge workers	222
	Key learning points	226
	Explore further	226
	References	226
Chapter 11	**Managing an international workforce**	**229**
	Introduction	229
	Learning outcomes	231
	Convergence and divergence	231
	Cultural differences	233
	Institutional differences	237
	Expatriates	240
	Culturally diverse teams	245
	Structural issues	247
	Key learning points	249
	Explore further	250
	References	250
Chapter 12	**Managing ethically**	**252**
	Introduction	252
	Learning outcomes	255

Ethical decision-making in HRM – theory   258
Ethical decision-making in HRM – practice   258
Equality and diversity   266
Key learning points   270
Explore further   270
References   271

Chapter 13   Developing HR strategies   273
Introduction   273
Learning outcomes   274
Alternative conceptions of HR strategy   274
Contingency models   278
Positioning an organisation in the labour market   282
Contemporary approaches to human resource planning   284
Key learning points   288
Explore further   288
References   289

Chapter 14   Managing the HR function   290
Introduction   290
Learning outcomes   290
Adding value   291
Outsourcing   292
Ulrich's models   294
Evaluating the HR contribution   297
Evaluation criteria   300
Evaluation methods   304
Cutting-edge approaches to evaluation   308
Key learning points   310
Explore further   311
References   311

INDEX   313

List of Figures and Tables

List of Figures

Figure 3.1 Jobs in the UK   35
Figure 3.2 Population structure: by age, sex and economic activity,
    autumn 2005   38
Figure 3.3 Percentage of the UK population born overseas   40
Figure 3.4 Recent trends in immigration and emigration   40
Figure 3.5 UK population projections in 2006   42
Figure 3.6 European fertility rates   43

Figure 5.1 Income distribution in the UK   84
Figure 5.2 Gini coefficient for equivalised disposable income in the UK   85
Figure 5.3 Trends in households, by household type (England)   99
Figure 5.4 Trends in the proportion of households that are single-person
    households in each age group (England)   100

Figure 6.1 Atkinson's model of the flexible firm   130

Figure 7.1 Four categories of reward   141

Figure 10.1 Typologies of human capital   211

Figure 13.1 Boston Consulting Group model   280
Figure 13.2 The Higgs model   283
Figure 13.3 External and internal labour market model   284

List of Tables

Table 3.1 Female participation rates   37
Table 3.2 Changes in occupations, 1951–1999   46
Table 3.3 Changes in occupations, 2001–2008   47

Table 5.1 UK GDP per capita   82
Table 5.2 Proportion of household income spent on different items   84
Table 5.3 Percentage of consumers claiming to have acted in one of the
    following ways 'at least once' during the year in question   104

Table 8.1 Job satisfaction   162

Table 12.1 Drivers of equality and diversity measures   267

Walkthrough of textbook features and online resources

LEARNING OUTCOMES

The objectives of this chapter are to:

- explain why organisations do not always have to pay wages at or above market rates in order to recruit and retain effectively
- introduce and discuss the concept of 'total reward' and its relevance for recruitment and retention in a resource-constrained environment
- assess the advantages and disadvantages associated with flexible benefits systems
- introduce and explain the concept of employer branding
- introduce and assess the prospects for contemporary ideas about labour market segmentation.

LEARNING OUTCOMES

At the beginning of each chapter a bulleted set of learning outcomes summarises what you can expect to learn from the chapter, helping you to track your progress.

CASE STUDY

From time to time attempts have been made to establish alternative methods of settling employment disputes which do not require a tribunal hearing.

The most recent has been the alternative process for determining unfair dismissal cases by arbitration that is offered by Acas (the Advisory, Conciliation and Arbitration Service). This option is available when both the claimant and the respondent choose to take it rather than to take the case to a full tribunal hearing. The scheme was launched in May 2001, but it has never been popular. In most years only a handful of cases are settled this way.

Questions

Why do you think the Acas alternative arbitration route is so rarely taken by the parties to an unfair dismissal dispute?

What would be the major advantages and disadvantages of a system which required many disputes to be settled via arbitration rather than at a full tribunal hearing?

CASE STUDIES

A range of case studies illustrate how key ideas and theories are operating in practice, with accompanying questions or activities.

CRITICAL REFLECTION

Linda Holbeche (2003) conducted a most interesting research project that looked in detail at how politics are played in organisations. Among her many findings was an apparent difference between the genders in terms of their approach to playing politics in organisations. The findings included the following:

- Men are more likely than women to admit to enjoying organisational politics.
- Women are more likely than men to respond by making a case in support of their position.

CRITICAL REFLECTION

These boxes contain interesting examples, questions and activities designed to get you reflecting on what you have just read and to test your understanding of important concepts and issues.

BIRMINGHAM CITY COUNCIL

Read the article by Anat Arkin entitled 'The Best Policy' featured in *People Management* (1 January 2009). This can be downloaded from the *People Management* archive on the CIPD website (www.cipd.co.uk).

In this article Anat Arkin reports on how a series of engagement initiatives championed by managers at Birmingham City Council failed to have much impact, until one called 'Best' was launched in 2006. This one, unlike the others, has improved staff perceptions of their employer and also those of key client groups.

Questions

1 What was the key difference between the approach taken in launching 'Best' and other less successful initiatives?

2 What unconventional features of the initiative might account for its relative success?

KEY ARTICLES

Current and thought-provoking academic articles from a range of sources encourage in-depth analysis and critical thinking, with accompanying questions or activities.

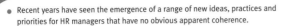

KEY LEARNING POINTS

- Recent years have seen the emergence of a range of new ideas, practices and priorities for HR managers that have no obvious apparent coherence.

- It is possible to argue that we are witnessing the evolution of a distinct new stage in the historical development of people management practice. Some writers and commentators have adopted the term *the new HR* to describe this trajectory.

- The new HR is characterised by a need to manage within and around environmental constraints such as tighter labour market conditions, increased regulation and the rise of ethical awareness on the part of organisational stakeholders.

- A further key contemporary business trend which is affecting HR practice is increased competitive intensity.

- It can be plausibly argued that the key professional debates that will dominate the next 20 years in HRM will derive from the interplay between these various environmental developments.

KEY LEARNING POINTS

At the end of each chapter, a bulleted list of the key learning points summarises the chapter and pulls out the most important points for you to remember.

EXPLORE FURTHER

Stephen Bach's introductory chapter in the 4th edition of his book *Managing human resources: personnel management in transition* (2005) provides a useful explanation of thinking about the key current trends in HR practice.

Bach, S. (2005) Personnel management in transition. In S. Bach (ed.) *Managing human resources: personnel management in transition*. 4th edition. Oxford: Blackwell Publishing.

You will also find a number of useful articles on long-term developments in HRM in *Reinventing HRM*, edited by Ronald J. Burke and Cary Cooper (2005).

Burke, R.J. and Cooper, C. (eds) (2005) *Reinventing HRM: challenges and new directions*. London: Routledge.

Lynda Gratton's recent book entitled *The shift: the future of work is already here* (2011) is an enjoyable and accessible read about environmental developments and how they will shape the experience of work in the future.

Gratton, L. (2011) *The shift: the future of work is already here*. London: Collins.

EXPLORE FURTHER

Explore further boxes contain suggestions for further reading and useful websites, encouraging you to delve further into areas of particular interest.

ONLINE RESOURCES FOR TUTORS

- PowerPoint slides – design your programme around these ready-made lectures
- Lecturer's Guide – including guidance on the activities and questions in the text

ONLINE RESOURCES FOR STUDENTS

- Annotated web-links – access a wealth of useful sources of information in order to develop your understanding of the issues in the text
- Multiple-choice questionnaires – these will test your knowledge of the chapters and help you revise

For Student and Tutor Online resources, visit: www.cipd.co.uk/olr
or scan the QR code on the back cover using your Smartphone

CHAPTER 1

Introduction

During the first decade of the twenty-first century, human resource management (HRM) thinking and practice have evolved in significant new directions. Issues and approaches that were previously seen in many organisations as being peripheral have moved to centre stage as HR agendas have been adjusted to take account of developments in the business environment. Hence we have seen much more interest in work–life balance issues, in HR ethics, partnership agreements and in the formal evaluation and measurement of HR practices. Ideas developed in the 1990s have moved from 'fringe' or 'fad' status to occupying a pivotal role in many organisations' HR strategies. This is true of employer branding, the use of balanced scorecards, the fostering of positive psychological contracts, the provision of flexible benefits and the range of activities collectively comprising 'e-HR'. Older, more-established approaches have been reconfigured and often relabelled to make them fit for purpose in the contemporary world. *Workforce planning* has thus been reinvented as *talent management*, *pay administration* has metamorphosed into *total reward management*, *equal opportunities* has become *diversity management*, while terms such as *coaching*, *mentoring*, *competencies* and *business partnering* have been accorded specific definitions in our professional vocabulary. We have also seen the emergence of some genuinely new areas of research and practice, such as strengths-based performance management, formal strategies aimed at fostering well-being and happiness at work and the evolving employee engagement agenda. At the same time we have seen a substantial increase in the amount of regulation to which the employment relationship is subject, the emergence of skills shortages across a range of occupations and additional pressure both to intensify work and to increase levels of employee commitment. Last, but not least, we have seen the development of a situation in which the need to adapt, evolve and restructure is a constant presence in many organisations. Whereas change used to be episodic in nature, it has for many become endemic, with major implications for the way we carry out HRM.

There are two major purposes behind this book. The first is to focus on these major contemporary issues and ideas in HRM, to explain their significance, assess some of the research that has been carried out into them, debate their advantages and disadvantages and seek to understand their implications for HR practice. In addition, the book aims to explore *why* this apparently diverse range of unconnected ideas and practices have come to prominence in recent years. While the bulk of the later chapters are focused on the key recent developments and emerging issues themselves, the early part seeks to put forward a coherent explanation for their rise rooted in an analysis of key, longer-term trends in the HR business environment. Not only does an analysis of this kind enable us to explain why the HR agenda has evolved in recent years in the way that it has, but it also provides a good basis for thinking usefully about its likely future direction. It is this feature which makes the book distinct from others. By focusing on the future as well as the present, it aims to help prepare you for a future career in HRM. In short, an attempt will be made to answer the following question:

● What will be the major issues and problems that are likely to shape HR work during the coming 20 years?

LEARNING OUTCOMES

The objectives of this chapter are to:

● place contemporary developments in HRM in historical context

● explain how current HR priorities differ from those that prevailed 20 or 30 years ago

● put the case in favour of the proposition that we are seeing the emergence of a distinct new era in the evolution of people management practice

● discuss the major environmental constraints that increasingly influence HR practice in organisations

● assess the likely future direction of HRM practice

● set out the key questions that are likely to dominate HR thinking and debate over the next 20 years.

KEY ARTICLE

WORKFORCE WAKE-UP CALL

2006 saw the publication of a book of articles by a variety of writers, consultants and researchers working in the field of HRM called *Workforce Wake-Up Call: Your workforce is changing, are you?* Addressed to a senior management audience, the book looks at key trends in the contemporary business environment and makes judgements about how the world of work and people management is likely to evolve and change in the coming decades in Western industrialised countries. In their introduction the editors sum up the key messages. Their conclusion begins as follows:

The workforce is in the midst of an unstoppable and dramatic transformation. In the coming years, organizations will confront challenges related to demographic trends, global mobility, diversity, work/life issues, technology changes and a virtual workforce. Competition will be global; capital will be abundant; leaders will be developed swiftly; and talented people will be keen to change jobs frequently. These changes will influence how work is performed, where it is performed and what

skills are required. While other resources will be abundant, the most important resource of all – talent – will become increasingly scarce. Organizations must ask themselves: Are we prepared for this global workforce revolution? Do we have the right strategies in place? (Gandossy et al 2006: xxiii).

Questions

1 How far do you agree with the view that in the future all the resources that organisations draw on will be 'abundant' with the exception of talent? What arguments could be advanced against this point of view?

2 Why should leaders be developed any more swiftly in the future than they are now?

3 Why should people be any keener to switch jobs in the future than they are now?

4 Thinking about your own organisation, how relevant are these points? What might be 'the right strategies' to adopt in order to prepare for the future?

CONTEMPORARY TRENDS: TOWARDS A NEW HR?

Throughout its history the profession or management function – now commonly titled 'human resource management' (HRM) and previously known as 'personnel management' – has evolved in definable new directions every 20 or 30 years (see Torrington et al 2011: 10–14). In its earliest incarnation more than 100 years ago, it was focused primarily on improving the welfare of workers in factories, down mines and on docks and shipyards. Some employers began to realise that they could secure greater loyalty, commitment and productivity if they looked after the interests of their workforce by providing a healthy, safe workplace and by providing paid holiday, sick pay and even subsidised housing. Between the two World Wars – as professional, white-collar work became more common and as the state welfare system started to develop – the focus shifted to improving efficiency with the application of scientific management and organisation design principles of the kind advanced by F.W. Taylor and Henri Fayol. Organisations became more bureaucratic and mechanistic, with clearly defined grading structures and a preference for recruiting people at a relatively young age with a view to promoting them over time. Workforce planning, occupational pensions and extensive staff rulebooks were introduced, as management became less personal. The profession then shifted gear again after the Second World War, as the trade union movement grew in strength, requiring personnel managers to negotiate new initiatives and to manage often difficult industrial relations disputes.

The last major change occurred in the 1980s with the emergence of the term *human resource management* signalling not just new rhetoric, but also significant new thinking on the part of managers. At the time much effort was expended debating what exactly 'HRM' was and how it differed from 'personnel management' – a debate that was never really satisfactorily concluded before the mainstream research agenda moved on to focus on establishing how and to what extent HR practices contribute to the achievement of organisational performance (see Guest 1987, Legge 1995, Sisson and Storey 2000). In retrospect, however, it is possible to see the evolution of HRM in the 1980s and 1990s very much as a response on the part of management to the sharp decline in trade union membership and influence that occurred at that time as a result of regulatory changes, increased individualism, the decline of traditional industries and the growth of the service sector. Over quite a short period of time managers found themselves firmly in the driving seat and in control of the direction of people management in their organisations. Particularly important was the demolition during the 1980s, at least in the private sector, of the established national-level collective bargaining system. Terms and conditions were no longer set for employers by a body negotiating with unions on their behalf for a whole industry. Bargaining was decentralised, and in many cases gave way altogether to a situation in which pay and conditions were determined by management without any need to negotiate with anyone at all. Power thus shifted sharply in many organisations towards management, high levels of unemployment and low levels of employment security reducing both the ability and willingness of employees to resist. Donkin (2001) neatly sums up the result as follows:

> Like an improved soap powder with a biological ingredient, HRM, equipped with something called strategy, promised a new set of tools and measures to reward, motivate and organise employees in the re-engineered workplace.

For a generation managers had been seriously constrained in terms of how they approached the people-related aspects of their activities. Now they had an opportunity to take control and shape approaches that were appropriate for their own organisations' particular circumstances. HR strategies were developed, new individualised pay arrangements introduced, formal performance appraisal systems established and competency frameworks defined. Employers also seized the opportunity to employ people more flexibly, establishing more part-time and temporary jobs, outsourcing 'non-core' activities to external providers and abolishing long-established lines of demarcation which determined where one group of workers' duties ended and another's began. At the same time new methods of relating to workers had to be established to replace union consultation and negotiation arrangements, so we saw the spread of a range of new involvement and communication initiatives along with a preference for single-table or single-union bargaining in circumstances where trade unions retained an influence. In short, HRM can largely be explained as a response on the part of organisations to a newfound freedom to manage their workforces in the way that they wanted to. Fewer compromises had to be made, allowing decisions to be made and strategies to be established which operated exclusively in the long-term interests of organisations.

The question that researchers and commentators are now starting to ask is whether or not, 30 years on, we are beginning to see the evolution of another new pathway in the historical development of 'people management'? Can we yet announce the arrival of a distinctly new era with any confidence, and if so, how can it be characterised and what should it be labelled?

The answer is that a credible argument can be put in favour of the proposition, but that it is too early to conclude with great confidence that we are entering a period which is clearly distinct from the 'HRM era' described above. Much will depend on the fate of the world economy over the next few years. At the time of writing (early 2011) the UK economy, along with those of most countries, is slowly recovering from a deep recession. As a result, we have seen a reversal of some key trends in HRM practice and thinking which had taken root and become established during the boom years of the 1990s and 2000s. If things follow the pattern of the two recessions we witnessed in the early 1980s and early 1990s, we will see a return to economic growth fairly quickly and a reasonably swift resumption of the earlier, established long-term trends. If this turns out to be the case, it is likely that we will soon be able to herald the arrival of a distinctly new period in the development of HRM. Alternatively, and much less agreeably, recessionary conditions could last for much longer, perhaps even leading to a prolonged period of sluggish economic performance as occurred in the 1930s. Were that to be the case the key recent long-term trends that established themselves 30 years ago would reverse. This might well herald a new direction in the development of people management, but it would in all likelihood simply point to the re-establishment of the kind of approaches first brought into being in the early 1980s and labelled 'HRM'.

However, let us assume for now that the first prognosis turns out to be fulfilled, that the economy recovers reasonably swiftly and that the long-term established trends in our business environment resume again. If this turns out to be the case, it will soon be common for HR thinkers and leaders to proclaim the establishment of a clearly defined, new trajectory. It is on this premise that some of the thinking behind this book is largely based.

The term *the new HRM* has been adopted by some in recent years to describe collectively some significant recent developments in professional thinking and practice. It is commonly used in the HR press and has also now found its way into books and articles authored by academic writers (see Price and Walker 1999, Bach 2005, Boroughs et al 2008). There is little coherent agreement about what the term means but it is a convenient label for a new trajectory which retains many features of HRM as established in the 1980s, yet is fundamentally distinct in key respects. More pretentious terms which could well end up being used in the academic community might be 'post-HRM' or even 'HRM 2.0' (both have been used from time to time), but for the purposes of this chapter we will stick with 'new HRM' simply because it has already been used quite widely.

So what is it that distinguishes 'the new HR' from HRM in the form it was established during the 1980s and 1990s? The short, concise answer is that the new HR operates under significant constraints of a type that were not present when HRM originally emerged and became established during the last two decades of the twentieth century. Three are of particular significance:

1 **Tight labour markets:** The first eight years of the new century saw labour markets tighten very considerably. While the supply of would-be employees remained larger than the demand for them in one or two areas of work and in some areas of the country, skills shortages emerged in most industries and began to dominate the HR agenda before recessionary conditions arrived in 2008 and the economy began to contract. Recruitment and retention thus moved to the top of the agenda in most HR departments as organisations struggled to source the people they needed. Importantly, the evolution of tight labour markets meant that skilled employees who were dissatisfied with their work, their organisations or, most commonly, their managers, could find alternative work with some ease. In a tight labour market this reality gives employees a degree of power and hence influence over the nature of managerial decisions which affect them.

2 **Regulation:** Since the 1990s the amount of regulation governing the employment relationship in the UK, as well as in other EU countries, has increased very markedly. Areas of employment which were completely free of regulation prior to this period, such as age discrimination, have been regulated for the first time, while others, where light-touch approaches were the norm previously, are now far more closely regulated. Disability discrimination and maternity rights are two prominent examples. As a result the number of employment tribunal claims lodged each year has increased very significantly indeed, reflecting an increased propensity on the part of aggrieved employees to seek redress in the courts.

3 **The nature of the jobs we do:** Increasingly in recent years demand for labour has been focused on higher-paid, higher-skilled jobs of a professional, managerial or technically sophisticated kind. Job-holders in these roles are well educated and typically have greater knowledge about their work than the people who manage the organisation. As a result, if they are wise, managers are required to take account of their employees' views and have increasingly found it necessary to involve them in decision-making. Moreover, because there is much truth in the saying 'knowledge is power', professional and managerial staff are well placed to resist attempts by managers to impose decisions on them with which they disagree.

In addition, there is another form of constraint which has had an impact, although as yet it has been of a good deal less practical significance than the first three:

4 **Ethical awareness:** Consumers, investors and job-seekers, particularly those who are from the younger generations, have started demonstrating both increasing awareness of ethical matters and also a willingness to take ethical considerations into account when making decisions about what goods and services to buy, where to put their savings and which organisations they seek to work for. As a result, organisations have begun to embrace 'corporate social responsibility', have actively sought to develop a reputation for ethical conduct and have tried to associate leading brands with ethical values. In the main the nature of ethical awareness has focused on green matters and on fair trade, but there are significant examples of concern spreading into the HR field, notably in respect of the working conditions established by multinational corporations operating in developing countries.

We will look in detail at these developments, as well as others in the business environment which are shaping the contemporary HR agenda, in Chapters 2, 3, 4 and 5. For now it is simply necessary to establish that together their impact has been to constrain the freedom of manoeuvre enjoyed by HR managers, thus restricting the extent to which decision-making can be taken uniquely in the interests of organisations and their shareholders. As a result there has been a change in what is generally considered to constitute 'effective HR practice'. In the 1980s and 1990s the dominant idea was that the prime role of the HR manager was to develop HR strategies which aimed to help 'deliver' the organisation's strategic objectives. The starting point was thus a clear understanding of the organisation's aims and priorities. An HR strategy would then be developed and implemented, organisational strategy being 'translated' accordingly into HR practice. There is nothing at all wrong with this approach – and in Chapter 13 you will find examples which set out the thinking behind it – but it can only be the focus of professional HR practice in circumstances in which managers are free to implement such strategies without substantial constraint. In other words, there is an assumption behind it that putting the defined HR strategy into practice will be unproblematic. During the first decade of the twenty-first century it became increasingly apparent that this is by no means the case. Constraints of the kind set out above have loomed ever larger, acting singly or in combination to restrict the capacity of the HR function simply to deliver objectives which underpin the organisation's long-term strategy. Major compromises are increasingly required.

We can therefore usefully conceptualise the distinction between the HRM era and that of 'the new HR' as being concerned with the priorities of the HR function and of HR work. Helping to deliver organisational objectives remains present in the 'new HR', but there are more fundamental matters to focus on first. Key is the need to ensure that the organisation has at its disposal the human resources it needs in order to function at all. Effective recruitment, retention and employee development are thus the prime concerns. The staff, once assembled, then have to be motivated and encouraged to perform at the highest achievable level. Thirdly, the function needs to manage the employment relationship (when seen from the perspective of both employer and employee) in an efficient and fair manner. Such is necessary if it is to gain and maintain a reputation as an effective, and indeed an ethical, manager of people.

As a result of the need to manage HR with these constraints, we are seeing the development of thinking and of approaches which are clearly different from those associated with HRM in the 1980s and 1990s. The most striking and significant is the increased tendency of HR functions to use language and ideas associated with customer relationships when talking about employees. It has for example become common for HR managers to refer to employees, as well as to line managers, as 'our internal customers', the implication being that the purpose of a well-run contemporary HR function is to provide a service to a client group which specifically includes employees. Moving on from this we are seeing a pronounced increased interest in undertaking staff attitude, satisfaction and engagement surveys, the purpose being to measure and track over time the perceptions of employees towards the organisation and its managers. Signs of growing dissatisfaction are then investigated and action taken to try to secure improved ratings the following year. HR practices are becoming increasingly employee-focused in other ways too. We can point, for example, to increased interest in and use of 360-degree appraisal systems in which staff are involved formally in providing feedback on performance to their peers and bosses. Further evidence comes from the increased use of self-managed teams, of flexible benefits systems which allow employees to determine the make-up of their own pay packages and of payment systems which link remuneration to the achievement of objectives which are agreed ahead of time between managers and staff. Finally, and most interestingly of all, HR managers are increasingly borrowing ideas long used by colleagues in the marketing function and applying them to the labour market. Employer branding is the most prominent of these (see Chapter 7), but we can also point to job sculpting (designing jobs around the preferences and qualifications of individuals) and to approaches which 'segment' staff into groups and design employment experiences around their perceived needs and aspirations.

One way of summing up this group of trends in HR practice is to argue that 'the new HR' is as concerned with effectively competing in the labour market as it is with supporting the efforts of the organisation in competing in the product market. It has to be – because if it does not, it will not deliver to the organisation the pool of human resources necessary to enable it to function at all.

RESOURCE DEPENDENCY THEORY

It is helpful in this context to draw on the ideas that underpin 'resource dependency theory' (see Hatch 1997). Adherents of this theory focus on the extent to which organisations rely on a variety of different 'sources of dependence', the main examples being labour, capital, raw materials, knowledge, plant and equipment, and a market for their products and services. These sources of dependence vary in terms of how critical they are to the organisation's success or survival and in terms of how scarce they are at any one time. The more critical and scarce a source of dependence becomes, the more attention the organisation must pay to it in order to ensure that it can continue to benefit from its supply, and the less freedom of manoeuvre managers enjoy in carrying out their job. Hence where an organisation is heavily reliant on one or two large customers, it is in a situation of high resource-dependence. Customers are relatively scarce and each is utterly critical to the organisation's future. Satisfying those customers becomes a priority. By contrast an organisation which has many thousands of customers is in a wholly different position. Customers are neither scarce nor, as individuals, critical. If one is dissatisfied and takes their business to a competitor it is a matter of concern, but it is not hugely damaging to the organisation. In such an environment individual customers inevitably have less power over how the organisation manages its relationship with them. The same analysis can be carried out in respect of access to financial capital (the more critical and scarce the more influence the provider of the capital has over the organisation), raw materials and any other potential source of dependence.

Resource dependency theory is useful as a means of explaining recent developments in HR because of these concepts of 'criticality' and 'scarcity'. In short, we can plausibly argue that in recent years, until the recent recession reversed trends somewhat, employees (as a source of dependence) became both more critical and more scarce. They became more critical because the jobs we are looking to fill increasingly require people who are more skilled, highly educated and experienced. Each individual's contribution to the achievement of the organisation's objectives is thus more significant. When they leave they are harder and more costly to replace with a satisfactory successor, not least because they walk away with a great deal of knowledge in their heads which it is going to take a successor some time to build up. The departure of such employees is thus damaging to the organisation, and indeed doubly so if they go on to work for a competitor and to deploy their knowledge and experience against the interests of the organisation. In short, the more skilled, qualified and experienced job-holders are required to be, the more critical each is from an organisation's perspective.

Over the long term, too, employees have become increasingly scarce. While this trend was interrupted to a degree by the onset of recession, there is no question that over a long period now many labour markets have become steadily tighter. Mainly because the skills that are in most demand are more specialised and higher-level in nature, the size of potential applicant pools has declined. Hence, in recent years we have seen a great deal of overseas recruitment, the development of a 'war for talent' between organisations seeking the best-qualified staff, the growth of headhunting agents and many examples of organisations seeking to position themselves in the labour market as 'employers of choice'.

In short, the first years of the twenty-first century saw a situation develop in which employees have started to become both increasingly critical and increasingly scarce, ratcheting up the degree to which organisations are dependent on securing their services. Arguably this can be seen as a fundamental change and is central to any understanding of 'a new HR'.

CRITICAL REFLECTION

Think about the recent experience of your own organisation. How far is it true in its case to state that employees are becoming 'increasingly critical' to its operations? How far is it true to state that would-be employees are becoming increasingly scarce?

FUTURE AGENDAS

Above I argued that we have seen a clear and decisive move towards 'a new HR' in recent years as a result of the rise of a knowledge-based economy, of tighter labour markets, increased regulation and increased ethical awareness. The big question for the future is, will this be sustainable? Is the 'new HR' as we have defined it here to stay for the long term, or are the trends that have brought it into being likely to cease, slow down or reverse direction?

The answer depends in part on the extent to which the economy is able to recover fully from the recent downturn. If recovery is strong and the longer-term trends are re-established, the answer will be 'yes'. If, by contrast, we enter a lengthy period of international depression, with high levels of unemployment for many years, a contraction in international trade and reduced demand for human resources, the answer will be 'no'. In these circumstances HRM will have to alter its orientation, but it will be in a wholly different direction from that of 'the new HR' as defined in this chapter.

It is important to introduce this caveat at the start of this section to make it clear that this book is not intended to be a work of prophecy. Its purpose is not to set out a vision of the future of HRM that *will* be fulfilled. Instead, one of its core aims is to speculate in an informed manner about how the future of HRM in the UK is most likely to pan out if these acknowledged, long-term trends in our business environment do continue to develop along their established lines in the future.

In the above discussion about 'the new HR' a number of these key contemporary trends were introduced. Each of those discussed so far is further explored in the chapters which follow, along with an assessment of its likely future impact on HRM. However, one further contemporary trend of major significance has not yet been discussed. It will form the focus of Chapter 2, but needs to be introduced at this stage as it is fundamental to any credible assessment of the future direction of HRM. This is increasing competitive intensity.

Over a long period now, in both the public and the private sectors, organisations have been faced, year on year, with increased competition from other providers. This trend is partly due to the globalisation of world economic activity, partly due to the rapid advance of technological developments in recent years, partly due to government policy aimed at increasing 'competition and choice', and partly due to increased customer expectations and a greater willingness on their part to switch suppliers or brands when they are unhappy with the quality or price of the product or service they are receiving. Moreover, it has not just been customers who have become increasingly demanding. The situation has been exacerbated by the increased tendency of shareholders to demand higher and faster returns on their investment. Markets for capital have become much more competitive as well as markets for goods and services.

The result is a situation in which organisations are obliged to compete harder in order to survive and prosper, leading to a situation in which pressure is placed on employees to work much more productively and efficiently. Aside from intensifying work in this way, increased competitive intensity has other significant effects too:

- Employers are required to rationalise, restructure and reorganise much more frequently. Mergers, demergers, acquisitions, sell-offs, outsourcing and downsizing exercises are thus more common than in the past. This means that HR managers are having to focus more than they did in the past on the effective management of major change episodes.

- Increased competitive intensity has brought with it increased volatility. As a result business is a great deal less predictable than it used to be. The time horizons in which we can plan with any degree of certainty have declined, while insecurity has become a good deal more common.

- The harder we are required to compete for business with others, the more important good HRM becomes. This is because those organisations which are most effective at recruiting, retaining and motivating a committed and productive workforce are better able to compete successfully than those who are less effective in these areas.

- A greater premium is placed on efficiency. Cost control becomes more important the more intense the competitive environment because price is one of the most significant determinants of which organisation secures business.

When thinking about the likely future evolution of HRM over the coming 10 to 20 years we need to take account of increasing competitive intensity alongside the further development of the other key trends we have identified, such as tighter labour market conditions, increased regulation of the employment relationship, the changing nature of the work we are employed to do and the rise of greater ethical awareness. The central argument of this book is that it is the *interplay* of these various trends that will determine the future character of the HR function in organisations, of HR priorities and the key problems that future HR professionals will have to grapple with.

So what does this kind of analysis suggest will be the key preoccupations of HR managers as the next two decades unfold? What will be the major professional issues that they will have to try to resolve? The following are likely to be the major questions that will need to be addressed and hence the defining issues faced by HR managers in coming years:

1 **How can an organisation compete for staff when its labour markets are tightening and its environment is increasingly resource-constrained?**

This may very well turn out to be the most significant question faced by HR managers in coming decades. What may develop is something of a 'perfect storm' in which people with the required skills and experience are in ever shorter supply, but at the same time due to increased competitive intensity organisations are less and less able to respond by paying recruits higher salaries.

2 **How can an organisation become more flexible and responsive to change while also successfully recruiting, retaining and motivating committed employees?**

This is another fundamental issue that could very well preoccupy HR managers in the years ahead. On the one hand, a capacity for flexibility is going to become increasingly significant in order for organisations to compete successfully in volatile and unpredictable market conditions. On the other hand, maximising flexibility is incompatible with the need to mobilise and motivate a highly committed workforce because it brings with it insecurity. Yet the nature of the work that we will increasingly be carrying out in the future will require committed staff.

3 **How can an organisation compete effectively, often in international markets, while also gaining and maintaining a reputation for high standards of ethics and legal compliance in its dealings with employees?**

This is another difficult issue to resolve. Increased competition makes it harder for organisations to survive and prosper. There is a need to keep a lid on costs and sometimes considerable temptation to cut corners in order to secure business. The extent to which it is possible to duck and dive sufficiently in order to maintain a competitive position while also adhering to high standards of employment practice – defined in ethical and legal terms – is questionable, particularly when international competitors are not required to maintain the same standards.

These three questions are not at all easy to answer. Moreover, of course, they can be answered in a number of very different ways. For these reasons they are likely to form the basis of the major professional debates in HRM that will evolve over the next few years. This book will not provide any easy answers, but readers will hopefully find it useful as a guide to the underlying issues and to some of the tools, techniques, ideas and theories that may be the basis of possible solutions.

CASE STUDY

Since the early 1980s the highly influential UK-based management guru Charles Handy, along with many others, has been predicting the arrival of a world of work in which most jobs are of a temporary nature. He has argued that in the future most people will progress through 'portfolio careers', moving from short-term assignment to short-term assignment, sometimes employed, other times in the capacity of a self-employed person. Long-term, stable employment for a single employer will become rare.

Handy's view has been much criticised in recent years, largely because he was predicting that these developments would be with us by the turn of the millennium. In practice, of course, the predictions proved to be faulty, making Handy and his ideas an easy target for critics. Long-term employment remains a reality for many, self-employment has become more common but is very much the preserve of a small minority, while job tenure rates have remained stable for many years. Handy himself, however, remains unrepentant and convinced that given time his vision of the future will turn out to be accurate.

Questions

1 Which environmental trends discussed in this chapter are compatible with Charles Handy's predictions and which are not?

2 To what extent do you agree with Charles Handy that portfolio careers will one day be the norm in countries such as the UK? Why?

KEY LEARNING POINTS

- Recent years have seen the emergence of a range of new ideas, practices and priorities for HR managers that have no obvious apparent coherence.

- It is possible to argue that we are witnessing the evolution of a distinct new stage in the historical development of people management practice. Some writers and commentators have adopted the term *the new HR* to describe this trajectory.

- The new HR is characterised by a need to manage within and around environmental constraints such as tighter labour market conditions, increased regulation and the rise of ethical awareness on the part of organisational stakeholders.

- A further key contemporary business trend which is affecting HR practice is increased competitive intensity.

- It can be plausibly argued that the key professional debates that will dominate the next 20 years in HRM will derive from the interplay between these various environmental developments.

EXPLORE FURTHER

Stephen Bach's introductory chapter in the 4th edition of his book *Managing human resources: personnel management in transition* (2005) provides a useful explanation of thinking about the key current trends in HR practice.

Bach, S. (2005) Personnel management in transition. In S. Bach (ed.) *Managing human resources: personnel management in transition*. 4th edition. Oxford: Blackwell Publishing.

You will also find a number of useful articles on long-term developments in HRM in *Reinventing HRM*, edited by Ronald J. Burke and Cary Cooper (2005).

Burke, R.J. and Cooper, C. (eds) (2005) *Reinventing HRM: challenges and new directions*. London: Routledge.

Lynda Gratton's recent book entitled *The shift: the future of work is already here* (2011) is an enjoyable and accessible read about environmental developments and how they will shape the experience of work in the future.

Gratton, L. (2011) *The shift: the future of work is already here*. London: Collins.

REFERENCES

Boroughs, A., Palmer, L. and Hunter, I. (2008) *HR transformation technology: delivering systems to support the new HR model*. Aldershot: Gower.

Donkin, R. (2001) A quiet revolution in human resource management. *Financial Times*. 16 August.

Gandossy, R., Tucker, E. and Verma, N. (eds) (2006) *Workforce wake-up call: your workforce is changing, are you?* Hoboken, NJ: Wiley.

Guest, D. (1987) Human resource management and industrial relations. *Journal of Management Studies*. Vol 24, No 5.

Hatch, M.J. (1997) *Organisation theory: modern symbolic and postmodern perspectives*. Oxford: Oxford University Press.

Legge, K. (1995) *Human resource management: rhetorics and realities*. London: Macmillan.

Price, K. and Walker, J. (1999) *The new HR: strategic positioning of the human resource function*. Chicago, IL: Human Resource Planning Society.

Sisson, K. and Storey, J. (2000) *The realities of human resource management: managing the employment relationship*. Buckingham: Open University Press.

Torrington, D., Hall, L., Taylor, S. and Atkinson, C. (2011) *Human resource management*. 8th edition. London: FT/Prentice Hall.

CHAPTER 2

Competition and choice

Introduction

The first major trend in the HR business environment that we need to examine and understand is the very significant growth we have witnessed over recent decades in the extent and intensity of competition between organisations. For many this is by far the most significant contemporary business trend and it is one that many commentators have found very difficult to welcome. Competitiveness has grown both in respect of product markets (ie markets for goods and services) and also, by extension, in the financial markets (ie gaining access to capital). As a result consumers have become more demanding and less loyal, while at the same time shareholders have placed managers under a great deal more pressure to ensure a swift and good return on their investments. While we may regret some of the consequences, there is every reason to expect that these pressures will continue in the future and that they will probably intensify further.

In this chapter we are going to explore the reasons why competitive intensity has increased so markedly over recent decades and to identify the major impact the trend has had on organisations and is likely to have in the future.

LEARNING OUTCOMES

The objectives of this chapter are to:

- explain how competitive intensity has increased over recent decades and shows every sign of continuing to increase in the future
- demonstrate how the globalisation of much economic activity serves to increase competition
- explain the role played by technological developments in increasing competitive intensity
- show how developments in governments' trade and industrial policies have also fuelled increased competitive intensity
- explore the impact of 'financialisation' on UK organisations and its causes
- set out the major ways in which HRM activity is increasingly being affected by increased competitive intensity.

COMPETITIVE INTENSITY

The extent of competitive intensity in any industry is difficult to measure in an accurate way. This is because there is no simple, straightforward calculation available which enables us to calculate the degree to which organisations face competitive pressures. Many economists use the Herfindahl index, which is a measure of industry concentration (ie the extent to which any one firm dominates a market), but this is widely acknowledged to be hugely unsatisfactory. Some of the most competitive global markets are dominated by two or three major players who fight fiercely with one another on a variety of fronts to maintain their relative market shares. Examples are the soft drinks industry, which is dominated by the PepsiCo and Coca-Cola companies, and the market for domestic detergents, which is dominated by Procter & Gamble and Unilever. Each of these companies produces numerous different brands and promotes them vigorously in order to differentiate itself. Competition could not be much more intense, and for that reason it is very difficult for any new producer to enter the fray. In other industries competition is less intense, despite the presence of numerous participants. Many other factors thus have to be taken into account.

In the absence of any simple measure, two other approaches tend to be used to establish the extent to which competition is increasing and becoming more intense:

1 We can use proxy measures. These are not in themselves indicators of competitive intensity, but they are associated with it. Each on its own proves little, but when several are examined collectively a compelling case can be made for the proposition that competition has intensified very significantly across most industries over the past 30 years. Examples of such proxy measures are the following:

   – reductions in the length of time leading firms are able to maintain dominance of a market
   – increases in the extent of churn in 'industry membership'
   – increases in the incidence of financial instability (among both established and newer entrants to a market)
   – increases in the length of time that episodes of financial instability last
   – increases in the extent to which a market is open to overseas competitors
   – increases in the number of small businesses/start-ups, and increases in their growth rates
   – increases in concentration ratios (ie the extent to which the top five or top ten companies in an industry contribute to its total output)
   – increases in the extent of 'discounting' – ie price reductions
   – decreases in 'perceived ability to increase prices' as measured in surveys of executives.

Studies that use these measures have found that while competitive conditions vary considerably from industry to industry (McNamara et al 2003), for most the commercial environment has become a great deal more competitive over the past 20 or 30 years. Indeed, in some industries, researchers claim that

a state of 'hyper-competition' has developed, making it impossible for any
organisation to achieve meaningful competitive advantage over others for any
length of time (see Wiggins and Ruefli 2005 and Thomas and D'Aveni 2009).

2 We can also make use of anecdotal evidence which involves asking managers
and others who have long experience of working in an industry what their
perceptions are of the competitive environment and how it is changing. Studies
of this kind invariably find that we have witnessed, at the very least, very
substantial increases in the *perceived* levels of competition across a range of
industries. Moreover, this is true of the public and voluntary sectors just as much
as it is of commercial sectors (eg Adcroft et al 2010, Chew and Osborne 2009).

Most studies into competitive intensity have a US focus, but there can be little
doubt that competitive pressures have increased in much the same way in the
UK too. This is a major theme in recent work on industrial relations in the
UK by Professor William Brown and his colleagues. They argue that increased
competitive intensity is one of the most significant, if not *the* most significant,
factor explaining the decline of collective bargaining in the UK over recent
decades. Drawing on data from successive Workplace Employment Relations
Surveys, while recognising that competitiveness varies from industry to industry,
they conclude as follows:

> All this confirms the intimate link between collective bargaining and
> the fortunes of the product markets within which it is conducted. Over
> our quarter century, collective bargaining has retreated fastest in those
> workplaces that, relative to others, were in product markets with particular
> competitive characteristics. Their workplaces faced more geographically
> local competition. They confronted more competitors. Their industries
> had lower profit levels. And their industries faced a relative worsening of
> profitability. The growth of collective bargaining in the twentieth century
> had been nurtured by imperfect competition. Tightening product market
> competition suffocated it.

We can only judge whether or not competition in markets for goods and services
will continue to intensify in future decades if we first gain an understanding of its
main causes. There are three major causes, which we will now look at in turn:

- the globalisation of product markets
- the pace of technological change
- government policy.

GLOBALISATION

The term *globalisation* is defined in a number of different ways. Some focus on its
cultural, social and political aspects, others on economic developments. For our
purposes in this chapter it is globalisation as an economic phenomenon which
we need to focus on. It is without doubt one of the most significant phenomena
of our times, transforming our economy and hence our lives to an extraordinary
degree.

Dicken (2011) sets out the size of the change that has occurred in recent decades. He explains that during the second half of the twentieth century, while total world output (ie the value of goods and services produced and consumed) increased six-fold, the volume of world trade increased twenty-fold. In other words, the proportion of goods and services that we traded across international boundaries increased at more than three times the rate that we produced them. He goes on to show that foreign direct investment (ie companies based in one country controlling assets based in others) increased at a faster pace than world trade. Since the early 1990s we have seen a significant acceleration of this long-term trend, largely as a result of the emergence of countries such as China, Russia, India and Brazil (the BRIC countries) as major participants in world trade. Between 2000 and 2007, the Indian economy grew by almost 8% each year and the Chinese economy by over 10%. Between them these two countries account for 40% of the world population, so the fast development of their economies is inevitably having a transformative effect on the world economy.

Globalisation inevitably has the effect of substantially increasing competitive intensity across a range of different industries. It means that UK-based firms that were once dominant players in a national market now find that they are small-fry in much larger international markets. Indeed, in many cases they have been subsumed into large multinational corporations which are based overseas. The number of competitors has increased, as has their size along with that of the available market.

Nowhere has the impact been greater as far as the UK is concerned than in the manufacturing sector. Let's look for example at the fortunes of the steel industry. In 1970 the world produced around 500 million tonnes of crude steel, of which 28 million tonnes was produced in the UK (5.6%), almost all by one nationalised company called the British Steel Corporation (later British Steel). Of the 19 million tonnes of steel consumed in the UK, less than 1 million tonnes was imported. So in 1970 only 30% of the steel produced in the UK was exported, while just 5% of the steel used in the UK was imported from overseas. By 2006 things had changed beyond recognition. World production of crude steel had increased to 1,240 million tonnes, of which the UK contributed just 12 million tonnes (less than 1%). However, only half of the steel used in the UK was home-produced, the rest was imported. British Steel was privatised in 1988, merging with a Dutch company in 1999. By 2006 it had been taken over by the Indian company Tata.

The UK steel industry's fortunes have largely been determined by increased international competition. Fifty per cent of world steel production is now based in Asia, compared with less than 20% in 1970. Chinese production alone has increased from 22 million tonnes in 1970 to around 200 million a year today. This is now a truly global market and one which is dominated by Chinese and Indian producers, leading to the existence of a world price for steel which fluctuates up and down and is wholly unaffected by market developments in countries such as the UK.

It is a similar story in the car industry. Back in 1967 19 million cars were produced globally, of which 1.55 million (8%) were manufactured in the UK. Our companies exported only 32% of the cars they produced, while the number of overseas imports was tiny, accounting for less than 10% of the UK market.

By 1997 world car production had doubled to 38 million, of which only 1.7 million were manufactured in the UK (4.47%). Of these 960,000 (56%) were exported, while UK consumers purchased 2.06 million cars manufactured overseas (around 66% of the total). Globalisation totally transformed the UK car industry in this 30-year period. It switched from being one which was largely serving a domestic market, and which faced little overseas competition, to one which exported over half its products and faced huge competition from overseas. By 2007, before the recession reduced the size of the market, globalisation had advanced far further still. In that year UK-based manufacturers exported 77% of the cars they produced, while imports accounted for some 85% of the UK market. Moreover, of course, the major car manufacturing facilities in the UK are now almost all foreign-owned. The biggest manufacturers are Nissan, Honda and BMW. Jaguar still produces a large number of vehicles each year, as does Land Rover, but these companies, like the bulk of the UK steel industry, are now owned by Tata.

Globalisation has not only affected manufacturing, though. Increasingly we are seeing the globalisation of the service sector too. This is most evidently true of the financial and business services sector in which UK-based institutions have performed very well. Here, as in most industries, global conglomerates increasingly have a presence in all the major markets of the world, carefully managing their global brand images and competing fiercely with one another for market share and the maximum returns. Higher education is increasingly becoming global as is the hotel industry, an increasing part of the media industry and legal services too.

 CRITICAL REFLECTION

Think about your own organisation and your industry. To what extent and in what ways is it being affected by globalisation?

The effects may be direct. Your industry may itself face competition for customers/clients/ service users from overseas. This is very likely to be the case if you work for a larger private sector organisation, although the extent varies greatly from industry to industry.

There will also almost certainly be significant indirect effects. Is globalisation affecting other organisations that you deal with or compete with? Your suppliers, for example, may be more affected as may other employers with whom you compete for staff.

TECHNOLOGY

Technological advances have been one of the major drivers of globalisation. Since the 1990s the World Wide Web has spread itself across the world as fibre-optic cables and satellite communication systems have served to make international communication speedier, more sophisticated and much much cheaper. The result is quite simply a situation in which pretty well anyone can sell anything to anyone else based anywhere in the world. Air freight services have proliferated, making it possible for a product to come out of a factory and to be delivered to an address on the other side of the world in less than a week. By container ship it takes about three weeks to deliver products manufactured in China to a shop in the UK.

Aside from their role in facilitating global economic exchange, new developments in information and communication technologies (ICTs) have also served to increase competitive intensity more generally. An important way in which this happens is through the capacity of the Internet to increase hugely our knowledge of possible alternative providers and also to make a choice between them. Online surfing allows us to track down a vast range of organisations with which to do business and to discover a good deal about them and what they have to offer very quickly and cheaply. In more recent years we have, of course, seen the rise of websites which help us to do this by acting as a guide or gateway to other organisations' sites. In the UK, so great is the potential demand for such services that vast investment is currently being devoted to the building up and marketing of price comparison websites. These are potentially highly lucrative businesses in themselves. Not only do they serve to increase competitive intensity by furnishing consumers with information, but they also engage in fierce competition between themselves. Not all will survive for the long term, but at the time of writing key players in the industry in the UK include Kelkoo (owned by Yahoo), Shopzilla and a number that specialise in financial services (Gocompare.com, Confused.com, Comparethemarket.com). In addition there are a plethora of online retail websites which sell goods and services on behalf of a wide range of others, taking a commission, but also fuelling competitive intensity in the industries that they are involved with. Expedia, Lastminute.com, Jellyfish.com and eBay are major examples.

ICT has also transformed the nature of the media that can be used to advertise products and services. An obvious example is the TV industry which has been transformed by new technologies in recent years, providing broadcasters with a far greater variety of channels and other platforms through which users can access their programmes. In the 1950s there was just one TV channel in the UK, by 1960 there were two, and by 1970 there were three. Channel 4 started in 1982 and Channel Five in 1997. Each launched as new technological developments allowed.

Satellite TV was launched in the UK in 1989, the two companies providing it sustaining huge losses in the first years. A breakthrough came in 1997 with the arrival of digitally transmitted satellite TV. This innovation permitted subscribers to access more than 5,000 channels through a satellite dish or cable. BSkyB moved into profit in 2003 and by 2010 was reporting annual profits of £878 million. Around 40% of UK households subscribe to their satellite service, while almost everyone else can now access dozens of channels free of charge through digital satellite systems.

Over time we are going to see the coming together of Internet and television technologies vastly increasing further the potential number of channels.

Super-fast broadband cables will not only make it possible to access any programme broadcast anywhere in the world through a computer system, but will also enable anyone to broadcast high-quality video content to anyone else.

Technologies also drive competition by enabling organisations to achieve step-changes in their productivity, often by introducing labour-saving machines. In manufacturing a lot of work that would once have been done by people is now carried out by robots and other machines, while computer-aided design allows much more flexibility. Customised production is fast replacing mass production, enabling manufacturers to develop bespoke products and small ranges aimed at niche markets. In supermarkets it is now routine for us to check out and pay for our items ourselves using scanning machines, while the use of virtual sales and learning environments is becoming a day-to-day experience. All of these innovations permit organisations to improve the quality and range of their offerings while also reducing their costs. Increased competitive intensity is the result. No provider can afford to be left behind in the race to adopt new technologies if they want to survive and prosper.

Book production provides a good example of the impact of new technologies on competitive conditions. In the last five years or so digital printing systems have started to be adopted to replace traditional offset printing methods. The cost per book is more, but the speed and quality mean that books can be printed on demand singly if necessary, instead of in batches of several hundred. This makes it far more economic to publish books which are not going to be big sellers. The technology has made self-publishing possible. An author can write a book and promote it on the Web, only getting copies printed when someone orders a copy. The publisher and the book retailer are thus removed from the process, cutting costs vastly. At the same time, of course, people are increasingly consuming books electronically, downloading text onto an e-reader rather than purchasing a physical book. The result over time will mean an explosion in the number of titles available.

It is not just information and communication technologies which are having the effect of increasing competitive intensity. Newer technologies are often said to have the potential to change our lives as profoundly in the next 50 years in much the same way as ICTs did in the last 50. This is particularly true of biotechnologies and nanotechnology. These offer the prospect of increasing life expectancy very considerably, eliminating our dependence on fossil fuels as a source of energy and, perhaps most importantly, the creation of wholly new materials with which to manufacture products and construct buildings. The result will be the development of new markets for new products and services, and inevitably the decline of existing ones. The competitive stakes for organisations will be raised further and faster as a consequence.

GOVERNMENT ACTION

The significance of the third great driver of increased competition in recent decades is often less well appreciated, but its role has been every bit as great as globalisation and new technologies. Starting primarily in the USA and in the UK during the 1980s, and later spreading across much of the world, governments have adopted policies that are explicitly aimed at increasing competition and choice. The consensus view now tends to be that markets provide the best means of ensuring efficiency, promoting innovation, providing high standards of service and hence encouraging economic growth.

It is only, however, relatively recently that governments have been so keen to embrace markets. It was very different in the UK 40 years ago, and much more recently in many other countries. The belief that it is the role of government to promote competition and choice and that such concerns should form the centrepiece of industrial policy is relatively new.

From the 1940s until the 1980s, and in most other economies until much more recently, a completely different approach was taken to the relationship between government and industry. The term *mixed economy* was often used to describe the situation that prevailed.

During this period, for example, a large portion of UK industry was owned by the government. In most cases, though not all, the government owned corporations which were either monopoly suppliers or which dominated the national market. Hence we had British Telecom, British Steel, British Petroleum, British Coal, British Airways, British Aerospace, British Leyland, the British Oxygen Company, British Gas, British Rail, the National Water Board, the Central Electricity Generating Board and the National Bus Company – all owned and directly controlled by central government, and in most cases with few competitors. However, it was not only these so-called 'commanding heights of the British economy' which were nationalised. Rolls-Royce was owned by the government at one stage, as was the travel agent Thomas Cook and the home removals firm Pickfords. In addition, local government owned bus companies and nearly all the nursing homes as well as 35% of the housing stock.

Until the 1980s industrial policy was decided in large part by a body called the National Economic Development Council (NEDC), which developed five-year national plans. Government ministers sat on the Council alongside senior industrialists and trade union leaders. Their plans involved some strengthening of competition, improving training and introducing new technology, but also building up state monopolies, directing subsidies to failing corporations and providing financial incentives for organisations to locate activities in less prosperous regions. A policy of 'picking winners' was pursued whereby government would decide which industries should be grown via public investment and played a role in facilitating that development. Where industries were flagging, investigations were carried out and government subsidies channelled to improve their productivity or help them to survive in the face of international competition.

The political consensus around the desirability of a 'mixed economy' broke down in the 1970s with the rise of competition from overseas – particularly from German and Japanese companies. The election in 1979 of the Thatcher Government signalled the start of a complete reversal of the policy. By the time of the election of the Blair Government 18 years later, a new political consensus had been established around wholly different industrial and economic policies.

At its root is the belief that fair competition between organisations is the best means of:

- satisfying customers
- raising productivity and quality
- growing the economy.

The view became established that government should not seek to run industry, but should concentrate on regulating competition and creating the right macroeconomic conditions for organisations to thrive and compete internationally.

Initially the switch in policy was highly controversial and caused great pain. Subsidies were withdrawn from organisations which were not productive, leading to millions of job losses and the destruction of communities that relied on particular employers (steel towns, coal villages, etc). Industrial restructuring led to major instances of industrial action as uneconomic pits and factories were allowed to close and labour-saving new technologies were introduced. Privatisation replaced nationalisation as all major corporations run by the government were either sold wholesale or divided up and then sold off.

Deregulation also occurred so that national and local monopolies had to face competition for the first time. As a result we now have several UK-based airlines competing with one another on the same routes, a multiplicity of phone companies and private courier mail companies.

Tariff reductions and the evolution of the European Single Market means that formerly nationalised companies now have to compete internationally. They have to satisfy their customers and make a profit in order to survive. In some cases they have become wholly-owned subsidiaries of large overseas-based conglomerates.

The privatisation programme continued under the Blair and Brown Governments (the Post Office, the Royal Mint, the Tote, Air Traffic Control), as did the policy of encouraging local government to 'contract out' services to the private sector. The NHS has also contracted out parts of its operation. Government ministers have been involved in trying to save failing organisations (eg Rover in 2005 and spectacularly in the case of the banks in 2008), but they do not generally provide large subsidies any more – and are not expected to.

In addition, the government has sought to import 'market disciplines' into the public services that remain under direct government control, by retaining/ strengthening internal market mechanisms in health care, higher education and some areas of social care. Private funding is attracted into the public services through policies such as the private finance initiative (which involves private firms undertaking major capital investment and renting the resultant facilities back to the government), foundation schools and direct involvement of the private sector in running defence and prison facilities.

The same big policy switch has occurred in most industrialised countries, although it came in the 1990s and 2000s rather than the 1980s in many cases. There is now a broad international consensus that governments should not seek to micromanage economic development centrally or own the commanding heights of their economies.

The evolving international consensus in favour of competition and choice has led to inter-governmental agreement about a range of measures which promote international trade, and thus international competition too. This process has involved a mixture of new regulation and deregulatory measures.

Unquestionably a major impetus for increased international trade has been the abandonment or relaxation, in recent years, of foreign exchange controls by more than 150 countries. These are forms of control imposed by governments on the purchase and sale of foreign currencies by their own residents or overseas residents. They allow governments to fix exchange rates and hence the price of imported and exported goods. Controls of this kind remain common in developing countries, including very significant international players such as China and India. They have, however, been largely abandoned in the industrialised countries, making it far easier and speedier to conduct international business.

The USA abandoned exchange controls in 1974 and the UK in 1979. The completion of the European Single Market removed all controls on the movement of capital, goods and services within the EU in 1986.

Free international trade remains restricted thanks to a range of informal and formal barriers in the form of tariffs, quotas, national licensing standards and state subsidies. But the movement over time has been towards liberalisation.

International competition has also been accelerated by a degree of new regulation in the form of cross-national standardisation in different fields. Examples are 40-foot containers for transportation, customs documentation, airline ticket formats, air traffic control conventions, accounting standards, insurance rules, global patents and international property rights.

Airlines provide a good example of an industry that has seen its competitive structure transformed in recent years, largely as a result of government action. Until the 1980s, the airline industry in the UK was very heavily regulated in such a way as to minimise competition. British Airways (BA) was the designated national carrier and was 100% government-owned. Other small private airlines existed, but in practice were only able to operate on routes that BA did not want to operate.

When awarding licences to fly routes, the Civil Aviation Authority was obliged to take account of the possible impact on BA and, in any event, only to license one carrier to fly each route. The same approach was used in all the European countries, resulting in a series of 200 separate bilateral agreements, mostly restricting competition to the national carrier of each country. British Airways was privatised in 1987, but it was not until 1993 that the EU introduced a single regulatory regime that permitted a much greater level of free competition.

The impact of deregulation has been profound. Hundreds of new airlines have been established, while previously small airlines have rapidly expanded. There is competition on all the major European routes and a far greater diversity of offers. Fares have fallen spectacularly, there is a far greater diversity of deals on offer and passenger numbers have soared. There are now 50 UK-based airlines operating more than 900 aircraft. Thirty years ago there were fewer than 200 aircraft operated from the UK.

In March 2007 the EU and the US Government signed an 'open skies' agreement covering transatlantic flights. This came into effect from March 2008. It is expected over time to lead to much greater levels of price competition between airlines. Over the long term ticket costs are expected to fall by a third or a half on the most profitable routes. Rising oil prices have so far served to hold back this development, but prices are lower than they otherwise would be were it not for deregulation.

 CRITICAL REFLECTION

CRITICISMS OF THE COMPETITION AND CHOICE AGENDA

Two major sets of arguments are commonly put against the competition and choice agenda. The first has regularly been articulated by government ministers in other EU countries and by EU advisers who wish to maintain what is often known as the 'European Social Model'. The basic economic argument runs as follows:

- Allowing consumers choice and encouraging increased competition leads to volatility in product markets.
- Volatility leads to insecurity for employees.
- Volatility in labour markets is undesirable in itself, but it also makes people less inclined to spend and take risks with their money.
- This is deflationary in its impact and so makes longer recessions and unemployment more likely.

The second argument involves stating that too much choice is a bad thing for consumers and for the long-term good of society generally.

It can be seen as an argument in favour of paternalism, being rooted in the idea that most of us are unqualified to exercise the choices that are now available to us.

We simply do not know what is the best choice to make. A good example is the decision that many employees are now confronted with when joining an occupational pension scheme – what investments they should invest in. Most go for the most secure option, even though this is likely to lead to the lowest pension. Experts describe this as acting in a 'recklessly conservative' manner.

Similar arguments are sometimes put against increasing choice for patients and parents about which hospital they go to or schools they send their children to.

The other major strand of the argument is broader. Choice leads us to make decisions about consumption which are to do with short-term gratification rather than our long-term good.

The result is a society which is less healthy, wealthy and satisfied than would be the case if the choices available to us were more limited. It leads to:

- obesity

- environmental degradation

- debt

- dysfunctional family relationships

- depression

- vanity/self-regarding individualism

- reduced trust

- inequality.

What is your view of these criticisms? Is it possible for government policy to embrace competition while also ensuring that these negative aspects do not become too damaging?

CONSUMERISM

As a result, primarily, of these three developments (globalisation, technological advance and government policy) market conditions for organisations based in countries such as the UK have become vastly more competitive than they used to be. The impact has been both positive and negative, but it is hard to conclude that these developments are not only irreversible but also likely to have an even greater impact in the future. Globalisation shows no signs of slowing down, while technological innovation is accelerating. Government thinking may change over time, leading to a reversal of the pro-market policies, but there is little sign of this happening. The recent banking crisis and subsequent recession tested governments severely, and while many major serious problems still face them, it looks as if the consensus in favour of competition and choice has come through unscathed.

A consequence of increased competitive intensity has been the rise of a society which is increasingly consumer-focused. There have been all manner of implications, many of which are negative and worrying. We will look at these further in Chapter 5 in the context of the major social trends that are shaping the evolving HR business environment. For the purposes of this chapter we need only to note that consumerism is a growing force and that its impact is to increase competitive intensity still further. Put simply, the more competition there is in an industry and the more choice consumers have about how to spend their money, the more inclined they are to exercise that choice. It means that we are becoming less loyal to suppliers and to brands over time. We are keen to try new products and to taste new experiences and are strongly influenced in our purchasing patterns by fashions and fads. This serves to drive greater levels of competitive intensity for organisations, making the commercial environment less stable and less predictable.

FINANCIALISATION

A major consequence of increased competitive intensity in product markets has been ever-increasing pressure to reduce costs as organisations are obliged to compete with one another on price as well as the quality of their products. Pressure to drive costs down is also increasingly coming from shareholders, and particularly from the institutional shareholders who own the lion's share of most UK publicly limited companies. For these organisations and their employees, increased competition for capital is as significant a development as increased product market competition.

Private sector organisations largely raise capital to fund new ventures and expansion plans by trading their shares on the capital markets. These are increasingly international in nature and dominated by large financial organisations (pension funds, unit trusts, insurance companies, etc) seeking to invest money on behalf of their clients and their own shareholders. Attracting and retaining investors, and gaining a positive reputation in the financial markets, has thus become an essential prerequisite of business success in the corporate sector.

What we are seeing, in short, is particularly intensified competition in the financial sector. Companies here have been affected as much as anywhere by globalisation, technological developments and the governmental deregulation agendas. They are obliged to compete fiercely with one another in order to recruit and retain clients. This means getting faster and larger returns on their money. There is a knock-on impact on the private sector more generally because the financial companies trade in their shares.

Above I referred to the abandonment of foreign currency controls across the Western industrialised world and explained its role in driving globalisation. No industry has been as affected by this development as much as the financial services industry. Not only has this industry, like many, now become international and highly competitive in its own right, but it has also had to adjust to the globalisation of financial markets.

A recent film about corporate life in the twenty-first century was given the very appropriate title *Money Never Sleeps*, a neat way of summing up the way that financial institutions now move money all around the world on an hour-by-hour basis in order to secure the best returns. Each day the London financial markets open just as the Tokyo markets are closing, to be followed five hours later by the opening of the New York markets. At no point, day or night, is money not being invested, often just for a few hours at a time by financial firms seeking quick and profitable returns. All the time, somewhere, unimaginably large amounts of money are being exchanged into different currencies and used to buy shares, bonds, commodities, futures and other financial derivatives or simply being invested by one financial intermediary in the activities of another. Well over 90% of all international financial flows are now speculative in nature rather than related to trade in visible products or services. As a result, foreign currency exchange rates – crucial to the people and organisations in a country – are increasingly determined by the actions of speculators and not by real trading relationships.

The globalisation of the money markets means that the world's financial system is to a very considerable extent 'unregulatable'. A loss of confidence in a corporation can spell its end overnight. Moreover, as we have seen in recent years, loss of confidence in a government causes a currency crisis and can require it to raise interest rates sharply and rapidly in order to raise finance to cover its short-term needs.

The increasing power of these unregulated, unpredictable, global markets for capital is having a profound impact on the way that larger private sector organisations are run. Moreover, because smaller businesses and public sector bodies are often reliant on PLCs, the practical impact is a great deal more widespread. Purcell and Sisson (2010) rightly conceive of these developments and their associated system of 'shareholder capitalism' as constituting a fundamental shift for UK management into 'an era of financialisation'. They sum up what this means as follows:

> First, a privileged position for shareholders and an overwhelming emphasis on shareholder value as the key business driver, as opposed to the interests of other stakeholders. Second, a focus on short-term profitability rather than long-term market share or added value, as the key index of business performance has been encouraged by institutional share ownership by investment trusts and pension funds. Third, takeovers are relatively easy, which not only reinforces the pressure on short-term profitability to maintain share price, but also encourages expansion by merger and acquisition rather than by internal growth, while reconfiguring the corporation through outsourcing, off-shoring and restructuring to remove parts of the business from the portfolio. Finally, there tends to be a premium on financial engineering as the core organizational competence, the domination of financial management over other functions and numbers driven as opposed to issue-driven planning (Purcell and Sisson 2010: 91).

A feature of the emerging system is the tendency for companies to be merged or taken over and becoming subsidiaries of parent companies with diverse interests. Purcell and Sisson (2010) show that 68% of UK workplaces are now part of larger organisations and that over half of all private sector organisations are part of companies with international interests. Nineteen per cent of UK workplaces are owned by companies that are based overseas. Every year the number of mergers and acquisitions involving British companies increases, as does the number of buy-outs (ie takeovers). Often these are financed through debt, creating greater incentives for a quick and substantial return to be made.

THE IMPACT OF INCREASED COMPETITIVE INTENSITY

The developments I have described above have had and continue to have a major impact on business priorities in UK organisations. The impact on HRM practices has been particularly significant.

Firstly, increased competitive intensity requires organisations to work harder at meeting their objectives effectively. In most cases this involves satisfying, if not delighting, their customers. The level of service and of product quality has to be maintained and continually improved in order for an organisation to thrive and survive. For HR this means added pressure to meet core objectives – recruiting, retaining, motivating and engaging good performers – more effectively than competitors are able to do.

Secondly, this needs to be achieved more efficiently. Competitive pressures require costs to be kept as low as possible, while financialisation often means that higher profit margins must be achieved in shorter periods of time. Quite simply, more has to be achieved all the time with less by way of resources. This has led to a substantial increase in the intensity of work.

Thirdly, the HR function itself is being continually placed under greater pressure to prove its own worth in financial terms. Being effective is no longer enough. HR managers have to prove it and demonstrate that they are creating greater value year on year.

Fourthly, organisations are increasingly likely to face an uncertain future. The more competitive the business environment becomes, and the more global the sources of competition, the less predictable things are. Volatility is the norm.

Fifthly, organisations are having to become a great deal more agile and opportunist. A capacity for flexibility is increasingly important to long-term success as is the ability to adapt to changed circumstances rapidly and fruitfully on a regular basis. Structural change (mergers, acquisitions, downsizing, upsizing, offshoring, outsourcing, etc) has become a much more common experience as organisations morph as required to meet changing opportunities and threats. Cultural change has often had to follow on fast behind.

Sixthly and finally, organisations are increasingly having to operate internationally in some form. UK companies have more overseas interests and overseas employees, while UK workplaces are increasingly likely to be owned or partly owned by overseas parent companies. The capacity to operate effectively internationally as well as nationally has thus become more important.

We will explore the consequences for HRM practice in more detail later in the book. For now we simply need to conclude that the trends in our competitive environment discussed in this chapter are profound, probably irreversible and likely to accelerate further in the future.

KEY LEARNING POINTS

- Increasing competitive intensity is the most significant contemporary trend in the business environment.

- The trend towards more intense competitive conditions is largely explained with reference to globalisation, technological developments and government policy over recent decades.

- Increased competition has been particularly significant in the financial sector. The effect has been to increase the pressure on larger private sector organisations to create value by cutting costs and intensifying work.

- The result is a business environment which is much more volatile and less predictable. Organisations are thus obliged to achieve more with fewer resources and to become more agile and opportunist.

EXPLORE FURTHER

An excellent discussion of the causes and consequences of increasing competitive intensity is provided by Keith Sisson and John Purcell in their chapter entitled 'Management: caught between two competing views of the organisation' in the third edition of *Industrial relations: theory and practice*, edited by Trevor Colling and Michael Terry (2010).

Sisson, K. and Purcell, J. (2010) Management: caught between competing views of the organisation. In T. Colling and M. Terry (eds) *Industrial relations: theory and practice*. 3rd edition. Chichester: Wiley.

Globalisation, its causes and impact are explored in many books from all manner of perspectives. A good, up-to-date, general introduction that covers most is provided by George Ritzer in *Globalization: a basic text*.

Ritzer, G. (2010) *Globalization: a basic text*. Chichester: Wiley-Blackwell.

Globalisation in general is covered splendidly by Peter Dicken in his excellent book *Global shift*, now in its 6th edition. Chapter 6 explains the central role that governments play in liberalising trade and promoting international competition.

Dicken, P. (2011) *Global shift: mapping the changing contours of the world economy*. 6th edition. London: Sage.

REFERENCES

Adcroft, A., Teckman, J. and Willis, R. (2010) Is higher education in the UK becoming more competitive? *International Journal of Public Sector Management.* Vol 23, No 6. pp578–588.

Brown, W., Bryson, A. and Forth, J. (2009) Competition and the retreat from collective bargaining. In W. Brown, A. Bryson, J. Forth and K. Whitfield (eds) *The evolution of the modern workplace.* Cambridge: Cambridge University Press.

Chew, C. and Osborne, S.P. (2009) Exploring strategic positioning in the UK charitable sector: emerging evidence from charitable organisations that provide public services. *British Journal of Management.* Vol 20, No 1. pp90–105.

Dicken, P. (2011) *Global shift: mapping the changing contours of the world economy.* 6th edition. London: Sage.

McNamara, G., Vaaler, P. and Devers, C. (2003) Same as it ever was: the search for evidence of increasing hypercompetition. *Strategic Management Journal.* Vol 24, No 1. pp261–278.

Purcell, J. and Sisson, K. (2010) Management: caught between competing views of the organisation. In T. Colling and M. Terry (eds) *Industrial relations: theory and practice.* 3rd edition. Chichester: Wiley.

Thomas, L.G. and D'Aveni, R. (2009) The changing nature of competition in the US manufacturing sector, 1950–2002. *Strategic Organisation.* Vol 7, No 4. pp387–431.

Wiggins, R. and Ruefli, T. (2005) Schumpeter's ghost: is hypercompetition making the best of times shorter? *Strategic Management Journal.* Vol 26, No 10. pp887–911.

CHAPTER 3

People and skills

Introduction

When thinking about the future of work and of human resource management over the next two decades, one of the more predictable aspects is the number of people of working age that there will be in the UK and the type and level of skills they are likely to have. We can thus predict with some accuracy, at least in broad terms, the probable size and shape of the labour market from which demand for staff will have to be met. Importantly, from the perspective of organisations, it looks as if many labour markets will tighten rather than loosen as the coming decades unfold, meaning that a good proportion of the skills that employers seek will be less available than has been the case in recent years. For human resource managers this means that more of their work will need to be focused on competing for staff with other organisations. Where skills shortages are most acute, which will be the case for organisations seeking more highly qualified or specialist people, effective competition in the labour market is likely to dominate the HRM agenda to a considerable degree. It follows that someone seeking to develop a successful career in HRM needs to develop an understanding of labour market dynamics, and of what these mean for the recruitment and retention of individual employees in different industrial sectors.

That said, the same long-term trends also suggest that lower-skilled workers will be a great deal less hard to recruit and retain. At the lower end of the earnings range, the skills sought are likely to be in greater supply than there will be demand for them. This has important social consequences in terms of inequality (see Chapter 5), but poses no great problems when seen purely from the point of view of HR managers seeking to recruit and retain people.

The purpose of this chapter is to put the case for the proposition that tightening of many labour markets will be one of the most significant trends for HRM over the next 20 years. We will start by looking at demographic trends and at long-term patterns in the demand and supply of labour in the UK. This will include discussion about key factors in determining population size such as fertility rates and patterns of international migration. In the second half of the chapter we will turn our attention to skills, focusing particularly on the question of how effectively the skills base of our future workforce will match the skills that employers will increasingly need.

LEARNING OUTCOMES

The objectives of this chapter are to:

- explain why many labour markets are likely to tighten during the next two decades as a result of demographic trends and the changing nature of the skills that employers seek

- demonstrate that demand for labour is likely to continue increasing as it has for more than 50 years

- outline the view that it will be harder to tap into the same sources of additional staff that have been used in the past to meet increased demand for labour

- review the long-term trends in the types of skill that employers look for when hiring staff

- assess the extent to which the stock of skills in the UK labour market is likely to meet demand from employers in the future.

 LOCAL GOVERNMENT

CASE STUDY

Nearly 3 million people are employed by local government bodies in the UK – around 10% of all employed persons. More than 70% are employed to work in the education service or in the social services, areas which are expected to expand in coming years as the population ages and the 'education leaving age' is raised to 18 years. The local government workforce is the oldest of all the sectors in the UK by some margin, more than 34% being over the age of 50 and fewer than 20% being under the age of 30. Staff turnover levels in general are relatively low (around 14%), but are rather higher in areas where skills shortages are most acute. Absence levels, which average 10 days per employee per year, are more than double national average rates. In 2008, 49% of councils reported having difficulty recruiting and retaining staff for non-professional roles, while as many as 87% had problems recruiting and retaining professional and managerial

staff. The most widespread skills shortages were among social workers, carers and occupational therapists. Tight budgets set by central government and limits on the amount of money that can be raised via council tax increases mean that there is only limited scope to increase salaries, while councils face increased competition for staff from the private consultancies and agencies which sell them core services and expertise. The costs associated with continuing to provide generous final salary pensions are increasing year on year, making it less and less likely that current levels of benefit provision will be able to be sustained in the future.

Questions

1 In what different ways are demographic trends likely to affect the ability of local councils to deliver core services in the future?

2 What are the main strengths and

weaknesses of local government in terms
of its ability to recruit and retain staff?

3   What steps would you recommend
senior HR managers working in local
government should be taking now in
order to reduce the impact of growing
skills shortages in key areas in the
future?

Source: Audit Commission (2008)

DEMAND FOR PEOPLE

For more than 50 years now the UK has seen a long-term trend towards
increased levels of employment. Since 1971 government statisticians have been
collecting data every quarter, giving us a good indication of how many men aged
16–65 and women aged 16–60 in the UK are working in jobs, are self-employed
or are unemployed at any time. This pronounced upward trend is illustrated
clearly in Figure 3.1. In the first quarter of 1971, 24.6 million people were
officially estimated to be 'in employment' in the UK, a figure that included people
who are self-employed as well as those working for employing organisations.
Of these, 15.6 million (63.4%) were men and 9.0 million (36.6%) were women.
Twenty-seven years later in the first quarter of 2008, there were 16 million men
in employment and 13.6 million women, a total of 29.6 million. During those
years, therefore, the total figure increased by 5 million, while the proportion
of the workforce that is female increased to 46%. In fact, the total number of
jobs in the economy is rather higher, because a good number of people over the
state retirement age are in employment, while some people always occupy more
than one part-time job at the same time. There were 31.4 million jobs in 2010
compared with 26.1 million in 1971.

Figure 3.1 shows the trend in the total number of jobs since records were first
published 50 years ago. It shows that while demand has increased in most years,
and particularly steeply since the mid-1980s, there have also been short periods
of recession in which the number of jobs has fallen sharply, before recovering
and resuming the pattern of growth. This increase in the total number of jobs
in the UK economy is remarkable when it is considered that in addition to two
major recessions, these years also saw the wholesale restructuring of the UK
economy, substantially increased international competition (see Chapter 2), the
exporting overseas of many jobs and the introduction of significant labour-saving
technologies. It is thus fair to observe that long-term demand for staff in the
UK is highly robust and that there are good grounds for anticipating continued
growth in demand in the future.

Given the strength of past trends, it is unsurprising that published projections
of the future level of employment in the UK point to further growth. Beaven et
al (2005), in their study carried out to help inform the Leitch Review of Skills in

Figure 3.1 Jobs in the UK

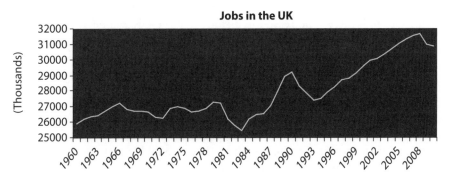

the UK, estimated that the total number people employed in the UK in 2020 is likely to be somewhere between 32.47 million and 32.79 million, depending on what set of variables are used in the analysis. This suggests a growth of around 1 million, but it is interesting to note that in the years since their study was carried out (2004) growth exceeded these expectations by a considerable margin until the onset of recession in 2008. It is thus reasonable to view them as conservative and to conclude that employment levels in 2020 will in fact be rather higher. They certainly will be if the pre-recession trends reassert themselves. The number of jobs in the UK economy grew by more than 2.5 million in the 10 years after 1997 (Gadenne et al 2006); were this rate of growth to resume over the next 10 years we can anticipate that there could be demand for people to fill more than 34 million jobs by the early 2020s.

MISLEADING STATISTICS?

Throughout the recent period during which we have seen the total number of jobs increase, along with overall rates of employment, the true significance of the trend has been the subject of political controversy. Governments always boast loudly about their record as job-creators, while opposition parties always look for opportunities to argue that the achievement is not as impressive as it looks on the surface.

People on the left politically have tended to argue that the government record on job-creation was not all it was cracked up to be because so many of the new jobs were of low quality and were often of a part-time or temporary nature. By contrast, critics coming from a right-wing perspective have often bemoaned the fact that so many of the new jobs that have been created in recent years have been in the public sector. The growth, therefore, was somewhat artificial, being a product of profligate government spending rather than genuine wealth-creation in the real economy.

There is some truth in both of these criticisms. The proportion of jobs which are part-time in nature has grown substantially since 1984 from 21% to 25%. So around 2.3 million of the 5.3 million 'new jobs' created in the UK economy over the past 25 years have been part-time. It is also true that much of the growth in jobs between 1998 and 2008 was in the public sector. Around 18% of all jobs are currently based in public sector organisations – 5.82 million in 2008. This compares with 5.18 million in 1998. So 640,000 of the 2.7 million additional jobs created between 1998 and 2008 – 24% – were public sector roles.

SUPPLY OF PEOPLE

On the face of it there is no reason to assume that the UK will have any difficulty finding sufficient numbers of people to fill the increased number of jobs that the economy is anticipated to need over the next 10–20 years. After all, as was demonstrated above, the growth in demand for labour is very much a long-term trend, and we have always managed successfully to meet increased demand with increased supply over the past five decades. Why then, it is reasonable to ask, are labour markets predicted to tighten particularly in the future? The answer lies in an appreciation of exactly how labour supply has managed to keep pace with increased labour demand in the past. It has been possible due to three distinct developments, the continuation of which, in the future, is highly questionable. These are female participation, the impact of the Baby Boom generation and overseas immigration.

FEMALE PARTICIPATION

First, the growth in the number of jobs over the past 50 years has coincided with a period in which what is known as 'female participation' has increased substantially. In other words, the proportion of women of working age who undertake paid work has grown, and this has hugely helped the supply of available labour to grow so as to meet demand from employers. Table 3.1 shows the proportion of women of working age who were classed as economically active in official figures published since 1951. This shows that while female participation has increased in each of the past six decades, the period of most rapid growth was during the 1960s. After that the rate of growth has steadily declined and has been much lower since the turn of the millennium. It is thus reasonable to argue that the potential for further extensive growth is limited. The male participation rate in the UK is currently 84%, and it will always remain higher than the female rate unless we see a profound change in the number of men taking up the prime child-caring role in families. A factor of significance in holding down female participation rates is the ongoing growth in lone-parent families (see Chapter 5). The employment rate for single mothers is only 55%, compared with 72% for women with dependent children who are married or cohabiting (National Statistics 2006). Female participation is thus unlikely to grow further while the number of single-parent households continues to grow.

Importantly, however, we are witnessing the start of a major change which will serve to increase female participation rates, and hence labour supply more generally. This is the planned increase in the state pension age for women from 60 to 66, which is taking effect in stages between 2010 and 2020. Once complete this will boost the number of people classed as being 'of working age' by more than 2 million. However, in practice the increase in the number who are economically active is likely to be considerably lower. Fewer than half of men aged between 60 and 64 (48%) currently work, while 30% of women in this age group already choose to remain in employment rather than to claim a state pension (Banks and Casanova 2004: 129). So the raising of the pension age is unlikely in practice to increase labour supply by more than around 300,000 people. Moreover, it will be counterbalanced with a bigger fall in the size of the working population resulting from the planned raising of the education leaving age from 16 to 18 from 2015. There are currently just under half a million 16–18-year-olds working, fewer than half of whom are undertaking any formal part-time programme of education or training (DfCSF 2007: 2). Notwithstanding the fact that many 16–18-year-olds will work part-time while in full-time education after 2015, raising the education leaving age to 18 is likely to have the effect of reducing labour supply by rather more than the increase that will be achieved as a result of raising the female state pension age.

Table 3.1 Female participation rates

1951:	42%	1961:	47%
1971:	59%	1981:	65%
1991:	72%	2001:	73%
2009:	75%		

THE BABY BOOM GENERATION

The second reason that the UK's labour supply has managed to keep pace with growing demand over the past 30 years has been the presence in our labour market of the so-called 'Baby Boom generation'. In the years immediately after the Second World War fertility rates in the UK, as was the case in most countries, increased rapidly. Later they declined. This means that there are considerably more people born between 1945 and 1964 (the Baby Boom years) than there are born between 1965 and 1984 (often referred to as 'Generation X') and between 1985 and 2004 (now variously labelled 'Generation Me', 'Generation Y' or the 'iPod Generation'). The significance of this demographic phenomenon can clearly be seen in Figure 3.2, which shows the number of men and women of different ages, starting with recently born children at the bottom and elderly people at the top. The white areas indicate those who are classed as being 'economically active' and who are thus either working or actively seeking work. This figure was published by the Office for National Statistics in 2005 and is the latest available. Since then, it is interesting to note that birth rates have increased markedly.

Between 1945 and 1964 there were 17.6 million live births in the UK, an average of 880,000 each year. During the following 20 years, 1965 to 1984, the total number of births fell to 16.1 million (803,000 each year on average). More recently, between 1985 and 2004 there were only 14.8 million births, an average of just 738,000 each year. Over the coming 20 years, therefore, the cohort of UK-born people that will be retiring (the Baby Boomers) is larger by some 2.8 million than the cohort that is now reaching working age, completing its education and entering the labour market. Inevitably this will contribute to a further tightening of the labour market.

However, the major impact of demographic trends in the near future from an employer perspective is going to be more specific. We are going to see a particular sharp tightening of the markets for school-leavers and for new graduates. This is a result of two distinct factors. First, due to the marked fall in fertility rates that occurred during the 1990s and early years of the current century, we are going to see a substantial fall in the number of people coming into the labour market for the first time. There will be a steady but pronounced reduction in the number of

Figure 3.2 Population structure: by age, sex and economic activity, autum 2005[1]

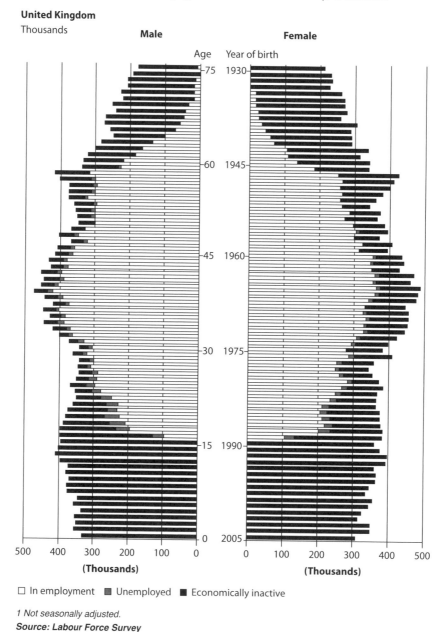

1 Not seasonally adjusted.
Source: Labour Force Survey

people in the 18–20 age group in the 10 years from 2011 until 2021. After that the numbers will begin to increase again, but are not expected to reach the pre-2011 level until at least 2027. Demographic projections estimate that the number of people reaching the age of 18 in the UK will have fallen by 16.2% between 2009 and 2020 (Universities UK 2008: 18). In terms of numbers this means that there will be around 300,000 fewer people in the 18–20 age group in 2020 than there were 10 years earlier. The second factor is the government's plan to increase the proportion of young people who stay on in full-time education until the age of 21. The target is 50%, but as we will see later in this chapter, there are good grounds for anticipating a moving upwards of this target in years to come. Taken together these two developments are going to have the effect of reducing the supply of young people coming into the labour market to a significant degree over the next 10–15 years.

IMMIGRATION

The third major way in which the UK economy has managed to meet the increased demand for labour over the past 50 years is through overseas immigration. This mechanism has been particularly significant over the past decade, but played an important role throughout the post-war period. Figure 3.3 shows the growth in the proportion of the UK population who were born overseas at each of the most recent national censuses. Official statistics define migrants as people who move overseas and settle in another country for at least a period of a year. Under this definition, according to Horsfield's (2005: 117) analysis of government figures, 8.9 million people came from abroad to live in the UK between 1975 and 2004 while 7.5 million left, giving a total net inflow of around 1.4 million people. In the most recent years, however, net inflow has

CASE STUDY

PATTERNS OF BIRTH RATES

Over time the number of babies born each year has fluctuated up and down. In recent years the trend has been in an upwards direction, largely as a result of high levels of immigration into the UK during the early years of the twenty-first century. Women who were born overseas tend to have more children than women born in the UK, and this accounts for recent increases. More than 50% of babies born in London now are to women who were themselves born overseas. However, explaining past peaks and troughs in birth rates is not always so easy. Since the Second World War the following five years saw the highest numbers of live births in the UK:

1 1947: 1,025,427 births

2 1964: 1,014,672 births

3 1965: 997,275 births

4 1963: 990,160 births

5 1966: 979,587 births

By contrast, the following years saw the lowest numbers:

1 1977: 657,038 births

2 2002: 668,777 births

3 2001: 669,123 births

4 1976: 675,526 births

5 2003: 695,549 births

Question for discussion

What explanations can you think of for why there is such a marked variation between the number of births in these years? Why did we see so many births in the late 1940s and mid-1960s, and so few in the late 1970s and early 2000s?

Figure 3.3 Percentage of the UK population born overseas

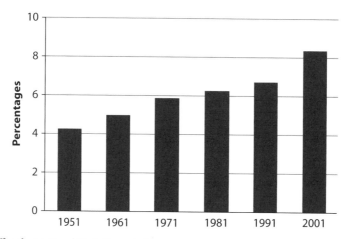

Source: Office for National Statistics website

Figure 3.4 Recent trends in immigration and emigration

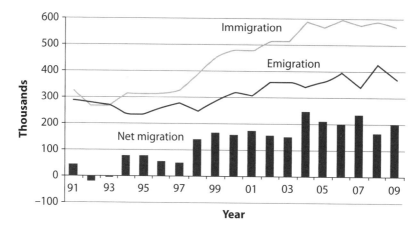

Source: Office for National Statistics website

exceeded net outflow by a wider margin than has been the case historically. As is demonstrated in Figure 3.4, the UK has been gaining approximately 165,000 more people each year than it has been losing over the past 10 years, contributing to an overall rise in our population from 58.5 million in 1998 to more than 61 million today. However, the precise figures are a matter of some controversy because it is difficult to measure with great accuracy exactly how many people who come from other EU countries settle in the UK on a semi-permanent basis, or indeed to measure how many return each year to their country of origin. Most independent commentators thus agree that the official statistics are conservative in their estimates, particularly as far as recent migration into the UK from eastern Europe is concerned (Blanchflower et al 2007: 6–11, Migration Watch UK 2005).

Whatever the precise statistics, it is clearly the case that migration from overseas has had a major impact on the UK labour market in recent years. It has enabled organisations to fill vacancies and has helped to prevent inflationary increases in wage levels. In some public sector organisations the impact has been huge. In the NHS, for example, until very recently more than 40% of newly registered doctors and nurses were being recruited from overseas (Batata 2005). But what of the future? Is international migration going to continue to be a major route whereby the demand for labour is matched by supply? The answer is unclear, because we cannot be certain how politically acceptable it will continue to be for the UK population to be allowed to continue rising at recent rates. Moreover, there are grounds for anticipating that it will be progressively harder for employers to source new staff from overseas than has been the case over the past few years.

In 2006 government statisticians produced figures projecting future population growth through the middle of the century. Some of the results are illustrated in Figure 3.5. This shows that if recent trends of immigration and emigration were to continue, the total population of the UK would grow by 10 million over the coming 20 years, the overwhelming majority of the population growth being in England and in the south-eastern region in particular. Longer-term projections point to a total UK population of 85 million by 2081 (GAD 2006). Were this scenario to unfold in practice, there would be few grounds for arguing that labour markets will tighten in a general sense over the coming two decades. But it is important to recognise that these statistics represent *projections* of current trends rather than *predictions* of actual likely outcomes.

In practice it is likely that the population will not grow anything like as quickly. It is widely agreed among politicians from all parties that the current rate of population growth is not economically sustainable. In terms of housing, transportation and public service provision, the stage has been reached at which further rapid increases in numbers will damage the economy rather than contribute to economic growth. Ways are thus being found to reduce the rate of growth and to try to ensure that migrants entering the UK are people who have the capacity to make a substantial contribution to future economic growth. Chief among these has been the recent introduction of new immigration controls by the government. They have been brought into effect in stages since 2008, their purpose being to simplify the system, to make it harder for illegal immigrants to sustain themselves in the UK and more generally to restrict the level of non-EU immigration. In the future, ministers argued as the legislation was being introduced, the system 'will ensure that only those with skills the country needs can come'.

Figure 3.5 UK population projections in 2006

						Thousands
	2006	2011	2016	2021	2026	2031
United Kingdom	60587	62761	64975	67191	69260	71100
England	50763	52706	54724	56757	58682	60432
Wales	2966	3038	3113	3186	3248	3296
Scotland	5117	5206	5270	5326	5363	5374
Northern Ireland	1742	1812	1868	1922	1966	1999

Source: Office for National Statistics website

In the case of skilled workers, the new rules make it much harder for UK employers to recruit from overseas than was the case in the past. It includes a requirement for any employer wishing to employ non-EU nationals to keep copies of documents and check their authenticity, to keep attendance records, to inform the authorities if a migrant worker does not come to work for 10 days or more, to purchase a sponsor's licence and to pay a fee to register an overseas worker as an employee. Substantial civil penalties (effectively fines) can be levied on employers who do not comply. In addition, before a job offer can be made to a potential overseas migrant, employers now have to demonstrate that they cannot fill a post with a UK resident and, except in the case of jobs on an official 'shortage occupation list', must be in a position to demonstrate that the vacancy has been unsuccessfully advertised in the UK. For potential immigrants there are also new restrictions. First, under the new rules they must get a job offer before they can apply for a visa to travel to the UK. Secondly, for the skilled and highly skilled categories, competence in the English language, backed up with appropriate certification, is required. The position in respect of low-skilled workers is now a good deal more restrictive. For them, if they are not citizens of EU countries there is simply no possibility of working legally in the UK under the new system except when the government decides there is a need to bring people in on a temporary basis to fill specific labour shortages, such as major construction projects. In 2011, for the first time, formal caps are being placed on the number of immigrants from outside the EU who will be permitted to enter the UK to settle for more than a year.

There are thus good grounds for anticipating a reduction in the number of people entering the UK from outside the European Union in the future. Overseas countries will remain a source of skilled employees, but it will be more costly and time-consuming to recruit them than was the case in the past. No such restrictions apply in the case of EU nationals, but here there is another good reason for anticipating a fall in the level of migration from member states into the UK – low fertility rates.

Figure 3.6 European fertility rates

Ukraine	1.12	World:	2.65
Czech Republic	1.17	Europe:	1.40
Slovakia	1.20		
Slovenia	1.22		
Bulgaria	1.24		
Greece	1.25		
Romania	1.26		
Latvia	1.26		
Poland	1.26		
Spain	1.27		
Italy	1.28		
Hungary	1.30		
Germany	1.32		
Croatia	1.35		
Estonia	1.37		
Portugal	1.47		
Malta	1.50		
Cyprus	1.63		
Sweden	1.64		
Serbia	1.65		
Belgium	1.66		
UK	1.66		
Netherlands	1.72		
Finland	1.72		
Denmark	1.75		
France	1.87		
Ireland	1.94		
Turkey	2.46		

Source: United Nations (2005)

The number of births across much of Europe has been falling for several decades now, creating a situation in which the total population of many countries is facing substantial decline over the next two decades. According to the United Nations (2005: viii), in 15 European countries the number of births is now so low that they 'have reached levels of fertility unprecedented in human history'. In order to sustain a population at its current level over the long term, assuming net immigration and emigration are at similar levels, each woman must (on average) give birth to 2.1 children. Taking account of infant mortality, this ensures that each mother and father is replaced in the population by two adult offspring. Fertility rates are now below replacement level in the vast majority of developed countries, but they have fallen below 1.3 across much of southern and eastern Europe. As a result, over the next two or three decades, unless current trends reverse, we are going to witness substantial falls in the populations of those EU countries from which a good deal of recent migration into the UK has tended to come. For example, the population of Poland (currently 38.5 million) is expected to fall to 32 million by 2050 (UN 2005: 37), that of Italy from 58.1 million to 50.9 million and that of Germany from 82.7 million to 78.7 million. Current fertility rates in the major EU countries and candidate countries (ie those likely to join the EU soon) are shown in Figure 3.6.

UNPICKED FRUIT

In 2008 it was reported that thousands of tonnes of strawberries and other soft fruits worth £20 million had been left unpicked in the UK in 2007 as a result of a shortage of people to pick them. In 2008 the situation was expected to be a great deal worse due to new immigration rules being introduced which prevent people from non-EU countries from entering the UK to work on farms during the picking season. Another factor of significance was the fall in the value of the pound *vis-à-vis* the euro and other EU currencies, making working in low-paid jobs in the UK a good deal less attractive to eastern European workers than it was in the past. The result was expected to be 50,000 tonnes of fruit being left to rot in the fields.

Source: Milmo 2008

MIGRANT WORKERS: AN ECONOMIC ADVANTAGE OR DISADVANTAGE?

CASE STUDY

In recent years as the number of people migrating into the UK has increased more rapidly than the number emigrating each year, an interesting debate has taken place between those who believe that this level of population increase is an economic boon and those who argue that the economy would perform as well, if not better, without such a sizeable influx of workers from overseas.

The economic argument in favour of increased immigration rests on three propositions. Firstly, it helps increase economic growth because immigrants are overwhelmingly of working age and earn slightly more, on average, than UK workers. They thus make a net contribution, helping to create wealth. Secondly, immigrants help to plug skills gaps by taking jobs that UK workers are either unable or unwilling to take. This enables organisations to invest, diversify and expand more easily than if migrant workers were unavailable. Finally, there is a fiscal argument deployed in favour of increased immigration. Migrant workers tend to earn rather more, on average, than UK workers. This is because they work longer hours and/or take up more highly skilled jobs. They thus make a positive and disproportionate contribution to public funds through taxation and help to finance the pensions and other benefits required by an ageing UK population.

The economic argument against increased immigration also has a number of separate strands. It is based, however, less on the overall national economic situation and more on the economic interests of existing UK residents. Firstly, it is argued that housing costs are increasing at too great a pace, particularly in areas such as London where the impact of immigration is greatest. Secondly, there is an impact on public spending simply because we need more schools, hospitals, roads and social housing in order to accommodate more people. Finally, there is a negative impact on people who are obliged to compete with migrant workers for jobs. Wage levels are lower than they would otherwise be because the labour market is loosened by

the arrival of so many people from overseas looking for work.

In 2008 the House of Lords Select Committee on Economic Affairs conducted an investigation into all of these arguments. Their conclusion was that there was an economic advantage being gained from immigration in terms of increased national wealth, but that it is relatively slight and is very limited when measured in terms of GDP (gross domestic product) per head. In other words, on average each individual UK resident hardly benefits at all economically, while some lose out. The government disagreed with this assessment, arguing that managed economic migration at a controlled pace and focused on meeting skills gaps, yields significant economic benefits.

The task

Download from the House of Lords website the Select Committee's report entitled *The Economic Impact of Migration*, published 1 April 2008. Then download the government response to this report from June 2008. You will find both documents at www. parliament.uk/hleconomicaffairs/. Read the conclusions and decide what your view is on this debate.

DEMAND FOR SKILLS

The direction of key demographic trends forms only a part of the case for anticipating a considerable tightening of labour markets in the future. The other major component concerns the ability of the people who are available for work to meet the requirements that employers are likely to have for skills. Here too there are pronounced, entrenched, long-term trends to consider whose broad direction is unlikely to reverse in the coming 20 years. As is demonstrated by the statistics presented in Tables 3.2 and 3.3, for many years now we have seen a reduction in demand for people to fill unskilled and relatively low-skilled roles and an increase in demand for employees with higher skills. The way that the government classified different occupations changed in 2000, so we have to study two tables containing different categories in order to see the extent of this trend. Particularly striking is the growth in demand for people to undertake managerial and professional roles. By their nature these tend to be specialised in nature, requiring a knowledge base that can only be gained via extensive study and relevant experience in a field.

The change in the occupational profile of the UK workforce has largely been driven by the revolutionary shift that has occurred in the nature of our industries during the past 30 years. In 1978 (the first year that data was collected on employment by sector), 7 million of us worked in manufacturing and a further 1.5 million in the energy, water, farming and fishing industries. These have all declined substantially since then in terms of the number of people they employ. Manufacturing employment now consists of only 3 million people (12% of all jobs). Agriculture and fishing account for just 200,000 jobs, energy and water for fewer still. The big growth areas have been in retailing, distribution, hotels and restaurants, finance, business services, public administration, education and health. Employment in the financial services sector has grown especially quickly, having more than doubled since 1978.

Published future projections of skills needs point to a persistence of these long-term, established trends into the future as the UK economy continues to see the development of knowledge-intensive industries and the growth of smaller business units in the service sector. According to the research commissioned by the Leitch Committee and carried out at Cambridge and Warwick Universities (Beaven et al 2005), the following can be expected between now and 2020:

Table 3.2 Changes in occupations, 1951–1999

Occupation	% in 1951	% in 1999
Higher professionals:	1.9	6.4
Lower professionals:	4.7	14.9
Employers and proprietors:	5.0	3.4
Managers and administrators:	5.5	15.7
Clerks:	10.7	14.9
Foremen, supervisors and inspectors:	2.6	3.1
Skilled manual:	24.9	12.7
Semi-skilled manual:	31.5	23.0
Unskilled manual:	13.1	5.9

Source: Labour Force Survey statistics accessed at www.statistics.gov.uk

Table 3.3 Changes in occupations, 2001–2008

Occupation	% in 2001	% in 2008
Managers and senior officials:	12.9	14.7
Professional occupations:	11.7	12.7
Associate professional and technical occupations:	13.2	14.2
Administrative and secretarial:	14.9	13.5
Skilled trades:	9.5	8.4
Personal services:	7.5	8.3
Sales and customer services:	8.6	8.6
Process, plant and machine operatives:	8.7	7.4
Elementary occupations:	13.2	12.1

Source: Labour Force Survey statistics accessed at www.statistics.gov.uk

- continued growth in demand for people to work in the service sectors, the highest levels of growth being in financial and business services
- continued reductions in demand for people to work in construction, manufacturing, primary and utility industries
- increases in demand for managers, professionals, associate professionals, sales and customer services, and personal services
- decreases in demand for administrative and secretarial roles, skilled trades, machine and transport operatives and (hugely) people to work in 'elementary occupations'.

The researchers estimate that UK employers will be creating around 2 million new management jobs over the next 15 years, 1 million new professional jobs and hundreds of thousands of new jobs in the customer services industries. However, they also reckon that there will be a fall of a few hundred thousand in the number of secretarial/administrative roles and skilled trades, and a fall of around 850,000 in the number of unskilled jobs by 2020. Their conclusion is thus that all the significant growth in the future is going to be in demand for people with skills – either soft skills (such as customer-handling), technical skills or higher-level skills requiring a degree-level education.

Another major recent report focusing on future demand for skills (Wilson et al 2006) was published by the Sector Skills Development Agency. Written by researchers based at the Institute for Employment Research at Warwick University, this too anticipates a continuation of established trends over the next few years, increases being anticipated in the demand for people to work in 'business and other services', 'non-marketed services' (ie public sector), distribution and transport. This study also presented evidence of likely future falls in the primary and utility sectors, construction and, particularly, in manufacturing employment. In terms of occupational groupings, the areas where significant growth is anticipated are as follows:

- managers, some professional and many associate professional occupations
- protective service occupations and culture/media/sports occupations
- caring, personal service and customer service occupations.

Falls are anticipated in the size of administrative skilled and unskilled occupational groups (Wilson et al 2006: xv–xvi).

The Leitch Review of Skills commissioned by the government also published its final report in 2006. Looking forward to 2020, it too stressed the likelihood that we will see a continuation of the established trend away from lower-skilled and towards higher-skilled work. Some of the most striking conclusions reached were as follows:

- Technological change increases demand for higher-level skills rather than reducing it, as is often claimed.
- There will be a 50% increase in the share of occupations classed as highly skilled.
- Skills that were once seen as being 'high level' will increasingly be regarded as 'basic' in nature.
- 45% of jobs are likely to require a degree-level education by 2020, a significant growing proportion will require a postgraduate qualification.
- 95% of jobs will require basic literacy and numeracy skills, while 90% will require a level 2 qualification (defined as 4 GCSEs at grades A–C).

CASE STUDY

ADMINISTRATIVE AND CLERICAL WORK

The one occupational group that appears to be bucking the historical trend in terms of its size and growth is the category that includes administrators, secretarial staff and clerks. The number of people employed in occupations of this kind grew steadily during the second half of the twentieth century along with other skilled, white-collar occupations. However, since the turn of the century or thereabouts, demand from employers for workers in this category has reversed and is now declining. Future projections show a continuation of this trend, it being predicted that the

UK economy will require several hundred thousand fewer people to fill administrative roles than is currently the case.

Question for discussion

What different factors can you identify which you think might explain:

- the growth in the number of secretarial and administrative roles between 1950 and 2000
- the decline in numbers since 2000
- an ongoing decline in the future?

SUPPLY OF SKILLS

The Leitch Report represents by far the most comprehensive and authoritative source of information on the readiness of the UK labour market to meet the likely future demand for skills outlined above, although McIntosh (2003) earlier reached similar conclusions in his rather shorter summary of key trends in the supply of skills. The government commissioned Sandy Leitch to undertake a review of the current stock of skills in the UK with a view to making recommendations about the actions that government, education providers and employers will need to take in order to ensure that the UK is well equipped to meet future economic challenges and opportunities. The final report, published in 2006, was forthright in its conclusions and recommendations.

The key conclusion was that despite the UK economy performing comparatively well in recent years, its capacity to continue doing so is seriously hampered by the fact that its 'skills base remains mediocre by international standards' (Leitch 2006: 10). The key recommendation is that in order to secure future prosperity in the 'new global economy, the UK must raise its sights and aim for world class skills' (Leitch 2006: 14). The report assesses the current level of skills in terms of three categories – basic platform skills, intermediate skills and high skills. It argues that substantial progress needs to be made in all three areas if the UK is not to fall behind its chief competitors as the global economy develops.

Some of the most worrying statistics highlighted by Leitch concern the proportion of adults in the UK who leave school without any qualifications or do so lacking a sufficient 'basic platform of skills' to enable them to gain employment in an economy which has less and less need each year for unskilled labour. The report defines the basic platform as being qualifications which are equivalent to 5 GCSEs at grades A to C. At the time that the report was published, 13% of adults lacked any qualifications at all, while a further 18% had left school without achieving the level 2 basic platform. This is 11 million people. However, rather more people are reported to lack either basic numeracy or literacy skills. More than 15 million people lack numeracy skills equivalent to Grades D–G in GCSE maths, while around 7 million do not meet basic 'entry level' numeracy – being unable, for example, 'to add or subtract money using decimal notation, or being able to work with fractions'. When it comes to literacy the majority had not achieved the level 2 qualification (ie grades A–C in GCSE English), while 5 million people (16% of the adult population) were not even at level 1 (ie grades D–G) and could be said to be 'functionally illiterate'. The future for people who lack these basic level skills is extremely bleak. There will be fewer and fewer jobs available for them in the future and thus very considerable incentives for them to improve their skills. In terms of international comparisons the UK performs badly in the area of basic platform skills, ranking 17th among the OECD countries, well behind major competitors such as the USA, Japan and Germany. In the USA only 10% lack this level of skill, compared with 38% in the UK.

The UK's position is also weak when comparisons are made about the number of adults who have intermediate skills – above level 2, but below degree level. Around 37% of UK adults have achieved this level of educational attainment, compared with 47% in Japan, 50% in the USA and 57% in Germany. Only in the final category – higher skills, being equivalent to degree level or above – can the UK claim to be performing at a level that is above average among OECD countries. Almost 30% of UK adults are educated to degree level, but this remains a smaller proportion than has been achieved in many competitor countries. In the USA and Japan, almost 40% of adults have a degree, while the figure is 45% in Canada. Other countries also spend a great deal more on higher education as a proportion of their national wealth than is the case in the UK.

The Leitch Report thus concludes that the UK suffers from a 'historic skills deficit' which will increasingly mean that the labour market is unable to supply employers with the skills they need. It goes on to make recommendations about the action that it is going to be necessary to take in order to rectify the situation, erase the skills deficit and ensure that by 2020 the UK the economy can draw on a 'world class skills base'. Most of the recommendations have since been taken up by the UK Government on behalf of England and by the devolved administrations in Scotland, Wales and Northern Ireland. The government White Paper *World Class Skills* published in 2007 sets the following targets for 2020:

- 95% of adults to be functionally literate and numerate

- more than 90% of adults to have gained a level 2 qualification

- 2 million more people to have level 3 qualifications

- 500,000 people to be in apprenticeships

- 40% of adults to have degree-level qualifications.

The paper confirms the aim to lift the age at which people can leave full-time education from 16 to 18. However, many of the proposals are focused on adult learners and on the role to be played by employers. We will focus on some of these initiatives in detail in Chapter 4. They include, for example, employers being given incentives to make a 'Skills Pledge', amounting to a public declaration that they will take responsibility for helping their staff to gain basic levels of educational attainment (ie literacy, numeracy and level 2 qualifications in areas of value to the employer). In return for making the pledge, the employer will gain access to the services of a government-funded 'skills brokerage service' and other support to help source appropriate training providers. Public funding will be made available for a proportion of the training. The government hopes that once employers work with skills brokers in raising these basic skills, and observe the benefits it brings to them, they will take advantage of opportunities to fund higher-level training for staff themselves. This is further being encouraged through the formation of a UK Commission for Employment and Skills with a devolved, regional structure, which will articulate employer priorities in the training field. The aim then is for public sector training and education providers to become much more 'demand-led' than they currently are – providing programmes which are tailored to meet the needs of employers. The other major proposal is the establishment of an Adult Careers Service, which will run a 'skills account' scheme. This will be something individuals join as a means of demonstrating the skills they have attained and where the funding has come from (employer, state or themselves).

These are all important initiatives, but the targets are highly ambitious and will require much more than government willpower and substantial public funding if they are to be achieved in practice. It must be remembered, as Leitch points out, that more than 70% of the people who will form the UK's workforce in 2020 had already left full-time education by 2006. Making radical improvements to the level of skills in the UK is thus going to require the active participation of employers, along with funding, and the willing participation of the millions of adults whose qualifications are below those the government wants to see them achieve. A real revolution in attitudes among the existing workforce alongside major injections of public and private money will be needed. While progress can and will certainly be made, it is highly unlikely that the targets set out above will be met by 2020. These are more government aspirations than firm commitments. It is necessary for leaders in all areas of life to set ambitious goals, but the likelihood in this case is that they will not be achieved in practice. We can therefore anticipate some growth between now and 2020 in the skills gap that employers face. The supply of skills, particularly at the higher, more specialised end of the market, will continue to be scarce, contributing to a further tightening of labour markets.

One of the consequences, as is hoped and expected by the Leitch Report and the White Paper, is that employers will in part respond by investing more in developing their own staff. So we are likely to see employee development, and particularly management development, rising up the HR agenda in the coming years. Another major consequence of the trends discussed in this chapter will be a greater willingness on the part of employers to look to new labour markets in order to recruit staff with the skills they need. Older people who have passed the age of retirement but who have key skills will be one target group. Others will include parents who have taken time out of work in order to bring up children and others who for one reason or another are currently 'economically inactive' and are not putting their skills at the disposal of the economy. Overseas recruitment will continue, but because it will become increasingly difficult and costly, there will be a need to take greater care over who is recruited and much more interest in the retention of overseas staff once they have been employed. Finally, we are also going to see greater competition between employers for staff in the groups with relatively scarce skills. This has implications for reward policy, management practice generally and the need to foster a positive reputation in the labour market. We will return to all of these issues later in the book.

SKILLS SHORTAGES

While it can be argued that acute skills shortages will worsen in the future, it is important to recognise that in some lines of work they are already very much with us. The most recent Learning and Skills Council survey of employers in England (LSC 2006) included the following findings:

- 17% of organisations in their sample had vacancies at the time the survey was conducted – a total of 571,000.

- 7% of organisations had vacancies at that time which they classed as 'hard to fill'.

- 25% of vacancies are considered by employers to be in areas where there are skills shortages (ie around 150,000 at any one time).

- 16% of organisations claim that there are 'skills gaps' among their existing staff.

- 6% of all staff are described by employers as not being proficient in their jobs due to skills gaps (that is 1.3 million employees in England).

However, the extent to which particular labour markets are affected varies considerably. In some lines of work there is no major problem for employers finding people who have the required skills and experience to carry out a job proficiently. This is true of administrative and secretarial roles and the elementary occupations. Here, according to LSC data, fewer than 20% of vacancies are hard to fill or subject to skills shortages. Skills shortages are most acute when recruiting people for roles in the 'skilled trades' category. Here, nearly half of all vacancies are perceived by employers as being hard to fill. Above-average figures are also reported for 'associate professionals', 'professionals' and 'transport and machine operatives'.

The most acute shortages are therefore in the more specialised areas of work where people are required to have particular skills of a technical nature or specific qualifications in order to carry out their roles. The same picture emerges from the survey data on skill gaps among the current workforce. High figures (ie more than 50% of employers reporting skills gaps) are reported in the more specialist, technical areas.

However, there are other important gaps too – principally softer, people-oriented skills. Teamworking, customer-handling skills and oral communication are also reported as being areas where employers perceive their own staff to be lacking in key skills.

When asked about the 'main causes of skill gaps', employers partly blame themselves for failing to train and develop staff effectively (29%) and partly blame staff for lacking the motivation to become fully proficient (34%). However, more often the problem is related to the tightness of labour markets. Some gaps are caused either by high staff turnover or an inability to find suitable people to fill vacancies (50%). More often, the problem arises from the recruitment of people who do not have sufficient experience and thus fail to perform to the expected level (73%).

THE HOURGLASS METAPHOR

Peter Nolan (2001) first adopted the metaphor of an hourglass to illustrate a key evolving trend in the UK labour market. This was subsequently developed by Goos and Manning (2003) in their influential article contrasting 'McJobs' with 'MacJobs' and has been debated in detail by other writers (see Grugulis et al 2004). The essential claim made is that over time we are increasingly seeing a polarisation of work into two core categories, one comprising highly skilled and highly paid roles, the other lower-skilled and lower-paid roles. This represents a change from the past when many jobs fell in between these two categories, being skilled manual and administrative roles which have largely now either been replaced by machines or exported overseas. Fitzner (2006) takes issue with this analysis, claiming that the hourglass thesis was based on data collected in the last quarter of the twentieth century and that there has been something of a reversal in the first years of the twenty-first century. He is particularly keen to skewer what he calls the 'myth of the disappearing middle', arguing that recent years have seen a halt in its decline.

In terms of future trends it is not possible to be certain, but the analysis set out above concerning demand and supply of skills suggests strongly that we will see a solidification of the hourglass occupational structure in the future. Fitzner (2006) makes some good points about developments between 2000 and 2006, but his statistics demonstrate that even during these years it was at the higher and lower ends of the income scale that most growth occurred. Moreover, of course, this period was one in which government spending on public services (particularly on health, education, the police and government administration) grew at an abnormally fast rate. Since then expansion of these sectors has slowed very considerably, the longer-term trends once again asserting themselves.

It is thus fair to conclude that the UK labour market will continue to polarise over the coming decade, maintaining and further developing this 'upstairs–downstairs' character which has become prevalent in recent years. On the one hand we will see strong growth in demand for people to fill 'upstairs jobs' and relatively slower growth in the supply of such skills. Upstairs labour markets will tighten, forcing employers to improve their offering, to treat job-holders well and to develop more-sophisticated approaches to recruitment and retention. On the other hand, we will see a relative decline in demand for people to work in lower-skilled roles and a surplus of labour supply. As a result in the downstairs world, labour markets will be loose, leading to poorer-quality working experiences as employers minimise costs in the knowledge that they can replace leavers relatively easily.

From the point of view of human resource management it is the upstairs world that will preoccupy because it is here that staffing will be problematic. Organisations which employ large numbers of lower-skilled workers will be able to continue to meet their objectives without the need for extensive HR input beyond the need for basic administration and training functions. It will be the growing higher-skill, knowledge-focused jobs which are hard to fill satisfactorily that will become the focus of most HR activity in practice.

- Employers have been creating increasing numbers of jobs over several decades. During periods of recession demand for people has reduced, but the long-term trend is strongly in an upward direction.

- Sources of new employees that have enabled supply to meet demand over past decades are beginning to dry up or become increasingly costly.

- In the future a good majority of new jobs will be higher-skilled, in many cases requiring holders to have specialist higher education. This too is a long-established trend.

- Despite ambitious targets being set by government, it is unlikely that skills levels among the UK workforce will increase sufficiently to meet increased demand for higher-skilled workers.

- Organisations will increasingly have to seek employees from among groups in the UK who are classed as 'economically inactive'. This will require both increased use of flexible working practices and higher standards of people management more generally.

- Specialised staff will increasingly be sourced from overseas. This will mean that UK workforces become increasingly diverse in terms of their cultural, national and racial backgrounds.

- The labour market will become increasingly polarised. Higher-paid, higher-skilled groups will be in relatively short supply. Employers will have to compete increasingly hard to recruit and retain these people. By contrast more people will be seeking lower-skilled, lower-paid jobs than there will be jobs available to them.

I would recommend anyone with an interest in skills development in the UK to read the Leitch Report and the supporting evidence published alongside it in 2006. You can download these from the HM Treasury website (www.official-documents.gov. uk).

Leitch, S. (2006) *Prosperity for all in the global economy – world class skills*. Final report. The Leitch Review of Skills. London: HM Treasury.

The best source of up-to-date information about British population trends is the National Statistics website.

The labour market in winter, edited by Paul Gregg and Jonathan Wadsworth (2011), is the latest in a line of their books covering all the most important contemporary developments in the UK labour market, including issues relating to population ageing.

Gregg, P. and Wadsworth, J. (eds) (2011) *The labour market in winter*. Oxford: Oxford University Press.

REFERENCES

Audit Commission (2008) *Tomorrow's people: building a local government workforce for the future*. London: Audit Commission. (www.audit-commission.gov.uk)

Banks, J. and Casanova, M. (2004) Work and retirement. In M. Marmot, J. Banks, R. Blundell, C. Lessof and J. Nazroo (eds) *Health, wealth and lifestyles of the older population in England: the 2002 English longitudinal study of ageing*. London: Institute of Fiscal Studies.

Batata, A. (2005) International nurse recruitment and NHS vacancies: A cross-sectional analysis. *Globalisation and Health*. Vol 1, No 7.

Beaven, R., Bosworth, D., Lewney, R. and Wilson, R. (2005) *Alternative skills scenarios to 2020 for the UK economy*. Cambridge: Cambridge Econometrics.

Blanchflower, D., Saleheen, J. and Shadforth, C. (2007) *The impact of recent migration from eastern Europe on the UK economy*. London: Bank of England.

DfCSF (2007) *Reducing the number of young people not in education, employment or training: the strategy*. London: Department for Children, Schools and Families.

Fitzner, G. (2006) *How have employees fared? Recent UK trends*. Employee Relations Research Series No. 56. London: Department for Trade and Industry (now Department for Business, Innovation and Skills).

GAD (2006) *Migration and population growth*. London: Government Actuary's Department.

Gadenne, L., Given, R., Stephens, M. and Wilkinson, C. (2006) *2.5 million more jobs*. Department for Work and Pensions. Working Paper 36. London: DWP.

Goos, M. and Manning, A. (2003) McJobs and MacJobs: the growing polarisation of jobs in the UK. In R. Dickens, P. Gregg and J. Wadsworth (eds) *The labour market under New Labour*. Basingstoke: Palgrave.

Grugulis, I., Warhurst, C. and Keep, E. (2004) What's happening to 'skill'? In C. Warhurst, I. Grugulis and E. Keep (eds) *The skills that matter*. Basingstoke: Palgrave.

Horsfield, G. (2005) International migration. In ONS (ed.) *Focus on people and migration*. London: Office for National Statistics.

Learning and Skills Council (2006) *National employers skills survey 2005: key findings*. London: LSC.

Leitch, S. (2006) *Prosperity for all in the global economy – world-class skills*. Final Report. The Leitch Review of Skills. London: HM Treasury.

McIntosh, S. (2003) Skills in the UK. In R. Dickens, P. Gregg and J. Wadsworth (eds) *The labour market under New Labour*. Basingstoke: Palgrave.

Migration Watch UK (2005) *UK population increase through migration*. Briefing Paper 9.17. London: Migration Watch UK.

Milmo, C. (2008) Tightening of immigration laws means farmers face losing 50,000 tonnes of fruit. *Independent*. 12 May.

National Statistics (2006) *Social trends 36*. Basingstoke: Palgrave Macmillan.

Nolan, P. (2001) Shaping things to come. *People Management*. 27 December.

United Nations (2005) *World population prospects: the 2004 revision*. New York: United Nations.

Universities UK (2008) *The future size and shape of the higher education sector in the UK: demographic projections*. London: UUK.

Wilson, R., Homenidou, K. and Dickerson, A. (2006) *Working futures 2004-2014: national report*. Skills for Business. Warwick: Institute of Employment Research.

CHAPTER 4

Regulation and public policy

Introduction

The very considerable growth in the volume and complexity of employment regulation that we have seen in recent decades constitutes a further major development in the HR business environment. In truth, we have seen nothing short of a transformation of the regulatory environment as UK labour markets have moved from being among of the most lightly regulated in the world to being among the most tightly regulated. This process was recently described by Heery (2010: 72) as comprising 'arguably the most significant change in the real world of work since the establishment of industrial relations as an academic field after the Second World War'. All manner of consequences have followed as trade unions have assumed a less significant role in determining how employee relations are regulated and the amount of litigation has grown exponentially. No analysis of the contemporary HR landscape can be complete without serious analysis of these trends and their practical impact on how people are managed in organisations. We also need to examine the reasons behind this shift, in order that we can explore how far it is likely to continue in the future.

In this chapter I am going to argue that the rise of employment law has had a significant impact on practical HR management in organisations and that by and large this has been positive when seen both from employer and employee perspectives. However, I also want to suggest that the 'era of regulation' which we have recently been living through is now reaching its end-point. We are unlikely, in coming decades, to see increases in employment regulation on anything like the scale of the past 20 years. Amendments will be made and we will certainly see some deregulation alongside some new regulation, but to a very great extent now our 'regulatory revolution' can be said to have run its course. We will see few further examples of really major reform, at least for the foreseeable future.

This does not mean, however, that public policy will not continue to impinge on HRM in important ways. In fact, there is a strong case for predicting that the extent of government involvement in activities that are HR-related in one way or another is likely to increase rather than decrease in the future. But this will not take the form of more employment law. Instead we are likely to see a greater tendency for pressure to be placed on employers, through various incentives and disincentives, to assist governments in the achievement of a variety of diverse public policy objectives.

LEARNING OUTCOMES

The objectives of this chapter are to:

- outline the extent of the regulatory revolution that the employment relationship has undergone in recent decades
- explain the major reasons for recent increases in employment regulation in the UK
- set out the major arguments for and against deregulating in the field of employment law
- argue that the regulatory revolution has now largely run its course
- discuss ways in which a range of public policy objectives in the employment field will only be able to be met with the co-operation and support of organisations.

A REGULATORY REVOLUTION

Until relatively recently there was very little statutory regulation of the employment relationship in the UK. The current mountain of regulation which employers are obliged to take account of has thus only been built up in the last two or three decades. There has been no grand strategy. Instead, UK employment law has been developed in a piecemeal way, governments legislating as and when they felt the need to, the pace of new legislation increasing in the last 10–15 years.

It is not wholly true to state that there was no employment regulation before the 1960s. As Davies and Freedland (1993) show in their excellent book on the history of employment regulation in the UK, some law existed in the early part of the twentieth century in the fields of health and safety, working time and arrangements for the payment of wages. It was unlawful, for example, to employ children under the age of 14 except in family-run businesses and to employ women on most night shifts. Health and safety standards in factories were reasonably well regulated, but not in other types of workplace. People also had the right to be paid 'in the coin of the realm' and had, of course, the general right for their contract of employment to be honoured by their employer. But that was about it. There was no protection from dismissal on spurious grounds, nothing in law to prevent discriminatory treatment on grounds of sex, race or any other grounds, no maternity or paternity rights and no right to any paid holiday each year.

The situation in the UK was very different from that in most European countries where, by contrast, lengthy and effectively policed codes which employers had to follow were in force, backed up both by criminal and civil sanctions. This situation prompted the legal scholar Otto Khan-Freund (1954: 44) famously to write that:

> There is, perhaps, no major country in the world in which the law has played a less significant role in the shaping of industrial relations than in Great Britain and in which the law and legal profession have less to do with labour relations.

The reason for this was a generally held belief that the state should 'stay out' of employment relations, leaving it to employees and their representatives to negotiate terms and conditions freely with their employers without any assistance or interference from the law. This principle of 'collective *laissez-faire*' was widely accepted among politicians, business people, lawyers and trade unions.

Things started to change in the 1960s with the introduction of legislation which guaranteed minimum severance payments to people who were made redundant. A fledgling employment tribunal system was set up to adjudicate disputes on these matters in 1965. After that, slowly and steadily, modern employment law began to take shape. Equal pay legislation was introduced in 1970, followed shortly afterwards in 1971 by a general right not to be unfairly dismissed. The major motivation behind these developments was a wish on the part of ministers to reduce the number of days being lost to strike action over disputes about these things. 1974 saw comprehensive health and safety regulation and basic maternity rights being introduced, followed in 1975 and 1976 by measures that sought to outlaw unjustified discrimination on grounds of sex and race.

By the 1980s further new legislation in the employment field was necessary in order to meet the requirement of European directives, the UK having joined the EEC (European Economic Community, subsequently the European Union) in 1972. Among other measures, these required significant extensions to be made to equal pay and health and safety regulations, alongside new rights for employees affected by the 'transfer of an undertaking' (ie a change in the identity of their employer). The 1980s also saw the introduction of extensive regulation intended to curb the influence of trade unions. Hence we saw the introduction of pre-strike ballots, the ending of closed-shop arrangements whereby union membership was a condition of employment in a workplace and attempts to outlaw secondary industrial action and mass picketing.

From the mid-1990s onwards the emphasis switched back to building up statutory rights for individual employees. Since then employers have had to take on board two or three major new pieces of employment legislation in most years. In addition, thanks to the provision of many new opportunities for aggrieved staff, we have seen a massive increase in the number of cases that employment tribunals are obliged to deal with each year.

Since 1997 it has become unlawful in principle to discriminate in employment on grounds of disability, age, belief, sexual orientation, people in civil partnerships, transsexuals and women who are either pregnant or new mothers. Discriminatory treatment of people who are employed on part-time or fixed-term contracts has also been outlawed in many circumstances as, since 2011, has been much unfair discrimination against agency workers. In addition, major extensions of family-friendly law have seen the introduction of more paid maternity leave, of parental and paternity leave rights, of regulations protecting people who take time off at short notice for family reasons and of a right to request flexible working arrangements.

Other major reforms included the introduction of a National Minimum Wage, new restrictions on working time and, in some circumstances, a legal right for unions to be recognised by an employer for the purposes of bargaining on pay, hours and holidays.

The net result is a situation in which aggrieved employees, would-be employees and former employees can now bring to employment tribunals more than 80 distinct types of claim (Shackleton 2005: 128) and in which a quarter of HR professionals are obliged to spend 40% of their working days dealing with employment law-related issues (CIPD 2002). A big, profitable industry has grown up which now employs thousands of lawyers and specialist consultants to advise clients on employment law, while the number of cases being lodged with tribunals has reached more than 250,000 a year.

The past 30 years have not just seen the establishment of new employment rights. They have also seen numerous new interpretations of what the law means in practice being made by judges in the courts. A bewilderingly large body of precedents has thus been established which employers somehow are expected to be aware of, to understand and to act on.

If we are correctly to predict the future trajectory of new employment law we need to get a grasp on why this regulatory revolution took place over the past two or three decades so that we can judge how much more regulated employment relationships should and/or will become. While there has been no single major cause, a number of key antecedents can be identified.

THE EUROPEAN UNION

A great deal of recent employment law originates at the European level rather than in the UK. It thus applies across all 27 member states and is intended to help ensure that no one country is able to steal a competitive march on the others by keeping a lid on the employment costs it imposes which organisations based elsewhere in the EU have to shoulder. Because most EU member states have long traditions of extensive employment regulation, the UK has had to make a much greater adjustment than most in order to bring its law into line.

Some recent innovations in employment law which have a European origin would almost certainly not apply in the UK was it not for our membership of the EU. This is true of the working time regulations, discrimination law covering age and belief, parental leave rights, the right to take time off to deal with family emergencies and the agency workers regulations that came into effect in 2011. In other areas we would probably have some regulation, but it would be less complex and burdensome in its operation than is the case due to EU requirements. This is true of the transfer of undertakings regulations, of European Works Councils and other compulsory consultative arrangements, and some health and safety regulations.

THE DECLINE OF TRADE UNIONS AND COLLECTIVE BARGAINING ARRANGEMENTS

The loss of members and, more importantly, of power in most industries by the trade union movement is another important explanation for the 'rise of employment law' in recent years. Prior to the 1970s and 1980s trade unions enjoyed much higher levels of membership than they now do (see Chapter 1), which enabled them to provide effective protection from injustice and sharp practice perpetrated by employers.

Alongside their decline, particularly in larger private sector organisations, has come a decline in the coverage and extent of collective agreements. In short, this means that managers enjoy a much more extensive prerogative than was the case in the past and can determine the rules that are observed in their organisations as far as employment is concerned without the need to negotiate with union officials or to take any notice of collective workforce opinion. In other words, collective *laissez-faire* of the kind that so impressed Khan-Freund in the 1950s has 'stopped working', requiring an alternative model to be established.

In order to offer decent protection to employees from unjust use of managerial prerogative and to deter abuse of power by managers, the state has had to step in to provide a floor of statutory rights.

In the early days of employment regulation in the UK, trade unions tended to oppose measures on the grounds that they served to undermine their position. Why join a union if your basic employment rights are protected just as effectively, if not more effectively, by the law? Over time, though, union opinion has moved. Trade unions have been in the vanguard of campaigns for changes to employment law in recent years and, for the most part, have actively supported the evolution of employment regulation at the European level. The shift has come about thanks to a recognition on their part that they no longer have sufficient power to achieve these objectives themselves on behalf of their members.

Moreover, some major employment rights were introduced specifically in order to reduce the need for industrial action on the part of trade unions, the aim being to reduce the incidence of strikes. This is true of unfair dismissal law, in particular, and also of some early anti-discrimination measures such as equal pay law.

In truth, therefore, we can conclude both that trade union decline has created a need for more employment regulation, but that the new regulation has to some extent also served to hasten union decline.

MAKING WORK ATTRACTIVE

Certainly in more recent years government policy in the area of employment has been underpinned by a belief that regulation has positive long-term benefits for the national economy. The clearest statement of this doctrine is found in the White Paper that the Blair Government issued shortly after coming to power in 1997. It was called *Fairness at Work* and its purpose was both to set the course and to justify the programme of increased regulation that ministers were then planning. Expressed simply, the idea was that one of the key challenges the UK economy faced was skills shortages and that government had a duty to intervene in order to help reduce these. Employment regulation helps to achieve such objectives in three major ways:

- by making it more attractive for people who have skills but are not working to rejoin the workforce (eg people who have taken early retirement and people who are full-time carers or homemakers)

- by seeking to offer employment conditions that are more attractive to people based overseas – particularly 'highly skilled migrants' – than those offered in other countries to which they might consider going to work

- by reducing staff turnover and providing incentives for employers to invest in their staff over the long term, providing them with training opportunities.

In addition, the *Fairness at Work* White Paper made a powerful case for improving communication and participation with employees. It argued in favour of the establishment of 'partnership arrangements' with trade unions and called, in a more general sense, for the creation of higher-trust, sophisticated employment relationships.

A lot of this thinking underpinned the legislation brought forward by the Blair Government, particularly in the area of family-friendly employment rights and flexible working. Similar arguments have been made more recently by the Coalition Government that came to power in 2010 with an ambitious agenda to extend flexible working rights to many more people.

OTHER MOTIVES

Aside from these three major factors that explain the rise of employment regulation can be listed some others too. One is very simply a belief in greater social justice. Sometimes laws need to be introduced simply because it is right that they should be in order to protect groups who have relatively little power. Such arguments were to the fore when Labour ministers were introducing the National Minimum Wage, for example, and when Conservative ministers were taking the Disability Discrimination Act through Parliament.

In addition, from time to time, governments have legislated in the employment field largely for reasons of political expediency. In the 1980s the laws which sought to restrict trade union power – particularly the Employment Act 1982 – were intended to garner positive headlines in the newspapers for a Conservative government that had been very unpopular and was soon to face a general election. More recently the Blair and Brown Governments legislated in response to demands from trade unions for specific reforms just before planned election campaigns for which the unions provided much-needed funding. These changes came out of the 'Warwick Agreements' of 2004 and 2008. They included the extension of the statutory annual holiday entitlement from 20 to 28 days and the law requiring employers to distribute tips earned by their staff in addition to paying them the National Minimum Wage.

KEY ARTICLE

HR MANAGERS' VIEWS ABOUT EMPLOYMENT REGULATION

The following article was published in *People Management* on 27 July 2005. You can download it from the CIPD website:

'Right and wrong sides of the law' by Adam Turner

This article describes the main results from an extensive survey of HR managers undertaken jointly by the CIPD and the law firm Lovells. You can also download the full survey from the CIPD's website in the surveys area. It is called *Employment and the Law: Burden or benefit?*

The survey found that HR managers are generally in favour of employment regulation, particularly anti-discrimination laws and regulations which are designed to promote flexible and family-friendly practices. Indeed, in many organisations, the HR department actively seeks to go beyond the requirements of the law in these areas. This is apparently true of a majority of public sector organisations.

HR managers are, however, collectively less impressed with the working time regulations and show little enthusiasm for collective employment rights designed to protect trade union members. They also tend to agree that much employment law is badly drafted and unclear in what it expects of employers.

Questions

1 Why do you think that HR managers generally are in favour of extensive employment regulation?

2 Why are they less favourable towards collective labour law than they are towards employment regulation which protects individual rights at work?

3 Why are line managers and managers in the small business sector usually found in surveys to be a good deal less keen on employment law?

CONTEMPORARY DEBATES

How employment regulation develops in the future will depend on which side prevails in ongoing debates about the need to reform the law. While many people have different views about different parts of employment law, Heery (2010) is broadly right to characterise the major current debate as being between 'regulationist' and 'deregulationist' camps.

Business opinion tends to be divided, the representatives of smaller enterprises (eg the Institute of Directors and the Federation of Small Businesses) generally being much more opposed to employment regulation than organisations such as the Confederation of British Industry (CBI) and indeed the CIPD, whose membership tends to be drawn from larger companies.

Those who approve of the development of employment regulation tend to argue that further reform is required in order to make it work more effectively. They draw attention, for example, to areas of law which are clearly not meeting their objectives and which thus need to be strengthened. A major target of such arguments is equal pay law, which we have had in broadly its current form since 1975. In its early days it had a big impact, helping to narrow the 'pay gap' between men and women from around 40% to 18%. But progress has apparently now stalled, and according to some analyses we are beginning to see a new widening of the gap between male and female earnings. It is thus argued that wholesale reform is now required, new regulation being introduced which will force employers to carry out equal pay audits and to rectify matters when a clearly unjustified gap is discovered between what predominantly male and female groups of workers are paid. In order to achieve this some form of new inspectorate would be required to undertake enforcement duties.

The case is also commonly argued for increasing the level of statutory redundancy payments and for tightening up on procedures for selecting people and consulting with them before redundancies take effect. This argument is often made with reference to the tighter regimes that are found in most other EU countries, where it is generally a great deal more expensive to make groups of staff redundant. The net result is that overseas companies who employ people across Europe tend to make their UK employees redundant rather than equivalent staff in other countries. UK plants are closed down in preference to Spanish, French or German ones purely because it is cheaper to do so.

A related point can be made about compensation levels in tribunals generally. The amount of money that claimants win is often too low to provide any serious deterrent for employers when they are considering whether or not to act in a way which is potentially unlawful. This is particularly true of dismissals on grounds of minor acts of misconduct or poor work performance. The hassle associated with managing these matters according to the expectations of the law – investigations, hearings, appeals, etc – is too great compared with the compensation that will have to be paid if a decision is taken to dismiss in any event. It is cheaper and much easier simply to dismiss and settle the case with a compromise agreement, rather than to meet the full expectations of the law.

In the opposite corner are those who take the view that employment regulation heaps unnecessary costs onto businesses, makes UK enterprises less competitive than they could be in world markets, and deters employers from taking on new staff. In particular, the point is often made that the level of costly regulation is now so great that the very groups it is intended most to protect actually suffer because of it. This happens because employers quietly decline to appoint them.

The major group which is believed to suffer most from employment protection legislation is young women, who it is argued employers avoid employing because of the wide range of maternity and parental rights that are now available to them. Lea (2001: 57) reported that 45% of Institute of Directors members 'felt that such rights were a disincentive to hiring women of prime child-rearing age', while a survey of younger women by the Equal Opportunities Commission (EOC) (2005) stated that 45% of its respondents had suffered some form of discrimination for reasons of pregnancy, while 7% (equating to around 30,000 women a year) had lost their jobs as a result of having become pregnant. More recently, Sir Alan Sugar, probably the most well-known employer in the country, expressed his view that many employers in practice simply bin CVs that are sent to them by women of childbearing age due to the potential costs involved (*Daily Telegraph* 2008).

To these arguments can be added a more cost-based case that is concerned as much with enhancing international competitiveness as it is with the impact of employment law on employment opportunities. Quite simply, it is argued, regulation places unnecessary and burdensome costs on organisations, which make it harder for them to succeed commercially. The actual extent of the costs involved is heavily disputed, but few doubt that it runs into billions of pounds each year for the UK economy as a whole. As long ago as 2004 the government's Better Regulation Taskforce estimated that the figure for business regulation in general was in excess of £100 million a year, while the CBI (2000) stated that the costs for companies associated simply with the implementation of the National Minimum Wage and Working Time Regulations had been more than £10 billion.

Particular concern has been raised recently about the number of cases that are being lodged with the Employment Tribunal Service. The figures have shot up in recent years, causing many people to question whether the whole employment law system has not simply grown too big and unwieldy. In 2009–10, the total number of claims that the Employment Tribunal Service received was 236,100. This represented an increase of 56% on 2008–09, but the extent of the growth over a longer period is more striking. Ten years earlier in 1999–2000, the figure was just 103,935 and 20 years earlier just 34,703. These figures reflect both the growth of employment regulation and an increased willingness on the part of employees to pursue grievances against their employers in court.

Unquestionably, as anyone working in the employment law field knows only too well, one of the major reasons for the growth in tribunal claims has been the arrival on the scene of legal firms who are prepared to take cases on a 'no win, no fee basis'. They tend to operate by sending employers threatening letters demanding large sums of money by way of compensation for their clients. In many cases the figures are hugely inflated and bear little resemblance to the kind of compensation that the individuals would win if they pursued their case to a full tribunal hearing, but the employers who receive them often don't know this. They are also concerned about the legal fees that they themselves would have to shoulder in order to fight the case. They therefore agree to settle for a few thousand pounds and a confidentiality agreement. This situation is made possible by the fact that tribunal litigation has essentially become a 'no risk' activity as far as claimants are concerned. Costs are only very rarely awarded against a losing party, while 'no win, no fee' claims mean that legal fees are only shouldered by a victorious claimant, or more often, one who achieves an out-of-court settlement ahead of the scheduled hearing.

No win, no fee settlements are, of course, only made possible by the unpredictable nature of so much litigation that is carried on in the field of employment law. The law, quite simply, is often very unclear, making it difficult to predict the outcome of cases. Too much hinges on the view that a particular panel (employment judge plus two wing members) will reach on a particular day. This happens because in employment law the tests that are used to determine the outcome of cases leave far too much to individual judgement. The major examples are all problematic when seen from this perspective:

- Did the employer's actions fall within the band of reasonable responses?

- Did the employer's policies amount to a proportionate means of achieving a legitimate aim?

- Did the employer/employee act in such a way as to breach a relationship of trust and confidence?

As a result employers often have no idea what they should be doing to comply with the law and, subsequently, once a case has been brought against them, often have no idea at all whether or not they have acted unlawfully. Settling cases that might in fact be won is thus the path that many choose to take. Indeed many larger employers now settle pretty well all cases as a matter of policy on commercial terms simply as a means of minimising their costs.

Another point that is often made is that the nature of some grievances that claimants now regularly take to employment tribunals are far too trivial in nature to deserve the attention of a formal court, let alone form the basis of a hearing lasting several days. This point tends to be made in response to press reports about hearings that relate to relatively minor acts of alleged unlawful discrimination, where the 'detriment' that claimants say they have suffered appears on the face of it to be pretty limited. The following quotation from a column by Boris Johnson (2011) makes the point very colourfully:

> Maybe I have this all wrong. It could be that Mr Konstantinos Kalomoiris will one day join the Tolpuddle Martyrs in the pantheon of those who have fought for the rights of working people. Perhaps Billy Bragg will strum an anthem in his honour and the trade unions will stitch his likeness to their gaily-coloured banners; and perhaps a street will be named after him in Islington and a plaque will be unveiled in Transport House, complete with a fiery speech by Tony Benn or Mr Tristram Hunt MP. Perhaps all future members of the British labour force – including my own grandchildren – will give thanks that Mr Konstantinos Kalomoiris decided he could take it no more.
>
> After three slaps on the bottom he took a stand, on behalf of himself and his entire gender. No matter that the bottom-patter (alleged) had worked for 40 years for the firm, with an 'unblemished record'. Never mind that she was a 68-year-old woman, who insisted that she had only 'touched his back in a caring way, like a mother or grandmother'.
>
> Mr Kalomoiris, 40, has sued the company, John Lewis – a notably tender-hearted employer – for sexual discrimination and harassment; and, as I

*say, my instincts could be completely out of whack. This could turn out to
be a ground-breaking case in the advancement of workers' rights against the
unfeeling boss class. But I sincerely doubt it. It sounds to me like a perfect
indication of the levels of barminess now being attained by our system of
employment tribunals. The hearing continues, it says at the bottom of the
reports, and my first thought is how mad, how incredible it is that this poor
man's grievance – whatever it really is – has come to court.*

The key point that Boris Johnson makes in this article is that a full court hearing,
staged at considerable cost to the taxpayer, is not the best place to sort out
relatively insignificant disputes between employers and employees of this kind.
Moreover, he is suggesting, that the motive for the litigation is often a desire to
bag compensation and not any really genuine sense of grievance.

Looking back through my own notes about employment law cases that have
been reported in legal journals in recent years (published on the CIPD website),
I cannot help but be struck by how trivial some of the issues at stake appear to
be. Of course, in many cases a legal principle of some genuine significance is
being decided, but nonetheless it is hard not to agree with Boris Johnson that
some other, much less costly way of sorting out these kinds of dispute between
employers and employees should be found. Here are some examples:

- *City of Edinburgh v Dickson* (2010) concerned the rights of a man who had
  been dismissed for downloading pornography from the Internet while at work.
  There had apparently been a failure to take account of the fact that Mr Dickson
  suffered from diabetes and of his claim that he had viewed the pornography
  during a 'hypoglycaemic episode' and was therefore unaware of what he was
  doing.

- *Eweida v British Airways* (2008) concerned the right of an airport check-in
  officer to wear a crucifix over her uniform.

- *Nixon v Ross Coates Solicitors* (2010) concerned a woman who became
  pregnant after having had two separate affairs with work colleagues. 'Who's
  the daddy' gossip was widespread in the offices at which she and they worked.
  Management had done nothing to stop it.

- *Chondol v Liverpool City Council* (2009) concerned the dismissal of a social
  worker who had discussed his Christian faith with clients, had given one a
  Bible and had told others that he believed in God and went to church regularly.

- *Grainger PLC & others v Nicholson* (2009) concerned whether or not a man
  who felt very strongly about climate change should be protected from unlawful
  discrimination.

- *Willoughby v CF Capital* (2010) focused on a situation in which a letter of
  dismissal had been sent to the claimant by mistake. Was Mrs Willoughby free
  to pursue an unfair dismissal claim in these circumstances?

- *English v Thomas Sanderson Blinds Ltd* (2009) concerned whether or not
  a heterosexual man who had been subjected to homophobic banter and
  innuendo by co-workers should be able to claim discrimination on grounds of
  his sexual orientation.

- *Parsons v Bristol Street Fourth Investments Ltd T/A Bristol Street Motors* (2008) concerned the alleged constructive dismissal of Mr Parsons, who alleged that his boss had subjected him to a campaign of bullying that involved grabbing him by the testicles, giving him 'the hairdryer treatment', calling him by nicknames such as 'the old parsonage' and 'old git', and 'engaging in dangerous behaviour in the workplace including the use of an air gun, a mini-motorbike and a go-cart'.

- *Campbell v Falkirk Council* concerned whether or not a claim for disability discrimination on account of baldness could be sustained. The claimant had been harassed on account of his bald head by pupils at the school he taught at.

It is difficult not to conclude that both the regulationists and the deregulationists identified by Edmund Heery (2010) have good points to make. On the one hand, there is a lot of seemingly trivial litigation that is motivated primarily by a desire to win compensation. It is also true that this places unnecessary costs onto employers and can deter them from taking on staff. On the other hand, the regulationists are right to argue that major injustices continue to be perpetrated by employers who abuse the power they have over their staff and the regulatory system would offer more by way of deterrence if it operated more effectively.

CASE STUDY

From time to time attempts have been made to establish alternative methods of settling employment disputes which do not require a tribunal hearing.

The most recent has been the alternative process for determining unfair dismissal cases by arbitration that is offered by Acas (the Advisory, Conciliation and Arbitration Service). This option is available when both the claimant and the respondent choose to take it rather than to take the case to a full tribunal hearing. The scheme was launched in May 2001, but it has never been popular. In most years only a handful of cases are settled this way.

Questions

Why do you think the Acas alternative arbitration route is so rarely taken by the parties to an unfair dismissal dispute?

What would be the major advantages and disadvantages of a system which required many disputes to be settled via arbitration rather than at a full tribunal hearing?

LIKELY FUTURE DEVELOPMENTS

It is unlikely that we will see anything approaching the same amount of new EU-initiated employment regulation during the coming decade that we saw during the past decade. Consolidation of existing legal rights is a more likely scenario than the creation of new ones. In theory there is considerable scope under the Social Chapter of the Maastricht Treaty to harmonise more areas of employment regulation across Europe, and no doubt some will continue to call for greater conformity across the member states in areas such as dismissal law, redundancy compensation, unfair dismissal, minimum wage levels and family-friendly employment rights. At the time of writing (early 2011), for example, there is a campaign being mounted at the EU level to standardise some maternity rights across the EU. It is proposed that full wages are paid for the first 20 weeks of maternity leave and that the period of compulsory maternity leave should be extended from two to six weeks.

However, it is unlikely that many initiatives of this kind will in fact be implemented for the foreseeable future. This is mainly because of the need across most EU member states to cut costs in the wake of the recent financial crisis. There is simply no appetite among the governments of a good number of countries to impose greater costs on their businesses at a time when they are desperate to boost the growth of their economies. Preserving the prosperity of the eurozone is going to dominate EU-level policy-making for some years to come.

It is also plausible to argue that the big EU social project that was launched in the early 1990s and which has driven the creation of much new EU-level employment regulation is now reaching completion. The Social Charter, which became the Social Chapter of the Maastricht Treaty in 1993, was principally concerned with achieving two objectives:

1 ensuring the free movement of workers across national boundaries in the EU

   and

2 harmonising employment regulation designed to protect vulnerable groups.

Both of these have now largely been achieved, although there remain big disputes about the extent to which all member states have in practice implemented some measures. For example, there has long been concern in the EU Parliament and among the leaders of other member states about the way that the Working Time Directive works (or does not work) in the UK. Future British governments can therefore expect regularly to come under pressure to bring UK practice into line with that of the other countries. This would mean, for example, abolishing the right of individuals to opt out of the 48-hour week entitlement. Such issues, however, are relatively insignificant in the greater scheme of things. For the time being, at least, there is not likely to be any major new programme of employment regulation coming our way from the EU.

At the UK level we are going to see more activity on the employment law front. But for the coming five to ten years this is as likely to consist of deregulatory measures as new regulation. The reason is the need for government to focus primarily on the reduction of the budget deficit, the reduction of national debt and on private sector job-creation. In order to achieve these objectives a key aim of ministers is to promote economic growth and to provide incentives for employers to hire people. The state of national finances mean that they have little scope for cutting taxes as a means of supporting growth, so it is inevitable that their attention will focus on finding ways of cutting business costs. A programme of reform which frees businesses of employment-related regulatory requirements is therefore highly likely to be brought forward.

The current signs are that ministers intend to adopt a policy of 'one law in, one law out' when it comes to business regulation in general. This may well lead to a lightening of health and safety requirements in low-risk employment environments such as office buildings, schools and shops. In September 2010 a government report entitled *Common Sense, Common Safety* was published, its recommendations being endorsed by the prime minister. It advocated reducing the bureaucratic obligations on businesses in low-risk environments to have written policies and risk assessments and to exempt homeworkers and self-employed people from many health and safety regulations. There should be fewer formal inspections, it argued, and more information about good practice provided online by the Health and Safety Executive.

The other major proposals in the report relate to the 'compensation culture' that has grown up around personal injury claims, leading often to lengthy legal proceedings and high fees for lawyers before compensation can be paid to victims of industrial accidents. The report proposes creating a simple, state-sponsored claims system for claims up to the value of £25,000 along the lines of the existing system that applies in cases of road accidents.

The other major deregulatory measure that is being planned is a good deal more controversial. This is the proposal to extend the period in which an employer can fire a new employee without running the risk of triggering an unfair dismissal claim from one year to two years. The main argument in favour of this proposal is that it will serve to encourage businesses to take on new staff. It is argued that the one-year rule that has applied for more than 10 years provides too short a period for managers to assess the competence of new staff to do their jobs. The effect is therefore to deter employers from taking people on who they might otherwise happily employ. There is no strong evidence to back up this argument and many disagree profoundly. Indeed, it is often argued that one year is too long a period and that basic dismissal rights should kick in after a few months' probation, as is the case across the vast majority of EU countries. It could, however, turn out to be the case that some employees benefit from the change. Sometimes employers fire staff just before the 12-month deadline when they are uncertain about their long-term prospects. Rather than risk the need to go through lengthy procedures in order to secure a fair dismissal later on, a decision is taken to dismiss after 11 months. With a two-year deadline employers are more likely to give people they are uncertain about the benefit of the doubt and keep them on for longer.

While government rhetoric is likely to boast of major moves towards deregulation, aside from these examples we are unlikely to see any general dismantling of existing employment law. Removing core rights would be politically unpopular and, in any event, in the case of EU law would only be possible to achieve with the consent of other European governments. This is highly unlikely to occur. Other ways will thus be found to reduce the number of cases going to tribunal. It is likely, for example, that claimants will soon have to pay a modest deposit when lodging a claim. Ministers believe that charging a fee of £50 or so, which would be returned if the case was won by the claimant, would serve to deter some weak cases that stand little chance of success, but which are costly and time-consuming for employers to defend. Another possibility is some extension to the number of situations in which losing parties are required to pay the legal costs of their opponents. This is routine in most areas of civil litigation, but has never been widespread in employment proceedings. Such a reform might serve to deter parties – employers and employees – with very poor cases from pursuing them through to a full hearing. Settlements would be much more likely to be made. Further mooted reforms include some reduction in the levels of compensation that claimants can win in discrimination cases and reduced obligations for employers when consulting ahead of a round of compulsory redundancies.

If greater flexibility for employers is likely to be a major theme underpinning developments in employment law reform over the coming years, greater flexibility for employees is also on the cards.

By moving in this direction, the Coalition Government would be building on legislation introduced by its predecessors (see Davies and Freedland 2007).

At the time of writing (early 2011) no definite plans have been announced by ministers, but it has been made clear that they regard the introduction of additional paternity leave and the extension of the right to request flexible working to parents of 17-year-olds as 'interim steps' towards greater flexible working rights. In both of these areas there is room for a broadening and deepening of existing rights. We may well, for example, see legislation which permits either parent of a newly born baby to take the bulk of the maternity/paternity leave, potentially allowing fathers to take nine or ten months of leave after the mother of the child has returned to work. In addition, we are likely to see a general extension of the formal right to request flexible working to everyone (ie not only parents of children and those with caring responsibilities for disabled adults). It has also been suggested that such requests could, in the future, be for temporary alterations to terms and conditions and not, as is currently the case, only for one-off, permanent changes.

THE WIDER PUBLIC POLICY AGENDA

While HR managers are less likely in the future to have to take on board new employment law at the rate that we have become accustomed to in recent years, it is probable that other types of regulatory issue will assume greater significance. This will happen because there are a number of public policy agendas that government ministers will find it hard to advance without the active support of employers. In many cases the policy objective is to alter customary ways of doing things over a period of time, sometimes in ways that people are likely to resist. Because people have votes, government is less likely to force changes on the general population, but it can and probably will take a harder line with organisations. The major examples are as follows:

PENSION REFORM

At present the total value of pensions in payment to retired people in the UK is 60% state-funded and 40% funded privately, mainly through occupational pension funds. This is widely considered to be an unsustainable position given the demographic trends we discussed in Chapter 3. As our population ages and the proportion of people who are 'of working age' shrinks over the next 40 years, a greater emphasis needs to be put on private pension funding. Over time the government aims to bring about a profound shift so that only 40% of pension income is sourced from state funds, 60% coming from occupational and private pensions.

To achieve this target it is going to be necessary to push people into saving more of their current income in order to help provide a good pension in retirement. One way of doing this is to enlist the help of employers and to compel them to make contributions as well. The first steps were the measures contained in the Pensions Act 2008, which are due to come into effect from 2012, although some aspects will be phased in at later dates. The key requirements will be as follows:

- From October 2012, everyone who is employed will either have access to an occupational pension scheme or to the government's 'personal pension account scheme', which will invest monies through a body to be known as the National Employment Savings Trust (NEST).

- People will be able to opt out if they wish, but otherwise they will be automatically enrolled into one scheme or the other when commencing a new job. Employers will not be able to opt out, but they will have 12 weeks in which to enrol new staff.

- Minimum contributions will be as follows:

  - employees will contribute 4% of earnings

  - employers will contribute 3%

  - tax relief will mean that a further 1% is effectively contributed.

This represents a major reform. The extent to which it will in practice meet its objective of ensuring that many more people save towards a private pension than has been the case will very much depend on the actions of employers.

Employers may decide to resist the new scheme and seek to avoid making the proposed 3% contribution by encouraging people to opt out. And there is some evidence to suggest that this is exactly what will happen in some smaller organisations that have no tradition of occupational pension provision (Blake et al 2005). Should that occur on a wide scale, there is no doubt that ministers will move towards a compulsory scheme.

The other big change being planned on the pensions front is the raising of the state pension age to 66 from 2016 for men and 2020 for women, followed by further rises in future years. Here too employer co-operation is going to be required to ensure that people are not retired compulsorily from their organisations at a lower age.

UP-SKILLING

In 2004 the former government set up a wide-ranging and formal review of skills needs and skills levels in the UK. The resulting Leitch Report was published in 2006, named after the review's chairman Sandy Leitch. In the last chapter I described its key findings about the future supply of and demand for skills in the UK. The key conclusion was that we face the prospect of a significantly widening skills gap as demand for people with higher-level, specialised professional knowledge and technical skills outpaces the capacity of our educational system to provide people with these skills. Moreover, at the other end of the skills spectrum, the report drew attention to the large number of people in the UK whose low level of basic literacy and numeracy is likely to make them all but unemployable in our emerging knowledge-based economy.

Both the last government and the present one have recognised the significance of the skills issue for the future prosperity of the UK economy. In 2007 the Brown Government set out its response to Leitch – at least as far as England is concerned – in a White Paper entitled *World Class Skills: Implementing the Leitch Review of Skills in England*. Here ambitious targets were set which it is intended we meet by 2020. The following are prominent examples:

- 95% of adults to be functionally literate and numerate (currently 85% and 79% respectively)

- more than 90% of adults to have gained a level 2 qualification (currently 69%)

- 2 million more people with level 3 qualifications

- 500,000 people to be in apprenticeships

- 40% of adults to have degree-level qualifications (now 29%).

In order to get anywhere near hitting these targets, government will have to forge constructive relationships with employers and educational providers. Improvement should occur when the education leaving age rises to 18 from 2015 and as a result of further expansion of higher and further education. But much more is going to be needed as the majority of the 2020 workforce has already left school and forms our existing, rather poorly skilled, adult working population.

Improving adult learning is thus a key strand of government policy and this will not be achieved without the active co-operation of employers. Organisations as a group will benefit over the longer term from the presence of a stronger stock of skills in the workforce to draw on, but that does not mean that there is necessarily a compelling business case for an individual business to invest in skills development now.

The approach chosen by the Brown Government, which has been broadly endorsed by the Cameron Government, is to put in place a series of incentives which, it is hoped, will lead to the active involvement of employers. They are, for example, being asked to make a 'Skills Pledge' (replaced in 2011 by an 'industry-sector pledge'). This amounts to a public declaration that they will take responsibility for helping their staff to gain basic levels of educational attainment (ie literacy, numeracy and level 2 qualifications in areas of value to the employer). In return for making the pledge, the employer gets access to the services of a government-funded 'skills brokerage service' and other support to help source appropriate training providers. Public funding is being made available for much of this training, but in a resource-constrained economic environment the extent is necessarily limited.

To date ministers have avoided proposing any compulsion in this area, for example by introducing a continental-style training levy. Such systems work by requiring employers who do not spend a sufficient portion of their turnover on training to pay an additional tax, which is then used to fund state-sponsored training. However, it is interesting to note that the White Paper raised the possibility of this happening following a review planned for 2011.

Here too, as with the pensions agenda, we have an example of a key set of public policy objectives which can only be met with active employer co-operation. The probability is that employers will, one way or another, be forced to comply if they do not do so voluntarily first.

CASE STUDY

THE SKILLS PLEDGE

An interesting initiative that was launched by the Government in 2007 was a campaign to persuade employers to sign the 'Skills Pledge'. Initially dismissed by many as being little more than a gimmick, this initiative proved successful. By the time the 'old scheme' was wound up in December 2010 to be replaced by a scheme that was more industry-focused, more than 30,000 employers had signed up, employing between them more than 8 million staff.

Of these, the vast majority were small businesses. The response from larger employers was much more mixed. Only 209 organisations with more than 5,000 staff signed before December 2010.

Questions

Aside from gaining access to government assistance for training and advice on skills, what other benefits might employers gain from signing a 'Skills Pledge'?

Why do you think that the scheme has proved to be more popular with small businesses than it has with larger organisations?

WELFARE TO WORK

A third example is the Government's aim to reduce the number of people who have not been working for a long period of time and have therefore become dependent on welfare.

A second White Paper published in the summer of 2007 was called *In Work Better Off: Next steps to full employment*, a title which appears in retrospect to have been naively optimistic in light of the deep recession which followed soon after its release. Nonetheless, it is an important statement of the long-term public policy agenda in this area, one which has since been given even greater prominence by the Coalition Government with its plans to 'nudge' vast numbers of people into work with a mixture of 'carrots and sticks'. The 2007 White Paper started by setting out the scale of the problems, most of which have worsened since then:

- There are more than 3 million people in the UK of working age who have been on benefit for more than a year.
- There are 3 million households, with 1.7 million children, in which no one is working.
- In total, a quarter of adults of working age are not currently working.

The paper goes on to set a target participation rate of 80%, although it set no date for its achievement. Here too a mixture of incentives and disincentives are proposed under the general heading 'Pathways to Work'. Specific objectives are:

- a reduction of 1 million in the number of people claiming incapacity benefit
- a reduction of 300,000 in the number of single parents who are not working
- an increase of 1 million in the number of over-50s who are working.

The 2007 agenda envisaged that these targets would be met partly by providing new state-funded programmes aimed at preparing people for work which are more personalised and responsive to individual needs and preferences than at present and partly by providing assistance to people once they have started work in order to facilitate retention and career progression. People should, for example, continue to see Jobcentre advisers after they have started working.

The White Paper also confirmed the establishment of the principle that people who can work and are offered it must take it, benefits being reduced or even withdrawn altogether when someone is offered a job that they can do and decide to turn it down. A further measure was a requirement for job-seekers to undertake a period of unpaid work experience once they have been claiming benefits for a year – again, the prospect of benefit withdrawal being implied for those who do not co-operate.

In order to help ensure that new job opportunities are provided, ministers decided to set up partnerships between government agencies and organisations to facilitate arrangements for long-term benefit claimants to take jobs and to benefit from a year's training funded jointly by government and employers.

All of these measures have subsequently been accepted and continued by the new government elected in 2010. The economic problems faced by the country in the years since 2007 make it harder to achieve these objectives, but that is clearly not going to prevent attempts being made to move in the same broad direction.

Here too, as with the pensions and skills agendas, public policy objectives require active employer co-operation if they are to be successfully met in practice.

GREEN INITIATIVES

Partly under its own steam, partly as a result of signing the Kyoto Protocol and partly as a result of EU policy, the UK Government has set ambitious targets for the reduction of carbon emissions. The principal objective is to get emissions to a level equivalent to 12.5% below 1990 levels by the end of 2012. After this, new targets will have to be agreed for the following six or seven years.

Current policy is heavily focused on domestic energy suppliers, the insulation of domestic properties and the switch towards low-energy light bulbs. Action is also being taken to reduce the energy consumed by domestic appliances. Over the longer term, though, if radical reductions are to be made, there will be a need to change our accustomed behaviour.

The Stern Report (2006) argued that the following type of public policy responses would be necessary in order to prevent global temperatures rising by amounts that would threaten world economic growth:

- carbon pricing, by which Stern means tax, fines for those who do not comply with stricter regulations and expanded 'carbon trading schemes'
- public funding of research aimed at the development and deployment of low-carbon technologies
- public investment in measures which educate the public about ways of greening their lifestyles and which remove barriers which prevent people from living in a more energy-efficient way.

It is likely that employers will be put under pressure to help achieve these and other measures, notably substantial reductions in car usage and persuading people to use public transport much more than they currently do. This will mean providing incentives and disincentives which combine to encourage people to commute to and from work on trains, buses and bicycles. It is also reasonable to expect pressure to be put on employers in the future to reduce the number of business flights their people take, moving for example to greater use of video-conferencing.

There are another set of green initiatives in the area of waste disposal. Here too government has set ambitious targets. The amount of waste generated per person in the UK has risen considerably in recent years as we have become more affluent and bought more consumer goods. The amount of packaging has also increased, so that each person in the UK now accounts, on average, for around 500 kilogrammes of waste each year.

The current targets set by government include the ambition to reduce to a third the total amount of our waste that ends up in landfill sites. By 2015 the aim is that a further third should be incinerated and the final third recycled. By 2010, 55% was being sent to landfill, so there is a great deal of progress still to be made.

Getting ordinary householders to recycle more and to separate their waste into separate bins is a long haul. We all have votes, and issues around bin collection have moved up the local government political agenda in recent years. The extent to which government can realistically do more than simply persuade is doubtful in the area of domestic waste collection. Organisations, though, have no votes. So it can be expected that greater pressure will be exerted on workplaces to move faster and further towards green waste disposal practices in the future.

Both in the areas of energy consumption and waste disposal there is a need to alter people's behaviour if meaningful progress is to be made. For this reason, it is on the HR manager's desk that the job of addressing these issues within workplaces is likely to land.

- Since the 1970s the employment relationship in the UK has moved from being one of the least to one of the most heavily regulated in the world.

- This regulatory revolution can largely be explained with reference to UK membership of the European Union, the decline of trade union influence and the need for successive governments to meet a variety of economic and political objectives.

- There are good grounds for arguing that the pace at which new regulation is introduced is likely to slow considerably in the future and that some de-regulation is likely.

- Both the regulationists and deregulationsists can marshal strong arguments to back up their cases.

- The public policy agenda in the field of employment is likely to shift in the future from regulation to the creation of incentives designed to secure employer co-operation for a range of other objectives.

EXPLORE FURTHER

The best general introduction to debates about what purpose is served by employment regulation and who benefits from it is provided by Anne Davis in her book *Perspectives on labour law*, now in its 2nd edition.

Davis, A. (2009) *Perspectives on labour law*. 2nd edition. Cambridge: Cambridge University Press.

In *Towards a flexible labour market: labour legislation and regulation since the 1990s* (2007), Paul Davies and Mark Freedland explore labour market policy and the evolution of employment law over the past two decades.

Davies, P. and Freedland, M. (2007) *Towards a flexible labour market: labour legislation and regulation since the 1990s*. Oxford: Oxford University Press.

Wider contemporary public policy issues and debates are covered effectively in *The Cameron-Clegg Government: coalition politics in an age of austerity* (2011) and in its predecessor, *Ten years of New Labour* (2008), both edited by Simon Lee and Matt Beech.

Beech, M. and Lee, S. (eds) (2008) *Ten years of New Labour*. Basingstoke: Palgrave.

Lee, S. and Beech, M. (eds) (2011) *The Cameron-Clegg Government: coalition politics in an age of austerity*. Basingstoke: Palgrave.

REFERENCES

Blake, D., Byrne, A. and Harrison, D. (2005) *Barriers of pension-scheme participation in small and medium-sized enterprises*. Discussion Paper PI0505. London: The Pensions Institute, City University.

Chartered Institute of Personnel and Development (2002) *Employment law: survey report*. London: CIPD.

Confederation of British Industry (2000) *Cutting through red tape: the impact of employment legislation*. London: CBI.

Daily Telegraph (2008) Sir Alan Sugar: Our children need enterprise. 2 February.

Davies, P. and Freedland, M. (1993) *Labour legislation and public policy*. Oxford: Clarendon Press.

Davies, P. and Freedland, M. (2007) *Towards a flexible labour market: labour legislation and regulation since the 1990s*. Oxford: Oxford University Press.

Equal Opportunities Commission (2005) *Greater expectations: summary final report. EOC's investigation into pregnancy discrimination*. London: EOC.

Heery, E. (2010) Debating employment law: responses to juridification. In P. Blyton, E. Heery and P. Turnbull (eds) *Reassessing the employment relationship*. Basingstoke: Palgrave.

Johnson, B. (2011) A slap on the bottom, and a kick in the teeth for the economy. *Daily Telegraph*. 6 February.

Khan-Freund, O. (1954) Legal framework. In A. Flanders and H. Clegg (eds) *The system of industrial relations in Great Britain*. Oxford: Blackwell.

Lea, R. (2001) *The work–life balance and all that: the re-regulation of the labour market*. London: Institute of Directors.

Shackleton, J.R. (2005) Regulating the labour market. In P. Booth (ed.) *Towards a liberal utopia?* London: Institute of Economic Affairs (pp128–143).

Stern, N. (2006) *The economics of climate change: the Stern Review*. Cambridge: Cambridge University Press.

CHAPTER 5

Social trends

Introduction

In this chapter we turn our attention to long-term developments in people's circumstances, behaviour and social attitudes. Clearly this is a vast subject about which many different views are held. So here we will focus primarily on three distinct, yet interlinked, trends which are having a considerable impact on human resource management practice. It follows that their impact will grow greater still if they continue in the future. We will start by focusing on the most important single social trend of the past 50 years – the rise of an affluent society. For the large majority of people, increased affluence has transformed lives. The standard of living enjoyed by people today is vastly better than that of their parents and grandparents. Increased affluence, however, has been achieved at the expense of social equality. By no means have the benefits been distributed equally. The richer have become richer, while far less improvement relatively has been enjoyed by people on the lowest incomes. We have thus become a less equal society and continue to become less equal each year. So there are positive and negative consequences from rising affluence, all of which have implications for the management of people at work.

The second trend we will focus on in this chapter is the rise in individualism and the consequent decline in collective thinking and identity. This trend is harder to pin down in terms of statistics, but it is a subject which has exercised the minds of many sociologists in recent years as they have pondered its causes and long-term consequences. In this chapter we will look at the phenomenon in general terms, before looking more practically at the rapid and ongoing increase in the number of people living alone. Here too there are significant implications for the effective management of people in the long term. Finally in this chapter we will focus on the increasing concern that people have with ethical and environmental matters, considering how the HR function will have to respond if the trend towards ethical consumerism continues to grow and accelerate.

LEARNING OUTCOMES

The objectives of this chapter are to:

- explain how rising affluence has transformed society over recent decades, altering values and allowing people much greater choice about how they live their lives

- show how occupational identity is changing as work becomes less of a status symbol and more an extension of our lives as consumers

- demonstrate how increased affluence has been achieved at the expense of social equality and thus has contributed to increased social problems

- explore debates about increased individualism and about solo living, discussing the impact of these trends on the employment relationship and on HRM

- outline the evidence for increasing ethical awareness on the part of would-be investors, consumers and job-seekers

- explain the potential significance of ethical awareness for HR managers.

CRITICAL REFLECTION

LOOK AT ME!

The journalist Peter Whittle recently published a highly entertaining and original critique of aspects of contemporary life in the UK. In *Look at me* (Whittle 2008) he identifies and describes the activities of a group of characters. These are not real people, but are representatives of types – all very recognisable – who Whittle argues behave, think and hold values which are very different from those of their parents' and grandparents' generations. These modern British archetypes include the following:

- Kayleigh is 18. She has always been told by her parents that she is special and is convinced that she will soon be famous. On her birthday she and her mates hired a white stretch limo in which they were driven around the West End of London, each taking it in turns to stand up and wave to passers-by through the sun roof. She is now saving up for a boob job. 'I'm not doing this for anyone else,' she says. 'I'm doing this for me.'

- Harriet is 28. She lives alone in a one-bedroom flat and works in public relations. She goes on dates from time to time but has no intention of settling down in a long-term relationship for the foreseeable future. She has never got to know her neighbours despite having lived in her flat for more than six years. Every night she goes out to eat and party with three close friends. *Sex in the City* is their favourite TV programme. They say that they identify with it 'totally'.

- Marc and Sue are partners. Both have well-paid jobs in creative industries which require them to travel around the world regularly. They have as many friends in New York and Tokyo as they do in the UK. They regard themselves as post-modern and post-political, living an organic lifestyle. It is rare that they see their parents as they have so little in common with them nowadays.

Questions

1 To what extent do these three archetypes accurately represent significant groups in contemporary British society?

2 Make a list of the ways in which their lives and values differ from those which their parents and grandparents would in all likelihood have shared.

3 Why do you think lifestyles, values and ethics have developed in these kinds of direction over the past 30 or 40 years?

AFFLUENCE AND INEQUALITY

At the time of writing (2010–11) the UK's economy, like those of the USA and most EU countries, is slowly recovering from a period of deep recession. Economic growth is sluggish, house prices are falling and the cost of living is increasing. At such a time it seems strange to be writing about the immense social significance of rising affluence. And yet when we focus on long-term trends we observe that economic growth has never proceeded upwards in a stable, steady fashion. The extent to which economic output, productivity, wages and average living standards increase each year varies considerably. Over the past 50 years there have been periods of quite rapid growth, such as was the case in the early 1960s, the mid-1980s and more recently during the 15 years between 1993 and 2008. But these have always been punctuated by slowdowns and recessions during which the economy has retracted for a number of months before starting to recover. Whatever the short-term outlook, the big picture since the UK recovered from the experience of fighting major wars in the first half of the twentieth century has been one in which both national income and individual standards of living have increased hugely, bringing about a real revolution in the way that most people plan and live their lives.

Affluence is best defined as being the extent to which a household has sufficient money available to 'live well'. An affluent person is someone who has a reasonable amount of disposable income left over to spend on non-essential goods and services after meeting their basic needs such as housing, water, food, heating and transport to and from work. It is not the same thing as 'income'. People's incomes can rise quite dramatically, but this only translates into increased affluence if prices are rising less quickly.

The extent of affluence in different countries and increases or falls over time can be measured in different ways. A straightforward measure is gross domestic product (GDP) per capita (or per person). This involves estimating the total income of a country in a particular year and dividing the figure by its population. Most countries publish official figures for their GDP each quarter, while international institutions such as the World Bank and the International Monetary Fund (IMF) collate comparative data from around the world each year. In 2009, according to these sources, UK GDP was between £1.2 and £1.3 trillion. The UK total population was 61.8 million, giving a figure for GDP per head of around US$45,600 or £20,500 depending on the method of calculation that is used, rather lower than it was in 2007 before the recession arrived. This means that the UK is ranked as the fifth largest economy in the world after the USA, Japan, Germany and China. However, in terms of GDP per capita, the UK ranks 13th in the world and only 23rd when the cost of living is taken into account.

Table 5.1 UK GDP per capita

YEAR	GDP (£ billions)	POPULATION (millions)	GDP/CAPITA (£)	GDP/CAPITA (£ – 2005 prices)
1947	10.77	49.29	219	5,858
1952	16.02	50.45	318	6,455
1957	22.11	51.43	430	7,266
1962	28.69	53.29	538	7,992
1967	40.19	54.96	731	9,103
1972	64.34	56.10	1,147	10,263
1977	145.66	56.19	2,592	11,318
1982	277.20	56.29	4,924	11,813
1987	421.56	56.80	7,421	14,033
1992	614.78	57.58	10,676	14,800
1997	815.88	58.31	13,991	17,064
2002	1,055.79	59.32	17,798	19,548
2007	1,381.56	60.97	21,700	21,695
2009	1,264.65	61.79	20,467	20,466

Except during periods of prolonged recession when an economy contracts, the annual estimate of GDP increases year on year. Because the increase is usually larger in percentage terms than the growth in population, GDP per capita also grows. During the twentieth century the UK's GDP grew on average by 2.6% a year, far exceeding population growth. As a result there was around a six-fold increase in the country's wealth. Table 5.1 shows how these figures have risen over time. The most significant figures are those on the far right of the table, which show the rise in the per capita income since 1947 taking account of price inflation. This is a good estimate of the real rise in the level of income per head. These figures demonstrate that the figure has increased around fourfold over 60 years and that it has almost doubled over the last 30 years.

Another method of demonstrating increasing affluence is to track increases in the level of earnings for those who are in work. Long-term trends are difficult to summarise simply because the manner in which official statistics were presented changed after 2003. Before then average figures were presented; since then we have had median figures. Nonetheless the overall picture is striking. In 1975, gross *average* earnings for full-time workers in the UK were £3,000 a year. This figure had increased to £12,500 by 1990 and was estimated to have risen to £24,200 by 2005. In 2007, gross *median* earnings for full-timers were £23,749, compared with an estimated figure of £16,692 in 1997 (Daniels 2008). Earnings have thus doubled on average since 1990 during a period in which the rate of inflation increased only by around 50%. The real value of earnings has thus increased at a far faster rate than prices in recent years, bringing further affluence to larger numbers of people.

The extent to which people in the UK perceive themselves to have become better off during recent years is demonstrated by questions asked as part of the substantial annual British Social Attitudes Survey. In 1984 respondents were asked to choose from a list of statements which best described their household income 'these days'. Twenty-four per cent responded by stating that they 'were living comfortably', a total of 26% stating that they were either 'finding it hard' or 'finding it very hard' to cope financially. The same questions were asked 20 years later in the 2004 survey. Now there were 39% claiming to be living comfortably and only 16% saying that they were finding it hard or very hard to live on their incomes. A further government-funded survey carried out in England during 2007 (ONS 2008: 65) found that 30% of respondents were 'very satisfied' with their standard of living and that a further 55% 'fairly satisfied'. Only 6% expressed dissatisfaction. Seventeen per cent expressed dissatisfaction with their 'future financial security', while many more (63%) expressed satisfaction.

The same pattern is reflected in the statistics on household consumption, recent years having seen marked increases in the amount we spend on non-essential or luxury items. This is demonstrated by the figures in Table 5.2 published in 2007 by the Office for National Statistics. In terms of actual cash spent, rather than proportion of income, rather starker patterns are observable. Taking inflation into account, since 1976 average weekly spending on the following categories of goods has fallen:

- tobacco (by 43%)
- fuel and power (by 23%)
- food and non-alcoholic drinks (by 6%).

While spending has increased on the following categories:

- clothing and footwear (by 5%)
- alcoholic drinks (by 12%)
- fares and travel (by 27%)
- miscellaneous goods and services (by 58%)
- housing (by 69%)
- personal goods and services (by 74%)
- household services (by 75%)

- leisure goods (by 79%)
- motoring (by 112%)
- household services (by 170%)
- leisure services (by 229%).

Table 5.2 Proportion of household income spent on different items

	1984	1995	2006
Food and non-alcoholic drinks	21%	18%	15%
Housing	16%	18%	18%
Motoring	13%	13%	14%
Household goods	8%	9%	8%
Clothing and footwear	7%	6%	5%
Leisure services	7%	11%	14%
Fuel and power	6%	4%	3%
Alcoholic drink	6%	4%	3%
Leisure goods	5%	5%	4%
Household services	4%	5%	6%
Tobacco	3%	2%	1%
Personal goods and services	3%	4%	4%
Fares and other travel costs	2%	2%	3%

Source: ONS (2007)

Figure 5.1 Income distribution in the UK

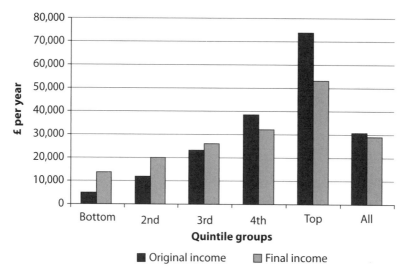

The benefits of affluence, while welcome, are very unevenly spread. In the UK levels of inequality have increased substantially over the past 30 years as incomes have risen faster among higher-income earners than among the lower-income earners. In other words, people and families who were already relatively well off have gained much more from the growth in affluence than those further down the income scale. In the UK the top fifth of households enjoy an average income before tax of more than £70,000 a year (see Figure 5.1). The figure for the bottom fifth is £13,000, two-thirds of which is accounted for by state benefits. The original income of the top fifth is thus now 15 times higher than that of the bottom fifth, the disparity reducing to four times once tax and benefits are taken into account (ONS 2010). The richest half of the UK population owns about 93% of the total wealth, leaving just 7% for the other half (ONS 2008: 64).

A widely recognised measure of inequality which allows trends over time to be tracked is the 'gini coefficient'. It captures in a simple manner the extent to which incomes are equally distributed in an economy. It operates on a scale of 0–1. A figure of 1 would indicate that all the income in the country concerned was earned by a single individual (ie as unequal an income distribution as is possible). A figure of 0 would indicate total equality of earnings between everyone. Over the past 30 years the UK gini coefficient has shown a considerable rise, indicating that we are becoming less equal over time. In 1977 a gini coefficient of 0.24 was recorded for the UK; now the figure is over 0.36.

There was a dip in the mid-1990s as a result of the property price crash, but the long-term trend is very much upwards. The World Bank computes a gini coefficient number for each country each year. The UK trend is illustrated in Figure 5.2. Developing countries are generally less equal than Western developed countries, some recording gini coefficients of over 0.5. But among the developed nations the UK is now among the least equal, having been one of the most equal three decades ago. Only in the USA, Hong Kong, Singapore and Portugal is there greater inequality.

Figure 5.2 Gini coefficient for equivalised disposable income in the UK

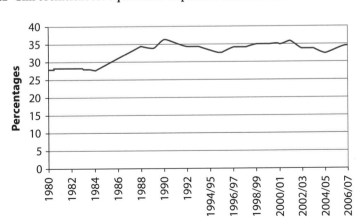

Source: Office for National Statistics 2008

These trends mean that more people each year in the UK are living in 'relative poverty', a commonly used measure which is defined as having an income which is less than 60% of median household income. This stands at 12.7 million people – slightly lower than the peak in 1997, but considerably higher than was the case 30 years ago. The figures for 'relative poverty' only measure inequality and can thus appear deceptive. Living standards are in fact rising over time for the large majority of people, it's just that the rich are advancing at a much faster rate than the poor. As time proceeds, those who are already well off are taking for themselves a bigger share of the cake; those lower down the scale only benefit at all because the cake itself (namely the national economy) has itself also grown.

The rise in inequality and hence in the statistics for relative poverty do not, however, mean that affluence has not increased very substantially for the majority of people in the UK over recent decades. The statistics on household consumption demonstrate that even among people in the lowest income groups in the UK – people who are unemployed or who have never worked – a fair proportion of weekly household expenditure goes on items such as 'alcohol and tobacco' (£8.79), 'restaurants and hotels' (£28.65), and 'recreation and culture' (£31.95). All in all this group spends less than 40% of its weekly income on essential, staple items such as food, clothing, housing and energy (ONS 2008: 83).

Much of the increased inequality over recent decades, according to Berthoud (2007), has occurred because of increased employment among women with children who have educational qualifications. By his calculation around 2 million adults, mostly from this group, are now in work who would probably not have been in the 1970s. We thus have many more families today in which both parents or partners work than used to be the case. Household income for these people has thus increased substantially. Meanwhile at the other end of the scale, there has also been a substantial increase in the number of households in which no one of working age works and hence are reliant on state benefits of one kind or another. These tend to comprise couples, lone parents and single people who have left school without qualifications and hence are finding it harder and harder to secure stable employment. The proportion of families in this category doubled from 7% in 1974 to 14% in 2003. It was higher during the recessions of the 1980s and 1990s, but did not go back to the previous low level during the long recent period of sustained economic growth.

HIGH-INCOME EARNERS

Rising inequality in the UK over recent years reflects, above all, the increase in the number of people who are very wealthy in comparison with the rest of the population. Inland Revenue statistics for the tax year ending in 2008 show that 7.5 million UK residents earned more than £30,000. That is a lot of people, but it represents less than a quarter of the total working population. 2.3 million of us earned more than £50,000, but only 571,000 earned more than £100,000. 30,000 declared earnings in excess of £500,000 and 8,000 of £1 million or more.

INEQUALITY AROUND THE WORLD

CASE STUDY

The extent to which levels of inequality vary, even in countries with apparently similar types of economy, is striking. Below are some of the gini coefficient scores for 2007–08 as calculated by the World Bank and published in the United Nations' annual *Human Development Report* (2008). The lowest recorded figure is that of Denmark, making it the most equal country in the world. The least equal according to these figures is Namibia, but it should be noted that some countries which are known to have a high degree of inequality, such as Saudi Arabia and other Gulf states, do not publish sufficient information to enable a gini coefficient to be calculated.

Country	Gini	Country	Gini
Namibia	0.74	Portugal	0.39
Sierra Leone	0.63	India	0.37
Bolivia	0.60	UK	0.36
Colombia	0.59	Italy	0.36
South Africa	0.58	New Zealand	0.36
Brazil	0.57	Australia	0.35
Chile	0.55	Spain	0.35
Peru	0.52	Switzerland	0.34
Argentina	0.51	Poland	0.34
Zambia	0.51	Irish Republic	0.34
Zimbabwe	0.50	Greece	0.34
Malaysia	0.49	Egypt	0.34
China	0.47	Canada	0.33
Uganda	0.46	France	0.33
Mexico	0.46	Belgium	0.33
Philippines	0.45	Pakistan	0.31
Turkey	0.44	Netherlands	0.31
Nigeria	0.44	Romania	0.31
Hong Kong	0.43	Croatia	0.29
Iran	0.43	Austria	0.29
Kenya	0.43	Germany	0.28
Singapore	0.42	Ukraine	0.28
USA	0.41	Finland	0.27
Ghana	0.41	Norway	0.26
Russia	0.40	Sweden	0.25
Sri Lanka	0.40	Czech Republic	0.25
Israel	0.39	Japan	0.25
		Denmark	0.25

Questions

1 What broad, general patterns can you observe in the above table?

2 How might these be explained?

3 Why do you think that gini coefficients are currently rising rather than falling in the majority of countries?

THE SOCIAL IMPACT OF AFFLUENCE

Just as improving levels of income have the capacity to transform the lives of individuals, increased collective affluence and particularly its spread transforms society as a whole. This happens primarily because more and more people have disposable income and thus enjoy the ability to choose how to spend their resources. The rise of a society in which a good majority live in a state of affluence, as has occurred in industrialised countries in recent decades, is unprecedented in human history. In a recent book about the social transformation brought about in the wake of increased affluence, Brink Lindsey (2007) develops ideas originally put forward by the economist J.K. Galbraith (1958) in his classic text *The affluent society* concerning the significance of 'the conquest of scarcity':

> *For all the preceding millennia, physical survival stood front and centre as the overriding problem that most people had to confront, day in and day out, for all their lives …. In this state of affairs, choices were relegated to the margins of life. What to do, how to contribute to the great social enterprise, where to live, whom to associate with, how to spend one's resources – these were questions that, for most people, required little thought, since the options were few and the relative desirability of this or that alternative was usually obvious.*
> (Lindsey 2007: 35–36)

As we have become increasingly affluent, so the business of ensuring that we have the capacity to feed ourselves and provide shelter have retreated to a relatively marginal place in our lives. In their place we find ourselves focusing on fulfilling other desires and on the consumption of non-essential goods and services. At the same time we are less tied to our families and to the communities in which we were born and grew up. Diverse career opportunities are open to us, along with the resources to make of our lives what we want, and this includes forging our own social identities. Thanks to increased affluence, the increased opportunities we have to travel, better education and to access multiple forms of media, we grow up knowing about and understanding alternative places, cultures and value systems. Thirty to fifty years ago most people had far less choice in these things and grew up with necessarily limited horizons and little expectation that their lives would be much different from those lived by their parents and grandparents. As a result a clearly defined class system flourished, holding people back from pursuing the careers that they wanted to and dictating the values that they lived their lives by. People did what their families and communities expected of them to a far greater degree than is now the case.

There are a number of very practical implications that flow from this development for employing organisations and for HR managers in particular. First, as Paul Ransome (2005) argues, we are seeing a very significant weakening of the link between social identity and occupation. As each year passes and more people born into affluence reach working age, people are defining themselves less and less in terms of what they do to earn a living. In other words people see themselves primarily less and less as a doctor or accountant, chef or local government officer, tinker or tailor, butcher, baker or candlestick-maker. Instead, they define themselves first and foremost as consumers. Social identity is thus increasingly determined by how we spend our money and what our tastes are rather than what we do for a living. What we wear, what we watch on TV, the music we listen to, the holidays we take, our sports and leisure activities all now influence which other people we identify with, how we see ourselves, how we label ourselves and how we react to others who have a different identity. Moreover, and equally significantly, how we spend our money is replacing how we earn our money as the prime source of our social esteem.

This is a highly significant shift which has an important consequence for an HR manager charged with improving an organisation's record in the fields of recruitment and retention. In almost all respects it makes the task harder. As people define themselves less than they did in terms of their occupations, the particular line of work that they carry out in order to earn a living takes a less central place in their lives. What matters is how they consume the money they earn, not the manner in which they earn it in the first place. If we are unhappy in our jobs we are thus far more willing to throw them in and try something different instead.

Indeed, according to some analysts, the process has gone further still for many people, our jobs becoming an extension of our lives as consumers (see du Gay 1996 and Bauman 2005). Svendsen (2008: 106–107), for example, argues that it is less a case of consumption replacing production as the source of social identity, but more one of 'the norms that govern the domain of consumption' starting to shape the expectations we have of our jobs. Increasingly we expect our work to amount to a pleasurable, interesting and fulfilling experience. When our employers fail to deliver on this expectation we start 'shopping around' for a new job:

> People who join the workforce today have expectations that differ from those of previous generations. We demand meaningful jobs in which we are self-governing and that form and confirm our identities. Work and consumption are just different arenas for what is essentially the same basic quest for self-realization. (Svendsen 2008: 107)

Both of these trends mean that employers increasingly have to persuade people to work for them rather than simply assuming that potential employees will approach them in pursuit of a particular job. It also means that people are likely to be less loyal to particular employers and much more relaxed about moving from job to job, or even career to career. A major consequence is thus that employers have to be more active in the way that they compete in the labour market. More resources must be devoted to the task and greater creativity employed. It is necessary, for example, to take up the opportunities presented by 'employer branding' (see Chapter 7). For larger organisations looking to employ new graduates, for example, this provides scope for selling jobs to potential recruits in the sophisticated kind of ways that products are sold to consumers. The need is to associate the image of the job with that of a particular lifestyle or defined set of values.

Another consequence of increased affluence with important consequences for employers has been identified and explored by Ronald Inglehart (1990). His central argument is that as more and more people are growing up in affluence and 'with the feeling that one's survival can be taken for granted', there is a reduction in the extent to which people adhere to well-established moral, ethical and religious norms. They are more willing to experiment by acting in ways that their parents and grandparents would disapprove of and a great deal more tolerant of alternative lifestyles. In short, Inglehart argues, people brought up in a world in which scarcity and war are absent, are less respectful of authority, more likely to question what they are told and keener to rethink what are perceived to be traditional ways of doing things. It follows that to be successful in the future, managers will increasingly need to adopt a more consultative and less authoritarian style. They will be less able to rely on their position or qualifications in order to garner respect. Instead, it will increasingly have to be earned, and re-earned with every new recruit signed. They will have to be good delegators and comfortable with democratic decision-making. Anyone who thinks of answering 'because I say so' to the question 'why' is going to be less and less likely to succeed. Far greater subtlety will be required than has traditionally been the case, more emotional intelligence and an acceptance that people will question significant decisions with confidence and expect that their voice is heard before they are made.

In recent years several high-profile writers have emphasised the negative aspects of rising affluence, arguing that for many, if not for a majority of, people, it is as much a curse as a boon. One of the more prominent critics is the economic historian Avner Offer (2006), who argues that affluence has the effect, in practice, of 'undermining well-being'. He argues that having more disposable income and choice as to how to spend it may give us short-term pleasure as consumers, but that it also tends to tempt us into courses of action that are not in our long-term interests. Aggressive marketing by companies trying to sell us things means that we often end up losing self-control and wasting money on unnecessary goods and services which they convince us that we need – often against our better judgement. The result is a tendency to eat foods which are not good for us and make us obese, to insist on driving cars which damage the environment and often to get into debt because we buy products that are really of little value to us. At the same time, he argues, we pay less attention to the things that really matter and which genuinely foster human well-being such as the development of human relationships with family members and the communities we live in.

Oliver James (2007, 2008) reaches similar conclusions from the perspective of human psychology. His prime targets are the growth in inequality referred to above and more generally the rise of materialistic values in society. The combination of these two processes leads large numbers of people to be dissatisfied with their material position. James likens this to a virus which he labels 'affluenza' and which he estimates has already spread to around a quarter of UK adults. The symptoms are a tendency to judge people's worth by how much money they have got and to envy people who are more successful than we are when judged against this rather narrow standard. The results are damaging both to individuals and society generally, taking the form of stress, mental breakdown, alcoholism, drug addiction, soaring personal debt and hence crime and family breakdown. In short, James blames affluence, and particularly its unequal spread in countries such as the UK, for most major, contemporary social ills.

This analysis too suggests major implications for the HR function in organisations. In particular it follows that managers will be called on increasingly frequently to deal with sensitive issues such as drug and alcohol abuse on the part of staff. There is likely to be an increasing incidence of absence due to stress and mental illnesses of various kinds which require care and expertise to handle effectively. Demand for flexible working patterns is also likely to increase as more employees have to juggle work with responsibility for bringing up children or the care of sick adults. Finally, these trends enhance the case from an employee performance and retention perspective for investment in counselling services, employee assistance programmes and initiatives aimed at improving the well-being of staff in a general sense.

 CRITICAL REFLECTION

Questions

1 Why do you think the rate at which affluence grew in the UK accelerated so much between 1993 and 2008?

2 In the contemporary world, is it possible for a society to increase its affluence without also increasing levels of inequality?

3 To what extent is Oliver James correct to ascribe so many current social problems to increases in both affluence and inequality?

Benjamin Barber (2007), writing from an American perspective, is even more damning in his analysis of the impact of affluence on contemporary societies. His central argument is that traditional characteristics of adulthood are steadily being replaced, adults in the process becoming 'infantilised'. In other words, the adult population is increasingly taking on characteristics traditionally associated with behaviour in childhood and adolescence. This, it is argued, has resulted from the spread of affluence and our expectation that we will enjoy lives which have perhaps become too comfortable. On the one hand, this 'enduring childishness' manifests itself in a shortening of our attention spans so that we are less willing to read adult books (or indeed read books at all), or to focus on a long film, conversation or meal. On the other hand, we are increasingly reluctant to age gracefully, preferring instead to dress like teenagers into middle age, to undergo cosmetic surgery in a bid to make ourselves appear youthful and to consume in vast quantities drugs which improve our sexual performance. Moreover, according to Barber:

Beyond pop culture, the infantilist ethos also dominates: dogmatic judgements of black and white in politics and religion come to displace the nuanced complexities of adult morality, while the marks of perpetual childishness are grafted onto adults who indulge in puerility without pleasure and indolence without innocence. Hence, the new consumer penchant for age without dignity, dress without formality, sex without reproduction, work without discipline, play without spontaneity, acquisition without purpose, certainty without doubt, life without responsibility and narcissism into old age and unto death without a hint of wisdom or humility. (Barber 2007: 6–7)

The potential implications of this trend for the management of workplaces are many and profound. Barber goes as far as to argue that it means the end of the dominance of the Protestant work ethic that has underpinned our attitudes to work for generations. Work is less and less seen as a 'worldly calling', a capacity for hard work and a willingness to carry it out being seen as much less admirable qualities than used to be the case. Instead, increasingly, there is a preference for play over work. What we do outside the workplace is of greater importance in our lives than what we do at work, except where the play forms part of the workplace experience. This suggests a decreasing level of commitment on the part of people to their work, to their profession and to any particular employer. It is likely to mean that absence management becomes increasingly significant in the future as people feel less obligation to their employers. Employee retention will also become increasingly significant and difficult to achieve as the sense of allegiance to employers, colleagues and careers lessens.

Barber develops the further idea that 'an ideology of entitlement' is steadily replacing 'the ethics of obligation and responsibility'. This, combined with increased materialism and a desire to increase our disposable income without necessarily having to work harder for it, has implications for the management of reward systems, the dynamics of employee relations management and, above all, the management of expectations from recruitment advertising through induction to performance management activities. Finally, of greatest day-to-day practical significance is the demand on the part of post-modern workers with their limited attention spans for experiences which are 'simple, easy and fast'. These need to be met with appropriately designed jobs, training and development materials, and recruitment and selection initiatives.

INDIVIDUALISM

Another contemporary social trend that dominates the thinking of leading sociologists and which has profound implications for future HR practice is our tendency over time to become increasingly individualistic in our approach to life. According to Beck and Beck-Gernsheim (2001: 39) 'the motor of individualization is going at full blast', while others describe ours as 'an age of rampant individualism' (Elliott and Lemert 2006: 36) or one in which 'excessive individualism' poses major threats to our children's lives (The Children's Society 2009). Psychologists have also stressed the significance of this trend, finding each succeeding generation of adults who reach maturity to be more individualistic than the previous one:

The Baby Boomers may be individualistic, but their Generation Me children (born in the 1970s, 1980s and 1990s) have taken this characteristic to the next level. (Twenge and Campbell 2008: 864)

There is some disagreement, however, about how the term *individualism* should be defined and about what has caused its rapid recent growth. The most widely quoted definition is that coined by Geert Hofstede in his studies of cultural differences between national groups. For him an individualistic society is one 'in which the ties between individuals are loose' and in which 'everyone is expected to look after him/herself and his/her immediate family'. This is contrasted with collectivist societies 'in which people from birth onwards are integrated into strong, cohesive in-groups, often extended families, which continue protecting them in exchange for unquestioning loyalty' (Hofstede 1997: 196–197). Others are more specific. Graham (1997: 117), for example, defines individualism in terms of the 'celebration of the entrepreneur as the basic creator of wealth', while Hyman et al (2004: 45), focusing on the workplace, characterise it as a decreased interest on the part of employees to join trade unions. A broad and very helpful definition is provided by Triandis (1995: 2), who sees an individualistic society as one that is made up of people 'who see themselves as independent of collectives; are primarily motivated by their own preferences, needs, rights, and the contracts they have established with others; give priority to their personal goals over the goals of others; and emphasise rational analyses of the advantages and disadvantages to associating with others'. This is contrasted with a collectivist outlook in which people value membership of groups, happily accept and are motivated by the duties and expectations of such groups, and put meeting collective aims ahead of individual goals. Critics of individualisation bemoan the way in which it is making our societies increasingly selfish, while those who welcome it tend to stress the way it increases choice, empowers us and frees us from oppressive social conventions.

Evidence for increased individualism comes in different forms. Robert Puttnam (2000), writing primarily about American society in his hugely influential book *Bowling alone*, focuses on the decline in the extent to which younger people spend their leisure time engaging in communal activities with family members or the wider community. He looks at data covering a huge range of such activities from the hosting of dinner parties, to charitable giving, participation in team sports and membership of churches, trade unions and political parties. In each field he notes significant decline starting in the early 1970s and accelerating in more recent years. While some of his detailed evidence has been questioned (for example by Fukuyama 1999), his overall conclusion is widely accepted. The same broad trends are apparent in the UK too. A study that formed part of the British Social Attitudes Survey for 2006–07 (Heath et al 2007) tracked changes over time in the extent to which we identify with religious groups, political parties, our national groups (English, Scottish, Welsh, British, etc) and any social class. This reported very substantial declines indeed in religious affiliation since the 1960s and significant if lesser declines in class and party identity. Changes in national identity were more modest.

Twenge and Campbell (2008) have carried out the most comprehensive recent study of these issues in their work on differences in the psychological traits that are observable between generations in the USA. Their work is particularly persuasive because of its scale (an analysis of studies reporting 1.4 million questionnaire responses) and because they compare the scores given by each generation of adults reaching adulthood at the same age. In other words, they compare the responses of current college students with those given by their parents and grandparents to the same questions when they were the same age.

They conclude that on a variety of measures very significant changes have occurred over the past 70 years. For example, they found today's young people have far more self-esteem, being much more likely than their parents to be satisfied with themselves and to see themselves in a positive light. Taking things a step further, they reveal that current college students are a great deal more likely than past cohorts to exhibit narcissism (self-belief taken to the point of arrogance), believing that they are 'special', that the world would be a better place if they ran it and that they can live their lives 'any way I want to'. Twenge and Campbell also report a striking decline since the 1950s in the extent to which young American adults need social approval. In other words, they are a great deal less concerned than previous generations were about what others think of them and are much less conformist in their outlook. They are also, according to this study, much more likely to exhibit 'an external locus of control', meaning that they perceive themselves to have less influence over what happens in their own lives than former generations did. They thus tend to blame others when things go wrong, rather than accepting personal responsibility. This may be a reason that young adults are much more likely to have experienced major depressive episodes than their parents and grandparents at the same age or at least to admit to themselves and others that they have. The final major conclusion reached by this study relates to a fundamental shift in the traits exhibited by women. Whereas in the past female respondents to personality questionnaires were a good deal less assertive and somewhat less analytical than men, by the 1990s such differences had disappeared.

 CRITICAL REFLECTION

Researchers who specialise in the study of generational difference have tended to compare the outlook and attributes exhibited by four groups:

- Seniors or veterans (people born before 1945)
- Boomers or Baby Boomers (people born between 1945 and 1965)
- Generation X (people born between 1965 and 1985)
- Generation Y, Generation Me or the iPod Generation (people born since 1985).

The precise years used to delineate the different generations vary somewhat, but these are the most common categories.

An underlying theme in such work is the idea that each generation's characteristics are shaped by the collective experiences they shared in their formative years. Hence, for example, the greater tendency of Seniors to conform to social norms and to respect authority figures such as politicians and police officers is explained by the fact that they experienced war and its aftermath in their youth.

What other formative experiences can you think of that could be said to have shaped the characteristics of subsequent generations? Are there such experiences which are uniquely shared by a large number of your own generation and which shape your collective outlook and attitudes?

While UK-based writers have tended to agree with their American counterparts that we are living through a period in which collectivist thinking is steadily being replaced by individualism, they do not agree with one another about its causes. For some it is largely the inevitable consequence of the increased affluence we discussed earlier in this chapter. Hobsbawm (2000: 105), for example, argues that financial deprivation leads people into collective action because it provides the best hope of alleviating their poverty. Once most people get past what he describes as 'the threshold of need' they are much more likely to pursue private interests. Giddens (2006: 67–68) stresses the significance of globalisation and the way that we now directly (through personal contact) and indirectly (via the media) come into regular contact with people from a vastly greater range of cultures than used to be the case. This has led us to be aware of the many alternative ways there are of living our lives and of the possibility of breaking free of traditional institutions and expectations as we forge our own identities. Elsewhere Giddens has stressed the importance of increased educational opportunities, and in particular the substantial recent growth in the proportion of young people attending universities (Kasperson 2000: 119). This leads people both to break familial ties physically because most people leave home to attend university, but also means that they are encouraged to question social norms and to develop their own thinking about life, the universe and everything.

Other British contributors to the debate put forward a more directly political point of view. For Elliott and Lemert (2006: 39), who take a negative view of increased individualism, the blame lies with the Thatcher Governments of the 1980s, which 'destroyed human communities and solidarity on a scale not previously witnessed' and 'promoted individualist forms as central to lifestyle and the maximising of individual potential'. By contrast, the Chief Rabbi, Jonathan Sacks (2007: 54), argues that the key change was the embracing by government and society of liberal thinking during and after the 1960s. Beck and Beck-Gernsheim (2001), writing primarily about German society, develop a series of closely argued explanations for increased individualism, but among these they give prominence to the role played in recent decades by the welfare state. The presence of social security, in their view, has led to 'a break in historical continuity' which has 'released people from traditional class ties and family support' and has 'increasingly thrown them onto their own resources and their individual fate in the labour market, with all its attendant risks, opportunities and contradictions'. Puttnam (2000) argues that a range of factors explain increased individualism in the USA, but he gives particular attention to the role played by television and newer forms of information technology in reducing the amount of time we spend socialising with others and hence developing a collective identity.

A further group of explanations are of particular relevance to readers of this book because they stress the role played by organisations and contemporary employment practices in fostering greater individualism. According to Collins and Boucher (2005: 9–11), this is particularly true in Ireland, where the recent transformation of workplace relationships and management practices has been particularly rapid and profound. Remuneration is increasingly negotiated individually and influenced by individual performance, we are increasingly made individually responsible for meeting personalised objectives by our managers and also are given more individual discretion about how we perform our own areas of work. Moreover, career trajectories are increasingly individualised too, each of us being expected to develop our own career rather than to follow an organisationally predetermined path. Reflecting on the development of labour markets in the UK, McGovern et al (2007: 142–148) agree that HR management practices have contributed to individualisation. Their prime focus is on the evolution of competitive external labour markets in which organisations hire people at all levels directly from other employers, paying the going rate and cutting down on their own training costs. Such approaches force employees to compete with one another in order to progress their careers and earn more money. Previously, when organisations had well-developed internal labour markets and a preference for internal promotion, employees wanting to progress career-wise would only have to compete with fellow employees.

INDIVIDUALISM AND HRM

What does this steady but apparently inexorable move towards greater individualism mean for the future of people management? It is difficult to know for certain, but worth speculating about. A few key points are made here, several of which we will return to in more detail later in the book in the context of specific areas of HR practice.

First and most obviously, increased individualism is bad news for traditional trade unionism. It suggests that the now well-established decline in the proportion of workers who join unions is likely to continue in the future and that their influence will continue to wither. Unless they are able to reinvent themselves quite radically so that they are seen primarily to represent individual rather than collective interests, their significance in employment relations is highly likely to erode further. There is a knock-on effect for HR practices which are union-focused or which assume that a recognised trade union speaks for employees in a genuine sense. The more individualistic the workforce becomes, the less it will be possible for any collective body to represent it effectively. Employees will increasingly expect to be consulted individually, to negotiate their own payment arrangements and to be able to organise their own work without the assistance or interference of any collective grouping, be that a union or the immediate team of colleagues with whom they work. Trends of this kind are already well established in private sector organisations where once powerful trade unions have ceased to have any significant influence. In the future it is likely that public sector organisations where unions retain a significant role will travel a similar path. This provides major opportunities for managers but also some major threats. Managing employment relationships individually allows greater flexibility, permits the reward and recognition of outstanding individual performance and generally licenses managers to exercise greater levels of discretion. But it also requires greater sophistication and emotional intelligence if the result is to be a satisfied, committed, well-motivated and high-performing workforce. Maintaining high-trust employment relationships is often harder in a non-union setting. Managers have more opportunity to impose their will, but also more opportunity to do so in a manner which is perceived as unfair and which demotivates and reduces trust as a result.

Another reason that rising individualism makes HR harder to achieve effectively results from the fact that individualists tend only to act in ways which they perceive to be beneficial to their own long-term interests and establish relationships with others (including their employers) on such a footing. Herriot (2001: 135) sums this up as follows:

> Individualist relationships are often isolated, in the sense that they are not anchored in a wider social setting. The parties relate to each other as individuals, rather than as representatives of groups. Hence they have only each other, and expect only the other(s) to provide all the benefits of the relationship. The temporary nature of so many individualist relationships is due to the failure of one or both the parties to achieve their expected outcomes.... Overall, individualists tend to belong to a lot of groups and form a lot of relationships; however most are temporary and superficial.

The key implication therefore relates to expectations on the part of employees when they enter an employment relationship. Whereas someone with a collectivist temperament or outlook will readily identify themselves as a member of an organisation, will develop loyalties to it and to colleagues who they work alongside and will feel a sense of duty towards it, individuals are far more focused on what is in it for them. This means that they will only stay employed somewhere for as long as they perceive that employment to be beneficial or fulfilling from their own individual perspective. If their careers stagnate, if they become dissatisfied with an aspect of their work or if they believe they could do better elsewhere, they will think nothing of leaving. The extent of their loyalty is strictly circumscribed. The same is true of the effort they are prepared to put into their work. They are happy to work hard, to exercise discretionary effort and to perform to the highest standards, but their continued willingness to do so is dependent on their own perception of the benefit they are personally deriving from doing so. This means that organisations dominated by individualists are much harder to manage effectively. There is a greater need, for example, to develop and invest in appropriate employee retention initiatives. Performance management also needs to be more sophisticated because each individual's personal ambitions and needs have to be considered and acted upon separately. The fostering of effective, thoughtful and sensitive line management thus becomes an increasingly important HR objective. Meeting employee expectations in an individualistic workplace leads to substantial dividends for the organisation. Dashing expectations has serious, negative consequences.

It is also true that high-trust employment relationships are simply harder to maintain when the workforce is more individualistic. This is for several distinct reasons. First, as Herriot (2001: 133) points out, collectivists tend to believe that 'attitude and behaviour should not necessarily be consistent' and that there are 'many occasions when it is right, rather than merely expedient, to comply, even though you may not agree with what you are doing'. Such an approach to workplace life jars with individualists who see it as lacking in integrity. They say what they think, aim to behave in line with their own values and respect managers who do the same. They will not trust or respect those who take a collectivist approach if this means compromising personal integrity. Moreover, as Twenge and Campbell (2008: 868–869) argue, today's more individualistic workforce is also unconcerned with what others think of them, having much less need for social approval than older people. They are thus relaxed by the thought that colleagues or managers may not rate them or may disapprove of what they do, say or how they dress. They admire non-conformism and are likely to mistrust managers who take a more conformist line and expect them to do the same. Being straight, honest and up front is often harder for managers than spinning a positive message or concealing the whole truth from employees. The more individualistic the workforce becomes, the greater the need to take the straight approach.

Fourthly, it is important to appreciate that while individualists are focused on themselves and their own interests, this does not mean that they are unconcerned or unaffected by the way that colleagues are treated. When a fellow employee is treated unfairly or in an unjust fashion, individualists may not feel much by way of collective solidarity, but they will be concerned because they fear being treated in a similarly unfair manner themselves. Indeed, in many respects the lack of a conformist outlook means that an individualistic person is adversely more affected by poor treatment meted out to colleagues than is the case with a collectivist. This results from the 'live and let live' credo of tolerance that underpins the individualist's view of life. It means that organisations will increasingly have to pay attention to the way that individual employees are treated more generally. Fair-dealing and being seen to act equitably are more, not less, important because of the greater impact perceived unfairness towards individuals has on individualists. In particular it means that organisations must be increasingly vigilant not to discriminate unfairly on any grounds.

SOLO LIVING

The most striking trend in behaviour, as opposed just to attitudes, that suggests growing individualism is the considerable and ongoing growth in solo living in the UK (see Figure 5.3). In the 1971 census it was reported that there were 18 million households in England, yet 30 years later the 2001 census recorded that there were 23 million (a third more). This is remarkable when it is considered that the population of the country remained broadly stable during this period.

The trend is explained by a very substantial, steady and sustained growth in single-person households – one of the most important social trends of our time. The statistics presented below are taken from two excellent reports on single-person households published by the Joseph Rowntree Foundation (Bennett and Dixon 2006, Palmer 2006).

There are three distinct types of single-person households, all of which have seen substantial growth in recent years and are forecast to grow further:

1 widows and widowers

2 people who have split up with or are divorced from former partners

3 single people of working age.

The increase in the numbers of households in the first of these groups is caused by falling mortality rates. People are living longer, and this means that there are more single, older people than there used to be. However, there has been no major change in the *proportion* of older people who live alone. It remains, as it always has been, around 50% (see Figure 5.4). The really significant social trend is the rise in the number of people of working age who live alone, the number having trebled since 1971. Only 2% of people in the 24–44 age group lived alone in 1971. More than 10% now do so. In 1971, approximately 5% of working age adults lived alone. The figure is now 15%. Moreover, all government and other authoritative forecasts suggest that this trend will accelerate over the next 20 years. It is projected that 20% of all working-age adults will be living alone by 2020 and that 40% of all households will be single-occupancy.

Figure 5.3 Trends in households, by household type (England)

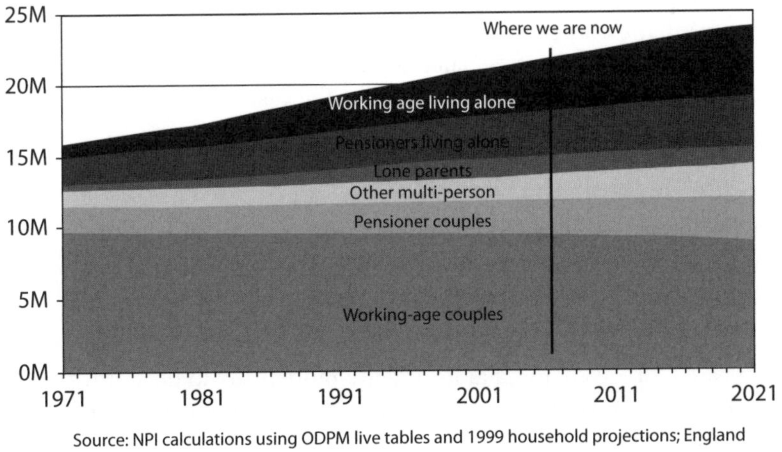

Source: NPI calculations using ODPM live tables and 1999 household projections; England

Source: Palmer (2006: 9)

Figure 5.4 Trends in the proportion of households that are single-person households in each age group (England)

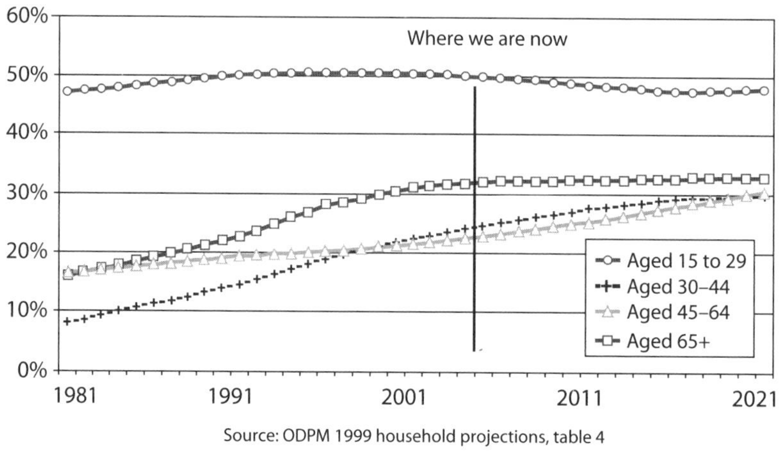

Source: ODPM 1999 household projections, table 4

Source: Palmer (2006: 10)

It is interesting to note that the biggest change is in the number of men of working age who live alone. In 1971, only 3% of households were occupied by single men; the figure has now reached 10%. More men than women of working age live alone, largely because when families break down, mothers typically continue to live with the children, while the father moves out. More women of working age are living alone too than used to be the case, but the reasons appear to be different. While similar proportions of men live alone across the social spectrum, for women the proportion (and trend) is far higher among professionals. This is mainly associated with financial independence and the choice this gives many more women than was the case in the past to live alone.

There are several discernible causes of the increase in solo living among people of working age:

1 Single people are less likely to form stable relationships and are more likely to wait until a later age before forming couples. The proportion of people aged 15–29 who describe themselves as 'single' doubled between 1981 and 2001, from 10% to 20%.

2 Couples are more likely to separate and are more likely to do so earlier in their relationship than used to be the case. Divorce rates have increased very substantially over recent years.

3 We have seen the development of relationships in which couples live apart for most of their time, seeing one another only at weekends or occasionally rather than living together in the same household. A proportion of these relationships involve couples living at some distance from one another.

4 More elderly people live independently than used to be the case. In 1961, 65% of single over-75s lived in their own homes. The figure is now 90%.

Sociologists disagree about how much solo living is 'forced' and how much is 'elective'. This is because the evidence is inconclusive and unclear. For example, most older single people are alone due to bereavement, but many prefer to remain alone than to move into sheltered accommodation or to live with relatives.

Among working-age solos, 84% say that they choose to do so, yet only 27% state that they wish to do so indefinitely.

There is also disagreement about whether we are seeing a major underlying change in the way people choose to live their lives, reflecting a shift of a profound nature towards individualist lifestyles. The alternative view is that we are not and that the trend is more simply explained by economic factors and observable life-course developments, such as:

- increased affluence/independence (among women and younger people in particular)
- more people going away to university and experiencing solo living early in life
- more geographical mobility among professional workers.

The extent to which work and employment trends are driving the trend towards solo living is much debated. It is probably the case that employers carry some responsibility, but this can be indirect and is less significant than the other factors set out above. In her critique of modern workplace cultures (*Willing slaves*), Madeleine Bunting (2004) argues that long-hours cultures, delayering, intensified competition and demands for flexibility on the part of employers are major causes of the solo living trend. Her research suggests that younger people are now required to be so committed to their careers that they have little time or energy left outside of work to build social networks, engage in community activities or, crucially, to develop personal relationships. The requirement to be geographically mobile also hinders relationship-building. It means that people take longer to form stable, long-term relationships and tend to become more distant from the family and social networks established before they leave home.

Much less has been written about the extent to which employment practices and HR policies are likely to/need to develop in response to the solo living trend. It is interesting to speculate about how things may change if the trend continues or accelerates. Firstly, it is likely that as the number of solos in the labour market increases, employers will have to prioritise retention initiatives. This is because single people living alone have fewer social ties, are less likely to own their own homes and are more likely to want and be able to make radical changes in their lives. Secondly, there are potential gains to be made in recruitment and retention terms from developing benefits and policies that attract single people to an employer. Interestingly, this may involve downplaying or running counter to the current trend for practices which are 'family-friendly' and which privilege parents as these tend to irritate and anger people without families. Thirdly, greater care needs to be taken when managing career expectations of solo-living people and when disciplining them. This is because they tend to have a more intense emotional reaction which lasts longer when they perceive themselves to have been treated unfairly. They are less likely to have robust support networks and are more likely to brood and let negative emotions 'get to them'. Finally, there is scope for actively providing opportunities for people to socialise in a work-related context (gym membership, social events, etc). Some employers discourage people from forming relationships with colleagues at work. Such policies are understandable but may be counterproductive from the point of view of recruiting and retaining solos, particularly where the culture is one of long hours.

CRITICAL REFLECTION

According to the Joseph Rowntree Foundation's research, people living in single-person households have different patterns of spending from those who live with others. On the one hand, they spend more on health-related products such as slimming pills, herbal teas and fruits. But they also drink much more, smoke more and are much more likely to be drug-users than people living in couples or families.

Single people are also more prone to depression, they get themselves in debt more easily, are more likely to be alcoholics and victims of crime. Moreover, when they get into personal or financial difficulties they tend to rely on the state rather than on partners and families to support them. The same is true when they fall ill. Lack of support in the home requires the state to provide care for longer during the recovery period. At present, single people find it harder to access public services such as housing because priority is given to households with children. They are thus many more times likely to end up homeless when they lose their jobs than people in couples or single parents looking after children.

Life is particularly hard for divorced people and particularly divorced men who live alone. They suffer from higher incidences of depression and anxiety than married people. They also live less healthy lifestyles and their mortality rates are higher. Divorced men under 60 have 75% higher mortality rates than married men. Lone mothers are 2.5 times as likely as mothers living in a couple to suffer from mental health problems.

Given this information, to what extent do you agree or disagree with the following propositions?

1 Employers should pursue policies which make it less likely that their employees are required to live alone (eg by refraining from moving people around the country at regular intervals and by restricting long-hours working).

2 Employers should provide as much specific support for single people as they do for families.

3 Employers should take active steps to help provide single people with a work-based social life.

ETHICAL AWARENESS

The final major contemporary social trend that we are going to focus on in this chapter is the rise in what might be best termed as 'ethical awareness', by which we mean an increased propensity on the part both of consumers and investors to make decisions, at least in part, according to their perception of an organisation's ethical record or reputation. As is the case with individualism, rising ethical awareness is in large part a product of increased affluence. Just as affluence brings us choice in respect of the lifestyles we can lead and in the social identity we seek to forge for ourselves, so it affords us choice to buy and invest ethically if we want to. In short, having disposable income allows us the luxury of acting ethically in the purchasing and investment decisions we make. Affluence is also a prerequisite for ethical buying and investment behaviour simply because it sometimes requires us to spend more on the products we purchase or to shoulder a somewhat greater investment risk than would be the case if we did not take account of ethics when making such decisions.

Affluence itself, however, is only part of the explanation. Another is the presence of technologies which give us access to information about the ethics of organisations competing for our custom. Here the rise of the Internet and, particularly, social networking sites have played and are increasingly playing a key role. The Internet plays an increasing role because it allows campaigning groups with an interest in ethical and wider political issues to address their audiences directly without the need to have their message 'filtered' by mainstream media organisations such as newspapers, radio stations and TV networks. This makes it easier for unethical activity on the part of corporations to be publicised and spread very rapidly across the whole world via email or through social networking sites such as Facebook. Indeed, so rapidly can such a message be spread that it is already widely disseminated nowadays before the corporation is able to rebut in the mainstream media or indeed to threaten a libel action.

ETHICAL CONSUMERISM

Each year since 2000, the Co-operative Bank has published its *Ethical consumerism report*. This tracks the growth of ethical consumerism in the UK, as well as ethical behaviour more generally, and is the largest and most influential survey of its kind. The Co-operative Bank surveys demonstrate substantial year-on-year increases over the past decade in the proportion of the UK population who claim to have acted ethically in various ways. Increases in any one year are relatively slight, although there are some examples of step-changes happening quite suddenly, but over the nine years that the survey has now been carried out, pronounced and significant trends are apparent. These are shown in Table 5.3.

Table 5.3 Percentage of consumers claiming to have acted in one of the following ways 'at least once' during the year in question

	1999	2009
Recycling	73%	96%
Supporting local shops/suppliers	61%	87%
Avoiding a product/service due to ethical reputation	44%	64%
Choosing a product/service due to ethical reputation	51%	60%
Buying primarily for ethical reasons	29%	52%
Feeling guilty about an unethical purchase	17%	43%
Seeking information on a company's reputation	24%	38%
Actively campaigning on environmental/social issues	15%	26%

From the point of view of producers of goods and services, it is the developments in the middle of the table which are interesting and perhaps (at least for some) alarming. This is because they demonstrate that a majority of consumers are now taking account of a corporation's ethical reputation when making purchasing decisions – either to buy or to avoid buying a particular product or service.

The Co-operative Bank reports also track year-on-year growth in purchases of organic, Fairtrade and ecologically sustainable products, the extent of charitable donations, ethical consumer boycotts, the use of public/private transports and usage of ethical banking and investment products. Current annual growth rates in most of the categories are between 13% and 18%. In 2008 particularly big increases were recorded in the purchase of Fairtrade items (up 61%), energy-efficient light bulbs (up 58%), rechargeable batteries (up 79%) and green cars (up 132%).

Interest in ethical consumerism has now grown sufficiently for it to have been worth the while of several publishers to commission handbooks on the subject (eg Clark 2006, Dolan et al 2006, Corkhill 2007, Hickman 2008, MacBride 2008). There are also at least two successful monthly journals on the subject in the form of the magazines *Ethical Consumer* and *Ethical Living*. Moreover, such research as there is (as yet quite limited) strongly suggests that the market for ethical goods and services will grow at an accelerated rate in the future. According to Crowe and Williams (2000) this is because growth takes off once a critical mass of consumers has been achieved, leading government and large corporations to 'transform niche markets, pushing ethics into the mainstream'. This has already happened, for example in the case of lead-free petrol, and is now happening with low-energy light bulbs. Another reason for anticipating substantial future growth is the finding that younger people are more committed to the ethical consumer agenda than older people. The largest UK-based academic study backs up the Co-operative findings, concluding that 'consumers are developing more socially conscientious mindsets' (Freestone and McGoldrick 2007: 461).

ETHICAL INVESTMENT

Like ethical consumerism, ethical investment – or 'socially responsible investment' as it is more commonly called – has grown substantially in recent years – but from a low base. As yet it remains very much a niche market, but one which is by no means insubstantial. Kurtz (2008) estimates that around 10% of 'assets under management' in both the USA and Europe 'is now invested according to some type of social constraint'. While it is only in very recent years that ethical investment funds have played any serious role in the markets, their significance is now growing substantially year on year (Blowfield and Murray 2008: 280–283). Moreover, there are good grounds for anticipating much greater growth in the future. This is because financial analysts and journalists are increasingly accepting the view that socially responsible organisations are more likely to give them a superior return on their investment than rivals that have a less ethical reputation. Where as in the past most 'ethical investors' accepted greater risks and lower returns in order to invest in line with their consciences, increasingly investors seeking good value and low risks are positively opting for socially responsible investment strategies.

The extent of the correlation between ethical investment and the relative size of any return on such investments remains controversial. While most studies demonstrate a statistically significant correlation with the pursuit of corporate social responsibility (CSR) on the part of organisations, there is no acceptance at all that the former leads to the latter. Indeed, it is commonly argued that only successful companies have the money available to pursue CSR initiatives and that profitability leads to ethics in corporate life much more frequently than ethical activities lead to increases in profit (Kurtz 2008: 268). From the point of view of the self-interested investor, however, this is a pretty insignificant chicken-and-egg argument. What matters is that there is a correlation and that ethical investment vehicles have a tendency to yield high returns. As a result it is increasingly believed that investors can 'do well by doing good'.

Kiernan (2005) argues that this change in attitudes among the investment community is largely occurring as a result of industrial restructuring and the impact of globalisation on Western economies. He argues that as the knowledge economy develops, interest grows among would-be investors in digging deeper into a company's activities than a simple analysis of its financial performance, and that this includes corporate ethics alongside other considerations:

> As we move deeper and deeper into the era of knowledge value and intangibles, conventional balance sheets and profit and loss statements are capturing and reflecting less and less of a company's true value, investment risk and competitive potential. What is needed instead is a new, more dynamic, 'iceberg balance sheet' approach, one that focuses investor and senior management attention where it properly belongs, on the roughly 80 per cent of companies' true value that cannot be explained by traditional, accounting-driven securities analysis: in short, one that provides a focus on leading indicators of performance, not trailing ones. (Kiernan 2005: 69–70)

ETHICAL AWARENESS AND HRM

Much, indeed most, of the contemporary corporate social responsibility agenda
has little to do with HRM. The emphasis tends to be on green issues of various
kinds, on charitable activities, on maintaining high standards of corporate
governance, on animal testing, embryo research and on sourcing supplies which
are themselves produced ethically. However, employment matters have a place at
this table and always have had, particularly in respect of working conditions in
developing countries. For well over a decade now campaigns to persuade people
to boycott products manufactured in sweatshops or using child labour have met
with considerable success in several countries (Harrison et al 2005: 156–159).
Several large corporations, including Nike and Reebok, have been targeted by
such campaigns and have had to adjust their practices in response.

In the future, though, there are good reasons to expect that organisations stand
to gain a good deal more than they currently do by developing and maintaining a
reputation for ethical HR practice. This is likely to happen if the extent of ethical
awareness continues to grow and more purchasing and investment decisions are
influenced by an assessment of a corporation's ethics. The main reason is that in
such an environment organisations will increasingly seek to compete for business
in part by deliberately fostering for themselves an ethical image. 'We are socially
responsible' will thus be a message that advertisers will increasingly seek to get
over and, crucially, to associate with high-value brands. While pursuing such
a strategy will pay dividends in an increasingly ethically aware marketplace, it
also carries considerable risks if the corporation is caught failing to live up to
the image it has created for itself. Negative stories in the media concerning the
way in which employees are treated in a company will have the capacity to do
great damage to a corporate reputation and seriously to contaminate a hard-won
positive brand image. The growth of new media and its global reach merely serve
to increase the potential damage.

It follows that many organisations in the future will have to take greater
care than they currently do to develop and then to maintain a reputation as
good, fair employers. This is particularly true of corporations whose survival
depends on sales of goods and services to a mass consumer market, but also of
those dependent on attracting investment from the market. Another group of
employers who may find that the business case for adopting ethical HR practices
becomes increasingly compelling in the future are those who have a particular
interest in recruiting people who have a choice about where they work. Increased
ethical awareness among younger people may well mean that those which
have a poor reputation as employers fail to attract the best minds even if those
individuals are treated well. This was a significant conclusion reached by a recent
survey of new graduate recruits in the USA, the UK and China carried out by
PricewaterhouseCoopers (2007). 2,739 recruits were asked to think about their
future careers and to answer a series of questions about their expectations. One of
the questions was as follows:

*Will you deliberately seek to work for employers whose corporate responsibility
behaviour reflects your own values?*

71.2% of UK graduates, 87.2% of the Chinese recruits and 90.2% of the US sample responded affirmatively to this statement.

Having concluded that ethics are more likely to play a central role in future HRM practices, it is necessary to point out that there is a big debate about what exactly does constitute 'ethical HRM'. We will return to this issue in Chapter 13.

CASE STUDY

Public relations professionals commonly make reference to the 'tabloid test' when advising business people about decision-making (see Zetter 2008). It is particularly useful to apply in the case of significant decisions which could be seen, at least by some people, as being unethical. The test simply involves judging an action, in part, according to how comfortable the organisation would be defending itself were it to be reported on the front page of a tabloid newspaper. In applying the test you need to bear in mind that journalists and editors working for such papers will always put the worst possible spin they can on a story and make it out to be as scandalous as they can. No attempt is made to be balanced or fair at all.

Think about the activities of your own organisation or one which you have worked for in the past. Also think about key decisions that have been made, either in the realm of HRM or more generally. Do these pass the tabloid test?

KEY LEARNING POINTS

- The most significant single, contemporary social trend is the rise of an affluent society whose members have a good degree of choice about their lifestyles, careers and patterns of consumption.

- Work and careers are being 'consumerised', many people now 'shopping around' for jobs which they will find enjoyable and fulfilling rather than which are simply a source of income.

- Greater affluence has been achieved at the expense of less equality. This is creating social problems which impact on the conduct of people at work.

- Society in the UK, as in most other countries, is becoming increasingly individualistic. The result is less solidarity with other workers and a need for a different emphasis in the way that they are managed.

- Employees are much more likely to live alone than was the case in the past. This trend will continue, with consequences for the type of employment experiences that they seek.

- Over time consumers, investors and job-seekers are becoming more ethically aware. Organisations with a poor ethical reputation or which do not have a positive ethical reputation are thus likely to be less successful in the future. An explicit commitment to ethical HR practices will thus become more common in the future.

EXPLORE FURTHER

In two books Oliver James debates affluence and its impact on society, concluding that its impact has been more negative than positive. These are *Affluenza* (2007) and *The selfish capitalist: origins of affluenza*. In *The spirit level*, Richard Wilkinson and Kate Pickett also debate the impact of inequality on society from a critical perspective.

James, O. (2007) *Affluenza*. London: Random House.

James, O. (2008) *The selfish capitalist: origins of affluenza*. London: Vermilion.

Wilkinson, R. and Pickett, K. (2009) *The spirit level: why more equal societies almost always do better*. London: Allen Lane.

A more impartial account of these and other significant social trends is provided in the Government's annual publication *Social and Labour Market Trends*. A web-based version is available to download at the Office for National Statistics website (www.statistics.gov.uk).

The impact of increased affluence on the workplace is discussed in many recent works by leading sociologists. Zygmunt Bauman's *Work, consumerism and the new poor* (2005) provides a good introduction to these debates.

Bauman, Z. (2005) *Work, consumerism and the new poor*. 2nd edition. Maidenhead: Open University Press.

REFERENCES

Barber, B.R. (2007) *Consumed: how markets corrupt children, infantilize adults and swallow citizens whole*. New York: W.W. Norton & Co.

Bauman, Z. (2005) *Work, consumerism and the new poor*. 2nd edition. Maidenhead: Open University Press.

Beck, U. and Beck-Gernsheim, E. (2001) *Individualization: institutionalized individualism and its social and political consequences*. London: Sage.

Bennett, J. and Dixon, M. (2006) *Single person households and social policy: looking forwards*. York: Joseph Rowntree Foundation.

Berthoud, R. (2007) *Work-rich and work-poor*. York: Joseph Rowntree Foundation.

Blowfield, M. and Murray, A. (2008) *Corporate responsibility: a critical introduction*. Oxford: Oxford University Press.

Bunting, M. (2004) *Willing slaves*. London: HarperCollins.

The Children's Society (2009) *A good childhood*. London: Penguin.

Clark, D. (2006) *The rough guide to ethical living*. London: Penguin.

Collins, G. and Boucher, G. (2005) Irish neo-liberalism at work. In G. Boucher and G. Collins (eds) *The new world of work: labour markets in contemporary Ireland*. Dublin: The Liffey Press.

The Co-operative Bank (2008) *The ethical consumerism report (2008)*. Manchester: The Co-operative Bank.

The Co-operative Bank (2009) *The ethical consumerism report (2009)*. Manchester: The Co-operative Bank.

Corkhill, M. (2007) *How to be an ethical shopper*. London: Impact Publishing.

Crowe, R. and Williams, S. (2000) *Who are the ethical consumers?* Manchester: The Co-operative Bank.

Daniels, H. (2008) *Patterns of pay: results of the annual survey of hours and earnings 1997–2007*. London: Office for National Statistics.

Dolan, S., Garcia, S. and Richley, B. (2006) *Managing by values*. Basingstoke: Palgrave Macmillan.

du Gay, P. (1996) *Consumption and identity at work*. London: Sage.

Elliott, A. and Lemert, C. (2006) *The new individualism: the emotional costs of globalization*. London: Routledge.

Freestone, O. and McGoldrick, P. (2007) Motivations of the ethical consumer. *Journal of Business Ethics*. Vol 79. pp445–467.

Fukuyama, F. (1999) *The great disruption: human nature and the reconstitution of social order*. London: Profile Books.

Galbraith, J.K. (1958) *The affluent society*. New York: Houghton Mifflin.

Giddens, A. (2006) *Sociology*. 5th edition. London: Polity Press.

Graham, P. (1997) Human relations. In A. Sorge and M. Warner (eds) *The IEBM handbook of organizational behaviour*. London: Thomson Learning.

Harrison, R., Newholm, T. and Shaw, D. (eds) (2005) *The ethical consumer*. Los Angeles: Sage.

Heath, A., Martin, J. and Elegenius, G. (2007) Who do we think we are? The decline of traditional social identities. In A. Park, J. Curtice, K. Thomson, M. Phillips and M. Johnson (eds) *British social attitudes: the 23rd report: perspectives on a changing society*. London: Sage.

Herriot, P. (2001) *The employment relationship: a psychological perspective*. Hove: Routledge.

Hickman, L. (2008) *The good life: the guide to ethical living*. London: Eden Project Books.

Hobsbawm, E. (2000) *The new century*. London: Little Brown.

Hofstede, G. (1997) Organization culture. In A. Sorge and M. Warner (eds) *The IEBM handbook of organizational behaviour*. London: Thomson Learning.

Hyman, J., Lockyer, C., Marks, A. and Scholarios, D. (2004) Needing a new program: why is union membership so low among software workers? In W. Brown, G. Healy, E. Heery and P. Taylor (eds) *The future of worker representation*. Basingstoke: Palgrave Macmillan.

Inglehart, R. (1990) *Culture shift in advanced industrial society*. Princeton: University of Princeton Press.

James, O. (2007) *Affluenza*. London: Random House.

James, O. (2008) *The selfish capitalist: origins of affluenza*. London: Vermilion.

Kasperson, L.B. (2000) *Anthony Giddens: an introduction to a social theorist*. Oxford: Blackwell.

Kiernan, M. (2005) Corporate social responsibility: the investors' perspective. In J. Hancock (ed.) *Investing in corporate social responsibility*. London: Kogan Page.

Kurtz, L. (2008) Socially responsible investment and shareholder activism. In A. Crane, A. McWilliams, D. Matten, J. Moon and D. Siegel (eds) *The Oxford handbook of corporate social responsibility*. Oxford: Oxford University Press.

Lindsey, B. (2007) *The age of abundance*. New York: Collins.

MacBride, P. (2008) *Ethical living*. London: Teach-Yourself Books.

McGovern, P., Hill, S., Mills, C. and White, M. (2007) *Market, class and employment*. Oxford: Oxford University Press.

Offer, A. (2006) *The challenge of affluence: self-control and well-being in the United States and Britain since 1950*. Oxford: Oxford University Press.

Office for National Statistics. (2007) *Family spending*. London: ONS.

Office for National Statistics. (2008) *Social trends 38*. London: ONS.

Office for National Statistics. (2010) *Increase in income inequality: the effects of taxes and benefits on household income 2008/9*. London: ONS.

Palmer, G. (2006) *Single person households: issues that the Joseph Rowntree Foundation should be thinking about*. York: Joseph Rowntree Foundation.

PricewaterhouseCoopers. (2007) *Managing tomorrow's people: the future of work to 2020*. London: PwC.

Puttnam, R.D. (2000) *Bowling alone: the collapse and revival of American community*. New York: Simon & Schuster.

Ransome, P. (2005) *Work, consumption and culture: affluence and social change in the twenty-first century*. London: Sage.

Sacks, J. (2007) *The home we build together: recreating society*. London: Continuum.

Svendsen, L. (2008) *Work*. Stocksfield: Acumen Publishing.

Triandis, H. (1995) *Individualism and collectivism*. Boulder, CO: Westview Press.

Twenge, J.M. and Campbell, S.M. (2008) Generational differences in psychological traits and their impact on the workplace. *Journal of Managerial Psychology*. Vol 23, No 8. pp862–877.

United Nations (2008) *Human development report 2007/2008*. New York: UNDP.

Whittle, P. (2008) *Look at me: celebrating the self in modern Britain*. London: The Social Affairs Unit.

Zetter, L. (2008) *Lobbying: the art of political persuasion*. Petersfield: Harriman Books.

CHAPTER 6

Flexibility and change

Introduction

In the first part of the book I argued that increased competitive intensity is one of the major trends in the contemporary business environment that has had, and will continue to have, a major influence on HR work in countries such as the UK. The major reasons are as follows:

- The more competitive markets become, particularly as they internationalise, the more volatile and unpredictable the trading environment becomes for organisations. This inevitably makes it much harder than is the case in relatively stable business environments for organisations to be able to offer their staff long-term, stable employment of a traditional kind.

- Increased competition almost always leads to increased pressure to keep a lid on costs. This is particularly so when organisations compete with others based overseas in places where wage levels are relatively low and where business-to-business transactions play a major role in the trading environment. The result is a need on the part of HR managers to restrain wage growth and to maximise operational efficiency.

- More-intense competition provides the pretext for organisations to change their structure more frequently. In some industries it has been observed that organisations are now engaged in 'permanent restructuring' as new opportunities present themselves and established businesses cease to generate the profits they once did.

As a result, the need to manage change effectively and the need to achieve greater operational flexibility have moved up the HR agenda in recent years. Moreover, there is every reason to anticipate that they will further grow in significance in the future.

As we discussed in Chapters 1 and 2, these external pressures are creating a very interesting set of conundrums for HR people to address. Professor Keith Sisson of Warwick University has articulated the core issue most effectively in his work on the 'financialisation' of employee relations (see Purcell and Sisson 2010). In it he outlines the emergence of two contrasting 'views of the organisation' which appear to pull in different directions. One he calls 'the firm as nexus of contracts'. Here the organisation is almost entirely conceived as a vehicle to enable its shareholders to increase their financial gain, if need be at the expense of all other objectives. The outlook is short term in nature, the role of managers being to extract as much value as possible as quickly as possible so as to maximise the return on investment. According to this view, labour is characterised as 'a commodity whose cost is to be minimised'.

The alternative, labelled by Sisson as 'the resource-based view', is very different. Here people are seen as being 'a resource to be developed' as part of an approach to management which aims to build market share over the longer term. The aim of the organisation is to provide goods and services, not just to make money, and to serve the interests of multiple stakeholders, including employees.

The two views look on the surface to be incompatible. But is this necessarily the case? It seems to me that the core purpose of the HR function in many organisations now is to find some way of serving the needs of both of these competing views. On the one hand, financialisation and increasing competitive intensity forces us to focus on maximising our organisations' flexibility and on managing near continual change. On the other hand, we also know that a key to prospering in the contemporary commercial world is to provide consumers with high-quality products and services which are increasingly sophisticated in nature. This is difficult to achieve without the assistance of an engaged, committed and well-motivated workforce which is prepared, as and when necessary, to work beyond contract and to take responsibility for its actions.

Reconciling these two sets of demands is a very difficult prospect and will often not be wholly achievable. Essentially it requires HR managers to find ways of securing commitment from staff to whom the organisation is unable to give much commitment back in return. It may not be at all easy to pull this off, but that does not mean that we shouldn't try.

In this chapter my aim is to explore possible ways forward for HR managers who are tasked with solving this conundrum or at least to begin to make progress in that direction. We will start by looking at how best to manage change in such a way as to maintain as much employee commitment and active engagement as possible. In particular we will consider the role that HR managers play in effective change management episodes. In the second part of the chapter we will go on to look at flexible working arrangements and at how these can be introduced in such a way as to enhance rather than reduce commitment and engagement.

LEARNING OUTCOMES

The objectives of this chapter are to:

- explore why change is often handled poorly by managers because they fail to take sufficient account of people's views, hopes and fears

- discuss the main models and theories which assist in the development of a planned approach to change management

- assess recent research that stresses the political aspects of effective change management

- explore knock-on effects of change and the need to manage these effectively

- describe the many different forms of flexible working arrangement that are found in contemporary organisations

- explain how the flexible firm model and the concepts of 'mutual' and 'intelligent' flexibility can enable organisations to increase their agility and efficiency while also maintaining high levels of staff commitment and engagement.

CHANGE MANAGEMENT

We need to start by acknowledging that organisational change comes in many different forms and levels of complexity. It also varies in its extent and significance from nominal to transformational. The term *change management* thus covers a huge number of diverse organisational situations, some being of far greater importance to different stakeholders than others. The major alternative types of change situation that require some managing are as follows:

- structural change
- cultural change
- technological change
- changing policies and practices
- relocations and ergonomic change
- new organisational objectives or strategic directions.

INEFFECTIVE MANAGEMENT OF CHANGE

Over the decades, but particularly in more recent years as change has become more regular and pervasive, the topic of 'change management' has generated a vast literature. Views on how it should best be managed by organisations vary greatly, but when reading these, one clear message comes through again and again. However much people disagree about many aspects of managing change, they all seem to agree that the chances of success are greatly enhanced when the 'people side' is taken into account and given full attention.

In practice, organisations often handle the people side of change very poorly. Decisions, even about major restructuring exercises, let alone mergers, acquisitions, downsizing and outsourcing initiatives, are frequently taken without consulting employees and, in many cases, without any genuine communication at all. Sometimes commercial confidentiality requires that this is the case. News of a proposed corporate takeover, for example, must not be allowed to leak ahead of time because the potential effect on the target organisation's share price might well make a deal unaffordable. But that does not mean that extensive communication and consultation cannot take place after the deal has been done. Experience suggests that these are often done too late and to an inadequate extent.

In most change management situations commercial confidentiality is not a major issue, but the literature is nonetheless full of examples of exercises that have gone wrong, or at least failed to meet their objectives simply because an organisation has pressed ahead willy-nilly without giving proper consideration to employees' needs, fears and prospects, let alone to their ideas.

The results can be spectacularly disastrous from a corporation's point of view. One well-known recent example was the debacle that followed the opening of Terminal 5 at Heathrow Airport in 2008. This great event had been 25 years in the planning. The new terminal cost around £4.3 billion and had taken six years to construct. It was to be used exclusively by British Airways, who contributed £330 million to secure a striking and flamboyant interior design. The building was opened by the Queen, guaranteeing a huge amount of publicity around the world. What followed was described by many commentators as a national disgrace. In the first few days of operation, a range of 'technical glitches' resulted in the cancellation of 300 flights. Lengthy queues formed at all the check-in and transfer desks, while an estimated 28,000 passengers found themselves separated from their luggage on departure or arrival. According to BBC reports, the immediate cost to British Airways was £16 million, but long-term direct costs were estimated at £150 million, not to mention those arising from the further erosion of an already tarnished corporate reputation.

The main reason for this mess, according to press reports at the time (see Done and Willman 2008, Blitz 2008, BBC 2008) was poor planning, and particularly mismanagement of people. Staff were not properly trained to use the new equipment in Terminal 5 and unable to solve the 'technical glitches' that arose when it opened for business. Many were not even able to find the staff car park or were unable to get through the security screening systems on time. Things were made worse, however, by the presence of long-standing poor, low-trust employment relationships between managers and staff within the company. Employees were simply not engaged sufficiently to speed up the rate at which they worked once difficulties developed. Many were not particularly committed either to their employer or to the success of the new operation. What was needed was goodwill, positive enthusiasm and, above all, flexibility. What BA staff tended to demonstrate was intransigence and a lack of co-operation.

Terminal 5 provides a striking and quite extreme example of the consequences of failing to take full account of people's needs and aspirations when planning and executing change. But it is not an uncommon type of situation. Baxter and Macleod (2008), for example, describe a longitudinal research project involving change management episodes in 20 diverse organisations. The aim, in each case, was to increase efficiency or quality. In practice all failed to meet their initial expectations due to poor management. Communication exercises were typically inadequate, while managers failed to take proper account of 'employees' feelings of insecurity and anger'. What was worse, though, according to this study, was that the senior managers who were responsible sometimes failed to accept that their initiatives had disappointed in practice. Great efforts were made to manipulate data so that the appearance of success could be proclaimed, even though the vast majority of employees knew this to be a fake. Further cynicism was then generated by the launch of newer initiatives aimed at achieving the same objectives, but with different names. According to Baxter and Macleod, it was only when employees were fully involved in planning and decision-making that the same problems were subsequently avoided, making second attempts at introducing change more successful.

The first clear lesson that can be learned from research into episodes of effective and ineffective change management is therefore to involve the people who will be most affected by the changes that are being proposed as fully and comprehensively as is possible at the planning stage. The old adage that 'people support what they help to create' is very true and should guide management in these types of situation.

What is remarkable in many ways is the apparent rarity with which these principles are adopted. They seem so obvious, yet managers appear reluctant to embrace them. Some pay lip-service, for example by organising extensive pseudo-consultation exercises. These give the appearance of taking on board diverse views from staff, but actually tend to generate anger and disappointment because in practice only senior management opinions are actually taken into account.

Why is this incompetent approach to change management so common? Sometimes it is simply due to ego, managers wanting to drive through changes 'their way' and to take the credit, presumably in a bid to impress their seniors and potential future employers. It appears to be a common vice of careerists whose motive in pushing through changes is as much to enhance their own positions as it is actually to improve an organisation's fortunes.

Just as often, though, poor management of change occurs because managers are put under too much pressure by parent companies, institutional shareholders or government ministers to drive major changes through quickly. They know full well that taking it at a slower pace and involving all stakeholders in decision-making will result in a more satisfactory outcome, but they are not given the time to take this approach.

A third explanation can be developed from the thinking of the influential economist Joseph Schumpeter (1942: 82), who saw continual change of a kind which undermines the status quo as being an essential feature of capitalism:

> *The opening up of new markets, foreign or domestic, and the organizational development from the craft shop and factory to such concerns as U.S. Steel illustrate the same process of industrial mutation – if I may use that biological term – that incessantly revolutionizes the economic structure from within, incessantly destroying the old one, incessantly creating a new one. This process of Creative Destruction is the essential fact about capitalism. It is what capitalism consists in and what every capitalist concern has got to live in.*

In principle an argument can thus be made in favour of driving change through in a destructive manner, on the grounds that genuine innovation cannot be achieved if gentler, more conciliatory approaches are taken. Necessary, radical change can only be achieved in a revolutionary fashion. This is a view that some managers articulate, as do radical politicians when they reflect on how to bring about what they consider to be genuinely necessary changes of a fundamental kind. They may well be right, but most organisational change is not so fundamental or revolutionary in its aims. It is not necessary in anything but extreme situations for managers to ignore the legitimate views and interests of their employees and to engage on a programme of creative destruction.

CASE STUDY

GEOGRAPHICAL DISPERSION OF BBC PROGRAMME-MAKING

One reason that organisations sometimes have to push change through without taking full account of their employees' views is when they know that staff will be fiercely opposed to what is being proposed, but nonetheless have every intention of going ahead in any event.

A recent example, which has been well publicised, is the moving of the production teams responsible for BBC programmes out of London to Glasgow and Manchester, along with whole divisions and a radio network. In all, more than 4,000 jobs will ultimately be relocated from London to other centres.

The decision to go ahead with the move was taken in 2007. Staff had to make decisions about whether or not they were going to move in March 2011, programme teams actually relocating later that year.

The purpose of the policy is to try to make the BBC's output less London-focused and to create a situation in which a wider range of regional voices and interests are reflected in national radio and TV programming.

For many staff, however, the requirement to relocate has been deeply unsettling. Unsurprisingly, a wide range of arguments have been developed in opposition to the proposals. Chief among these is the view that current affairs-based programming needs to come from London so that producers can readily secure live interviews with newsmakers, politicians and celebrities. Such arguments have been made in opposition to the relocation of the *Question Time* production team to Glasgow and the *Breakfast News* and Radio Five Live network to Manchester. An attempt was even made, though rather less convincingly, to deploy the same argument in favour of the children's show *Blue Peter* remaining at its London base.

BBC managers have responded by refusing to budge at all or to rethink their proposals. They have, however, offered very generous relocation terms, including full removal expenses, advice on schooling and job-hunting for spouses and partners, relocation bonuses of £5,000 (or £8,000 for staff who do not qualify for other aspects of the scheme), £3,000 for carpets and redecorating on arrival, £350 per house-hunting trip made 'up north', and three months' free storage of effects. In addition, all staff moving will retain their London weighting payments and will benefit from a house price guarantee scheme which means that they will be paid a figure of 95% of their London house's value if they cannot sell it. Any losses made will be shouldered by the BBC (ie the licence payer!). The total cost of the moves is estimated to be over £1 billion, making this one of the most ambitious change management episodes in UK corporate history.

Press reports in the weeks leading up to 31 March 2011, when final decisions had to be made, suggested that only around half of the staff offered the chance to relocate would actually be doing so.

Questions

1 Which aspects of this major change management project could be judged to have been successful and which unsuccessful?

2 Why do you think that the generous relocation terms appear to have failed to ensure that a good majority of staff have agreed to relocate?

THE NEED TO PLAN CHANGE

Aside from needing to involve people and to enable genuine two-way communication about proposed changes, the other major conclusion that can be made from decades of research into change management is that major advantages follow when the introduction of change is planned with some care. In particular strategies need to be developed for winning over people's hearts and minds. This is a side of change management which HR managers are well placed to take responsibility for.

Over the years a number of influential models have been published which, while being somewhat simplistic in their approaches, are nonetheless useful tools for us to use when planning a 'hearts and minds' campaign. Any survey of this field must start with the work of Kurt Lewin (1890–1947), whose theories and models are the most widely quoted. Lewin was a brilliant Jewish academic who left his native Germany in 1933 following the rise of Hitler. He settled in America, where he devoted the rest of his life to thinking through the ways in which Germany could be transformed into a leading Western democracy. He is best known for two simple propositions.

The first was his idea that in order to change people's views and to get them to support rather than to oppose change, leaders (be they politicians or managers) had to adopt a simple three-stage process summed up by the mantra:

'unfreeze – move – refreeze'

The starting point is therefore to gain acceptance for the need to change by putting forward a convincing case. Once people have accepted that, you introduce your changes, before taking steps to embed them effectively through a 'refreezing' process. The metaphor of ice is used in part to demonstrate that time needs to be taken in order to bring about successful change. It takes time to unfreeze and even longer to refreeze, allowing new ways of doing things to take root.

Lewin's second major contribution took the form of 'force field analysis'. The idea here is that in any change situation there are likely to be winners and losers. The winners will tend to support proposed changes, while the potential losers will resist. The key, according to Lewin, is for leaders to take steps to strengthen the forces of change so that their strength and influence gradually comes to outweigh that of the resistors. Lewin's force field analysis goes beyond persuading employees of the need to change; it also incorporates other potential blockages such as legal, technological and institutional impediments of one kind or another.

Later researchers have built on Lewin's ideas to develop rather more sophisticated models of effective change management. John Kotter's (1996), for example, is widely cited as a useful tool for managers to use when planning and executing change in organisations. He proposes that the following eight steps are taken:

1 **Establish a sense of urgency:** discuss the need to change with people, putting the case and explaining the risks associated with failing to change.

2 **Create a guiding coalition:** assemble a team of people who have power or influence in the organisation who can act as change agents.

3 **Communicate the change vision:** develop words and images that convey quite simply and compellingly what the change will achieve for the organisation.

4 **Communicate the vision:** make the case repeatedly to the target audience in a variety of different ways

5 **Empower others to take action:** break down resistance by allowing people to experiment with changes, perhaps piloting proposed changes in a small area of the organisation.

6 **Generate short-term wins:** where improvements are made as a result of stage five, celebrate these loudly and publicly reward those who are responsible to demonstrate the organisation's approval,

7 **Consolidate gains and produce more change:** maintain momentum and keep up energy levels by further promoting the need to change and rewarding those who embrace it.

8 **Institutionalise the new approaches:** cementing the change by making it clear that the organisation expects all to accept the change and to demonstrate appropriate attitudes and behaviours.

There are clear echoes here of Lewin's thinking, Kotter's ideas serving to put more meat on the bone as well as to using more contemporary business language (quick wins, empowerment, etc). Kotter's contribution is also important because of the stress he places on the potential role to be played by 'change agents', defined as individuals or groups who are enthusiastic backers of proposed changes and who are in a position to persuade others of its potential advantages.

We can also find echoes of Lewin's models in Everett Rogers' influential 'diffusion of innovation model', which develops some of the thinking behind force field analysis. Rogers proposed that when change is being proposed and introduced, those who are affected tend to fall into one of five distinct categories:

1 innovators

2 early adopters

3 the early majority

4 the late majority

5 the laggards.

The first group consist of winners and others who are readily persuaded of the need for change. These people are won over very easily. The next group to seek to persuade are the early adopters; like the innovators, they are quite a small group in most organisations. Once their support has been secured, managers can turn their attention to persuading the majority of staff, who typically fall into categories 3 and 4. Finally are the laggards, another relatively small group consisting of the people who are hardest to convince. In many cases these will be people who stand to lose most from the proposed changes.

In order to successfully persuade the doubters of the need for changes that are being proposed, it is important for managers and other change agents to understand what the major sources of resistance may be. Researchers tend to make a distinction here between resistance which is rooted in concerns about the content of the change and that which is focused more on process issues (ie the way that the process is being managed). Doubters tend to emphasise one or the other. In response, change agents need to be able to articulate different types of argument to employ when trying to persuade them to accept and even embrace the changes that are being mooted.

The CIPD (2005) has also contributed to this area of management thinking with its plan for making change happen successfully. Based on research carried out in partnership with Oxford's Said Business School, the CIPD recommends that organisations focus on all seven of its 'seven Cs' when seeking to manage change effectively. The role that HR professionals can play is a particular feature of this model. The seven are as follows:

- choosing a team
- crafting the vision and the path
- connecting organisation-wide change
- consulting stakeholders
- communicating

- coping with change

- capturing learning.

All of these well-respected models have stood the test of time because they provide practical help to managers who are planning to introduce change and are persuaded of the need to bring people with them if the process is ultimately to be successful. Nonetheless, two particular criticisms can be made of them. The first is that they all assume a situation in which a discrete change management initiative or episode is being embarked upon. Burnes (2009) rightly argues that this is less and less an appropriate characterisation of the type of change which organisations now have to manage. In the twenty-first century, change in many organisations is continual and endemic rather than episodic. There is therefore no point in 'refreezing', as Lewin would have us do, and not much point in 'institutionalising' changes, as Kotter recommends. No sooner have we done that, than we face the need to start all over again as new pressures demand further change.

The second criticism that is increasingly made of these and other rather formulaic models of change is that they fail to reflect the messy reality of effective change management in many organisations. In particular, it is often argued, they downplay the vital role that politics typically plays in bringing about the outcomes that managers are working towards.

THE NEED TO PLAY POLITICS

In 1999 David Buchanan and Richard Badham published a book entitled *Power, politics and organizational change: winning the turf game*. Here they drew on their research into change management in organisations, concluding that the reality was almost always a lot more complex and political than theories such as Lewin's, Rogers' and Kotter's supposed. Their book has proved to be highly influential, not least in signposting a new direction for change management research.

The conclusion that Buchanan and Badham reach is quite straightforward. They argue that change in organisations, even when it is of a relatively modest kind, tends to serve some people's interests more than others. In other words, there are winners and losers, which inevitably makes the process of change management political in nature. Those who stand to lose most will fight a turf war to prevent or to minimise the extent of a victory for those who stand to gain most.

It follows that in order to bring about change, managers need to hone and deploy political skills.

However, they also make two further important points. The first is that change tends to create opportunities for people to gain more influence because it shakes up the status quo. Working out whether or not you are likely, over the long term, to be a winner or a loser is thus not always obvious. Secondly, they make the point that organisations are typically made up of coalitions of interest groups that assemble over time. Proposed changes may thus be opposed or supported by people who are not themselves hugely affected, but are allied to people who are.

The central point is that whether we like it or not, organisational politics are pervasive and often complex. Power and influence may shift over time, as does the make-up of the coalitions, but it is quite impossible for people to push through any major changes without being part of such a coalition of interests and playing the political game. Simply making a good case in order to sway opinion, as is implied in the major published models of change, is thus not enough. Those who rely on this approach without also mastering the politics are likely to fail, however strong the case they are making may be.

It is important to make clear that people do not simply play politics in order to enhance their own economic interests – although many do. Often the motives are not selfish at all but rooted in honestly held but widely divergent views about the direction an organisation should take. Sometimes there is a clash of values or ethics leading to political battles over just causes. In some situations people clash politically over an issue, but become personally hostile to one another in the process. As a result future battles are as much motivated by personality as they are by principle.

What does this mean for HR managers operating in a commercial world which is continually forcing organisations to change, leading to the evolution of ongoing, never-ending debates about what direction should be taken?

It means that HR people need to develop the capacity to play the political game as effectively as other managers, not simply in order to protect and enhance their influence for personal reasons, but more importantly so as to ensure that the people side of change is given full consideration.

If it is the case, as decades of research clearly suggest, that change management episodes are more likely to succeed if they take proper account of the needs and interests of employees, it follows that ensuring this happens requires HR managers to act politically. First and foremost this means that they need to maintain a good understanding of the politics of their organisations:

- Where does power and influence really lie?
- Whose support needs to be gained in order to ensure that change is carried through in a people-friendly manner?
- Who has influence over those whose support is required?
- What types of argument are persuasive to these people?
- Who will gain and who will lose from proposed changes?
- Who is allied to the winners and losers?

Knowing the answer to these questions is essential if an HR function is to play a central role in the management of change. After that it is a question of thinking politically before acting.

Paton and McCalman (2008: 256) have adapted some of Buchanan and Badham's thinking to develop a list of eight 'turf game tactics' that they suggest all would-be change agents need to be adept at deploying if they are to be in a position to secure a win for their causes.

1 Image-building
Consciously taking steps to enhance your personal reputation in an organisation. This might involve sporting an air of self-confidence, taking care to be seen to support the causes of powerful people in an organisation and generally adhering to the 'norms' of the most powerful groups/coalitions.

2 Selective information
Manipulating how and with whom information is shared. Some will only tell powerful people what they want to hear, or will restrict useful knowledge to themselves rather than sharing it with others.

3 Scapegoating
Manipulating perceptions so that others or no one in particular gets the blame for your mistakes and misjudgements. The other side of the coin is taking the credit when things go well even if your own contribution is minimal.

4 Formal alliances
These are labelled 'formal' but can also be rather informal. Managers in organisations often form cross-departmental alliances with like-minded people and will support one another's causes and oppose those advanced by shared opponents.

5 Networking
Getting known by powerful people in an organisation and making a favourable impression on them.

6 Compromise
A straightforward tactic used by diplomats for centuries. Here you concede relatively unimportant points in order to get your way on what matters most to you.

7 Rule manipulation
Sticking to the rules of an organisation when it suits you and your allies, but veering in another direction on the grounds that 'special circumstances' apply when that suits your cause.

8 Ruthlessness
Carrying out the other seven 'turf war tactics' in a single-minded and determined way, even if this sometimes involves trampling on or undermining others.

 CRITICAL REFLECTION

Linda Holbeche (2003) conducted a most interesting research project that looked in detail at how politics are played in organisations. Among her many findings was an apparent difference between the genders in terms of their approach to playing politics in organisations. The findings included the following:

- Men are more likely than women to admit to enjoying organisational politics.
- Women are more likely than men to respond by making a case in support of their position.

- Men are more likely to seek influence by increasing their visibility.

- Women prefer to build up a network through which to influence decision-making.

- Men are more comfortable adapting themselves and their behaviour to a new situation or group of people.

- Women are less likely than men to admit to being motivated by the desire to enhance their personal careers.

Questions

1 In your view, what do these findings tell us about the relative success of men and women in influencing change management processes?

2 To what extent might these findings provide an answer to the question of why so few women are appointed to top jobs in major corporations?

MANAGING THE CONSEQUENCES OF CHANGE

No survey of the potential role played by HR managers in change management can be complete without briefly considering one or two other issues that can be seen as by-products of change.

MANAGING CONFLICT

The political aspects of change as well as the fact that it tends to create winners and losers inevitably leads to conflict between individuals and groups within organisations. Moreover, this conflict can last for many months or even years after the original issue over which parties clashed has been forgotten. Put simply, change can very easily serve to make co-workers into enemies.

Some recent researchers who have examined conflict in organisations (see Jehn and Rispens 2008) have tended to argue that it is an inevitable feature of modern organisational life and, moreover, that it can have positive benefits for organisations. It tends, for example, to lead to better decisions because it ensures that they have to be properly justified. It is also often the source of valuable innovation.

All this may be true, but for the most part conflict between individual organisation members is unhealthy. It may be inevitable, but that does not mean that it should be left to develop unchecked. Conflict, particularly when it becomes personal in nature, is destructive. It makes teams less effective, adds to the burden of stress that people carry and generally makes working life a lot less pleasant both for those who are in conflict and others who are obliged to work closely with them. It tends to decrease organisational performance and increase staff turnover rates.

HR mangers therefore need to engage in conflict management. They need to be aware of problems of this kind and work as best they can to:

- prevent the development of damaging conflict

- seek to reduce its impact
- find ways of reducing conflict between individuals/groups

  and

- try to channel conflict so as to enhance its potential positive benefits.

The key to this is quite straightforward. HR managers need to intervene in order to prevent conflict from taking on a personal dimension. Conflict becomes damaging – often severely damaging to an organisation or a team within an organisation – when it becomes personal in nature. Vigorous disagreement between people who genuinely like and respect one another is not problematic because the underlying relationship is strong and positive. They may have opposing views and this may spill over into rows occasionally, but these are of short-term duration. The damage is caused when people fall out. When that happens, the emotional wounds that are created on either side can make it very difficult to ever heal the relationship satisfactorily.

Obviously no HR professional is going to be in a position to step in personally to prevent developments like these from occurring. But they are in a position to flag up the issue and, particularly, to develop training interventions which help individuals to manage conflict themselves. Similarly, a well-respected HR function will be able to encourage line managers to recognise warning signs and to take appropriate action before a conflict in their department becomes personal.

MANAGING STRESS

As is the case with conflict, there has been a vast amount of research published in recent years on the subject of organisational stress. Moreover, as is true of conflict in organisations, it is widely recognised that a moderate amount of stress is a good thing both for individuals and their organisations. It becomes problematic for both when levels of stress become impossible for people to cope with.

Research into the incidence of stress is notoriously unreliable because it is always based on self-reporting. While we can therefore conclude with some confidence that people perceive working life to be becoming more stressful over time, it cannot be proved that this is in fact the case. It may simply be that people are more prepared to admit that they are finding it difficult to cope with work-based stressors than they were in the past.

This should not, however, stop us from treating the subject seriously and acknowledging that when employees find it difficult to cope, there are significant negative consequences both for the individual and the organisation.

Change is by no means the only cause of stress at work. There are many others including increased work intensification, increasingly demanding customers and, importantly, the increasing extent to which the boundary between our home and working lives is becoming permeable or blurred (Jex and Yankelevich 2008: 504). Change, however, is inherently stressful for many people because it has the effect of increasing their insecurity and, as we saw above, tends to draw them into conflict with others.

The very extensive literature on the impact of serious stress demonstrates clearly that it has important negative consequences. Weinberg et al (2010: 24–35) provide a useful summary. They cite the following consequences:

- mental health problems
- increased likelihood that mistakes or misjudgements are made
- reduced tolerance of challenging situations
- low levels of morale and job satisfaction
- reduced preparedness to work beyond contract or to engage in positive organisational citizenship behaviour
- lower productivity
- low-trust employment relations
- higher absenteeism
- higher staff turnover
- more bullying-type behaviour.

Some research has attempted to quantify the losses. The National Institute for Health and Clinical Excellence (NICE) (2009) estimated the typical annual cost per 1,000 employees of absenteeism, presenteeism and voluntary turnover caused by stress. Their estimate was £835,355.

Research into stress at work has also been able to demonstrate that interventions by organisations can have a major positive impact. This is therefore a further way in which the HR function can take active steps to ameliorate the consequences of change management exercises.

Weinberg et al (2010: 153–243) set out in some detail all the types of intervention that can be made by managers which are known to have a positive effect on reducing stress levels. I don't have the space here to deal with all of them in detail, but it is possible to summarise the various approaches under three basic headings.

1 Preventative measures
Steps can be taken over a prolonged period of time to address and move towards the reduction of causes of stress. These include leadership style, the prevailing organisational culture, physical working conditions, overly burdensome workloads and the prevalence of bullying. All of these have a relevance to the way that change management is handled. Of particular significance is a perception on the part of employees that they lack control over their own area of work. This appears to be a major cause of damaging stress. This is another argument for genuine and extensive employee involvement when change is being planned and implemented. The key aim is to manage change in such a way as to reduce or even eliminate unnecessary stress.

2 Training

The second type of intervention available to managers who are aware that staff are suffering from an inability to cope with stress involves devising constructive training and development programmes. Formal training events typically cover issues such as time management, anger management and cognitive coping skills. A different approach focuses on building up resistance to stress rather than merely coping with it. These commonly include training interventions which encourage people to take exercise and to develop a more healthy, balanced lifestyle. Central is teaching people to recognise the symptoms of stress for themselves, and to take their own steps to deal with it.

Another common approach involves one-to-one coaching on relaxation, work–life balance and becoming more assertive. Interventions of this kind are particularly valuable in the case of people, and especially leaders, who have what psychologists refer to as 'Type A personality traits'. These people are highly ambitious, impatient, competitive workaholics who tend to be self-focused. They are more vulnerable to avoidable stress and are likely to react badly to any situation in which they perceive themselves to be losing control. They are thus likely to have a strong, negative reaction to change which they see as threatening to their position.

3 Counselling

The final type of intervention that can be shown to have positive effects is the provision of well-designed and effective counselling programmes. The most common is some form of employee assistance programme, which involves providing specialist counsellors who employees can speak to face to face or by telephone. Some organisations have also reported having successfully reduced stress in their organisations by training their managers in counselling skills.

FLEXIBLE WORKING

Increased competitive intensity requires organisations to do more than change more frequently and more profoundly. It also requires them to become more flexible. This is partly in order to increase efficiency and productivity, but developing a capacity for flexibility also allows them to respond more quickly to changed and changing circumstances. New opportunities can thus be seized and capitalised upon more effectively than their rivals are able to. The term *organisational agility* is increasingly used in this context.

In Chapter 7 we will look at the aspects of flexible working which are primarily concerned with helping employees to achieve a better work–life balance and, more generally, to manage their work commitments more flexibly. My purpose here is to focus on moves towards more flexible working that are initiated by employers in order to further commercial or financial objectives. In particular I want to explore some possible answers to the conundrum I outlined at the beginning of the chapter: namely, how far is it possible for organisations to increase their flexibility while also maintaining and enhancing employee commitment?

TYPES OF FLEXIBLE WORKING

There is nothing at all new about most flexible employment practices. People have been employed on various forms of flexible contract and have worked flexibly across job boundaries for centuries. Nor is there anything at all new about variable pay or homeworking. What is a relatively recent development, however, is the use of a wide variety of such approaches in combination as part of a defined employment strategy across all forms of organisation.

The term *flexible working* potentially encompasses a wide variety of different types of initiative:

- part-time working
- job-sharing
- term-time working
- compressed hours (full-time hours worked over fewer days)
- annual hours (varied patterns of hours worked at different times of the year)
- agency working
- zero hours (casual working)
- homeworking
- flexitime (flexibility over when work is carried out across the working week)
- sabbaticals and career breaks
- outsourcing
- multi-skilling
- variable pay (eg profit-sharing or performance-related)
- flexible benefits (employees choose how their benefits package is made up).

Each of these approaches, in their different ways, represents a departure from a traditional type of working contract (ie full-time, permanent, with fixed hours and pay with clearly defined job duties).

It is easy to see why they are attractive to employers:

- They increase efficiency, and hence competitiveness, by allowing managers to deploy staff where they are most needed at any time.
- They reduce the total amount of time that people are being paid to work during slack periods.
- They provide a close link between total wage costs and the quantity and quality of the work performed.
- They reduce the extent to which overtime needs to be paid.
- Some, but not all, are liked by employees and thus help employers to recruit and retain able performers.

From an employee perspective, however, moves in the direction of greater flexibility have major downsides. First and foremost, they often serve to make employment less secure and income less predictable. This is because effectively the employer is passing on some of the financial risks associated with doing business in unpredictable markets on to their staff. They also tend to reduce overall income levels.

Secondly, flexible working initiatives tend to increase work intensity, requiring staff to work harder during the periods that they are at work. There are fewer slow periods and many more hectic periods of work experienced by each employee.

There are thus considerable potential dangers associated with moves towards greater flexibility when seen from an HRM perspective. Enhancing flexibility serves to reduce costs and make an organisation more efficient, but at the same time it can serve to reduce levels of commitment and engagement among staff – attributes which are essential if an organisation is to perform competitively. This is particularly true of existing staff whose established working arrangements are altered, leaving them less secure in their jobs than they were previously. Not only can flexible working arrangements serve to reduce people's willingness to work beyond contract, but they can also make it harder for organisations to recruit and retain skilled and experienced staff who are looking for greater job and income security.

The key question the HR manager thus needs to grapple with is how to help their organisations increase their flexibility using these kinds of approaches while at the same time retaining and, if possible, increasing levels of employee engagement and commitment.

To date I am aware of three distinct answers to this question that are found in the published literature on flexibility. None is perfect, but all three help to provide some guidance about possible ways forward in a world in which HR managers need both to maximise efficiency and to ensure that their organisations have access to the skills they require.

ATKINSON'S MODEL OF THE FLEXIBLE FIRM

John Atkinson, a senior civil servant, published his model back in 1984. Drawing heavily on his understanding of Japanese management practice, he set out some ideas about how firms in the UK could develop greater flexibility. It was not made at all clear in the article that accompanied the model whether Atkinson was describing existing good practice, predicting likely future approaches or setting out his prescription for changes to existing employment practices. What is clear, however, is that the model can be applied equally well across the private, public and third sectors. The use of the term *firm* does not mean that it only has relevance to private companies. The model has been highly influential, and usually serves as the starting point for serious discussions on increasing organisational flexibility (see Figure 6.1).

Figure 6.1 Atkinson's model of the flexible firm

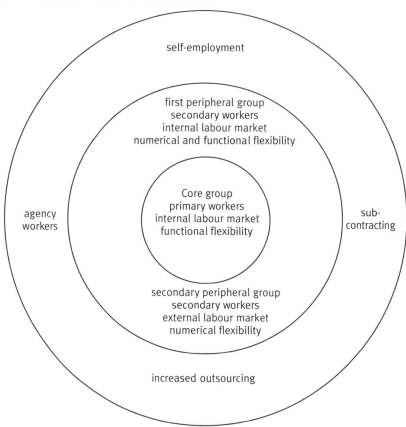

self-employment

first peripheral group
secondary workers
internal labour market
numerical and functional flexibility

Core group
primary workers
internal labour market
functional flexibility

agency
workers

sub-
contracting

secondary peripheral group
secondary workers
external labour market
numerical flexibility

increased outsourcing

The key feature of Atkinson's model is the distinction that he makes between core employees and peripheral staff. Indeed, he suggests that organisations employ three distinct groups of worker. In the centre of the model are the core staff. These people are employed on a traditional permanent, full-time basis. They thus enjoy considerable job security and can look forward to progression within the organisation. Their contribution to increased flexibility is entirely focused in the area of functional flexibility. That means that they are, as far as is practicable, multi-skilled and able to work across traditional job boundaries. A particular feature of functionally flexible arrangements is that there are fewer hierarchical layers than has tended to be the case in UK organisations. So core employees may find themselves carrying out duties that would, in a more traditional type of organisation, be 'reserved' for their bosses and subordinates.

There are then two separate groups of peripheral staff, represented by the outer and inner rings. Those in the inner ring are employed directly by the organisation, but on some form of atypical contract. Some are part-time, others are fixed-term. Then beyond them, on the outer ring, are people whose skills the organisation draws on, but who are not employees. They may be self-employed, employed by a contractor or employed via agencies, but one way or another can be hired and fired with considerable ease.

Here then is one answer to the difficult issue of how to combine flexibility with commitment. Atkinson's solution is to segment the workforce. The firm has at its core a substantial cadre of permanent employees in whom considerable investment is made and who can look forward to a relatively long and fruitful association with it. They occupy key positions and can thus reasonably be expected, all other things being equal, to be fully engaged and to go the extra mile for the organisation when needed. These people work flexibly, but they are not insecure. The big financial gains come from the employment of peripheral staff who may be less committed over the long term, but whose contractual arrangements permit the organisation to thrive in an increasingly competitive commercial environment.

In practice, organisations which operate according to the flexible firm model proposed by Atkinson often find that the staff in peripheral positions are just as committed as those in the core group. This is because there is movement across the boundary. People are, for example, often initially recruited on a fixed-term basis, but can then move on into a core role over time. The possibility of achieving this serves as an incentive and tends to mean that fixed-term staff are among the hardest working and most engaged workers that the organisation employs.

REILLY'S NOTION OF MUTUAL FLEXIBILITY

A second potential approach to solving the conundrum was articulated very effectively by Peter Reilly (2001) in an excellent book on flexible working in the UK.

Reilly's key point is that employees have a shared interest with employers in some, but by no means all, of the flexible working initiatives set out above. He shows, for example, how multi-skilling and systems which promote functional flexibility benefit employees if it means that they upskill and make themselves more employable. Secondly, many other forms of flexible working are actively sought by would-be employees who are looking to achieve a better work–life balance. Flexitime, term-time working, career breaks, homeworking, job-sharing and part-time working are the main examples. Reilly also argues that fixed-term contracts can be attractive if they pay well and provide opportunities for people to develop a career working for themselves.

It follows that organisations can, if they take care to introduce flexible working thoughtfully and in consultation with their staff, evolve practices which create a win–win situation. They increase efficiency and organisational agility, while also enhancing commitment and making the organisation more attractive in the labour market.

The problem, according to Reilly, is that too many organisations in the UK have failed to opt for mutually flexible solutions, preferring instead to take a 'cyclopic' or one-eyed approach which only considers the short-term financial needs of the organisation and which ignores the longer-term advantages associated with employing a well-motivated and highly engaged team of staff. Some employers have taken advantage of loose labour market conditions to employ macho-management approaches that involve mistreating staff, and are often unlawful too. They have forced greater insecurity on them through the use of zero-hours contracts and fixed-term contracts of short duration, by employing them indirectly through agencies or by outsourcing them to 'cowboy contractors'. Reilly rightly argues that such approaches can only ever bring short-term improvements to an organisation's financial performance. That may serve the needs of a careerist looking to make a quick splash before moving on to another post, but it is deeply damaging to the long-term financial prospects of an organisation.

WHITE, HILL, MILLS AND SMEATON'S NOTION OF INTELLIGENT FLEXIBILITY

A third approach is advocated very effectively in the book *Managing to change?* by Michael White and his colleagues (2004). Drawing on an extensive survey which looked at practice in UK organisations in 2002, they argue strongly that major advantages can be gained if organisations steer clear of 'buying in more flexible labour' and choose instead to follow an approach they label as 'intelligent flexibility'. The rationale is explained as follows:

> *Not all business uncertainty is a numbers problem. The market may shift towards a new product or service, as when CDs put an end to vinyl, or EasyJet and Ryanair challenged traditional airlines with their no frills service. To meet such a qualitative change in demand requires employees with new skills or capable of learning new approaches. It is unlikely that this kind of change can be met just by buying in temporary assistance, especially not of the 'pairs of hands' variety.... If the workforce is adaptable and versatile, it will be able to cope with this kind of change much better than where people work in a rigid way.* (White et al 2004: 39)

White et al are therefore arguing that the type of flexibility that enhances an organisation's adaptability and agility is increasingly more necessary for organisations to achieve than pure cost-based approaches that only serve to increase efficiency.

There are three major elements to their conception of 'intelligent flexibility'. Firstly, White et al argue in favour of a sophisticated approach to functional flexibility. The key is to develop a workforce which can undertake a wider variety of organisational tasks and where individuals are competent to cover one another's jobs as and when necessary. Efficiency savings are made because people can be deployed across the organisation to where the demand for their skills is highest at any one time. If someone is absent or leaves, there are others present who are in a position to cover their duties to a high standard immediately. There need be no loss in efficiency or quality in such circumstances.

Secondly, both this and future adaptability are facilitated by significant investment in training and development initiatives. White et al argue in favour of formal training, but also advocate job rotation as a strategy for developing an adaptable workforce and managers who are able to coach staff effectively.

The third element of 'intelligent flexibility' is teamworking – the aspect that White et al (2004) believe has not been as widely adopted by UK organisations as it should have been. Central here is the proposition that employees work best and most flexibly in a functional sense when they are placed in teams which are able to self-manage to a considerable degree. This is very different from the alternative and widely used approach in which managers deploy their staff here and there as and when required. Teamworking serves to enhance flexibility in many different ways:

- Individuals learn from one another, thus enhancing the range of skills that they have.

- They support one another through periods of change.

- They cover for one another during absences or when someone leaves.

- Teams enhance motivation and commitment, especially when rewards are team rather than individually focused.

- Teamworking enhances job satisfaction because it allows people to make their own decisions about the organisation of their areas of work.

KEY ARTICLE

FLEXIBLE WORKING AT NEWI

The following article was published in *People Management* on 26 November 1998. You can download it from the CIPD website:

'Pool position' by Colin Grethe

This article is a few years old now, but it is still well worth reading. It describes how the Welsh higher education provider NEWI changed the way that it achieved greater flexibility by moving away from the employment of agency staff to the establishment of its own bank of flexible workers. The approach they chose to follow aimed specifically to enhance their flexibility while also improving levels of employee engagement significantly.

Questions

1 What was the main motivation behind the change in policy?

2 To what extent did NEWI adopt thinking of the kind advocated by Atkinson, Reilly and White et al?

3 To what extent did the change succeed in enhancing both flexibility and commitment?

CONCLUSIONS

Increasing competition is putting great pressure on organisations to become more efficient, to change in significant ways more frequently and to become much more agile and flexible. Achieving these objectives while also retaining and enhancing levels of commitment and engagement among staff is a difficult task, but it is one that is becoming increasingly central to evolving HR strategies. In the future it is likely to become one of the central conundrums that HR managers are tasked with solving.

Achieving this is not easy, especially when finance directors, institutional shareholders and often government ministers are keen to achieve quick improvements in efficiency which serve short-term expedients, but are often damaging in their long-term impacts. HR managers thus need to be in a position both to develop strategies which maintain commitment while also increasing efficiency and to argue the case for such approaches convincingly.

In this chapter we have looked at the management of change and at increasing flexibility through this lens. Having done so we can conclude that there are strategies available which have proved successful and that effectively combine efficiency with commitment. It is partly a question of avoiding approaches which ignore the interests, fears and hopes of employees, and partly a question of championing methods which are beneficial to both organisations and their staff.

KEY LEARNING POINTS

- Change management is often carried out poorly because insufficient attention is given to understanding and accommodating the people side.

- Managers are more likely to ensure that a change episode meets its objectives if they plan it carefully, taking account of the hopes and fears of their employees.

- Maximising employee involvement in planning and executing change makes good sense because people support what they help to create.

- It is necessary for HR managers to develop and deploy effective political skills in order to influence change management processes in organisations.

- It is very difficult to increase an organisation's flexibility while also maintaining a high level of commitment and engagement on the part of staff.

- Three promising alternative approaches to increasing flexibility effectively are the 'flexible firm model', 'mutual flexibility' and 'intelligent flexibility'.

EXPLORE FURTHER

Peter Reilly's wise and thoughtful book entitled *Flexibility at work: balancing the interests of employer and employee* (2001) provides the best general survey of the complexities associated with developing more flexible working practices.

Reilly, P. (2001) *Flexibility at work: balancing the interests of employer and employee*. Aldershot: Gower.

The CIPD's (2005) contribution to the debate about how best to go about managing change in an organisation with plenty of HR input can be downloaded from the Institute's website. It is called *HR: making change happen*.

CIPD (2005) *HR: making change happen*. London: Chartered Institute of Personnel and Development.

David Buchanan and Richard Badham's work on change management, with its emphasis on politics, represents the most important recent development in this field of study. Their book is *Power, politics and organizational change: winning the turf game*.

Buchanan, D.A. and Badham, R. (2008) *Power, politics and organizational change: winning the turf game*. 2nd edition. London: Sage.

REFERENCES

Atkinson, J. (1984) Manpower strategies for the flexible organisation. *Personnel Management.* August.

Baxter, L. and Macleod, A. (2008) *Managing performance improvement.* London: Routledge.

BBC (2008) BA's terminal losses top £16 million. *BBC News* website. 3 April.

Blitz, R. (2008) The trouble with great expectations. *Financial Times.* 26 March.

Buchanan, D.A. and Badham, R. (2008) *Power, politics and organizational change: winning the turf game.* 2nd edition. London: Sage.

Burnes, B. (2009) *Managing change.* 5th edition. London: FT/Prentice Hall.

CIPD (2005) *HR: making change happen.* London: Chartered Institute of Personnel and Development.

Done, K. and Willman, J. (2008) Goodwill of staff is often in short supply. *Financial Times.* 5 April.

Holbeche, L. (2003) The politics of work. *People Management.* 26 March.

Jehn, K. and Rispens, S. (2008) Conflict in workgroups. In J. Barling and C. Cooper (eds) *The Sage handbook of organizational behaviour.* London: Sage.

Jex, S. and Yankelevich, M. (2008) Work stress. In J. Barling and C. Cooper (eds) *The Sage handbook of organizational behaviour.* London: Sage.

Kotter, J. (1996) *Leading change.* Boston: Harvard Business School Press.

NICE (2009) *Public health guidance: development process and models.* London: National Institute for Health and Clinical Excellence.

Paton, R. and McCalman, J. (2008) *Change management: a guide to effective implementation.* 3rd edition. London: Sage. Chapter 12.

Purcell, J. and Sisson, K. (2010) Management: caught between competing views of the organisation. In T. Colling and M. Terry (eds) *Industrial relations: theory and practice.* 3rd edition. Chichester: Wiley.

Reilly, P. (2001) *Flexibility at work: balancing the interests of employer and employee.* Aldershot: Gower.

Schumpeter, J. (1942) *Capitalism, socialism and democracy.* London: Allen & Unwin.

Weinberg, A., Sutherland, V. and Cooper, C. (2010) *Organizational stress management: a strategic approach.* Basingstoke: Palgrave.

White, M., Hill, S., Mills, C. and Smeaton, D. (2004) *Managing to change? British workplaces and the future of work.* Basingstoke: Palgrave.

CHAPTER 7

Competing for people

Introduction

In Chapter 3 I argued that, at least in organisations which employ skilled staff, recruitment and retention are soon likely to move back to the top of the HRM agenda and to stay there for the foreseeable future. Skills shortages and tight labour markets will increasingly require organisations to think more creatively and strategically about the way that they recruit and retain their people. In Chapter 2 the point was made that increasingly competitive market conditions will put an additional premium on an organisation's ability to recruit and retain stronger performers than its competitors are able to. At the same time, however, competition will also require organisations to maintain tighter profit margins and continually to keep a lid on wage costs. The combination of these trends is creating one of the thorniest conundrums in contemporary HRM, namely how do we recruit and retain effective performers in an environment which is both increasingly resource-constrained and characterised by tight labour conditions?

A number of the remaining chapters will touch on important aspects of this question and propose some possible answers. Here we will tackle it very directly. We will start by looking at reward management issues and particularly at ways in which managers can act to ensure that they achieve the greatest return in terms of staff performance from their investment in wages and salaries. We will go on to explore the concept of 'total reward', which has much to offer when the amount of money available to reward good performers is limited. In the second half of the chapter our attention will switch to the issue of how best to communicate the 'employee value proposition' that an employer is offering. This will take us into the very interesting and still undeveloped area of employer branding.

LEARNING OUTCOMES

The objectives of this chapter are to:

- explain why organisations do not always have to pay wages at or above market rates in order to recruit and retain effectively
- introduce and discuss the concept of 'total reward' and its relevance for recruitment and retention in a resource-constrained environment
- assess the advantages and disadvantages associated with flexible benefits systems
- introduce and explain the concept of employer branding
- introduce and assess the prospects for contemporary ideas about labour market segmentation.

REWARD

Much conventional economic and management thinking about labour markets places a considerable emphasis on pay. Like any other type of market, it is assumed, where price determines demand and supply and vice versa, pay is the key variable that underpins the operation of these factors in a labour market. It follows that an organisation seeking to recruit and retain strong performers and to fill its vacancies rapidly must pay people a good salary if it is to stand any chance of success. An organisation that wishes to be seen as 'an employer of choice' will therefore seek to 'lead the market', paying rather more than the going rate for a particular job in order to make quite sure that it attracts large numbers of applications from well-qualified, experienced applicants. Leading the market pay-wise also makes it harder for people to leave in order to take up alternative jobs.

Leading the market has other advantages too when seen from a management perspective. It means, for example, that pay can be used as an effective lever of control. If losing your job will mean a considerable fall in income, even if you do go on to find another similar job, there is inevitably a tendency to work hard and to conform to your manager's expectations. It thus becomes possible for organisations to pursue an HR strategy that combines high pay with relatively low levels of job security, high workloads and a fairly brutal style of management. People will be attracted by the money, will demonstrate high levels of commitment and will stay for a long period of time, not because they are achieving a high level of job satisfaction, but because it allows them to achieve a high standard of living. This approach is used routinely in the financial sector in the UK and is characteristic of that used in many larger American corporations, where a 'hire and fire' culture operates successfully due to the simultaneous presence of relatively high pay. Andrew Neil (1996: 184, 192), for example, shows how this has been the favoured approach to HRM for Rupert Murdoch's News

International corporation, allowing the company to buy acceptance from its staff of a range of 'low commitment/high control' management practices.

The extent to which this type of macho approach to management is workable in all industries and across all labour markets is highly questionable. There is plenty of good evidence to suggest that many people will only put up with so much unpleasant treatment and a long-hours culture for a limited period, however well remunerated they are. This appears to be particularly true of younger workers who seem less inclined than Baby Boomers and colleagues from Generation X (ie people born in the 1950s and 1960s) to work under such conditions.

Of course it helps if the work itself is enjoyable and interesting. If it is not, high levels of pay will not serve to recruit and retain effectively.

Sturges and Guest (1999), for example, in their interviews with graduate recruits, concluded firmly that:

> As far as they are concerned, while challenging work will compensate for pay, pay will never compensate for having to do boring, unstimulating work.

While it is remarkable how many organisations manage to make the case for 'leading the market' when it comes to the determination of senior management remuneration packages, for most taking such an approach for the generality of its staff is not an option. This is either because money is not available due to tight profit margins or limited public funding, because it is possible to attract and retain good staff without paying high rates or simply because the economics in highly labour-intensive industries preclude high pay. Here the best that can be achieved is 'meeting the market' (ie paying at the going rate), but in many cases organisations are required to 'follow the market' and pay wages below those of key competitors. This is particularly true of companies that are based in developed countries but which compete with others who employ staff to undertake similar roles in developing economies where labour costs are much lower. It is also true of a wide range of organisations operating in the private service sector in markets characterised by intense price-based competition. Retailing, hotels, nursing homes, fast food restaurants and call centres are all good examples. In all of these industries the need to keep costs low means that pay rates inevitably remain low *vis-à-vis* those that are available to similarly qualified staff working in other industries.

The likelihood is, as was shown in Chapter 2, that competition, and particularly international competition, is likely to intensify considerably in the future, making it harder and harder as time goes by for organisations to lead the market. Whereas in the past we have tended to deal with skills shortages by lifting pay rates, there will be less flexibility available to achieve this in the future. That would not be a problem if labour markets were loose and skilled people had little choice about where to work, but as we saw in Chapter 3, there are good grounds for expecting much tighter skilled labour market conditions to evolve in the future. It thus follows that organisations will increasingly look to maintain pay policies which follow the market rather than lead it, while seeking out other alternative methods of recruiting and retaining skilled people.

There are of course other alternatives. As Jeffrey Pfeffer (1994, 1998, 2006) has pointed out repeatedly and very wisely, it is possible for organisations to pay well while also keeping costs low if they can achieve superior levels of productivity to those that their competitors are able to manage. This is achieved by employing fewer people of higher calibre who are collectively able to achieve more in their time at work. Where new technologies permit the achievement of productivity savings of this kind, pay levels can be maintained at a relatively high level. But the more competitive the environment becomes, and the wider and more rapid the spread of the relevant technologies, the harder it becomes to sustain this approach over time, particularly in labour-intensive industries. While there may be exceptions, in my view the general direction in the future will inevitably be towards the reining in of pay for most people, despite the evolution of more competition among employers for skills and experience. Good individual performance will still be rewarded and people will continue to progress up career ladders, but the extent to which this happens will be less in the future than it has traditionally been in the past.

FOLLOWING THE MARKET

Gomez-Mejia and Balkin (1992), in their classic survey of research into reward management, clearly demonstrated that it is possible to attract, motivate and retain effective employees without paying as much money in the form of wages as other employers do. In other words, following the market is a feasible potential approach for employers to take. Where money is available to pay employees more, but employers choose not to in order to maximise share dividends or to reward senior staff, low levels of staff satisfaction and high levels of turnover will result due to perceived inequity of treatment, particularly when labour markets are tight. However, when resources are constrained and there is limited scope for pay increases, it remains possible, even when tight labour market conditions prevail, for an organisation to source skilled and experienced staff and to keep them.

This occurs because a good proportion of people are looking for much more from their jobs than just money and will trade other advantages for higher pay if an employer is able to provide them. The following are examples cited by Gomez-Mejia and Balkin (1992):

- job security
- flexible working arrangements
- benefits such as car parking, holidays, pensions, health insurance
- career development and training opportunities
- convenience of a work location
- work which is intrinsically satisfying, worthwhile or meaningful
- a pleasant working environment
- friendly and considerate colleagues.

Others appear to be happy to forgo high pay now for the possibility of higher pay later. Small organisations with growth potential can thus attract staff by promising a greater share of rewards in the future when the company expands. There also appears to be scope for big-name organisations to pay rather less than those with a low profile. This is because people perceive that gaining a period of work experience in a well-known and respected organisation will help to further their future career ambitions. This is why some of the most desirable graduate training programmes provided by the largest, best-known organisations often pay a good deal less to their recruits than equivalent graduate schemes offered by smaller employers.

TOTAL REWARD

Over time employers appear to be increasingly aware of the wide range of options that are available to them when it comes to reward management. They are also thinking about these matters more strategically and basing decisions on extensive, formal research about staff expectations. The language used by HR managers is developing too, use of terms such as 'formulating an employee value proposition' reflecting the strategic nature of contemporary thinking in this area and an understanding that reward is about much more than pay. Another expression which is increasingly widely used in this context is 'total reward', defined neatly by Armstrong and Murlis (2007: 12) as follows:

> *A concept which recognizes the importance of considering all aspects of reward as an integrated and coherent whole. Each of the elements of total reward, namely base pay, pay contingent on performance, competence or contribution, employee benefits and non-financial rewards, which include intrinsic rewards from the employment environment and the work itself, are linked together. A total reward approach is holistic; reliance is not placed on one or two reward mechanisms or levers operating in isolation. Account is taken of all the ways in which people can be rewarded and obtain satisfaction through their work.*

Total reward thus involves designing a rich mix of complementary initiatives which aim to maximise the chances that employees will find their work to be 'rewarding' in the widest sense of the word. It therefore has a great deal to offer organisations that are looking for ways of competing effectively in tight labour markets, but have limited resources available to allow them to increase pay rates appreciably.

Before we start to look at some of the most influential tools and models that have been published to help employers develop total reward strategies, there is a significant caveat to be aware of: this is the absence of any really major research studies carried out into the approach and into its practical impact. Corby and Lindop (2009: 255), in their survey of the subject, agree that as an approach it is appealing and 'makes sense', but point out that they were unable to locate any rigorous evaluation of a scheme anywhere in the academic literature.

In their conceptions of total reward, Armstrong and Murlis (2007) make a clear distinction between 'transactional rewards' and 'relational rewards'. The former category contains pay and benefits, including performance-related remuneration of various kinds. The latter, by contrast, contains a variety of non-financial rewards, including quite unspecific elements such as 'responsibility' and 'autonomy'. Armstrong and Brown (2009) go further, drawing on work by the consultancy firm Towers Perrin. They subdivide the various types of reward into 'individual' and 'communal', creating the four categories illustrated in Figure 7.1.

Figure 7.1 Four categories of reward

Individual	**Transactional**
base pay	pensions
contingent pay	holidays
bonuses	health care
incentives	other perks
shares	flexibility
profit-sharing	
Relational	**Communal**
learning and development	leadership
training	organisational values
career development	voice
	recognition
	achievement
	job design
	work–life balance

Another widely cited model of total reward is that which has been advanced by the American consultancy WorldatWork (2007). There are three categories here:

1 compensation (pay of various kinds)

2 benefits (pensions, insurance, holidays, perks, etc)

and

3 the work experience.

This third category is then further subdivided into five categories, which are framed as follows so as to follow the first five letters of the alphabet:

- acknowledgement
- balance
- culture
- development
- environment.

The term *acknowledgement* refers to recognition that can be either formal (eg employee awards) or informal (thanks/a pat on the back). *Balance* in this context means opportunities to achieve a better work–life balance and includes initiatives such as sabbaticals and flexible working arrangements designed to help parents of young children and those with caring responsibilities to combine work with domestic responsibilities. The term *culture* is less well defined in this framework. It is explained as concerning 'collective attitudes and behaviors that influence how individuals behave' and as encompassing sets of 'unspoken expectations, behavioral norms and performance standards'. It thus appears to comprise the way that people are managed in an organisation and the way that things get done. The term *development* refers to career development opportunities, formal and informal, internal and external, while *environment* in this context refers to 'the total cluster of observable physical, psychological and behavioral elements in the workplace'. This will thus encompass job design, relationships with colleagues and managers as well as the physical environment in which employees work.

This WorldatWork framework thus ranges rather more widely than the Towers Perrin/Armstrong approach, encompassing more by way of intangible, cultural experiences alongside more readily defined HR initiatives designed to enhance work satisfaction. The relational side of the employment experience is given even greater prominence here *vis-à-vis* the transactional side.

A further total reward framework labelled 'the engaged performance model' is described in detail by Armstrong and Murlis (2007: 14–26). This has been developed by the Hay Consulting Group and is notable for the range and detail with which 'relational rewards' are described. Here effective people management is given greater emphasis along with other factors that are not associated with the other models, such as the benefits that accrue from working for a well-regarded organisation and various social aspects of work. The Hay model is the most comprehensive, well-thought-through and readily understood model published to date. It includes the following sets of potential 'relational rewards':

Inspiration and values

- quality of leadership
- organisational values and behaviours
- reputation of the organisation
- risk-sharing (ie fairness and avoiding a 'blame culture')
- recognition
- communication

Future growth and opportunity

- learning and development beyond the current job
- career advancement opportunities
- performance improvement and feedback

Quality of work

- perception of the value of work
- challenge/interest
- achievement
- freedom and autonomy
- workload
- quality of work relationships

Enabling environment

- physical environment
- tools and equipment
- job training for the current position
- information and processes
- safety/personal security

Work–life balance

- supportive environment
- recognition of lifecycle needs/flexibility
- security of income
- social environment

It is important to stress that most people writing about total reward advocate the use of *both* transactional and relational rewards in combination. That, according to Thompson (2002), is where the 'real power' of the idea derives from. Developing the relational side of the employee value proposition is thus seen as a way of adding to and enhancing the impact of a well-designed, high-value package of transactional rewards (ie pay and benefits). These models do not thus envisage the use of relational rewards as an alternative to transactional rewards. Yet it seems to me that it is here that the influence of total reward thinking will develop over time. As organisations increasingly struggle to remunerate people as highly as they would like to, it is surely inevitable that considerably greater emphasis will be placed on the relational side. Moreover, I would argue that there are good reasons for doing so in a competitive labour market situation irrespective of the affordability of generous payment packages. The key point is that remuneration in the form of pay and associated benefits is readily imitated by competitors. It is not at all difficult to match a rival firm's pay package and to enhance it somewhat in a bid to out-recruit it or even to poach its star performers. Matching relational rewards is far, far harder and, in many cases, will be completely impossible, largely because so many of them are 'intangible' in nature and culturally generated. Managers can influence their development over time, but will never be able simply 'to draw up a package' as can be done with tangible, transactional rewards.

Since 2004 the fast food restaurant chain McDonald's has made significant changes to its HR practices in the UK. Its primary aim has been to transform its reputation as an employer from a provider of 'McJobs' (defined by the Oxford English Dictionary as 'unstimulating, low-paid jobs with few prospects') into an employer of choice, providing the best opportunities available for staff working in its industry.

One of the aspects of working for McDonald's that its staff said that they disliked was the relatively low wages that they are paid. The company always pays at a level that is above the National Minimum Wage, but the economics of the fast food industry preclude any possibility of paying a great deal more. It is very labour-intensive, highly competitive and necessarily therefore has to control its wage costs very carefully in order to stay in profit.

The approach taken was therefore to think in terms of 'total reward'. Emphasis was placed on the non-remunerative aspects of the contract that was established with staff. Great stress in particular was placed on promoting and providing developmental opportunities. A corporate university was established at the company's UK headquarters in north London at which staff can study towards a range of accredited qualifications from NVQs and GCSEs to full degree programmes. The company has also developed a range of flexible working

opportunities which are as good as those provided by any other major employer in the country.

However in addition, the company was able significantly to improve the total value of its remuneration package while avoiding increasing its wage costs. It did this by exploiting its size as an employer (80,000 staff in the UK) and negotiating a wide range of discounts on products and services offered by other companies. As a result, McDonald's employees are able to access all manner of goods and services at discounts of 10% to 30% – 1,600 retailers now participate in this scheme, allowing McDonald's employees to save collectively more than £1 million each month. The discount scheme has been tailored to be particularly attractive to the younger, less affluent groups who McDonald's typically employs. It includes, for example, mobile phones, Apple products, holidays and, most popular of all, driving lessons.

Questions

1 In what different ways do you think that the company has benefited financially from taking this 'total reward' perspective?

2 What other initiatives might you suggest were introduced that might further improve the employment experience without also increasing the wage bill?

FLEXIBLE BENEFITS

Another development in reward management that may well have a good deal more to offer employers in the future than it has in the past is flexible benefits. Sometimes referred to as 'cafeteria benefits systems', the idea here is that each individual employee has an opportunity to tailor their own reward package in such a way as to suit their personal circumstances. There are many different types of system in use. At one end of the scale are systems which provide only very limited choice over matters such as the level of pension contribution, the type of company car, or via a flexitime scheme (see Chapter 6) of the amount of holiday days. In each case employees can choose whether to take more by way of take-home pay and less by way of benefits, or whether to sacrifice salary for more by way of different benefits.

At the other end of the scale are highly elaborate schemes such as those offered by most banks and the bigger professional services firms. Here there is a wide range of benefits on offer, all of which can be traded with one another or with cash to make up a total package which best suits the needs of each member of staff. The number of alternatives can be substantial, including items which will only appeal to small numbers of staff, such as pet insurance. The following is a typical list:

- paid holiday (in excess of statutory minimum)
- occupational pensions
- company cars
- meals and accommodation
- relocation expenses
- private health insurance
- dental insurance
- child care benefits – crèche/vouchers
- occupational health and employee assistance programmes
- staff discounts
- mobile phones
- loans
- share schemes
- maternity/parental pay and leave (in excess of statutory minimum)
- career break schemes
- parking facilities
- life assurance
- club/gym memberships
- store vouchers
- dry cleaning.

A good many of these are made available due to the ability of a large company to negotiate discounts with suppliers. Health insurance can thus be offered at a much lower cost than would be available if it was purchased individually.

Another feature of the more elaborate flexible benefits systems is their considerable technological sophistication. In some cases employees are able to access their own accounts to alter the balance of their benefits packages when they wish to. So someone who has just had a new baby, for example, can access child care vouchers and perhaps 'pay for them' by reducing take-home pay or downgrading their company car.

In the USA cafeteria systems of this kind are provided in some shape or form by a majority of larger companies. This development, which dates from the 1980s, is widely considered to have occurred because of the significance of health insurance in the average pay package and because the tax system in the USA generally makes it more advantageous than is the case in the UK to take a good slice of one's total remuneration in the form of benefits rather than cash. To date, take-up in the UK has been a great deal slower (Wright 2009) and where flexibility is provided it is most likely to be limited to a small range of benefits. E-enabled, fully flexible systems of a kind which are common in the USA are still relatively rare in the UK. The CIPD's 2009 *Reward Management* survey reported figures in the range of only 5% to 9% when it asked employers whether the most common types of benefits were made available through a flexible benefits scheme. Moreover, despite this being a subject which has generated a great deal of discussion, only a small minority of employers report that they are actively considering introducing a scheme. Interest in the public sector is very limited indeed.

Research demonstrates though that where employers provide flexible benefits, take-up on the part of employees is quite high and that most, if by no means all, appreciate the opportunity 'to flex' (see Wright 2009).

There are considerable advantages from an employer perspective in introducing flexibility into reward management in this way. Firstly, it provides a means of communicating to staff the real monetary value of the benefits that an organisation provides. The outcome should be improved job satisfaction, because all the published evidence strongly suggests that employees hugely underestimate the value of benefits. Secondly, and more importantly, it can act as a very powerful tool to use in recruiting and retaining staff. Because each individual is able to design their own tailored package, it is evidently difficult for a rival employer which does not provide flexible benefits to match the deal without spending a good deal more. As a tool which helps to make an employee value proposition hard to imitate, flexible benefits scores very highly indeed.

The big drawback is the cost. Flexible benefits schemes which are administratively inexpensive are only very limited in their impact, while the more sophisticated approaches which serve to recruit and retain effectively tend to be costly both in terms of staffing and technology. Regular changes in taxation arrangements for different benefits add to the complexity for employers and employees alike. These cost considerations tend to rule out most types of elaborate scheme altogether for smaller employers.

What is really needed are systems which meet the objectives of a fully flexible scheme, but which are less costly to provide. There are ways of doing this, yet UK employers have been reluctant to develop them. The simplest approach involves offering staff a choice between five or six distinct menus of benefits, all of which are of equal value, but which are designed to meet the needs of different groups. For example, one menu can be designed to appeal to parents with young children, another to single people at the start of their careers and a third to older workers. Some can be biased towards benefits that women tend to appreciate most, while others can be designed with typical male employees in mind. Pre-packaging benefits in this way is much less costly than allowing full flexibility, yet retains the element of choice. Employees can move from one menu to another as they age and their circumstances change.

Provided the cost issues can be dealt with satisfactorily, there is every reason to anticipate that interest in flexible benefits systems will grow again in the future. Using the menu-driven type of approach in particular should offer employers a method of recruiting and retaining staff in tight labour markets, which is both powerful in its impact and also cost-effective.

EMPLOYER BRANDING

Having formulated an employee value proposition which takes account of all forms of reward, an employer which wishes to maximise its capacity to recruit and retain superior performers then needs to communicate its offering effectively. The more competitive the labour market and the more restricted an employer's capacity to buy its way out of skills shortages, the more important it is to communicate key messages about what makes an organisation a good place to work in.

In the case of canny knowledge workers for whom working is about much more than simply earning money, the nature of the message and the methods used to communicate it need to be subtle and intelligent if they are to have any serious effect.

In recent years, as a means of meeting these objectives, HR managers have begun to develop a serious interest in the range of tools that are borrowed from the world of consumer marketing and which are often collectively labelled as 'employer branding techniques'. This makes a great deal of sense. An organisation stands to gain a great deal from fostering a positive reputation as an employer, and employer branding provides a means of gaining a degree of control over the processes by which such a reputation is formed.

In Chapters 3 and 5 I drew attention to some long-term trends in the HR business environment which should, if they continue, mean that employer branding increasingly becomes a central part of the work of the HR function in the UK. One is the growth in the proportion of the workforce that is engaged in knowledge work of various kinds; another is the developing tendency for us to approach our relationship with the labour market in a similar way to our relationship with product markets. Consumerisation is affecting the latter as much as the former as dissatisfied staff 'shop around' for new jobs which they hope will give them greater satisfaction and opportunity.

As was the case in our discussion of total reward thinking above, employer branding remains a field that is seriously under-researched. Despite its having excited the interest of many HR managers and of the CIPD in particular, there is yet to be any serious research study carried out which evaluates its practical impact. What we do have to draw on is a fair amount of published theory, plenty of thoughtful debate and some individual case studies (see Backhaus and Tikoo

2004, Barrow and Mosely 2005, Edwards 2005, CIPD 2007, IDS 2008, Moroko and Uncles 2008, Martin 2009 and Rosethorn 2009).

There is also a clear consensus evolving about how organisations should go about employer branding in order to maximise their chances of success. Here the key first principle is that the brand message that is ultimately developed must genuinely reflect the lived reality of working for the organisation. In consumer marketing the mantra 'to your own brand be true' is frequently cited. The same principle holds true for employer branding. Claims should not be made, nor even hinted at, if they serve to do no more than raise false expectations among would-be recruits and generate cynicism among existing employees.

Instead the starting point for any employer branding exercise must be research into the perceptions of existing employees. Managers need to establish from the outset what qualities the employment experience they provide has which:

1 are positive

and

2 differentiate the organisation as an employer.

The best people to speak to, perhaps using a focus group approach, are those who have joined the organisation having previously worked in similar roles elsewhere in the industry. The process of getting them to articulate the ways in which your organisation outperforms its rivals as an employer can often lead directly to the formulation of core employer branding messages. Wider staff attitude surveys are often used too in a bid to gather useful data to form the basis of employer branding initiatives.

EMPLOYER BRANDING FRAMEWORKS

A number of consultants working in the field of employer branding have developed some useful frameworks for managers to use when seeking to identify how they wish to differentiate themselves from other employers in their key labour markets. Lievens et al (2007) and Davies (2007) both make use of a similar five-trait model in their research, although the precise words they use differ somewhat. The idea here is that organisations can usefully be categorised according to their prevalent personalities. Lievens discusses the following:

- sincerity (honest, sincere, friendly)
- excitement (trendy, spirited, innovative)
- competence (reliable, secure, successful)
- sophistication (upper class, prestigious)
- ruggedness (masculine, tough).

Davies labels his rather similar framework as 'the Corporate Character Scale'. His work uses the following formulations:

- agreeableness (warmth, empathy, integrity)

- enterprise (cool, trendy, innovative, daring, imaginative)
- competence (leading, achievement-oriented, technical)
- chic (charming, stylish, exclusive)
- ruthlessness (arrogant, aggressive, controlling).

Another rather different approach focuses less on the idea of corporate personality traits and more directly on different types of employee value proposition (EVP). An example is the model developed by the McKinsey consulting organisation which suggests four distinct types of employer brand (see Fields 2001: 101–102):

1 **Prestige** – ie we have a great reputation in our business; working for us will enhance your long-term career opportunities.

2 **Cause** – ie we undertake work which is meaningful and socially important; working for us will provide you with the opportunity to help humankind.

3 **High risk/big potential** – ie we are a small but growing organisation; working for us will enable you to grow alongside us to reap big long-term rewards.

4 **Work–life balance** – ie we will provide you with a good job, but also allow you plenty of time to spend doing other things.

It is not difficult to come up with further distinct types of EVP to add to the McKinsey four. For example:

5 **Secure** – ie we will not be able to offer you an exciting career, but we can provide you with steady, long-term employment so that you can achieve security for yourself and your family.

6 **Friendly** – ie we are a family-oriented organisation which looks after its people's welfare and treats them with respect.

7 **International** – ie we are a global organisation that can provide you with great opportunities to travel and work overseas.

For many organisations, more than one of these formulations will apply and can be built on when developing a distinct employer brand identity. In other cases, another, different type of proposition or set of character traits will be appropriate. What matters most is that whatever form of words is used, it genuinely articulates the nature of the workplace experience available to staff.

COMMUNICATING THE MESSAGE

Once the analysis is complete and the key factors that differentiate the employment experience have been clearly established, the next step is to develop slogans, statements and, sometimes, accompanying visual imagery, which can be used to communicate the key messages to existing and would-be staff. A feature of employer branding is the need to repeat the core message again and again and again over a prolonged period using every available opportunity. Employer branding exercises typically last for a number of years, so getting the wording right first time is very important indeed.

It took some time, but we are now fortunate in having a number of excellent examples to read about in a variety of publications. IDS, for example, have devoted two of their studies to examples of employer branding in action (see IDS 2005, 2008). A recent book edited by Helen Rosethorn (2009) of the Bernard Hodes consultancy contains some good examples too, while others are found in the CIPD publication *Employer branding: a no-nonsense approach* (Walker 2007).

Each example is necessarily different, but some common themes emerge. One is the frequent extent to which the perception that people have of employment in an organisation often varies very considerably in practice from the reality as experienced by the staff that work there. Employer branding exercises are particularly useful in such circumstances because they are able to provide a coherent and well-resourced route for adjusting an inaccurate, and perhaps an unfair, reputation.

For example, David Russell (2009) describes how he and his team at the bookmakers William Hill used branding thinking to alter perceptions of their organisation as an employer. The typical vision that people had was of 'smoke-filled, male-dominated' working environments full of men in flat caps focusing on horse and dog racing. The words that were used to describe the organisation tended to be 'dependable', 'solid', 'reliable' and 'honest'. There was thus a need to shift perceptions in order to reflect the modern, IT-driven reality of working for William Hill and its much broader range of products. After carrying out much research, the slogan 'Thrilling Gambling Action' was developed. The aim was to try to make 'people feel that they are at the heart of the action and that, as well as the traditional values of fairness and trustworthiness, the brand stimulates excitement and passion and is bold and pioneering' (Russell 2009: 146).

Another interesting example is the employer branding activity undertaken in recent years by the Prison Service. Here too the reality of the work differs in key respects from the popular image, the result being that many people do not consider embarking on such a career, even when in fact they might be ideally suited to it, and it to them. Walker (2008) describes how consultants worked with managers in the Prison Service to use employer branding as a means of adjusting popular perceptions. The starting point was research among existing staff. This led to the identification of six 'key attributes' which were believed, between them, to sum up the reality of prison work:

- human insight
- thoughtfulness
- realism
- courage
- competence
- humour.

A rather longer statement was then developed to sum up the 'brand promise' and is now used in recruitment literature and all manner of internal employee communications:

> 'If you are fascinated by people and can relate to them effectively, you'll find long-term interest and satisfaction in a career with the Prison Service.'

Lloyds of London (see IDS 2008) faced a rather different type of image problem when they first embarked on an employer branding exercise. The perception here was of a stuffy, old-fashioned organisation that only dealt with very wealthy people. In fact, it is a highly successful, innovative, future-focused organisation which makes use of the latest technologies and is distinctly global in its activities. Research among staff here resulted in the identification of the following list of 'core values' or descriptors:

- commercial
- accountable
- clarity
- collaboration
- flexible
- excellence.

From this analysis slogans such as 'constant originality' and 'do something that matters' were derived and used in employee and recruitment communications.

Marks & Spencer (Cameron 2009) ended their branding process not with a short slogan, but with a ten-point statement of intent which sets out the nature of the employment relationship they wish to establish and maintain with their staff. It is framed in the form of a contract, which gives it added power because it suggests that it is genuinely meant:

Join M&S and we will:

1 Make you feel valued and proud to work for M&S.

2 Reward you well against our retail competitors.

3 Make sure you have inspirational, effective line managers who value and support you.

4 Tell you how the company is doing.

5 Give you opportunities to share your ideas on improving the business.

6 Listen and deal with your issues and concerns.

7 Train you thoroughly to do your job.

8 Offer you career opportunities and support to take advantage of them.

9 Tell you how you are doing.

10 Treat you fairly, using modern, transparent employment practices.

CRITICAL REFLECTION

There has been a tendency for some commentators and academics specialising in HRM to be dismissive of employer branding during the past ten years or so. Despite the growth in interest in the approach and its widespread use in practice, there remains a reluctance to accept it as a mainstream HRM activity. It tends to be seen as peripheral, faddish and lacking in importance. This could have something to do with the words/label 'employer branding', which suggest that it is no more than a technique associated with recruitment advertising.

Questions

1 Why do you think that employer branding has tended to be dismissed as a passing fad?

2 What are the main arguments for and against this proposition?

3 How might 'employer branding' be re-labelled in order to encourage commentators to take it more seriously as an idea?

LABOUR MARKET SEGMENTATION

Employer branding is an area of HR thinking which has been borrowed directly from the marketing function and applied to the world of competitive labour markets. As we have seen, the idea has had very considerable influence and may well become more central to the HR agenda in the future. There are, however, good grounds for arguing that other approaches could also fruitfully be borrowed from the marketing world and used by HR specialists when developing strategies for recruiting and retaining people. An obvious example is market segmentation, long used by marketers to identify and analyse distinct target markets.

The basic idea is that HR managers should analyse in some detail the data that they have on their staff to establish if, and in what way, distinct groups can be identified who may have different needs and aspirations. This type of thinking informed my discussion of menu-driven approaches to the provision of flexible benefits (see above), the proposition being that there are potential advantages associated with tailoring reward packages to meet the needs of six or seven groups of staff delineated according to age and family circumstances. A remuneration package is then developed which is designed to appeal to each of these.

It seems to me that there is a lot to be said for taking this thinking forward to encompass much more than the development of distinct remuneration packages or even more generally framed employee value propositions. Why not take steps to ensure that the whole experience of being employed in an organisation adequately reflects the needs of all major target groups in a labour market? The more competitive the market and the greater the risk of damaging long-term skills shortages, the stronger the business case for developing sophisticated and subtle approaches to HR that take this kind of approach.

As yet very little has been published on this idea and pretty well no serious research carried out. There is, however, evidence to suggest that some larger employers with innovative HR divisions are experimenting with approaches to recruitment which explicitly make use of segmentation thinking. For example, Lynda Gratton (2004) briefly discusses research carried out by Tesco which identified five alternative 'employee identities' among its staff – distinct categories into which almost all fitted somewhere. The aim was to differentiate between groups according to their predominant attitude towards their jobs. The five were labelled as follows:

- work–life balancers
- want it all
- pleasure seekers
- live to work
- work to live.

Zemke et al (2000) were among the first of several authors and consultants who have recently proposed segmenting employees according to their age. The idea is that each generation differs somewhat in its expectations of work due to the diverse formative experiences that its members experience as they are growing up. They go on to argue that each must be treated rather differently if they are to be successfully managed. The four categories Zemke et al identify are Veterans (born before and during the Second World War), Baby Boomers (late 1940s and 1950s), Generation X (1960s and 1970s) and a group labelled 'Nexters' (born after 1980). Some of the points made about each are as follows:

- Veterans are attracted to workplaces which offer stability and which value experience.
- Boomers place a high value on effective employee participation.
- Xers enjoy ambiguity and are at ease with insecurity.
- Nexters are wholly intolerant of all unfair discrimination.
- Boomers do not object to working long hours.
- Xers require a proper work–life balance.
- Veterans are loyal to their employers and are less likely to look elsewhere for employment opportunities than younger colleagues.
- Xers are strongly resistant to tight control systems and set procedures.
- Nexters, being serious-minded and principled, prefer to work for ethical employers.
- Xers and Nexters work more easily with new technology than Veterans and Boomers.

Where a workforce is dominated by a particular age group, it makes sense to manage the workers in a way with which they feel comfortable. Organisational performance as well as turnover rates can improve as a result. Similarly, where a recruitment drive is aimed at a particular age group, it is important to give out appropriate messages about what the organisation is able to offer. Zemke et al (2000) go on to discuss the practical experience of several US-based corporations that have sought explicitly to manage the mix of generations differently, including Ben and Jerry's and TGI Fridays. Their initiatives include ensuring that there are benefits on offer which appeal to each major group and creating rest areas in their buildings which are decorated and furnished in ways which each group tends to find most comfortable.

CONJOINT ANALYSIS

Boudreau (2010: 89–120) outlines the potential advantages that an employer can gain from undertaking a detailed analysis of the strengths and weaknesses of each segment which is identified in terms of its contribution to the meeting of organisational objectives. Just as marketers are always keen to establish which customer group has the most potential for further exploitation at the lowest outlay (eg is most likely to spend more on a company's products or services per extra pound spent on advertising), HR managers should adopt the same approach when managing staff.

This idea is attractive because of its sophistication. It accepts, for example, that it is rarely economically viable, let alone practicable, to provide a bespoke employment experience or reward package for each individual member of staff. Technology has allowed companies to move in this direction in their dealings with customers, but there is a limit to how far it can go. The same is true of employees. Just as customers aspire to 'have all the features at the lowest price', employees would mostly, if asked, want both a highly sophisticated and pleasurable employment experience (perhaps involving few hours of work) and a high wage. Because this is impossible economically, there are trade-offs that have to be made. In marketing, 'conjoint analysis' is used to establish what these should be. Boudreau (2010) argues persuasively that HR managers should take a similar approach.

The type of analysis that Boudreau envisages involves extensive 'market research' using questionnaires sent to employees that take the form of extended staff attitude surveys. These, he argues, should include all kinds of questions about possible new forms of benefit or other initiative, including training opportunities and improvements in the effectiveness of management. Further questions should then ask about leaving intention, so that cost savings resulting from HR changes could be calculated. The aim is to enable managers to establish the costs and benefits in financial terms associated with a range of different types of HR intervention. Boudreau works through an example based on the experience of Microsoft. The conclusion was that the most cost-effective interventions for the company were those which focused on improving management effectiveness and providing more developmental opportunities. Increasing pay would help to reduce staff turnover, but only at considerable cost. The savings in staff turnover terms associated with management and development improvements were fewer, but the costs were a great deal lower.

Conjoint analysis draws on segmentation theories because it establishes where the 'sweet spots' are – for which groups of staff there is the greatest scope for generating improved performance or lower staff turnover through HR interventions. Armed with this information and an estimate of the likely financial implications, HR managers can go ahead and develop appropriate new policies and practices.

A rather different approach to segmentation is suggested by Becker et al (2009) in their recent book entitled *The differentiated workforce*. Here they put the case for identifying the jobs in an organisation which have the greatest strategic importance in terms of the ability of their occupants to make a contribution to improved profitability, productivity or whatever other objectives are of greatest importance. These are labelled 'A roles' and should, according to Becker et al, be those which the organisation focuses most of its HR effort on. They also advocate labelling the other jobs as 'B' or 'C' roles, the first of which gets more attention than the second, but neither as much as is enjoyed by the occupants of the A jobs. They go on to argue that the priority must be to ensure as far as possible that A-level performers are in the A-rated posts, before suggesting ways in which this group of high-performers needs to be managed in order to maximise its performance. This, it is argued, is one of the approaches that differentiates high-performing from low-performing organisations.

Thinking about labour market segmentation generally is as yet ill-defined and quite vague. It is also possible to criticise it, not least because it raises the danger that some groups will perceive that they are being treated less favourably than others, and react badly as a result. The approach does, however, have considerable potential, and is thus likely to be developed further in the future. It has particular attractions for organisations that wish to improve their recruitment and retention capabilities without spending a great deal more on wages.

KEY LEARNING POINTS

- It is possible for organisations to recruit and retain good performers without leading the market in terms of the pay and benefits that they offer.

- Those who seek to follow the market can only be viable if the employment experience that they offer is more attractive in a variety of respects than that offered by their competitors.

- The concept of 'total reward' with its emphasis on forms of reward that are 'relational' in nature rather than 'transactional' has a great deal to offer employers.

- Flexible benefits systems permit employers to provide payment packages which better suit the requirements of each individual employee.

- Employer branding involves adapting long-used approaches from the marketing function and applying them to an organisation's communication, both with existing and would-be employees.

- Labour market segmentation has the potential, if managed carefully, to increase an employer's ability to recruit and retain quite dramatically.

EXPLORE FURTHER

Paul Thompson's book on total reward (2002) written for the CIPD is a good general introduction to this approach.

Thompson, P. (2002) *Total reward*. London: CIPD.

Incomes Data Services (2005, 2008) have to date published two excellent studies setting out what employer branding involves and illustrating developments in the field with case studies.

IDS (2005) *Employer branding*. IDS Study 809. November. London: Incomes Data Services.

IDS (2008) *Employer branding*. IDS Study 872. June. London: Incomes Data Services.

An academic perspective on employer branding which raises key questions and sets out a research agenda is provided by Backhaus and Tikoo in one of the first articles to be published on employer branding in an academic journal.

Backhaus, K. and Tikoo, S. (2004) Conceptualising and researching employer branding. *Career Development International*. Vol 9, No 5. pp501–517.

REFERENCES

Armstrong, M. and Brown, D. (2009) *Strategic reward: implementing more effective reward management*. London: Kogan Page.

Armstrong, M. and Murlis, H. (2007) *Reward management: a handbook of remuneration strategy and practice*. London: Kogan Page.

Backhaus, K. and Tikoo, S. (2004) Conceptualising and researching employer branding. *Career Development International*. Vol 9, No 5. pp501–517.

Barrow, S. and Mosely, R. (2005) *The employer brand*. Chichester: Wiley.

Becker, B., Huselid, M. and Beatty, R. (2009) *The differentiated workforce*. Boston: Harvard Business Press.

Boudreau, J. (2010) *Retooling HR: using proven business tools to make better decisions about talent*. Boston: Harvard Business School Press.

Cameron, K. (2009) From poor M&S to your M&S – the historical perspective. In H. Rosethorn (ed.) *The employer brand*. Aldershot: Gower.

CIPD (2007) *Employer branding: the latest fad or the future for HR?* London: Chartered Institute of Personnel and Development.

CIPD (2009) *Reward management*. Annual survey report. London: Chartered Institute of Personnel and Development.

Corby, S. and Lindop, E. (2009) Drawing the threads together. In S. Corby, S. Palmer and E. Lindop (eds) *Rethinking reward*. Basingstoke: Palgrave.

Davies, G. (2007) Employer branding and its influence on managers. *European Journal of Marketing*. Vol 42, No 5/6. pp667–681.

Edwards, M.R. (2005) Employer and employee branding: HR or PR? In S. Bach (ed.) *Managing human resources: personnel management in transition*. 4th edition. Oxford: Blackwell Publishing.

Fields, M. (2001) *Indispensable employees*. Franklin Lakes, NJ: Career Press.

Gomez-Mejia, L. and Balkin, D. (1992) *Compensation, organizational strategy and firm performance*. Cincinnati: South Western.

Gratton, L. (2004) *The democratic enterprise: liberating your business with freedom, flexibility and commitment*. Harlow: Pearson Education.

IDS (2005) *Employer branding*. IDS Study 809. November. London: Incomes Data Services.

IDS (2008) *Employer branding*. IDS Study 872. June. London: Incomes Data Services.

Lievens, F., Van Hoye, G. and Anseel, F. (2007) Organizational identity and employer image: towards a unifying framework. *British Journal of Management*. Vol 18. pp45–59.

Martin, G. (2009) Driving corporate reputations from the inside: a strategic role and strategic dilemmas for HR? *Asia Pacific Journal of Human Resources*. Vol 47, No 2. pp219–235.

Moroko, L. and Uncles, M. (2008) Characteristics of successful employer brands. *Journal of Brand Management*. Vol 16, No 3. pp160–175.

Neil, A. (1996) *Full disclosure*. London: Macmillan.

Pfeffer, J. (1994) *Competitive advantage through people*. Boston: Harvard Business School Press.

Pfeffer, J. (1998) Six dangerous myths about pay. *Harvard Business Review*. May/June. pp109–119.

Pfeffer, J. and Sutton, R. (2006) *Hard facts, dangerous half-truths and total nonsense: profiting from evidence-based management*. Boston: Harvard Business School Press.

Rosethorn, H. (ed.) (2009) *The employer brand*. Farnham: Gower Publishing.

Russell, D. (2009) What's the deal? The impact of legislation and new technology. In H. Rosethorn (ed.) *The employer brand*. Farnham: Gower Publishing.

Sturges, J. and Guest, D. (1999) *Should I stay or should I go? Issues relating to retention of graduate recruits*. Warwick: AGR.

Thompson, P. (2002) *Total reward*. London: CIPD.

Walker, P. (2008) *Employer branding: a no-nonsense approach*. London: CIPD.

WorldatWork (2007) *The WorldatWork handbook of compensation, benefits and total rewards: a comprehensive guide for HR professionals.* London: John Wiley & Sons.

Wright, A. (2009) Flexible benefits: shaping the way ahead? In S. Corby, S. Palmer and E. Lindop (eds) *Rethinking reward.* Basingstoke: Palgrave.

Zemke, R., Raines, C. and Filipczak, B. (2000) *Generations at work.* New York: AMACOM.

CHAPTER 8

Managing expectations

Introduction

A major contemporary business trend that we discussed in the first chapters of this book is increased competitive intensity. For a variety of different reasons organisations in all sectors are having to compete harder with one another for both customers and effective employees. It has long been recognised that a key to ensuring that a business satisfies and retains its customers is the effective management of their expectations. The same is true of employees. In competitive labour markets, if an organisation wants to help ensure that its staff maximise their effort and their performance, and that voluntary turnover is kept to a minimum, it needs to provide its people with a satisfying experience. The effective management of expectations is central to achieving this.

In this chapter we are going to focus on a number of influential perspectives on the management of people which, in their different ways, involve the management of expectations. In particular we need to explain contemporary thinking on psychological contracts, an area of HR research which has developed hugely in recent years and which provides a very useful practical lens through which we can examine the impact of met and unmet expectations.

LEARNING OUTCOMES

The objectives of this chapter are to:

- demonstrate how the management of expectations is central to effective HRM
- discuss the expectations that employers and employees have of their relationship in a general sense
- debate how these are changing over time
- explore why levels of job satisfaction appear to be in decline
- introduce key management theories that concern the management of expectations
- explain what is meant by the psychological contract and why thinking in this field is helpful to practising managers
- show how the effective management of expectations can enhance the several core areas of HRM responsibility.

HOPES AND EXPECTATIONS

It is not at all difficult to understand what the major expectations of employers are as far as their staff are concerned. Expectations are generally set out quite clearly in writing in contracts of employment, job descriptions, role profiles and other documents. Hours of work, the locations from which people will work and job duties, along with any specific areas of responsibility are set out for would-be employees before they start work and often before they have even been offered their jobs. Organisations also generally use staff handbooks and intranet sites to communicate expectations about standards of conduct, methods of working and a host of other matters ranging from dress codes to the use of company credit cards and even personal relationships at work. In more general terms employers have reasonable expectations that their employees will act loyally and professionally while carrying out their duties and that they will not act outside work in such a way as to damage their organisation's reputation.

In addition to these very reasonable expectations, employers usually hope for more. In particular there is an expectation that people will 'work beyond contract', going beyond what is strictly required of them in a legal sense (ie going the extra mile) in the service of their employers. In recent years thanks to leading researchers in HRM such as Appelbaum et al (2000) and Purcell et al (2003), the term *discretionary effort* has become widely used to express this aim. They and many others show that the creation of a work environment in which employees are prepared to demonstrate discretionary effort is key to the achievement of superior performance and hence to achieving competitive advantage.

Job satisfaction, active engagement and a strong degree of commitment to organisations are prerequisites of discretionary effort. By definition it is not something that employers can force out of people; it is a matter of choice. It is therefore incompatible with management practices which serve to reduce trust and lead to dissatisfaction on the part of staff.

For this reason employers who are serious about getting a high level of performance out of their staff and subsequently maintaining it must seek to meet employee expectations. Indeed, as is the case with customers, enhanced employee commitment and discretionary effort tends to occur when employers exceed their employees' expectations.

So what do employees expect from their working lives? It is a most interesting question and one to which the answer is considered by many sociologists to be shifting in important new directions. On a basic level, as Taylor (2001: 15) points out in his survey of contemporary research in employment relations, employees have fairly straightforward expectations of their work, all of which should be eminently achievable in many organisations:

- an interesting job
- employment security

- a feeling of positive accomplishment
- influence over how their job gets done.

There is no question, however, that a good proportion of employees now expect rather more than this – and the more highly skilled and 'in demand' they are, the higher are their expectations. For example, most now expect that they will be able to achieve a reasonable work–life balance and that their career development aspirations will be met by their employers. Moreover, increasingly employees also expect to be treated with respect by their employers, and with integrity, professionalism and fairness.

It is often asserted that employees are becoming increasingly demanding of their employers and less tolerant of those who are unable to meet their expectations. This is a theme that comes out of much of the intergenerational research that has been carried out in recent years (eg Zemke et al 2000, Eisner 2004 and CIPD and Penna 2008) and is also a feature of sociological research by figures such as du Gay (1996), Bauman (2005) and Svendsen (2008) (see Chapter 5).

Loyalty, it would seem, is more conditional than it used to be. And that means that any employer seeking to lift performance levels and improve its employee retention rates should be focusing more on ensuring that it delivers job satisfaction to its employees and avoiding unmet expectations.

WORK SATISFACTION TRENDS

A great deal of research has been carried out in recent years looking at how satisfied people are with their work. The message it conveys is mixed. On the one hand, employees across most Western industrialised economies report pretty high levels of job satisfaction when asked in surveys. A good majority of people, when asked, say that they are either 'satisfied' or 'very satisfied' with their working lives, most studies reporting figures in the 70–80% range. International comparative studies typically show that the highest levels of job satisfaction are found in EU countries, followed by the USA, with Japan and other Asian countries lagging behind a bit. But the differences are slight. High levels of satisfaction are the norm across the industrialised world.

The UK is no exception. Most people say that they are generally satisfied with their work and with their jobs. The latest Workplace Employee Relations Survey (carried out in 2004 and 2005) surveyed 22,451 employees across all industrial sectors in the UK, including many smaller workplaces (Kersley et al 2006). The findings on job satisfaction are listed in Table 8.1.

Table 8.1: Job satisfaction

	% satisfied/very satisfied
sense of achievement	70%
scope for using initiative	72%
influence over job	57%
training	51%
pay	35%
job security	63%
the work itself	72%
involvement in decision-making	38%

Table 8.1 suggests that the majority of employees are reasonably happy in their jobs and that their expectations are being met, except in respect of their pay and the extent of their involvement in decision-making.

Importantly, however, two significant caveats need to be stated:

1 A substantial minority of the UK workforce is clearly not satisfied; and

2 Over time, satisfaction levels appear to be falling.

Evidence from other surveys in the UK, such as the General Household Survey, show that the proportion of UK workers who say that they are either 'very satisfied' or 'completely satisfied' with their work has declined steadily over recent decades from what were previously very high levels. Francis Green (2005) in his excellent book *Demanding work* analyses why this is by looking at responses reported in a wide variety of different surveys published in the UK and in the USA.

Why, he asks, is our level of job satisfaction apparently falling year on year, despite increasing living standards, improved job security and upskilling of work generally? Far fewer of us are employed in lower-skilled, tedious, physically tiring, low-paid work with few prospects than used to be the case. Yet we are less happy with our working lives.

The answer he comes up with is that 'employee well-being' is falling. He concludes that half the recent decline in job satisfaction is 'directly attributable to a decline in "task discretion"' – by which he means the extent that we can control how hard we work and how we carry out our work. He concludes that around a further third of the decline is due to increased intensification of work, and that the rest principally is down to an increasing mismatch between qualifications and jobs, by which he means a tendency for people to be overqualified for the jobs they actually carry out.

It must be remembered, of course, that job satisfaction is a relative rather than an absolute concept. We judge our satisfaction in a particular job with reference to our satisfaction in previous jobs or at previous points in our current jobs. Our judgement is also influenced by the experiences of friends and relatives. It is quite possible, therefore, that people express dissatisfaction with their jobs even though working life is better than it was historically. A general improvement in conditions of work may have occurred, which has had the effect of raising expectations and making us 'harder to please'.

Alternatively, the reverse may be true. Increased job insecurity and work intensification may have lowered expectations, so that we report higher levels of job satisfaction than is really justified by any objective measure.

Bussing (1997) is very critical of the studies which report high levels of job satisfaction, arguing that these need to be taken with a big pinch of salt. In particular he claims that many survey respondents are either experiencing 'resigned work satisfaction' or 'constructive work dissatisfaction', which are not examples of genuine satisfaction at all.

He defines 'resigned work satisfaction' as a natural response to dissatisfaction at work. It involves lowering our expectations to such an extent that we again start to experience a positive state of satisfaction. It does not mean that people are really satisfied, and it will not have any positive impact on productivity. 'Constructive work dissatisfaction', by contrast, is a common state which involves people taking active steps to deal with their dissatisfaction, finding ways of tolerating their frustration via 'coping strategies'. In other words they accept that their work is tedious or unfulfilling and 'deal with it' through the development of mutually supportive interpersonal relationships with colleagues and strategies designed to take back a degree of control from managers. Here, too, no real job satisfaction is experienced, although it may be reported in surveys.

A further group of critics are sceptical about all satisfaction surveys – not just employee ones, but consumer and client-based ones too. This view starts with the idea that most people do not like complaining or being seen as negative or ungrateful or awkward. They only do so when really pushed beyond their limits.

 CRITICAL REFLECTION

Think about your own experience of work. When have you been most satisfied in a job and when have you been least satisfied? What were the key factors that determined the extent of your satisfaction?

CONCLUDING THOUGHTS ON EMPLOYEE EXPECTATIONS

The evidence on this important subject is somewhat mixed and unclear. But it seems to be the case that most of us are broadly satisfied with some aspects of our jobs, if less satisfied with other aspects. This leaves a sizeable chunk (at least a quarter of us) who are not particularly satisfied. There is thus a great deal of scope here for HR managers to develop strategies for lifting satisfaction levels. There is also good evidence to suggest that over time things are slowly moving in the wrong direction. This should be a matter of concern because at the same time, at least in theory, our experience of working life should be improving. Generally, the jobs that we do are more challenging, less tiring and more comfortable than they used to be.

The big change is increased competition and increased competitive intensity. Over time this is having a positive effect on productivity and, indirectly, on living standards. But it brings with it reduced job security, a tendency for managers to make decisions without involving people properly and downward pressure on wage budgets. As Robert Taylor (2001) explains, these include major items on the list of employee expectations.

My conclusion is thus that while meeting employee expectations is becoming more important as the basis for securing high levels of performance, achieving this in practice is becoming much harder than it used to be. It follows that there is a strong case from an HRM perspective for thinking seriously about how employee expectations could be better managed in practice.

EXPECTANCY THEORY

A number of respected and well-established management theories help us to shed light on possible approaches that managers can use in order to manage employee expectations more effectively. While they are sometimes rather too simplistic simply to follow uncritically in anticipation of positive outcomes, they can and should inform our thinking about practical HR management issues. Expectancy theory is a good place to start because it deals directly with the question of how best to gain an understanding of individual employee expectations.

Expectancy theory was first developed in the 1960s by the American psychologist Victor Vroom (1964). Since then it has been refined and empirically tested by several others, notably by Porter and Lawler (1968) and most recently by Chiang and Jang (2008). Although it can be made to seem complex and is difficult to test empirically, the basic underlying idea is both straightforward and useful. Vroom expressed his theory in the form of the following formula:

motivation to achieve an outcome = expectancy $\times$ instrumentality $\times$ valence

This is a cognitive theory which accepts as its underlying premise the idea that people make rational choices about how much effort they will put in to achieving a task and how much time they will devote to it. Vroom proposed that a lot depends on the extent to which we expect that we will gain some kind of reward as a result of our actions. In his model the term *valence* concerns the value that the reward has for us. It can be very positive indeed when the reward is something that we desire greatly, much more limited or even negative when the reward that we expect is something that we actively do not desire. Individual preferences will vary greatly here. Some people, for example, are much more motivated by the desire to earn more money than others are. One person may be prepared to put a great deal of effort into a task in order to achieve a relatively modest pay rise, whereas someone else would only put equivalent effort in if the proposed pay rise was much bigger. Negative ratings for valence are possible when the reward that is proposed is something that an individual does not want. A promotion is a good example. This might be something one employee desires very much, while colleagues may have no wish whatsoever to do a job further up their organisation's hierarchy.

The term *expectancy* refers to our evaluation of the probability that the effort we put in will lead to the desired performance outcome. The stronger the link, the more motivated we are to put the required effort in. Much depends here on our evaluation of other factors outside our control which we consider may prevent us from fully achieving our goals, despite putting the effort in. For example, I may be asked by my manager to lead a major sales drive with the prospect, if I am successful in meeting targets, of receiving a big bonus. The extent to which I will be motivated to work hard on this project, according to Vroom, will in part be determined by my assessment of how achievable the sales target is. The less achievable, the less effort I am going to expend.

Finally, the term *instrumentality* refers to the probability that achieving the performance outcome will actually lead to receipt of the reward. There needs to be a strong probability in the employee's mind if effort is to be maximised. I may for example be told that if I accept an overseas posting and do it well for three years before returning, my career prospects in the company I work for will be greatly enhanced. I may agree and take the assignment, or I may be suspicious of how far my manager's assessment is accurate or doubt his or her ability to deliver on such promises in practice.

The theory is thus all about expectations and it contains within it very useful lessons for managers wanting to ensure that effort is maximised and that teams meet or exceed the objectives we set for them. Firstly it stresses the significance of individual differences between people. We vary in terms of what kinds of reward motivate us. It follows that managers need to get to know their staff as individuals, to understand what makes each person tick and to try to avoid adopting a 'one size fits all' approach to their motivation. Secondly, expectancy theory reminds us that we need to ensure as far as possible that when someone puts in additional effort they can achieve the goals we have set them and that anticipated rewards will follow. Vague promises and unachievable targets need to be avoided. If you want to ensure that an objective will be met, the people charged with meeting it must have a realistic prospect of doing so and must receive any reward promised to them for doing so. Thirdly, the model reminds us that failing to meet people's expectations is likely to reduce their motivation in the future. Vroom argued that we assess expectancy and instrumentality with reference to our past experiences. If we feel we have been let down in the past and that our efforts have not been rewarded, we are less likely to put in extra effort in the future.

As is the case with many theories in management science, it is not difficult to spot some inherent difficulties with the practical application of expectancy theory. It is the case, for example, that different people assess the extent of the effort that they put in very differently. What I consider to amount to very considerable effort going well beyond the call of duty might well be seen as being pretty limited by my manager. There can also be differences of perception about some types of reward. Praise and recognition are good examples. Managers might consider that a letter of commendation from the MD constitutes a strong form of praise for a job well done, but if the letter the employee receives is a standard one that is sent to several people, the extent to which the praise is really meant or counts for anything is hugely diminished. The MD has probably not even noticed the name of the recipient, but has simply signed a heap of letters and sent them out *en masse*. Moreover, when it comes to intrinsic forms of reward, things are very unpredictable. I may feel ahead of time that the task I am being asked to perform will give me great satisfaction and a strong sense of achievement. But this does not mean that it actually will do so in practice. Such matters are outside the control of managers to a great extent, and often outside employees' control too.

So fundamental differences in perception can limit the extent to which following the principles of expectancy theory will pay off in practice. But this does not mean that the thinking behind the theory does not have a great deal to offer practically. There is much to be said for introducing it to managers in training sessions and encouraging them to use it as a basis for their own self-development. If nothing else, it flags up some common traps into which managers sometimes fall when trying to motivate people and to assign objectives to them. It also reminds us of the importance of managing expectations effectively when seeking to improve individual performance.

More generally I think that applying expectancy theory helps to push managers towards establishing and maintaining adult-to-adult relationships with their staff, rather than taking the very common adult-to-child kind of approach. It promotes a mature approach to supervising staff in which individuals are treated as individuals, generalised thinking about what motivates people is avoided and, most importantly, less than honest manipulation of employee expectations for short-term management advantage is avoided. These are all important contributors to work satisfaction in contemporary organisations.

EQUITY THEORY

Equity theory is often paired with expectancy theory, an argument being made that both have equal validity as a means of explaining the willingness of employees to put effort into their work. Alternatively, equity theory can be seen as something of a development of expectancy theory. Either way the principles are as important for managers to take on board if they are serious about enhancing organisational performance.

Equity theory, like expectancy theory, was first clearly articulated in the early 1960s by an American occupational psychologist, in this case John Stacey Adams (1963). Similarly it has been subjected to criticism and has been tested and refined accordingly over the years. The central premise is that an individual's preparedness to work hard and demonstrate commitment is in large part dependent on their perceptions of equity in the workplace. When we perceive that we are being treated inequitably, the result is a tendency to reduce effort and, in more extreme cases, to leave the organisation. The presupposition is therefore that workers expect to be treated equitably and that the extent of their engagement with their work is dependent on their perceptions of how far this expectation is actually being met.

Adams believed that employees consciously make decisions of this nature, adjusting their effort upwards or downwards in response to employer actions. The idea is that we compare our 'inputs' (time, effort, enthusiasm, commitment, flexibility, loyalty, etc) with the 'outputs' that we receive (salary, benefits, job security, recognition, etc) and with those that we perceive others to be receiving. When we believe that others are being treated more favourably than we are, our reaction in a sense is to 'get even' by taking steps to reduce inequity. This will generally involve reducing our inputs, but it can also involve adjusting our perceptions of ourselves and of others. It follows that managers need to act in order to ensure that as far as possible people do not perceive that they are being treated unfavourably *vis-à-vis* other colleagues, or as far as is possible, comparators who do similar work in other organisations.

A controversial aspect of Adams' theory which many find hard to accept was his view that negative feelings of inequity apply when someone is treated better than they feel they deserve in comparison with others. He argued that a worker will adjust their inputs, for example by putting in extra effort in order to compensate for feelings of discomfort generated by a situation in which they perceive themselves to be overpaid or rewarded to too great a degree in some other way. This may be true of some people, but as with other aspects of equity theory, people vary considerably in how far they are motivated in this way (Huseman et al 1987).

Equity theory, like expectancy theory, may not be a perfect guide to how managers should treat people. But it is helpful as the basis for thinking about the way that a team should be managed. For example, it provides a strong practical rationale for avoiding favouritism. Inevitably any manager will have team members who they personally like, trust and admire more than others. But it is important, if the performance of the whole team is to be maximised, that people do not perceive themselves as being treated less favourably for an undeserved reason.

It is important to point out that Adams and those who have further developed his ideas in more recent years are not arguing for equality. They accept that people have different strengths, that levels of performance between individuals will vary considerably and that rewards should too. Instead, what they are arguing for and putting a good business case for is fair dealing on the part of managers. This principle should apply across an organisation from the way an individual supervisor manages a team to the remuneration policies that determine how much everyone in a company is paid.

PSYCHOLOGICAL CONTRACTS

The establishment of the concept of the 'psychological contract' is one of the most significant recent developments in the study of employee relations and in HRM. The term was first coined in the late 1950s by the American psychologist Chris Argyris, who borrowed the concept from writing on the mutual expectations of doctors and patients who were undergoing therapy. Argyris both invented the term and was the first to apply it to the employment relationship. The idea was then picked up and developed by other US academics such as Edgar Schein and Harry Levinson in work published in the 1960s, but it was not until the publication in 1989 of a seminal paper by Denise Rousseau that the full possibilities of the concept of the psychological contract were widely recognised.

Since then hundreds of books and papers have been published on the subject and it is increasingly being seen internationally as providing a significant new means of:

1 analysing changes in the nature of employment relationship over time,

and

2 providing a most useful means for managers to think about the way they manage people in practice.

As with many apparently new concepts, management thinking based around psychological contracts is not really new at all. The term *psychological contract* is relatively new, but the idea behind its management really amounts to no more than managing people's expectations effectively.

It is often the case when a new term is developed and then widely used in academic circles there is a debate about what exactly it means. This is true of the concept of the 'psychological contract', the debate about precise definitions being dry and of little practical relevance. The core idea is easily expressed. It is that employers and employees have a relationship that is much more complex and sophisticated than is set out in formal contracts of employment.

The legal contract sets out the expectations and obligations each side has towards the other in respect of pay and terms and conditions of employment, but the reality of the relationship consists of much more than this. The psychological contract can thus be defined as comprising expectations and obligations that the two sides have of one another and their relationship above and beyond what is formally agreed/written in any legal contract.

Schein conceives it as a set of 'unvoiced expectations and obligations' that employees have of employers and employers of employees in a particular organisation, while Rousseau puts greater stress on the idea of reciprocity in psychological contracts, arguing that we all have in our own minds an understanding of the 'deal' we have struck with our employers. This is crucial because it raises the possibility that either side can through its actions 'breach' the psychological contract.

When an employer breaches the legal contract of employment there are legal consequences. For example if pay is cut or the work location changed without contractual authorisation the employees who are affected can go to court to get injunctions or to sue for damages. If an employee breaches the legal contract (eg by going on strike), the employer responds by cutting wages. By contrast, when the psychological contract is breached the consequences are psychological – reduced commitment and loyalty, lower levels of motivation, higher levels of staff turnover, lower levels of performance, reduced levels of trust both individually and collectively.

THE IMPACT OF BREACHING THE PSYCHOLOGICAL CONTRACT

The psychological contract is breached when the employer is perceived by the employee (either individually or collectively) as having reneged on its deal or broken its promises. In other words, expectations are established and then dashed due to the action (or inaction) of the employer. Common examples of breaches are as follows:

- policy changes which affect someone's ability to do a job in the way they have been accustomed to doing it and want to continue doing it
- changes in payment arrangements or in practices which impact on earning capacity
- changes in hours of work or job duties
- reduced promotion opportunities
- the dashing of 'promises' made in the past about future opportunities
- reduced levels of employee involvement
- promotion/favouring of colleagues who are perceived as being less deserving
- unsatisfactory changes in the physical work environment.

It is important to recognise that inaction on the part of management is just as likely to lead to a perception of breach/violation over time as action does. Minor, one-off breaches or breaches that are not unexpected lead to minor and temporary reductions in morale and have no serious, long-term consequences for the health of the employment relationship. However, a series of minor breaches in a relatively short time, or a single major breach, have the potential to 'violate' the employment relationship by provoking damaging emotional reactions on the part of employees. The bigger the breach, the stronger the sense of violation.

Substantial numbers of studies have now been carried out into the impact on employees and on organisations when major breaches in the psychological contract are perceived to have occurred. They include the following:

- reduced levels of trust
- feelings of inequity
- greater levels of cynicism
- reduced psychological well-being/depression

- dissatisfaction with the job/employer/manager
- reduced commitment
- less 'organisational citizenship behaviour'
- increased staff turnover
- damaged reputation in the labour market
- reduced effort
- increased absence
- reduced willingness to work 'beyond contract'.

In some cases the sense of violation is so great that employees look for ways of 'getting back' at the organisation or 'getting even' with it. This involves taking active steps to retaliate. Examples include breaching of rules, arriving late/ leaving early, taking days off when not sick, malingering on the job, sabotage and pilfering equipment or supplies. More damaging still are situations in which a perceived breach provokes the spread of discontent among colleagues who may not themselves directly be affected. In extreme cases, where unions are present, this leads to formal industrial action.

KEY ARTICLE

BREACHING PSYCHOLOGICAL CONTRACTS

The following article was published in *People Management* on 24 November 2005. You can download it from the CIPD website:

'Love me or lose me' by Stephen Deery

In this article Stephen Deery, Professor of HRM at Kings College London, describes some research he carried out in a large UK company in which levels of staff commitment had fallen in recent years. He concludes that much of this was due to a violation of psychological contracts.

Questions

1 In what different ways had managers in this company failed to manage employee expectations effectively?

2 What were the consequences?

3 What could/should have been done differently?

MANAGING THE PSYCHOLOGICAL CONTRACT

There is a question mark over the extent to which a concept as complex and vague as the psychological contract can be managed in any direct sense by managers. At base, after all, it consists of a set of expectations held by employees. These will vary among the different people in the same departments, let alone across the organisation as a whole, and will vary over time.

However, research suggests that employers and individual managers can take active steps to reduce instances of perceived breach/violation and hence to avoid the negative organisational consequences that can occur. Moreover, there are things that can be done which reduce the emotional impact precipitated by breaches of the psychological contract. It is also possible to take steps to foster a positive psychological contract and hence to benefit from higher trust, more commitment, lower staff turnover and a greater willingness on the part of employees to work beyond contract. Finally, extensive research shows that organisations which take care to manage psychological contracts consistently outperform those who do not.

Two basic points can be made in this context:

1 Organisational change is inevitable. It is increasingly pervasive because the business environment is becoming steadily less predictable and more volatile. The number of situations in which perceived breaches/violations occur is thus increasing and the danger of breach is arising more frequently.

2 A major step can be taken towards the effective management of the psychological contract in an organisation simply by knowing about the concept and making sure that line managers understand it too. Once the idea is embedded in management thinking about the employment relationship, taking steps to improve it/to reduce the seriousness of breaches become much easier to introduce.

Conway and Briner (2005) in the most authoritative recent UK-based book on the subject suggest the following general approaches to managing the psychological contract:

- lower expectations by refraining from making promises that cannot be kept
- only make explicit promises – avoid implicit promises which may be misunderstood
- involve employees in the management of change
- communicate clearly and repeatedly the employer's view of the psychological contract
- negotiate changes in the psychological contract rather than imposing them
- carefully monitor workforce opinion for early signs of perceived violation
- redress breaches with compensation and/or better/more equitable treatment in the future.

Adams (2007) suggests ways of strengthening the psychological contract and maintaining a positive psychological contract:

- reward employees when they work beyond contract
- ensure equity of treatment between employees
- maximise the extent of control employees enjoy over their own work
- maximise individual developmental opportunities
- design jobs so as to maximise the extent of challenge and stimulation
- maximise the extent of employee involvement, information-sharing and communication
- embrace work–life balance initiatives.

Strengths-based management is a fashionable approach to the management of people which also serves to enhance the psychological contract. The approach involves managers focusing on people's strengths rather than on their weaknesses when seeking to improve their performance. This is the opposite of what traditionally happens. Strengths are often taken for granted in discussions between managers and staff, the focus of developmental efforts being firmly on identifying weaknesses and putting in place plans to improve performance in those areas. In fact, according to extensive research carried out by the Gallup Organisation and popularised by the writer Marcus Buckingham (2007), a more fruitful approach involves downplaying weaknesses and encouraging people to focus more on their strengths. According to Buckingham, organisational performance increases when managers match people to tasks at which they excel and allow them to achieve their objectives in ways which they find work best for them.

Another stream of contemporary HRM research which is relevant to the fostering of a positive psychological contract is that on 'happiness at work'. It is suggested that the following managerial characteristics can play an important part in fostering 'a culture of positive emotion':

- encouraging good humour
- giving plenty of positive feedback
- exhibiting confidence and enthusiasm
- discouraging aggression between colleagues
- encouraging celebrations of success.

Linked to this body of research is another which focuses on the relationship between physical and mental well-being. Increasingly it is being recognised that physical fitness has a major contribution to make to the development and maintenance of positive emotional states. Encouraging employees to take exercise, for example by providing subsidised gym memberships, and to eat healthily can thus play a role in improving long-term performance, as well as reducing absence.

Physical well-being, however, is about much more than fitness. Someone may eat well and have a fit body, but nonetheless be unfit if they are overworking, overstressed and sleeping badly. It is thus helpful to think in terms of a broader category increasingly labelled as 'wellness' and to encourage its development. Examples of initiatives in this field are employee assistance programmes, relationship counselling and lifestyle coaching courses, all of which help to foster 'wellness' and hence to increase positive emotion, improve job performance and reduce the chances of a negative psychological contract establishing itself.

MANAGING EXPECTATIONS IN PRACTICE

Having established what employer and employee expectations are, and having discussed the key theories in the field, we now need to think about how expectations can be managed from a day-to-day perspective.

RECRUITMENT AND SELECTION

The key here is to be honest with would-be employees about what they can expect from the job if appointed. In tight labour market situations there is a natural tendency for employers to exaggerate the positive aspects of a job or a workplace while downplaying the negative aspects. This is notoriously true in the field of graduate recruitment where employers compete quite fiercely with one another to hire the best graduates each year. It is, though, increasingly seen to be an unwise approach. Just as customers get irritated when they are oversold a product or service, so would-be employees can be seriously demotivated when they are oversold a job. A new employee starts a new job with over-inflated expectations and soon finds those to be dashed. The reality falls short of what was promised or, more often, some issue of significance such as the nature of the physical work environment or an area of responsibility was simply not discussed at interview or set out at all in any recruitment literature.

The result can be an early resignation. UK employers have a very poor record when it comes to retaining new starters; around 17% of new starters leave within three months and 40% within the first year (Gregg and Wadsworth 1999). Many, though – particularly those employed in more senior roles – will not resign quickly. Instead they will stick it out and stay for a couple of years. But very often the decision to go at an early date is made in the first few weeks of employment. The result is reduced commitment, which serves the interests of neither the employer nor the employee.

There is thus a compelling case for 'warts and all' recruitment practices, often termed 'realistic job previews' in the academic literature. For some time the leading researcher in this field has been John Parcher Wanous (1992), who has shown in a number of studies how much more satisfactory the outcomes are for everyone when someone enters a job with an accurate understanding of what it will entail. This does not mean that employers have to be negative in their approach or even to highlight the more unpleasant aspects of their jobs, but it does mean that an active attempt should be made not to distort the picture that is painted for candidates during the recruitment stage.

Interestingly it is for this reason that many researchers have argued in favour of internal recruitment and informal methods such as the employment of friends and family of existing staff. Their view is controversial because it conflicts with commonly held views of what constitutes 'good practice' in recruitment. But the business case can nonetheless stack up well (see Kirnan et al 1989, Blau 1992, Iles and Robertson 1997, Barber 1998, Castilla 2005 and Breaugh 2008). The truth is that internal promotees and those with close connections with existing staff tend not to gain an unrealistic impression of what the organisation is going to be like to work for. They enter the role with their eyes wide open and are also usually able to get up to speed more quickly.

INDUCTION

Formal induction and socialising exercises, sometimes referred to as 'onboarding' these days, have many functions and are often quite poorly managed. We have a strong tendency to treat all new starters in the same way, putting everyone through a standard programme, irrespective of whether or not that is really what they need. For some reason managers generally, HR managers included, tend to downgrade the significance of induction and fail to give it the attention it deserves. One reason for thinking about it more seriously than we do is the opportunity it gives to shape expectations at a time when employees are likely to be very receptive to messages about what is expected of them and what they can expect to receive in return. In other words, the induction period provides a great opportunity for managers to establish an effective psychological contract with new members of staff.

So what does a serious, well-designed induction programme look like? First of all it has individual aspects as well as collective ones. It is not simply about attending a day-long training programme, but about establishing good relationships and gaining an understanding of an organisation's culture. Secondly, it should be regularly reviewed and updated in response to feedback from new starters six months or so after they have completed an induction programme. Finally, it should be a two-way exercise. It is the manager's opportunity to learn about their new employee and what makes them tick as much as it is an opportunity for new staff to learn about what is expected of them.

PERFORMANCE MANAGEMENT

When managing individual performance, and particularly when carrying out formal appraisal exercises, it is equally important to manage expectations effectively. Here the keys are clarity of communication and delivering on promises made. The principles of expectancy theory that we discussed above need to be applied.

Firstly it is important that achievable goals are agreed with employees for the year ahead (or whatever time frame the organisation chooses to use). Setting objectives that someone is going to struggle to meet either because they lack the required skills or because they are just too stretching for anyone to meet is a major potential trap. Even when performance appraisal is used in order to determine pay rises or bonus payments, the presumption should be that each employee will in practice meet the targets that have been set for them. The alternative, inevitably, is going to be poorly managed expectations and a situation in which hopes are raised only to be dashed.

Secondly, there must be some form of reward which the organisation gives to employees when they meet their objectives. Moreover, the nature of this reward should be clarified up front as precisely as possible. Here too the key is to deliver on promises. Managers should not make such promises, or hint at them, if they cannot ultimately deliver them. This is particularly true of promotions and any financial rewards where the capacity for dashed expectations to have a serious impact on employee morale is greatest. But it is also important to deliver on lesser rewards if they are anticipated, such as praise and recognition. It is very easy for managers to act inconsistently in the way that they treat people who perform well, simply through carelessness. Praise and thanks are given one year, but not the next, despite the fact that someone has maintained a high level of performance across both periods.

CONDUCT ISSUES

All organisations need to have rules to govern the way that people work and the standards of professional behaviour that all are expected to observe. Breaking such rules is generally classed as being an act of misconduct which will lead to disciplinary action being taken. Ultimately breaches of conduct, particularly those deemed to amount to gross misconduct, can lead to dismissal. In this area much management activity is in effect determined by the requirements of unfair dismissal law which include an assumption that expectations in this area will be managed properly and equitably.

When someone is suspected of breaking the rules and committing an act of misconduct, the law requires that the matter is fully investigated and that the accused person is given every opportunity to defend himself or herself at a formal hearing. The outcome is often a formal written warning which makes it clear that further breaches of the rules may lead to dismissal. Expectations are thus being managed very formally and clearly.

In the case of acts of gross misconduct, the law requires employers to make clear to everyone in staff handbooks or on intranets what will be considered gross misconduct in the organisation. This matters hugely because an employee who is found to have committed an act of gross misconduct can lawfully be dismissed without notice. Some types of offence, such as theft or violence, are always accepted to amount to gross misconduct, but organisations also develop their own rules. The key is that these must be communicated widely so that when someone commits one of the prohibited acts an employment tribunal can be satisfied that at the time they did so they knew or should have known that their actions might lead to summary dismissal without notice.

CHANGE MANAGEMENT

In Chapter 6 we focused on various aspects of effective change management. There is no need to repeat those here. But it is worth pointing out that during change management exercises the effective management of expectations is key to a successful outcome. Communications need to be regular, as full as possible and accurate. If managers do not take the trouble to manage people's expectations properly, rumour mills will always rumble away, often allowing false expectations to develop.

ARE EXPECTATIONS CHANGING?

Above we discussed the case for establishing positive psychological contracts with staff and for avoiding breaches. There is, however, also another important stream in research on psychological contracts. This concerns the extent to which we are generally witnessing a change in the nature of the psychological contract that employers and employees establish. In other words, are the expectations that both sides have about the nature of their relationship changing, and if so, how?

This is an area of research in which people have rather different ideas. On the one hand, there is an established case in favour of change, the argument being that employers have no choice, given the environmental developments that we discussed in Chapter 2, but to alter the basis of employee relations in their organisations by developing new psychological contracts. Uncertainty and volatility, in particular, need to be reflected in the nature of the expectations that employers and employees have of each other. It is thus often argued that an 'old psychological contract', which can be summed up as follows –

> I will work hard for and act with loyalty towards my employer. In return I expect to be retained as an employee provided I do not act against the interests of the organisation. I also expect to be given opportunities for development and promotion should circumstances make this possible…

– is over time being replaced by another, which takes something like the following form:

> I will bring to my work effort and creativity. In return I expect a salary that is appropriate to my contribution and market worth. While our relationship may be short term, I will remain for as long as I receive the developmental opportunities I need to build my career.

The key change is a switch from an assumption that the relationship will be long-lasting, if not in theory 'permanent', to a much looser arrangement in which there is no expectation on either side of a long-term relationship. Instead, employers are tending to emphasise their capacity to provide people with development opportunities that will enhance their career prospects. This change matters hugely because of its impact on the extent of employees' commitment, and hence on the most fundamental aspects of human resource management. How can managers expect loyalty from their staff if they do not return it in kind?

The extent to which we are seeing a change of this kind happening is a contested question. Coyle-Shapiro and Kessler (2000), Schalk and Freese (2007) and Blickle and Witzki (2008), for example, are researchers who have found considerable evidence of a shift from the 'old' model to something like the 'new' model summarised above. Others, notably Guest and Conway (2000, 2001) in their studies carried out on behalf of the CIPD (2005), have tended to downplay the extent of change in most UK organisations. Their studies have picked up some evidence of a limited move from 'old' to 'new' in some organisations, but no substantial general shift.

Over time we are likely to see moves in the direction of new psychological contracts simply because employers are going to find it increasingly difficult to offer people guarantees of long-term employment. But in labour markets which are tight and in which the skills and experience required by employers are in short supply, there will inevitably be a resistance to doing so. As we established at the start of this chapter, job security is one of the key things that employees expect and look for when job-seeking. Employers who want to recruit and retain good performers will thus always try to provide it if they can. Those who suggest that the old psychological contract is dying may well have to wait a long time for their prophecy to be fulfilled.

 CRITICAL REFLECTION

No employer which is obliged to operate in an increasingly volatile and unpredictable business environment can guarantee job security to people, but there remains the world of difference between an employer which seeks to provide a high degree of job security for its people and one which is unconcerned about the issue.

Questions

1 What steps can employers take to maintain job security in turbulent times?

2 What are the major advantages and disadvantages of taking this approach?

3 What degree of job security is your employer able to offer? How might this change in the future?

KEY LEARNING POINTS

- Employers and employees have different expectations of each other both in terms of work generally and in terms of particular people and jobs.

- The effective management of expectations is central to much HRM practice.

- Job satisfaction levels appear over time to be falling as employers increasingly struggle to meet employee expectations.

- Expectancy theory, equity theory and theories of the psychological contract have much to teach us about how to manage expectations effectively.

- The management of expectations is central to key areas of HR practice such as recruitment, performance management and the effective management of change.

- Over time, as result of changes in the business environment, organisations are under pressure to alter the nature of employee expectations by replacing traditional psychological contracts with new ones which provide less by way of job security.

EXPLORE FURTHER

A great deal of excellent work has recently been published on psychological contracts and their significance. The books by Rousseau (1995) and Conway and Briner (2005) are good starting points for exploring this work.

Conway, N. and Briner, R. (2005) *Understanding psychological contracts at work: a critical evaluation of theory and research*. Oxford: University Press.

Rousseau, D. (1995) *Psychological contracts in organizations*. Thousand Oaks, CA: Sage.

The CIPD report *Gen-up: how the four generations work* (2008) is a good introduction to thinking about the different expectations each generation has of work and workplaces.

CIPD and Penna (2008) *Gen-up: how the four generations work*. London: Chartered Institute of Personnel and Development.

John Parcher Wanous's classic work on realistic job previews and its practical implications are covered effectively in his book *Organizational entry* (1992).

Wanous, J.P. (1992) *Organizational entry*. Reading, MA: Addison-Wesley.

REFERENCES

Adams, J. (2007) *Managing people in organizations: contemporary theory and practice.* Basingstoke: Palgrave.

Adams, J.S. (1963) Towards an understanding of inequity. *Journal of Abnormal and Social Psychology.* Vol 67. pp422–436.

Appelbaum, E., Bailey, T., Berg, P. and Kalleberg, A. (2000) *Manufacturing advantage: why high-performance systems pay off.* London: Economic Policy Institute/Cornell University Press.

Barber, A. (1998) *Recruiting employees.* Thousand Oaks, CA: Sage.

Bauman, Z. (2005) *Work, consumerism and the new poor.* 2nd edition. Maidenhead: Open University Press.

Blickle, G. and Witzki, A. (2008) New psychological contracts in the world of work: economic citizens or victims of the market? *Society and Business Review.* Vol 3, No 2. pp149–161.

Blau, G. (1992) An empirical analysis of employed and unemployed job search behavior. *Industrial and Labor Relations Review.* Vol 45, No 4, July.

Breaugh, J.A. (2008) Employee recruitment: current knowledge and important areas for future research. *Human Resource Management Review.* Vol 18, No 3. pp103–118.

Buckingham, M. (2007) *Go put your strengths to work*. New York: Simon & Schuster.

Bussing, A. (1997) Motivation and satisfaction. In A. Sorge and M. Warner (eds) *The IEBM handbook of organizational behaviour*. Andover: Thomson Learning.

Castilla, E.J. (2005) Social networks and employee performance in a call center. *American Journal of Sociology*. Vol 110. pp1243–1283.

Chiang, C.F. and Jang, S.C. (2008) An expectancy theory model for hotel employee motivation. *International Journal of Hospitality Management*. Vol 27. pp313–322.

CIPD (2005) *Managing change: the role of the psychological contract*. London: Chartered Institute of Personnel and Development.

CIPD and Penna (2008) *Gen-up: how the four generations work*. London: Chartered Institute of Personnel and Development.

Conway, N. and Briner, R. (2005) *Understanding psychological contracts at work: a critical evaluation of theory and research*. Oxford: Oxford University Press.

Coyle-Shapiro, J. and Kessler, I. (2000) Consequences of the psychological contract for the employment relationship: a large-scale survey. *Journal of Management Studies*. Vol 37, No 7.

Deery, S. (2005) Love me or lose me. *People Management*. 24 November.

du Gay, P. (1996) *Consumption and identity at work*. London: Sage.

Eisner, S.P. (2004) Managing Generation Y. *SAM Advanced Management Journal*. Vol 70, No 4. pp4–15.

Green, F. (2005) *Demanding work: the paradox of job quality in the affluent economy*. Princeton, NJ: Princeton University Press.

Gregg, P. and Wadsworth, J. (1999) Job tenure 1975–98. In P. Gregg and J. Wadsworth (eds) *The state of working Britain*. Manchester: Manchester University Press.

Guest, D.E. and Conway, N. (2000) *The psychological contract in the public sector*. London: CIPD.

Guest, D.E. and Conway, N. (2001) *Public and private sector perceptions on the psychological contract*. London: CIPD.

Huseman, R., Hatfield, J. and Miles, E. (1987) A new perspective on equity theory: the equity sensitivity construct. *Academy of Management Review*. Vol 12. pp222–234.

Iles, P. and Robertson, I. (1997) The impact of selection procedures on candidates. In P. Herriot (ed.) *Assessment and selection in organisations*. Chichester: Wiley.

Kersley, B., Alpin, C., Forth, J., Bryson, A., Bewley, H., Dix, G. and Oxenbridge, S. (2006) *Inside the workplace: findings from the 2004 Workplace Employment Relations Survey*. Abingdon: Routledge.

Kirnan, J., Farley, J. and Geisinger, K. (1989) The relationship between recruiting source, applicant quality and hire performance: an analysis by sex, ethnicity and age. *Personnel Psychology*. Vol 42.

Porter, L.W. and Lawler, E.E. (1968) *Managerial attitudes and performance*. Homewood, Illinois: Irwin-Dorsey Press.

Purcell, J., Kinnie, N., Hutchinson, S., Rayton, B. and Swart, J. (2003) *Understanding the people and performance link: unlocking the black box*. London: CIPD.

Rousseau, D.M. (1989) Psychological and implied contracts in organizations. *Employee Responsibility and Rights Journal*. Vol 2. pp121–139.

Schalk, R. and Freese, C. (2007) The impact of organizational changes on the psychological contract. In K. Isaksson, C. Hogstedt, C. Eriksson and T. Theorell (eds) *Health effects of the new labour market*. New York: Springer.

Svendsen, L. (2008) *Work*. Stocksfield: Acumen Publishing.

Taylor, R. (2001) *The Future of Employment Relations*. ESRC Future of Work Seminar Series. Swindon: Economic and Social Research Council.

Vroom, V.H. (1964) *Work and motivation*. New York: Wiley.

Wanous, J.P. (1992) *Organizational entry*. Reading, MA: Addison Wesley.

Zemke, R., Raines, C. and Filipczak, B. (2000) *Generations at work*. New York: AMACOM.

CHAPTER 9

Engaging people

Introduction

There is no doubt that the term *employee engagement* has recently become a highly fashionable expression that is very widely used in HR circles. Most large employers and many smaller ones too have invested in programmes aimed at increasing engagement levels, many under the guidance of consultants who have spotted a new opportunity to develop lucrative business. In the UK the CIPD has done a great deal to raise interest in engagement among decision-makers in industry, government ministers also contributing with the launch in 2009 of a national awareness campaign.

Interestingly, however, despite its very wide usage, there remains considerable confusion and precious little agreement about what exactly the term *employee engagement* means. What does an engaged employee look like and how does such a person differ from a disengaged employee? Is engagement best defined as a set of behaviours, a state of mind or an attitude towards work? What is the difference between engagement and longer-established notions such as motivation? Does it represent a genuinely new contribution to management thinking, or is it just a case of old wine in a shiny new bottle? It is difficult to be sure because everyone who has written about the subject seems to have a rather different understanding of how the term *engagement* should be defined. As a result we have a situation in which one researcher correctly observed that engagement has come to serve as an 'umbrella term' for 'whatever one wants it to be' (Saks 2008).

Due to this lack of definitional clarity, while the term has now been widely used for 15 years or so, it is only in much more recent years that any serious research has been carried out into employee engagement programmes, the extent to which employees are engaged and the approaches managers can use to enhance engagement among their staff. While the research agenda on engagement is still in its infancy, the conclusions strongly suggest that engagement need not simply be a new word for an old idea, but that as used in the contemporary HR world it does incorporate some genuinely new perspectives. Moreover, a number of large-scale research projects have now been carried out which demonstrate impressive links between the extent to which a workforce is engaged and a variety of measures of business success. Employee engagement is thus unlikely to prove to be a passing fad and much more likely to become an idea increasingly central to HR policy and practice as awareness of its potential spreads further.

LEARNING OUTCOMES

The objectives of this chapter are to:

- explore the different definitions of the term *employee engagement* that have been used
- explain why there is so much current interest in the notion of employee engagement
- set out the major advantages for employers and employees of achieving high levels of engagement
- consider the major ways in which employers can improve levels of employee engagement in their organisations
- explore the major criticisms that have been made about thinking in the field of employee engagement
- set out the main ways in which line management in organisations can be improved so as to enhance engagement levels.

DEFINING ENGAGEMENT

The use of the terms *engagement* and *disengagement* appear first to have been used in the employment context by the American psychologist William Kahn in a journal article written in 1990. They were then popularised in a bestselling and very influential book written by Marcus Buckingham and Curt Coffman called *First break all the rules*, published in 1999. Since then the usage of the term has become very widespread indeed, lifting employee engagement to the top of many HR management agendas in organisations.

However, there remain as many subtly different definitions of the terms *employee engagement* and *work engagement* as there are books and articles written about the subject. For the most part they are in broadly the same ballpark, but the emphasis varies considerably from writer to writer. Here are some examples which seem to me to be useful in helping us to distinguish *engagement* from other allied concepts such as *motivation, job satisfaction, well-being* and *organisational citizenship behaviour*:

> *A positive attitude held by the employee towards the organisation and its values. An engaged employee is aware of business context, and works with colleagues to improve performance within the job for the benefit of*

the organisation. The organisation must work to develop and nurture engagement, which requires a two-way relationship between employer and employee. (Robinson et al 2004: ix)

Work engagement is a positive, fulfilling, affective-motivational state of work-related well-being that can be seen as the antipode of job burnout. Engaged employees have high levels of energy and are enthusiastically involved in their work. (Leiter and Bakker 2010: 1–2)

The extent to which employees thrive at work, are committed to their employer, and are motivated to do their best for the benefit of themselves and their organisation. (Stairs and Galpin 2010: 158)

Engaged employees have a desire and commitment for always doing the best job. They grip any task with energy and enthusiasm, often going above and beyond to increase or influence quality, costs and customer service. They bring fresh ideas, infuse their teams with their own engagement and are less likely to seek opportunities to work elsewhere. They believe in the purpose of the organisation and demonstrate that belief through their actions and attitudes. (Macleod and Brady 2008: 11)

A combination of commitment to the organisation and its values and a willingness to help out colleagues (organisational citizenship). It goes beyond job satisfaction and is not simply motivation. Engagement is something the employee has to offer; it cannot be 'required' as part of the employment contract. (Daniels 2010)

The first thing we can observe about these definitions is that they are not neat and succinct. In each case the term *engagement* is defined in such a way as to encompass a group of distinct attributes. As an idea it is thus multidimensional, building on concepts such as *motivation* and *satisfaction*, and integrating them, rather than replacing them in any way. Engagement requires satisfied staff, motivated staff, committed staff and staff who are keen to act in their employer's interests, but it involves more besides.

Secondly, it is apparent that engagement is associated with the expense of energy. As Schaufeli and Bakker (2010: 20) argue, engaged staff are excited by their work, whereas those who are merely satisfied demonstrate 'contentment'. Others use the term *vigour* to describe the way in which engaged employees approach their work, that is to say with considerable positive enthusiasm, leading them to put a good deal of effort into achieving their core objectives.

Thirdly, of particular importance, is the two-way nature of employee engagement. The definitions clearly insist that this is a state which is mutually beneficial, both employers and employees gaining when their employment relationship is characterised by engagement.

In many respects it is easier to define engagement in terms of what it is not, and a number of writers have preferred to take this approach. Schaufeli and Bakker (2010: 13), for example, argue that engagement is the opposite of 'burnout', defined as a settled state in which employees demonstrate exhaustion, cynicism, low levels of energy and poor identification with their work. By contrast, engaged employees demonstrate vigour, dedication, absorption, high levels of energy and strong identification with their work. Others have focused their research primarily on 'disengagement', seen as a situation in which employees 'decouple themselves' from their work (May et al 2004), demonstrating a lack of enthusiasm and only doing what they have to do in order to retain their jobs. Engagement is thus defined in the way that we use the term when talking about 'engaging the gear' when driving a car. Engaged employees are fully involved with their work, genuinely interested in helping to achieve key objectives and keen to put effort and enthusiasm into the task.

An important contribution to the debate about what engagement really means in the workplace was made by Truss et al (2006) in a CIPD report when they suggested that there are in fact three distinct types of engagement which can be identified:

- emotional engagement (being involved in one's work)
- cognitive engagement (focusing hard while at work)
- physical engagement (being willing to go the extra mile for an employer).

No doubt these definitional debates will proceed for some time to come, a different emphasis being placed on the various elements as more research is carried out. In the meantime, from a practical management perspective, it is fair to state that while we may not yet have a neat, clear, snappy definition that all subscribe to, as a general idea it is pretty clear what we are talking about when we observe that a person is either engaged, actively engaged, disengaged or actively disengaged with their work, their organisation or their profession. As several interviewees who contributed to the government-commissioned Macleod Review (2009) said, an engaged workforce is something that you know when you see it.

CURRENT INTEREST IN ENGAGEMENT

In the first part of this book I discussed a variety of environmental trends which in their different ways are shaping the contemporary and future HR agenda. A number of these are relevant to the great growth in interest in employee engagement we have seen in recent years and explain why we are likely to see further interest develop in the future.

The key question is, why are employers keener *now* to secure the services of employees who are actively engaged than they were in the past?

One answer lies in the increasingly competitive business conditions that are emerging as a result of the trends we discussed in Chapter 2. The lack of stability means that organisations are having to become more agile and opportunist in the way that they operate. Less and less do we have the luxury of time to pass decisions up and down a hierarchy, while standardised and centralised approaches which assume all customers are the same are increasingly unsustainable. Teams and individual employees thus have to be empowered to make decisions themselves and to act on their own initiative, particularly when they deal directly with demanding customers who are very ready to switch their business elsewhere when not fully satisfied. This is not going to happen effectively unless the empowered employees are fully engaged with their work, keen to help the organisation achieve its objectives and fully signed up to its values.

A second consequence of increasing competition is a much enhanced need for organisations to innovate pretty well continually and to think creatively about the ways in which they operate. To maximise the capacity for innovation and creativity, organisations need to be able to draw on ideas from everyone who they employ in whatever capacity. A fully engaged workforce which is willing and able to participate is a prerequisite if this is going to happen. The same is true when it comes to the effective management of change (Chapter 6) and the sharing of knowledge (Chapter 10). Without the assistance of an engaged workforce the chances of succeeding in an increasingly competitive world are going to diminish rapidly.

Over time, labour market trends are also having an impact. As was explained in Chapter 3, we are moving steadily towards a situation in which demand for people to carry out higher-skilled roles in organisations is outpacing their supply. Yet at the same time, increasing international competition restricts our ability simply to pay people more in order to attract and retain them. The upshot is a need to enhance the quality of working life, to treat our people with greater respect and to involve them more in decision-making. Highly skilled people who have a choice about where to work are unlikely to hang around in a job that they find to be unengaging, nor is a corporation's reputation as an employer likely to be enhanced if it fails actively to engage its staff. It is thus reasonable to conclude that the tighter labour markets become, the more important it becomes purely from an employment perspective to take the engagement agenda seriously.

And this is not just a question of a preference for a more enjoyable job. As Leiter and Bakker (2010: 5) point out, employees in the future are likely to need engagement in order to develop their careers:

> Career tracks in the twenty-first century anticipate many more changes and larger shifts than was the case in the twentieth century. As active participants in the job market, individuals benefit from demonstrating their personal productivity. Demonstrating one's personal energy, dedication and efficacy will open more and better opportunities while building a dynamic and rewarding career.

Demand from employees and would-be employees for engaging jobs is also likely to become more pronounced as the members of the so-called 'Generation Me' enter the workplace in increasing numbers to replace retiring Baby Boomers. As we discussed in Chapter 5, this generation appears to be characterised by a higher degree of individualism than previous generations. Their approach to work is not that different in many respects from their lives as consumers. They are going to expect interesting jobs which energise them, managers who value their contribution and are also likely to avoid working for organisations with values they do not share. In other words, they want to be engaged and will not settle, unless there is no alternative, for a working life that does not provide them with this opportunity. Macleod and Brady (2009: 56) also point out how more effort needs to be put into engaging younger generations of workers in response to 'the death of deference' in organisations. The point is a simple but important one, and it also derives from the trend towards individualism. Over time many have observed that we are becoming a great deal less deferential as a society than we used to be. Managers cannot therefore automatically expect to be respected simply because of their position. Respect has to be earned, and re-earned again and again as each succeeding cohort of staff joins the organisation. Moreover, this is true even in organisations such as the military where most would not expect it to be the case:

> The difference in leadership qualities of our people in the services now to those fifty years ago is that the 'why' culture now exists.... Fifty years ago if you said jump and you had one stripe on your arm people did so, you were respected as an officer; people are now respected for things they ought to be respected for, which is who they are, what their qualities are, what their characters are, what their ability to lead is (or not). (Quotation from an interview with Admiral Sir Mark Stanhope, Deputy Supreme Allied Commander Transformation, NATO, in Macleod and Brady 2008: 56).

If people will no longer jump when asked to, and insist on knowing 'why' before considering whether or not to comply, it follows that managers need to develop more sophisticated approaches if they are to lead an organisation forward. Employee engagement offers a set of ideas that can help to achieve this.

Finally it is important not to neglect the role of government in pushing the employee engagement agenda (see Chapter 4). Macleod and Clarke (2009), in their *Report to Government* on employee engagement, argued that there is now compelling evidence to associate improved levels of employee engagement with increased productivity. The former is a key driver of the latter. For this reason, in recent years, raising awareness of employee engagement among managers in all sectors and actively promoting this agenda has become a significant plank in the government's industrial policy, particularly in light of research which suggests that UK employees are not currently an especially engaged population.

BENEFITS FOR EMPLOYEES

One of the points that emerges from the debates about what distinguishes an engaged employee from one who is merely motivated or satisfied is the supposedly win–win nature of employee engagement initiatives. This is something which critics have tended either to ignore, to discount or to be very suspicious of. But the research evidence suggests that considerable and very genuine benefits can accrue to people when they become more engaged with their work. Employees benefit as much as employers do, albeit in different ways.

Employers gain economically in a very direct sense because of increased productivity. Employees may benefit economically over the longer term, due to enhanced career development opportunities and the presence of profit-sharing plans, but for the most part the benefits for staff are psychological and not financial. Quite simply the research evidence suggests that engaged employees are happier and healthier people than those who are not engaged. There is a clear association between well-being and being engaged at work.

Macleod and Clarke (2009: 30–32, 59–61) set out the main findings from published research on individual benefits arising from increased engagement. For example, they cite the extensive Gallup studies, which we will return to later (Harter et al 2002), which found that:

- 86% of engaged employees 'very often feel happy at work' compared with only 11% who are disengaged.

- 45% of engaged employees 'get a great deal of their life happiness from work' compared with only 8% of people who are not engaged.

- 54% of actively disengaged staff state that 'work stress has caused them to behave poorly with friends or family in the past three months' compared with only 17% of engaged staff.

- 54% of actively disengaged staff also report that their work lives 'are having a negative effect on their physical health' compared with just 12% of engaged staff.

They also summarise the findings of CIPD research which found that people who are cognitively engaged with their work are three times as likely to 'have six key positive emotions' while they are at work, namely enthusiasm, cheerfulness, optimism, contentment, feeling calm and relaxed, as they are to experience negative emotions such as depression, gloominess and tension (CIPD 2006).

Further evidence comes from several studies which show clear and significant relationships between the extent of absence and rates of employee turnover and levels of engagement.

Stairs and Galpin (2010) go further in arguing that being actively and positively engaged at work is a central requirement of human happiness in contemporary society. Drawing on studies on human happiness, they advance the view that key outcomes of employee engagement mirror pretty closely the three 'pathways to happiness' advanced by Martin Seligman (2003) in his groundbreaking work in this area. The three are:

- enjoyment

- challenge

- meaning.

In short, they argue that work that is engaging serves as the key to achieving genuine fulfilment in life.

Others show that there is a knock-on effect in other areas too. Black (2008) for example, in her report on the health of the UK's working population, argues that positive experiences of working represent a central factor in determining our self-worth, the esteem in which others hold us and our standing within the community more generally – all of which are correlated with positive health outcomes. Waddell and Burton (2006) also stress the links between being happy and fulfilled at work and physical and mental health.

One possible caveat should be pointed out here. While the published literature on well-being and engagement demonstrates a correlation, it does not demonstrate causation. In other words, it is by no means clear that being engaged at work leads to improved well-being. Indeed, it is very possible that the cause and effect are the other way around and that people who experience well-being are more likely than those who do not to be engaged in their jobs.

BENEFITS FOR EMPLOYERS

A number of studies have been published over recent years which link measurements of employee engagement with a variety of positive business outcomes. Studies undertaken in private sector organisations tend to suggest strongly that increases in engagement lead to improved levels of profitability. In the public sector studies, a range of other outcomes have been linked to engagement, improved productivity being found across all sectors.

The most often cited and best known studies have been those which have drawn on data collected over a number of years by the Gallup Organisation. The sheer size of this data set and its international, cross-industry character makes these studies compelling. For many years now Gallup has been working with companies on a consultancy basis in order to help improve levels of employee satisfaction. One of the methods it has used has been to administer to employees a simple 12-question instrument (ie a questionnaire) which measures employee attitudes about a variety of aspects of their working lives. The main purpose is to ascertain where strengths and weaknesses lie as far as employee morale and commitment are concerned so that steps can be taken to improve them. Care is taken to analyse different business units separately so that managers can compare staff attitudes across different parts of their organisation with a view to identifying good practices and spreading them more widely. Often Gallup returns a few months later to administer the questionnaire again to see what, if any, improvements can be discerned.

In carrying out this work over a number of years, Gallup had by 2006 amassed a huge amount of data from employees based in all manner of companies around the world. What is more, the instrument asked questions which matched closely with the type of elements that were by now seen to constitute measures of employee engagement.

The 12 questions comprise simple statements about individual perceptions of work. Respondents are then asked to say whether they strongly agree, agree, disagree, strongly disagree or neither agree nor disagree, and scores are then generated for a unit's employees' level of engagement. Examples from the 12 statements are as follows (Buckingham and Coffman 1999: 28):

- I know what is expected of me at work.
- At work, I have the opportunity to do what I do best every day.
- In the last seven days I have received recognition or praise for good work.
- At work, my opinions count.

Data has now been collected from 200,000 people based in some 8,000 separate business units, and this has enabled researchers drawing on the database to identify statistically significant correlations between the extent of employees' emotional and cognitive engagement and other variables such as profitability, productivity, customer satisfaction and employee turnover rates.

Some of the key findings are as follows (Harter et al 2002):

1 There is greater variation in terms of the level of employee engagement between different business units within the same organisation than there is between organisations. This is significant because it implies that the variability in levels is not related to the type of industry or characteristics of employees – but is in most cases due to the quality of line management.

2 Impressive correlations were found to exist between relative levels of employee engagement in a business unit and the success of business units. Business units with the highest rates of employee engagement are twice as successful as those with the lowest when measured against indicators such as productivity, customer responses and profitability.

3 A particularly strong relationship was found between levels of employee involvement and rates of staff turnover. The size of the data set allows separate analysis of high-turnover industries and low-turnover industries.

   In high-turnover business units (above 60% turnover rate), staff turnover was, on average, 29% lower in units which scored in the upper quartile for employee engagement than in the lower one. The variation, however, ranged between 14 and 51 percentage points. In low-turnover units, the average difference was 10% (ranging from 4 to 19 percentage points) between upper and lower quartiles.

Another significant study on a global scale was carried out by Towers Perrin–ISR in 2005. Their data came from 664,000 people working for 50 different corporations. As in the Gallup studies, patterns were then sought linking engagement as measured using an employee attitude questionnaire with business outcomes over a 12-month period. These included rises in operating income, net income and earnings per share. The findings were striking.

The companies that scored highest in terms of employee engagement saw an average improvement in their operating income during the 12-month period of 19.2%. This compared with falls on average of 32.7% in the operating income of companies with low levels of employee engagement. Net income grew by 13.7% in the high-engagement companies and declined by an average of 3.8% in those with low engagement scores.

Other less extensive studies have been carried out by firms of consultants looking at engagement across a range of organisations and many by researchers focusing on single organisations. A good summary of the headline findings is provided by Macleod and Clarke (2009: 37–59). Not all measure exactly the same things because *engagement* is defined differently, but all provide some evidence to suggest strong links between high levels of engagement and a variety of measures of business success.

The most compelling evidence of the gains for employers arising from increased involvement is found in studies that compare different units within the same company which provide essentially the same services in the same way. Boots, the Standard Chartered Bank and the Nationwide Building Society have all recently carried out such research, all finding evidence that business outcomes are positively associated with high levels of engagement. Nationwide, for example, found that its branches which scored high for engagement performed better to the tune of 14% when it came to sales of banking products and 34% higher in the case of insurance sales than branches with low engagement scores. The same was true of scores on customer service, staff turnover and absence. Standard Chartered and Boots identified significant differences between high- and low-engagement branches on measures of profitability.

We do not yet have sufficient evidence to reach absolutely definite conclusions on the extent of the link between engagement and business outcomes, but the evidence base is growing each year and is compelling. At the very least it demonstrates that organisations can substantially improve their chances of increasing productivity and profitability by taking active steps to improve levels of employee engagement.

HOW ENGAGED ARE WE?

In contrast to studies which measure 'work satisfaction', the findings of those that look more specifically for evidence of active employee engagement have tended to be quite disappointing. A CIPD survey carried out in 2006 (see Truss et al 2006) included the views of 2,000 employees about their work. Some of the findings were as follows:

- Only two in five employees get regular feedback on how they are performing.

- Only half of employees are confident that problems they have at work will be dealt with fairly.

- Fewer than half believe that senior managers have a clear vision of where their organisations are going.

- Fewer than 40% say that senior managers treat employees with respect.

- Fewer than 40% are satisfied with the opportunities they get to feed their views and opinions upward.

- Only 52% find their job activities to be personally meaningful for them.

- Fewer than half employees are satisfied with the opportunities they get to use their abilities.

IMPROVING LEVELS OF EMPLOYEE ENGAGEMENT

Because the various studies that have been carried out to define *employee engagement* do so in rather different ways, it is unsurprising to find that they also vary somewhat in their conclusions about the steps managers can take to improve engagement levels. There is, nonetheless, a good deal of agreement about the kind of actions that are necessary and also about what organisations need to stop doing (ie pulling down barriers to improving engagement levels).

Robinson et al (2004), in a study of NHS employees, concluded that the following are the key 'drivers of employee engagement':

- involvement in decision-making
- employees feeling able to voice their ideas, managers listening to those ideas and valuing the contribution that employees make
- opportunities for employees to develop their jobs
- concern for employees' health and well-being.

This is all summed up by the simple idea that employees should be given an opportunity to feel both 'valued and involved'.

CIPD researchers (see Daniels 2010) came up with the following list of quite similar 'key drivers':

- employees having opportunities to feed their views upwards
- employees feeling well informed about what is happening in the organisation
- employees believing that their managers are committed to the organisation.

Leiter and Maslach (2010) take a rather different perspective that is focused on the 'how' as much as the 'what' of enhancing engagement levels. They argue that two separate sets of HR interventions are required in order to enhance engagement levels. The first involves 'building and sustaining employees' energy', the second 'confirming commitment to corporate values that inspire employees'. This leads them to develop the following six points which sum up their thinking:

1 Collaborate (ie involve people).

2 Establish an ongoing process (ie continually take new steps aimed at enhancing engagement).

3 Know your target (ie understand exactly what you are trying to achieve).

4 Be creative (ie adapt general principles to the situation the organisation is in).

5 Evaluate (survey employees regularly to track improvements over time).

6 Share (feed back survey results to everyone).

Macleod and Clarke (2009) in their review for government looked at a wide variety of studies and also interviewed managers in organisations which had seen improvements in their engagement levels. This led them to conclude that there are four major, distinct drivers of employee engagement:

- The organisation's leaders provide a strong and clear 'strategic narrative' which is owned by managers and employees at all levels.

- Managers are engaging, treating staff with respect and managing in a style which is facilitating and empowering rather than controlling and restricting.

- Employees have an effective voice. Their views are listened to and acted upon.

- The organisation's values are characterised by high levels of trust and integrity.

A number of conclusions can be reached from this survey of the research into the drivers of employee engagement. Firstly, many of the points made are consistent with and little different from established notions of 'good practice' in the management of people. The literature on engagement thus serves to reinforce messages that are already widely understood. Its main practical contribution is thus not to provide new insights but to enhance decisively the business case for effective people management. Secondly, the research findings make clear that employee engagement cannot be built quickly. We are not talking here about a single initiative lasting a few months, but a long-term commitment to a style of people management which needs to be continually reviewed and renewed over time. Thirdly, it is fair to conclude that the steps that need to be taken are not going to be easy ones for many organisations because they jar against established cultures and ways of doing things. Managers in many organisations are too autocratic in their style, too reluctant to share information with staff, possessed of essentially self-serving values and insufficiently interested in the well-being of their staff even to be at the starting point when it comes to engaging staff in any genuine sense. The learning curve is thus a very big one and it is not going to be easy for HR managers to convince leaders and line managers of the need to take a radically different approach.

KEY ARTICLE

BIRMINGHAM CITY COUNCIL

Read the article by Anat Arkin entitled 'The Best Policy' featured in *People Management* (1 January 2009). This can be downloaded from the *People Management* archive on the CIPD website (www.cipd.co.uk).

In this article Anat Arkin reports on how a series of engagement initiatives championed by managers at Birmingham City Council failed to have much impact, until one called 'Best' was launched in 2006. This one, unlike the others, has improved staff perceptions of their employer and also those of key client groups.

Questions

1 What was the key difference between the approach taken in launching 'Best' and other less successful initiatives?

2 What unconventional features of the initiative might account for its relative success?

CRITICISMS OF EMPLOYEE ENGAGEMENT INITIATIVES

Aside from concerns among academic researchers about the lack of clarity surrounding the precise meaning of the term *employee engagement* and inconsistent use of the term by managers and consultants, a number of other critical views have been voiced which we need to consider.

First, there is considerable unease about the agenda among those who distrust the individualistic nature of much thinking about employee engagement. This is a very valid point. Discussion about employee engagement and initiatives designed to promote it have tended to be very focused on the individual employment relationship. It is about *my* feelings and attitudes towards *my* work and does not take collective perspectives much into account. On one level this could be seen as a managerial response to the rise of greater individualism in society that we discussed in Chapter 5, but for many critics it is less a case of management responding and more a case of management taking steps to promote individualism at work. In particular there appears to be no obvious role at all for trade unions in employee engagement initiatives. Indeed, some have seen moves towards employee engagement as part of a wider strategy aimed at undermining unions.

Moreover, it is also clear that employee engagement is essentially a unitarist concept. That is to say, at its heart is an acceptance of the assumption that managers, shareholders and employees share the same basic set of economic interests. All benefit from an organisation's financial success. This is a perspective which is highly controversial among employee relations specialists, most of whom share pluralist assumptions about employment relationships. According to this perspective, employers and employees have fundamentally different interests. The idea that both could benefit more or less equally from a development such as employee engagement is thus something which is highly questionable. The suspicion is that engagement simply represents another in a long line of initiatives promoted by managers with the aim of intensifying work without paying their employees any more money. The pill is sugared in a positive rhetoric, but the reality is more work and harder work for no additional pay. Indeed, the whole notion of any initiative aimed at securing 'discretionary effort' is often seen by those who take a pluralist perspective as being no more than a strategy to extract more work from labour without fully sharing the return in the form of bonus or overtime payments.

These are strong arguments. One defect of the existing research into employee engagement is the lack of focus on increasing levels of engagement effectively in unionised organisations. It may well be that managers are using the rhetoric of engagement in a bid to undermine union influence, but it is also reasonable to argue that this need not be the case. It seems to me to be entirely possible and desirable in organisations with a heavy union presence to develop approaches which embrace a role for unions in enhancing levels of engagement. In particular it should be possible to ensure that employees, as a collective, benefit economically as well as psychologically from initiatives of this kind. Moreover, the concept of engagement fits well with that of a partnership approach to the union–management relationship.

Another set of criticisms come from those who are concerned more generally about trends towards greater occupational stress, job burnout, poor work–life balance and 'workaholism'. Despite the presence of academic papers which view recent thinking about engagement as a positive development and which seek to distinguish it from these negative outcomes of work, the fear remains that employees who are pressurised (however willingly) into expending greater energy at work are inevitably going to be susceptible to ills such as stress and burnout. This is particularly true when being seen to be engaged with one's work is a major criterion used when selecting people for new jobs, for promotion or is used as a criterion when selecting people for redundancy.

These too are very valid criticisms, but they seem to me to derive from an analysis of the misapplication of employee engagement thinking on the part of managers rather than employee engagement initiatives *per se*. It remains the case that employees can benefit from being more engaged without that necessarily leading them to work excessive hours, to overstress themselves through work or to become addicted to their work in a damaging way. Indeed, it makes no sense in the long term for employers who are serious about engagement to push people so hard that they end up suffering from undue stress or burnout. When that happens it reduces levels of engagement. The key is thus to be aware of the dangers and to ensure that being an actively engaged employee does not conflict with the need to enjoy a good work–life balance.

A third set of criticisms questions the extent to which management-led employee engagement initiatives can, in truth, increase engagement levels to any great extent. This argument derives from the view that our propensity to be engaged in a job is largely explained by our personalities, the choices we make about the role work plays in our lives and the particular assessments we make of our current jobs in comparison with those of others or our own past experiences. In other words, engagement is to a great extent outside the control of managers. Stairs and Galpin (2010: 166–168) estimate that these 'internal drivers' account for around 80% of the influence on employee engagement, leaving only 20% for 'external drivers' such as management initiatives:

> We would suggest that it is not so much the context in which the person works, as their perception of that context, which matters most to feelings of engagement.

There is also now a considerable amount of research published which strongly suggests that people with particular personality traits are much more likely to be engaged in their work than others. Some psychologists argue, for example, that reasonably high levels of conscientiousness are necessary in order for an employee to be genuinely engaged (see Macey and Schneider 2008 and Kim et al 2009). These studies have also found negative associations between neuroticism and engagement, suggesting that employees who have a tendency to anxiety and are more easily stressed find it harder to become actively engaged than those whose personalities are more emotionally stable. There is also some evidence linking extroversion with employee engagement, particularly those aspects which involve high levels of energy and dedication to a job or organisation (Langelaan et al 2006).

All of these arguments are persuasive in their different ways and should make us think twice about accepting uncritically the case for extensive expenditure by organisations on employee engagement initiatives. However, none really undermines the core case. What they demonstrate above all is that a great deal more research needs to be done into engagement before we can say that it is fully understood.

LINE MANAGEMENT

Pretty well all the research that has been carried out into employee engagement programmes recognises the pivotal role played by line managers. Without their commitment, no organisational-level programme aimed at enhancing engagement levels is likely to succeed. Poor standards of supervision act as a major barrier to the building of an engaged workforce, just as it scuppers other types of HR intervention such as drives to improve employee retention. The job of the first-line supervisor is a difficult one and it is one that few are really able to carry out to an excellent level of competence. But we do appear in the UK to have a particular problem in this area. In short, too many first-line managers are neither rated highly nor respected by their teams and this prevents organisations from making progress across the whole range of HR activities, including, crucially, employee engagement.

HOW DO UK EMPLOYEES RATE THEIR BOSSES?

In 2011 the online job advertising website Monster conducted an international survey to see how highly employees in different countries rated their managers. As far as the UK was concerned, the results were very poor indeed. 9,000 employees from 52 countries took part in the survey, the results of which show that workers in the UK have a lower opinion of their managers than is the case anywhere else in the world. Here are some of the headline findings:

- Only 10% describe their manager as 'brilliant'.

- 73% say that their manager 'fails to invest properly in staff development or training'.

- 70% believe that they could do their manager's job to a higher standard.

- Only 18% believe that their managers are more capable than they are.

- An astonishing 41% of UK workers described their manager as being 'almost totally incompetent'.

Managers are rated rather more highly by American employees and by those working in other European countries. The ratings were far higher in Far Eastern countries. In China, for example, only 15% questioned the competence of their manager, a third stating that they were 'brilliant'.

Another survey carried out in the UK by ICM on behalf of People First also reported quite damning results about the way that employees judge their managers. 2,000 took part, some findings being as follows:

- Over a quarter of respondents said that they did not respect their manager.

- Nearly half stated that their managers did not help them to develop their careers.

- 36% said that their supervisors failed to provide clear instructions.

- 27% said that their supervisors talked down to them.

The results accord pretty closely with those reported by the CIPD in its research on employee engagement. I also reached similar conclusions after carrying out interviews with dozens of people about why they left their last job. Incompetent, ineffective supervision appears to be a major problem which HR functions are failing to address as vigorously as they should.

(Sources: CMI 2011 and *People Management* 2011)

The term *poor supervision* can of course cover a wide variety of different types of situation. The following are the most common types of complaint made by staff about their supervisors in interviews carried out by myself and members of my research team when we looked into the reasons that people resigned voluntarily from their jobs in the early 2000s:

1 Supervisors who fail to respond to grievances. Managers often avoid confronting issues that are important to employees, preferring to sweep problems under their office carpets.

2 Supervisors who act autocratically, often imposing their views on others for no apparently good reason without discussion, irrespective of the effect such decisions have on their working lives.

3 Supervisors who abuse their positions, treating members of their teams rudely, making jokes at their expense or criticising them unfairly (often when they are under pressure) without subsequently issuing any kind of apology.

4 Supervisors who show undue favouritism to some staff. Those who see their colleagues being given more responsibility, praise, interesting tasks or pay than they are getting – *when this is not justified* – develop very negative feelings and often quit.

5 Supervisors who fail to appreciate their subordinates' efforts. Another common cause of dissatisfaction is situations in which people put in extra effort, complete a project or make a special contribution in other ways and get insufficient recognition or even feedback.

6 Supervisors who are very self-centred. Another common situation is one in which career-minded supervisors give the appearance of running their domain in their own interests rather than for the good of their teams, or in some cases their customers.

7 Supervisors who fail to deliver on their promises. This covers situations where indications are given that things will improve in the near future or that other commitments will be met. If in practice the promises are not subsequently delivered, the result is greater resentment than was felt at the start.

Before we go on to discuss how these issues can be addressed, it is important to recognise that industries vary considerably in terms of the quality of supervision.

The biggest problems often occur when people are promoted into supervisory roles at a young age before they have had the opportunity to observe and experience other supervisors at work. Promotion of inexperienced people occurs mainly in high-turnover, low-paying service industries such as catering and retailing. However, there are also major problems in the professional services sector and others in which supervisors are put under very considerable pressure to produce results without being given sufficient resources. In my research I found fewer examples of really poor supervision in the public sector and also in manufacturing, but there is no question that there is room for considerable improvement across the board.

KEY ARTICLE

Read the article by Graeme Buckingham entitled 'Same indifference' featured in *People Management* (17 February 2000). This can be downloaded from the *People Management* archive on the CIPD's website (www.cipd.co.uk).

This article briefly reports the results of Gallup surveys and others into the links between effective supervision, employee engagement and the performance of different business units within the same organisations. The variations between the relative performance of different shops in the same chain were found to be substantial and largely explicable with reference to the people management skills of local line managers.

Questions

1 Why do large corporations allow a situation to develop in which there is so much variation in the effectiveness of their line managers?

2 What are the key HR lessons that should be learned from this research?

WHY IS THE STANDARD OF SUPERVISION SO POOR?

It is not difficult to answer this question. In many ways it is a good deal harder to establish why we persist in allowing the standard of supervision to remain so poor. The main reason is simply because good supervision is difficult and good supervisors are therefore a rarity. Like good parenting, good supervision is not something that comes naturally to everyone. It is a skill that is gained over time through experience and by learning from one's own and others' mistakes. Yet despite this evident truth, it is only relatively rarely that organisations offer people formal training in supervisory skills either before or after they take up their first posts which carry responsibility for the management of others. It should therefore come as no surprise that so many supervisors are ineffective. The problem is compounded by our tendency to appoint people into supervisory positions for the wrong reasons. Appointing people in recognition of their supervisory skills appears to be insufficiently common. Instead we tend to promote people who are good at doing their present jobs, assuming wrongly that this will make them good supervisors of others doing that job. Such people are often respected for their technical abilities, which helps, but many turn out to be poor managers of others. Another common situation involves the promotion of the longest serving member of a team into a supervisory role, or the most highly paid. Sometimes we simply choose the person who wants the supervisor's role most, or worse still, allow the former occupant of the post to select their 'favourite' as their successor. The same is true in the case of many external appointments. Proficiency in the current role is used as the yardstick as much as or more than someone's supervisory potential. The result is an inexperienced and ineffective supervisory cadre in the organisation, often more concerned with establishing their own authority over disrespectful subordinates than motivating a team of individuals to achieve organisational objectives. Finally, having appointed someone for poor reasons, we have a tendency to judge their subsequent performance without reference to their achievements as supervisors. Provided organisational goals are accomplished, we see no need to question how effectively someone manages their team. Because managers who lose their staff or fail to engage them as a result of their incompetence pay no penalty, they do not concern themselves too much with these matters.

SIX GOLDEN RULES FOR EFFECTIVE SUPERVISION

As I pointed out above, supervisory skills do not necessarily come naturally. They need to be learned. This means formally training people in the principles of effective supervision both before and after they take up posts which carry responsibility for the management of others. The following seem to me to be the most important lessons that need to be learned.

1 Give praise where praise is due

Supervisors often forget to praise staff when they do their jobs well. It's almost as if we expect our employees to perform at the highest level consistently and expect no less. Why praise someone just for doing their job? The same principle, of course, does not apply when people slip up or perform badly. Then the supervisor steps in and is quick to criticise. This is a tendency which all supervisors must guard against. We need to remember that most staff, especially the average performers, see themselves as being more effective employees than their bosses do. The majority of people, when asked, rate their own performance as being 'above average'. They therefore expect this to be recognised and are disappointed when it is not. If they then receive criticism on the occasions when they do perform poorly, it is seriously unappreciated. As a general rule, except in the case of genuinely poor performers, managers should try to praise at least twice as often as they criticise.

2 Avoid the perception of favouritism

Treating people fairly is a fundamental principle of effective supervision. Again it is a question of managers looking at what goes on, as far as possible, through the eyes of subordinates. Whatever their views about the relative merits of their team members and however much they personally like and trust some more than others, it is essential that they are not seen to be acting unfairly. Once the perception of favouritism is established it is difficult to regain the trust and support of those who believe they are being denied opportunities that are their due. Managers may succeed in motivating their apparent favourites, but they demotivate everyone else.

3 Talk to every team member regularly

Another common reason that supervisor–subordinate relationships deteriorate is simply a lack of contact and basic communication between the parties. Irrespective of whether they want to praise or criticise, it is above all necessary to notice staff, to show an interest in what they are doing and to give them feedback. Even when managers have nothing significant to say to their staff, they should make the effort to talk to them, ask them what they are doing and provide some kind of support. This goes equally for work-based and non-work-based activities. The alternative is the fostering of a distant relationship which works against the development of trust and loyalty. It is not necessary to be over-friendly or gushing in any way. It is just a question of ensuring that some kind of genuine relationship of mutual respect is established and continues over time.

4 Act when you suspect there are problems

It is very easy for busy supervisors who have important work of their own to do to 'act deaf' or 'turn a blind eye' when they believe their subordinates to be unhappy with some aspect of their work. Sometimes this means that small problems grow into very much bigger ones, making them far harder to deal with later on. The aim should always be to sort out difficulties at an early stage. This requires supervisors to make sure that they get to know their subordinates sufficiently well so that they can tell something is wrong from their body language and the tone of their voice. It may be a problem inside or outside of work. Either way, in many cases judicious and early intervention by a well-meaning supervisor can defuse such problems and serve to retain individuals for longer.

5 Give people as much autonomy as you possibly can

A view that it is pretty well unanimously shared by management researchers across all disciplines is the damaging effect of overly close supervision. This is particularly true of research into employee engagement. The effective supervisor should therefore minimise the extent to which their subordinates perceive themselves to be supervised at all. Wherever possible they should find ways of allowing staff the freedom to carry out their own work in the way that they want to. They should be encouraged to use their own judgement and to develop systems of working with which they are comfortable. Where standardisation across an organisation or part of an organisation is genuinely necessary, rules should be drawn up and agreed with the consent of the supervisees. The more highly qualified and experienced employees are, the more advantage is to be gained from allowing them the strongest possible measure of autonomy. Some management control usually needs to be exercised to ensure that an organisation achieves its objectives effectively, efficiently and fairly. But control for the sake of control is unhealthy and simply serves to make an organisation less effective.

6 Involve people in decision-making

As well as allowing people, and indeed encouraging them, to take responsibility for their own areas of work, good supervisors also involve staff in the decisions that they have to take themselves. This need not be done in a formal way. All that is usually required is to ask employees their views ahead of time. Doing so shows in a very direct way that each individual's contribution is valued and that management is carried out by consensus rather than by diktat. Involving people in decision-making also serves to boost their self-esteem, while failing to do so serves to depress, demotivate and promote disengagement. It is particularly important in my view to involve new staff as far as is possible. Asking someone who has just joined your team to contribute their views helps to build trust in the early weeks. However, involvement on an informal scale only works if it is genuine. Going through the motions for the sake of appearances may well actually make matters worse than if decisions are simply imposed from above. Pseudo-consultation builds mistrust and decreases engagement levels.

ADDRESSING INEFFECTIVE SUPERVISION

The chances of good supervision becoming a reality are greatly aided by the presence of appropriate policies and practices being in operation across whole organisations. The most important are as follows:

1 selecting supervisors, to a greater degree, on the basis of an assessment of their supervisory skills

2 providing training for supervisors (new, established or potential) in the skills of effective supervision

3 appraising supervisors, at least in part, on their capacity to supervise effectively – the use of 360-degree appraisal systems are particularly useful here.

However, a great deal more can be done too. It is mainly a question of putting in place policy which conspicuously backs up the principles of good supervision set out above and helps to make them part and parcel of an organisation's people management culture.

KEY LEARNING POINTS

- The term *employee engagement* is now very widely used in HRM. There remains some uncertainty about what exactly it means and much inconsistency in the way it is used.

- Employee engagement is best understood as a multidimensional concept which builds on and incorporates longer-established concepts such as motivation, commitment, job satisfaction and organisational citizenship behaviour.

- Employers and employees both benefit when levels of engagement are high. The gains are, however, of a different nature. Employers benefit economically while employees, in the main, benefit psychologically and through improved well-being.

- Research into the main drivers of employee engagement stress the significance of effective line management and of genuine employee involvement at the individual level.

- Evidence suggests that line management in many UK workplaces is very poor. It follows that there is a strong business case for taking steps to improve it.

EXPLORE FURTHER

By far the most informative and thorough publication to date on employee engagement is the report that David Macleod and Nicky Clarke wrote for the Department for Business in 2009.

Macleod, D. and Clarke, N. (2009) *Engaging for success: enhancing performance through employee engagement. A report to government*. London: Department for Business, Innovation and Skills.

Recent debate and research evidence on engagement is discussed effectively in *Employee engagement: a review of current thinking* by Gemma Robertson-Smith and Carl Markwick (2009).

Robertson-Smith, G. and Markwick, C. (2009) *Employee engagement: a review of current thinking*. Brighton: Institute for Employment Studies.

REFERENCES

Arkin, A. (2009) The Best policy. *People Management*. 1 January.

Black, C. (2008) *Working for a healthier tomorrow: review of the health of Britain's working age population*. London: The Stationery Office.

Buckingham, G. (2000) Same indifference. *People Management*. 17 February.

Buckingham, M. and Coffman, C. (1999) *First break all the rules: what the world's greatest managers do differently*. London: Simon & Schuster.

CIPD (2006) *Reflections on employee engagement*. London: Chartered Institute of Personnel and Development.

CMI (2011) *33 per cent of workers say their boss is totally incompetent*. London: Chartered Management Institute. Available at: www.managers.org.uk

Daniels, K. (2010) *Employee engagement*. Factsheet. London: Chartered Institute of Personnel and Development. Available at: www.cipd.co.uk

Harter, J., Schmidt, F.L. and Hayes, T.L. (2002) Business-unit-level relationship between employee satisfaction, employee engagement and business outcomes: a meta-analysis. *Journal of Applied Psychology*. Vol 87, No 2. pp268–279.

Kahn, W. (1990) Psychological conditions of personal engagement and disengagement at work. *Academy of Management Journal*. Vol 33. pp692–724.

Kim, H.J., Shin, K.H. and Swanger, N. (2009) Burnout and engagement: a comparative analysis using the Big Five personality dimensions. *International Journal of Hospitality Management*. Vol 28, No 1. pp96–104.

Langelaan, S., Bakker, A., Van Doornen, L. and Schaufeli, W. (2006) Burnout and work engagement: do individual differences make a difference? *Personality and Individual Differences*. Vol 40, No 1. pp521–532.

Leiter, M. and Bakker, A. (2010) Work engagement: introduction. In A. Bakker and M. Leiter (eds) *Work engagement: a handbook of essential theory and research*. New York: The Psychology Press.

Leiter, M. and Maslach, C. (2010) Building engagement: the design and evaluation of interventions. In A. Bakker and M. Leiter (eds) *Work engagement: a handbook of essential theory and research*. New York: The Psychology Press.

Macey, W. and Schneider, B. (2008) The meaning of employee engagement. *Industrial and Organizational Psychology*. Vol 1, No 1. pp3–30.

Macleod, D. and Brady, C. (2008) *The extra mile: how to engage your people to win*. London: FT/Prentice Hall.

Macleod, D. and Clarke, N. (2009) *Engaging for success: enhancing performance through employee engagement. A report to government*. London: Department for Business, Innovation and Skills.

May, D., Gilson, R. and Harter, L. (2004) The psychological conditions of meaningfulness, safety and availability and the engagement of the human spirit at work. *Journal of Occupational and Organizational Psychology*. Vol 77. pp11–37.

People Management (2011) Quarter of UK workers do not respect their manager. News item. *People Management*. 21 March.

Robinson, D., Perryman, S. and Hayday, S. (2004) *The drivers of employee engagement*. IES Report 408. Brighton: Institute for Employment Studies.

Saks, A. (2008) The meaning and bleeding of employee engagement: how muddy is the water? *Industrial and Organisational Psychology*. Vol 1. pp40–43.

Schaufeli, W. and Bakker, A. (2010) Defining and measuring work engagement: bringing clarity to the concept. In A. Bakker and M. Leiter (eds) *Work engagement: a handbook of essential theory and research*. New York: The Psychology Press.

Seligman, M. (2003) *Authentic happiness: using the new positive psychology to realize your potential for lasting fulfilment*. London: Nicholas Brealey.

Stairs, M. and Galpin, M. (2010) Positive engagement: from employee engagement to workplace happiness. In A. Linley, S. Harrington and N. Garcea (eds) *Oxford handbook of positive psychology and work*. Oxford: Oxford University Press.

Towers Perrin-ISR (2006) *The ISR employee engagement report*. London: Towers Perrin.

Truss, C., Soane, E., Edwards, C., Wisdom, K., Croll, A. and Burnett, J. (2006) *Working life: employee attitudes and engagement 2006*. London: Chartered Institute of Personnel and Development.

Waddell, G. and Burton, A. (2006) *Is work good for your health and well-being?* London: The Stationery Office.

CHAPTER 10

Managing knowledge and learning

Introduction

In Chapter 3, among other long-term trends, we looked at the changing nature of the jobs that people do in the UK. The major trend for several decades now has been a move away from lower-skilled manual work towards higher-skilled white-collar work of various kinds. In recent years the big growth areas in terms of jobs have been managerial, professional and technically complex roles – jobs which involve what is often referred to as 'knowledge work'. While there is some disagreement among commentators about the true extent of the trend towards jobs which require higher-level skills, the general direction of travel is not in dispute. Increased demand for people to carry out professional roles reflects the shift in the UK's industrial structure in recent decades as our manufacturing sector has declined in relative terms and our services sector has grown. Globalisation has required economies such as the UK's to adjust their activities. Increasingly we now import cheaper manufactured products, food and energy from regions of the world which are able to produce these cheaply. In return we sell back to them goods and particularly services. Hence the fastest growing sectors in the UK in recent years have been health, education, financial services, cultural industries, business services and design. Some areas of manufacturing have grown too. These have mainly been those which make use of cutting-edge technologies such as medicines and military equipment.

Brinkley and Lee (2006) estimate that 48% of the UK workforce is now employed in knowledge-based industries, the number having grown significantly over the past decades, and up from only 17% at the start of the twentieth century (see Storey and Quintas 2001: 346). In 2009, the Department for Children, Schools and Families (now the Department for Education) reported that for every one job created in the previous ten years in more traditional industries, 12 had been created in the knowledge sectors (DCSF 2009). Furthermore, most authorities are of the view that this established trend will continue and strengthen in the future. The Leitch Review (2006), in particular, stressed this point. Their research suggested that around 2.3 million new jobs would be created by 2020, but that *all* the growth would be at the upper end skills-wise. They predicted a net decline overall in demand for unskilled and lower-skilled people, famously suggesting that by 2020 around 40% of all jobs in the UK would require a degree. A result has been a renewed focus by government ministers on the development of an upskilling agenda, which we discussed in Chapter 4.

For some years now it has been generally accepted in the academic community that knowledge – an asset which is intangible and very hard to measure – has become a major determinant of an organisation's relative success. This is a consequence of the decline of our established 'industrial economy' and its replacement over time by an evolving 'post-industrial economy'. It follows that knowledge is increasingly central to wealth creation:

> In these environments, wealth creation is less dependent on the control of resources and more dependent on the exercise of specialist knowledge, or the management of organizational competences. We can no longer blame the mismanagement of tangible resources for failures in a knowledge-based society. We now need to turn our attention to the management of the intangible. Managerial systems remain important, but it is the management of intangible assets that is now argued to be at the heart of the managerial process. (Swart 2007: 450–451)

The aim of this chapter is to discuss the impact that these developments are having on HRM and, more importantly, are likely to continue having in the future. We are going to start with a discussion of human capital theories and explain why these are increasingly useful for HR managers to take on board as the number of employees carrying out knowledge work grows. We will then go on to explore the field of knowledge management and to discuss the prospects for the development of 'learning organisations'. We will finish the chapter with a brief, practical overview of what published research tells us about the best way to manage 'knowledge workers' if we are to successfully attract, retain, motivate and engage them more effectively than our competitors.

LEARNING OUTCOMES

The objectives of this chapter are to:

- explain what is meant by the term 'human capital'
- discuss ways in which HR managers can help organisations to invest in human capital efficiently and effectively
- introduce the field of knowledge management
- explore the idea of 'learning organisations'
- debate the ways in which people engaged in knowledge work are best managed.

HUMAN CAPITAL

Rather like the concept of the psychological contract, which we introduced in Chapter 8, human capital theory provides HR managers with a useful way of thinking about key parts of their job which is of great help when developing policy and practice to meet organisational needs in the contemporary business environment. The ideas that underpin it are not at all new, having been traced by a number of commentators back to the work of the eighteenth-century economist Adam Smith. But they have increasing practical resonance for organisations as a result of the increase in knowledge work. Credit for first recognising this development is often given to the Nobel Prize-winning economist Gary Becker, who published a seminal book entitled *Human capital* in 1964 and has, along with many others, continued to develop thinking in this area since then.

It is probably helpful if we start by thinking about the term *capital* and its significance to organisations. The term, as used by economists in this context, is neatly defined by Griffeths and Wall (2008: 92) as follows:

> *Any man-made asset which can be used in support of the production of further goods and services.*

The terms *asset* and *used* are key here. Capital comes in a variety of different forms, such as land, buildings, machinery, stocks of raw materials and finance (often described as 'working capital'). All of these are used by organisations in order to produce goods or services which have economic value. They are assets because they can be accounted for on the corporate balance sheet and can be used to value an organisation's net worth. In the case of a private company, the price at which it can be bought or sold will depend to a large extent on its 'capital value', namely the accumulated worth of its various forms of capital.

Another key feature of capital is the way that investment is required in order that it can be formed and enhanced. To produce goods and services, therefore, an organisation invests in capital assets (ie incurs costs) with a view to creating value and thus benefiting from returns. In the case of fixed capital such as buildings, plant and machinery, there is a need for regular investment in order to maintain or increase value. Upgrades and replacements are required from time to time to prevent these forms of capital from depreciating too quickly as a result of being intensively used. Organisations typically set aside money each year in the form of 'capital budgets' for this purpose.

Historically accountants, as well as economists, tended to focus exclusively on tangible assets when thinking about capital – that is, forms of capital that can be seen and measured with a high degree of accuracy. However, in more recent years there has been greater recognition of the part played by intangible assets in creating value, namely forms of capital that are not readily measured. In the corporate world these can be very significant indeed because they mean that the value of a company is often very much higher than what is known as the 'book value' of its tangible assets (ie the value of its land, buildings, machinery, equipment, stocks of raw materials and unsold products). Indeed, in some cases the lion's share of an organisation's worth is in the form of intangible rather than tangible assets. Frappaolo (2006: 4) gives some examples:

- 82% of the net worth of the General Electric corporation (GE) is estimated to be made up of non-tangible assets.

- In the case of Google, 98% of the overall capital value consists of intangible rather than tangible assets.

- When IBM bought Lotus for $3.5 billion in 1995, it paid 14 times more than the company's 'book value' (ie the value of its tangible assets.

Some brands (along with their accompanying trademarks and advertising slogans), for example, are so well known and so commercially lucrative that their value towers over the physical assets of the corporations that own them. Coca-Cola is an often quoted example, as is Google. Other forms of intangible assets that can have considerable value for organisations include patents, copyrights and trade secrets of various kinds (such as the recipe for Coca-Cola). Corporate reputation and the rather vague term *goodwill* represent other forms of intangible asset which need to be taken into account when valuing a company. Human capital, in the form of an organisation's people, can be seen as another form of intangible asset. The people themselves are not the asset, of course, but their collective knowledge, skills and experience most definitely can be.

Since the 1960s, and increasingly widely more recently, it has been accepted that human capital is just as significant a form of capital as far as many organisations are concerned as physical capital and financial or working capital. Moreover, we increasingly see the same language being used to describe our collective social assets. Economists write about 'the stock of human capital' that is available in a society, a region or a nation and debate how best government policy can be deployed in order to enhance the size or value of this stock.

Precise definitions of human capital vary, some being rather narrower in their scope than others. Some conceive it in terms of 'collective know-how', others more broadly to encompass the whole range of skills, experience, knowledge, values and attitudes that organisations may draw on in order to achieve their objectives. One of the clearest and most succinct definitions is provided by Morris et al (2005: 59). It refers to the private sector, but the basic components are as relevant to organisations in the public and voluntary sectors too:

> Human capital value is determined by the accumulated knowledge and skills of employees that enable a firm to enact strategies that improve efficiency and effectiveness, exploit market opportunities, and/or neutralise potential threats.

One influential formulation, originally developed by Stewart (1997), sees human capital as being part of a wider category that is labelled *intellectual capital*. There are two other forms of capital that combine with the human variety to create intellectual capital:

- *structural capital*, which encompasses the culture, routines and processes that organisations develop as well as their IT systems, networking and management processes and their overall strategies

- *relational capital*, which relates to all the relationships which organisations establish over time with customers, suppliers, industry bodies, government and regulatory agencies, investor communities and the public at large.

In this model, while human capital is presented as one of three key forms that together give an organisation its overall intellectual capital, the other two (structural and relational) are only made possible by the activities of people. So human capital is very much the linchpin. From a practical management perspective the model is useful because it reminds us that merely having at our disposal a stock of skills, knowledge and experience (ie human capital) is of no use at all. It needs to be actively engaged through effective people management so that the processes and relationships that deliver value for the organisation can be fully developed.

 CRITICAL REFLECTION

Different kinds of capital

In his recent book on the publishing industry, John Thompson (2010: 5) sets out what he calls a list of 'key resources of publishing firms':

- economic capital (the accumulated financial resources that publishers have access to such as stock, plant, equipment and capital reserves)
- human capital (the staff they employ and their accumulated knowledge, skills and expertise)
- social capital (networks of contacts built up over time)
- intellectual capital (the intellectual property rights, copyrights, etc, owned or controlled by the publisher)
- symbolic capital (prestige and status accumulated over time as a reputation is built up).

Think about your own organisation. To what extent does it have similar resources to draw on in the form of capital? How does your industry differ from publishing in this regard?

The idea that an organisation's employees, along with other people with whom it has some form of employment relationship (consultants, casual staff, etc), represent an asset rather than simply a cost is still an idea that some managers struggle to accept. But increasingly the language of capital is being used in the context of employment and staffing, and this has long been the case in larger organisations, particularly those which are knowledge-oriented in their activities.

The implications as far as human resource management is concerned are of fundamental significance because assets and capital have to be treated very differently from mere costs. Assets need to be maintained and their value enhanced. We invest in assets and only dispose of them and replace them when they cease to have a value to us. Hiring and employing 'human capital' thus involves a rather different type of managerial mindset than simply employing and hiring staff. Capital is something that we only purchase after careful consideration about its capacity to generate value in the future. We then take care to invest in it judiciously, to nurture it and only dispose of it after careful consideration. In the case of human capital this translates as investing time and resources in recruiting and selecting people, investing in their professional development and only dismissing them once it has become clear that their capacity to add value in the future is limited or non-existent.

Lengnick-Hall and Lengnick-Hall (2003: 54) argue strongly that HR managers should see themselves in today's business environment primarily as 'stewards of human capital', viewing their role in respect of human resources much in the same way as stewards were traditionally employed on large country estates to oversee and nurture natural assets:

> Stewardship metaphors are commonly used with natural resources, such as land, fish and forests. These metaphors focus on preserving, conserving, sustaining, growing and developing the natural resources. Furthermore, these metaphors focus on the future and on ensuring that the resources will be available and thriving beyond the current time horizon.

The case for seeing human assets as a form of capital is thus well made and very convincing. However, it is important to point out that this form of capital varies from others in a number of key respects. Most importantly, human capital cannot be controlled by an organisation in the way that physical capital such as land, machinery or buildings can be. People will always own their own know-how, skills and attributes and in the vast majority of cases (professional footballers being an exception), there is little an organisation can do to stop a human asset from leaving and taking with them the capital they carry around with them in their heads. The products of human endeavour can be owned and traded, but not the human capital itself. In practice, therefore, organisations lease human capital, but on terms which make it difficult for them to exercise full control over their assets. The way that human capital is managed thus has to be different. We have to be subtle, collaborative and emotionally intelligent in the approaches we use. This is why HRM is different from other forms of asset management and another reason why the metaphor of the steward is so helpful to employ.

HUMAN CAPITAL IN THE KNOWLEDGE ECONOMY

Thinking about human capital and how it can be most efficiently and effectively enhanced has developed in recent years as the Western industrialised economies have become more knowledge-oriented. Human capital is about much more than just knowledge; it encompasses all the attributes that people bring to an organisation, including all manner of skills, abilities and experiences. But as a concept human capital has a great deal more resonance in an organisation which employs people whose knowledge is central to its ability to meet its objectives than is the case in one where the employees' knowledge is of less overall significance. There are a number of reasons for this. First, as is pointed out by Burton-Jones and Spender (2011: 5), it is the case that human capital is simply 'of qualifiedly higher importance' in a knowledge economy than it is in one where most jobs do not require their holders to make use of much by way of specialised knowledge.

This point is best illustrated with an example. Take a firm of solicitors which employs dozens of people in a variety of roles, some of which are much more knowledge-intensive than others. The receptionist or security guard who sits at a desk by the entrance may well be a great asset to the firm because of their personality or attitude, but their knowledge is never going to be at all central to the ability of the firm to succeed commercially. By contrast, a senior partner in the firm who has 30 years of experience and is an acknowledged expert in an area of law is someone whose knowledge is likely to be central to the firm's success. Not only will such a person have significant technical knowledge, but over time he or she will also have developed long-term relationships with a range of clients and will have briefed barristers with whom further, close relationships will have been established. The partner's know-how thus encompasses the law itself, but also intimate understanding of the firm's customers and suppliers. Indeed, from the perspective of many clients and barristers, the individual partner *is* the firm to a great extent. They see themselves as interacting with him or her and not so much with the firm as a whole, because it is that individual with whom they deal.

Were the security guard to resign, the consequences for the firm would be at worst mildly irritating. A replacement would need to be recruited and trained at some cost, but no more damage would be sustained. By contrast, the loss of the senior partner would be many times more serious from a commercial point of view, simply because of the extent of the knowledge that would leave along with its owner. Were that individual to join a rival firm, this knowledge could then be deployed against the interests of the original firm. In addition, clients might well move over too so as to retain their long-term relationship with *their* solicitor.

This simple example illustrates how much more important human assets with relevant knowledge are to an organisation than those who do not have such knowledge. Viewed as human capital, the solicitor has vastly more value to the firm as an individual than the security guard has. The two examples here are at opposite ends of a continuum, but over time what is gradually happening is that more of us are moving into roles that are towards the end of the continuum represented by the solicitor. The more reliant organisations are on knowledge workers, the more resonance human capital theory and human capital thinking has.

Secondly, the more knowledge-intensive an economy becomes, the greater its complexity. It follows that the ability of an organisation to negotiate and weave its way through this complex world becomes increasingly central to its ability to compete. The world of financial services, for example, with its plethora of different instruments, investment vehicles, regulations, alongside its apparently impenetrable jargon is bewildering to most of us. The same is true of scientific work, engineering, legal work and even politics. These are fields in which only specialists with very considerable ability and experience can thrive. It follows that an organisation wishing to compete effectively needs to recruit, develop and subsequently retain people with the required knowledge. The more complex the environment becomes, the greater the premium on those people and the more important it becomes to see them as representing capital assets in whom the organisation needs to invest. No more is this true than of multinational organisations that operate globally in a variety of very different cultural settings. Internationalising an organisation generates vastly increased complexity and, if the outcome is to be successful, necessitates the recruitment and development of a cadre of people who have the required knowledge and understanding of these complexities. Ng et al (2011) give this the label 'cosmopolitan human capital' as a means of demonstrating the value that human capital thinking has for the management of complexity.

A third feature of the contemporary business environment which is knowledge-related and which is often judged to be giving human capital theory greater prominence is increased uncertainty and volatility. We discussed this in Chapter 2, where I pointed out that the unpredictable nature of many product markets is an inevitable consequence of increasing competitive intensity, the globalisation of markets and the acceleration of technological developments. Several researchers working in the field of human capital have observed that the more uncertain the business environment becomes, the more reliant organisations become on the good judgement of their people (eg Foss 2011 and Loasby 2011). Making the right decision becomes harder, and the number of situations in which strategic decisions must be made becomes more frequent. Similarly, volatility creates more situations in which people have to respond to unexpected and unprecedented sets of circumstances, and to do so in an innovative or creative way.

In short, the rarer and more crucial someone's skills or knowledge are to their employing organisation, and the longer it takes to acquire those skills, the more sense it makes from a management perspective to view them as assets: part of a body of human capital in which investments are made in order to secure additional value for the organisation. And as time goes by more and more of us are moving into posts which fit these criteria.

DIFFERENTIATING MODELS

Some of the most significant recent contributions to thinking about human capital have been those which differentiate between groups of people employed in organisations in terms of their capital worth. While over time the general movement is towards higher skills, at any one time most organisations employ a variety of personnel whose human capital value varies considerably. In a world in which resources for investment in the development of human capital is limited, it makes sense for organisations to identify where these resources are best directed in terms of the long-term returns they are likely to bring.

A straightforward and widely quoted model which helps achieve these aims is that of Lepak and Snell (1999). Drawing on the work of many other economists, their model focuses on two distinct dimensions of human capital. Firstly, they are concerned with 'human capital value', which they define as the amount of added value an employee or group of employees brings to an organisation. Secondly, they focus on 'human capital uniqueness', which is defined as being the extent to which a set of skills or a stock of knowledge is either specialised in nature or firm-specific in its nature. The more specialised human capital is, the harder an organisation has to compete to recruit and retain it. Firm-specific human capital is valued for a different reason. Because it relates only to what goes on in a particular organisation, its usefulness to competitors is limited. However, it may also be hard for others to imitate and thus be very valuable indeed in terms of its capacity to assist an organisation to maintain competitive advantage. An example of firm-specific human capital would be intimate knowledge of an organisation's procedures, culture and organisational politics.

Lepak and Snell combine these two dimensions to provide us with a two-by-two matrix. An adapted version of this is provided in Figure 10.1. The aim of the model is to provide a tool for managers to identify the groups of people they employ whose human capital is of most value to them with a view to concentrating their resources appropriately.

Figure 10.1 Typologies of human capital

High HC uniqueness **Low HC value** **ALLIANCE PARTNERS**	**High HC uniqueness** **High HC value** **CORE KNOWLEDGE EMPLOYEES**
Low HC uniqueness **Low HC value** **CONTRACT WORKERS**	**Low HC uniqueness** **High HC value** **TRADITIONAL EMPLOYEES**

Source: adapted from Lepak and Snell (1999)

The group in the top right quadrant are those whose human capital value is greatest or has the greatest potential. These people, labelled 'core knowledge employees', have knowledge and skills that rank highly both in terms of its value and in terms of its uniqueness. It is thus very much in the interests of the organisation to keep them for as long as possible and to invest in their development so as to increase the stock of valuable human capital that they provide. It makes sense that these people are employed and that long-term, high-trust relationships are established with them. Those in the quadrant below them, labelled 'traditional employees', also have a high capital value to the organisation. They have knowledge and skills which are relied on in order that key business objectives are met. Individuals in this group can, through exceptional performance, add considerable value, but this is not something that occurs inevitably as a result of the jobs that they do. Their knowledge and skills are not 'unique' in any way. In short, when they leave, they are readily replaceable. There is a case for investing somewhat in their development, but when resources are constrained priority should be given to the core knowledge workers in the quadrant above.

On the left-hand side are two groups whose human capital value, by comparison, is relatively low. The authors of the model thus propose that these people are not employed directly by the organisation, but that they are instead 'externalised'. However, the alliance partners in the top left quadrant are of greater value because their human capital scores highly in terms of its uniqueness. These are people whose skills or knowledge are 'not easy to find on the market' and which are required from time to time, but not continuously or frequently. Consultants, trainers and providers of professional services of various kinds are typical examples. According to Lepak and Snell, there is no case for an organisation which buys such services investing directly in the development of these people, but there is a strong case for investing in the maintenance and development of the relationship, so that high levels of trust are maintained and long-term productive collaboration is made possible. The final group have least to offer in terms of human capital value. They are labelled 'ancillary' because their skills and knowledge are neither of great value nor unique in any way. Lower-skilled workers mostly make up this group. Their skills are in plentiful supply and, while they are needed collectively to help meet organisational objectives, no individual makes a particularly valuable contribution. The authors of the model thus propose that they are employed as and when required on a contract basis.

Other models have also been proposed and refined, all being broadly similar in terms of their practical usefulness from a management point of view. Some authors have, for example, introduced the concept of 'industry-specific human capital' as a type which falls between the general and firm-specific categories, while others emphasise the importance of seeing human capital as dynamic in nature. Their models are more concerned with flows of human capital and also with increases and decreases in stocks of human capital. One way or another, all are concerned with identifying groups of people from whose development an employing organisation has most to gain over the long term. Many are associated with resource-based thinking of the kind that we will discuss in Chapter 13.

INVESTING IN HUMAN CAPITAL

Having identified where resources should be focused in order to maximise the benefits that are gained from investing in human capital, the next stage is to put in place HR practices through which that investment can fruitfully occur. The key here according to Lengnick-Hall and Lengnick-Hall (2003: 57) is to 'create both competence and commitment to the firm'. They suggest that there are five avenues through which these objectives can be achieved:

1   buying human capital (ie hiring talented individuals with the potential to add value)

2 building human capital (ie providing suitable training and development opportunities)

3 borrowing human capital (ie forming long-term partnerships with external advisers and consultants)

4 bouncing human capital (ie dismissing or engineering the resignations of low-performers)

5 binding human capital (ie retaining the most talented).

Lengnick-Hall and Lengnick-Hall (2003: 65–66) go on to discuss the ways in which the 'human capital steward', namely the HR manager, can go about trying to 'leverage' human capital in order to maximise its value. They suggest that the following methods have most to offer:

- Concentrating human capital by focusing available resources more effectively on the achievement of key strategic goals: this involves using tools such as performance appraisal to agree objectives with staff which prioritise the organisation's major current objectives.

- Accumulating human capital by recruiting new employees and also by developing long-term and productive external relationships with people who have a contribution to make to building stocks of human capital: external trainers are a good example.

- Complementing human capital by designing jobs, selecting people for project teams and introducing technologies which serve to enhance individual contributions.

- Enhancing human capital by improving the extent and quality of knowledge: this is mainly achieved through a variety of developmental interventions.

- Conserving human capital by ensuring that the efforts of key groups are not 'wasted' on low-value-adding activities: tasks need to be allocated so that the core knowledge workers spend as much of their time and effort as possible doing things which they are best qualified to do. Support staff need to be employed to pick up other duties.

- Recovering human capital by speeding up the rate at which new staff and newly promoted staff are working at full capacity: induction and socialisation processes are central here as are formal developmental activities aimed, for example, at speeding up the rate at which someone becomes more proficient at using new technologies.

KNOWLEDGE MANAGEMENT

In a post-industrial, knowledge economy, the extent and quality of the knowledge that an organisation has and is able to make use of plays a major part in determining its relative performance. For some, such as the renowned management guru Peter Drucker, knowledge is now absolutely central to an organisation's chances of succeeding:

Knowledge has become the key economic resource and the dominant – and perhaps the only – source of competitive advantage. (Drucker 1995: 271)

Laudon and Starbuck (1997: 299) agree, suggesting that in a post-industrial economy most, if not almost all, jobs involve some kind of knowledge-based activity:

- people who process or preserve data
- people who interpret information and act upon it
- people who generate new information
- people who apply accumulated knowledge.

Others are less accepting of the idea that knowledge has now become quite such a crucial factor for organisations. Hislop (2009: 6), for example, is critical of the idea that 'all work is knowledge work', arguing that many jobs in the service sector cannot properly be characterised in this way. In fact, in many cases (office cleaning, jobs in fast food restaurants, security) jobs that have become more common in recent years are 'low-skilled, repetitive and routine'. A certain amount of knowledge is required to carry them out, but no more than is required by workers in traditional manufacturing, mining or agricultural jobs, and possibly rather less. He argues that the term *knowledge-intensive work* is more useful because, while being somewhat vague, it focuses attention on occupations which involve extensive 'creation and use of knowledge'. It is these which are growing particularly rapidly at present and which are occupied by people who can reasonably be described as being 'knowledge workers'. When seen from an HR management perspective it is this group which present particular challenges and who perhaps have to be managed in a qualitatively different way from people whose work is not knowledge-intensive in nature.

While arguments about definitions will undoubtedly continue, all agree that we are living through a period in which the number of organisations which are reliant on 'knowledge' in order to achieve their objectives is increasing along with the proportion of us who are engaged in knowledge work of one kind or another. Of course there is a continuum ranging from work which is very knowledge-intensive in nature (eg lawyers, engineers, architects, etc) to that which is largely unskilled but which requires job-holders to make use of a limited amount of specialised knowledge. What is significant is that over time there is a movement occurring along this continuum in the direction of more knowledge-intensive occupations.

It follows that an organisation – particularly one that is operating in a knowledge-intensive sector – has much to gain from seeking to manage knowledge proactively. As most knowledge exists only in the heads of employees, this is no easy task. In particular there is the problem we identified above in our discussion of human capital that organisations cannot own their employees' minds. People can, if they want to, keep their knowledge to themselves rather than choosing to share it with others. In addition, of course, their knowledge leaves with them when they move on from the organisation.

In large part knowledge management concerns trying to find ways of tackling these two problems. On the one hand, it involves encouraging people to share useful knowledge with one another so that the total stock of knowledge available to the organisation grows. Sharing knowledge is also one way of helping to ensure that it remains in the organisation when people leave, but other more formal approaches are also used to help ensure that this occurs. A further aspect of knowledge management is the creation of useful knowledge and its dissemination around the organisation to those whose ability to achieve their objectives benefit as a result. These processes will occur in any organisation spontaneously and informally in any event. Knowledge management involves managers trying to exercise a degree of control over the process with a view to enhancing and improving it.

TYPES OF KNOWLEDGE

At the heart of most debates and research about the practicalities of knowledge management is a distinction between two different types of knowledge which has relevance for an organisation:

1 Explicit knowledge
Explicit forms of knowledge are those which can be readily identified. The material contained in this book and which you are reading now is a good example, as is any form of idea or information that can be readily communicated either in writing, via some other form of media or face to face in a lecture or training event. Explicit knowledge can also be measured to an extent. For example, organisations can maintain databases on who has completed certain training courses and which of their staff have particular qualifications, etc.

2 Tacit knowledge
Tacit knowledge, by contrast, is rather harder to define. Nonaka and Takeuchi (1995) state that it comprises 'subjective insights, intuitions and hunches', while Holbeche (1999) sees it as consisting of 'intangibles such as know-how, information on stakeholder relationships, experiences and ideas'. Micklethwait and Wooldridge (1996: 143) define it more colloquially as follows:

> *The informal, occupational lore generated by workers grappling with everyday problems and passed on in cafeterias, not the official rules written down in company manuals and transmitted in compulsory training sessions.*

In short, it is the kind of knowledge which we all pick up over time working in any organisation which is useful to us in our jobs but which is not conveyed to us formally in any organised way.

The distinction between explicit and tacit knowledge is fundamentally important in theories about knowledge management because of the different approaches that have to be adopted when trying to manage the creation and sharing of the two forms. In short, it is much easier to manage explicit knowledge than is the case with tacit knowledge. Yet it is now widely recognised that tacit knowledge is as important, if not more important, in terms of its influence on organisational learning than explicit knowledge.

It is also the case that explicit knowledge often starts out as tacit knowledge. A brilliant business idea may, for example, originate as a hunch. It is then shared informally with colleagues who assess its possibilities and bring their experience to bear on it. After this it is raised more formally and discussed at formal meetings before being developed further. At some stage in the process it becomes explicit knowledge, but it did not start out that way.

Another important distinction needs to be made between knowledge which is held by individuals and that which is collective in nature. Of course, in strictly scientific terms, knowledge can only exist within a person's head and must therefore be individual in nature. But it is also true that knowledge is shared across a group of people collectively and that groups also create knowledge collectively through discussion and the development of approaches to work which evolve over time. Recent research has tended to focus on shared knowledge of this kind, the concept of 'communities of practice' being the major way in which theory has been translated into practice.

Hislop (2009: 10) defines these as 'informal groups of people who have some work related activity in common'. They may work for the same organisation, but they just as often comprise members of the same profession who work for different organisations, networks of people which evolve over time and through which knowledge along with values and attitudes get shared. There is no formal membership of a community of practice, and no hierarchy. People come and go all the time and engage at different levels and in different ways. For this reason the community can reasonably be said to have an identity which is separate from the people who make up its rather loose membership at any one time, and hence that the community has its own 'knowledge base.'

FORMAL KNOWLEDGE MANAGEMENT INITIATIVES

Some organisations in knowledge-intensive industries now take the whole process of knowledge management very seriously, treating it as a strategic activity which is central to their operations. Job titles such as 'knowledge engineer', 'knowledge analyst' and 'chief knowledge officer' have become common (Frappaolo 2006: 58–59), alongside substantial investment in IT systems which are designed to improve organisational knowledge. Grant et al (2010) give the following examples:

- Knowledge repositories act like electronic libraries, which contain documents and search engines which allow staff to locate information they need quickly. Wiki-type features also allow people to add and amend these so as to provide colleagues with further potential knowledge.
- Case-based reasoning (CBR) is an approach to problem-solving which makes use of the experience of handling similar past cases. Individuals use the approach all the time. CBR software provides a method for this type of knowledge to be shared across an organisation so that it is available to everyone irrespective of whether or not they have personally handled a similar case before. In its simplest form it works by asking staff to record their

experiences and then makes this information available electronically across the organisation. The more sophisticated systems present their users with information automatically when they carry out certain procedures. Hence a salesperson dealing with a customer enquiry (eg a travel agent booking flights and hotels) will be provided with prompts on their screens which let them know about other agents' experiences of dealing with similar enquiries.

- Expert listings are directories of staff with contact details and information about their areas of expert knowledge (sometimes described as a 'corporate yellow pages'). Colleagues can then email or call them for assistance with issues and problems, drawing on their knowledge and experience in the process. Systems of this kind are particularly useful in larger, multinational organisations with large numbers of experts based at different locations around the world.

- Discussion forums are also electronic most of the time these days. These allow staff to ask for advice about a situation which anyone with access to the relevant intranet pages can then reply to, hence placing their knowledge at the disposal of a colleague.

To these can be added more traditional ways of conveying knowledge around an organisation such as through training events, seminars, conferences and briefing sessions. All of these can also be e-enabled to make them available to a wider range of colleagues.

INFORMAL KNOWLEDGE MANAGEMENT INITIATIVES

A great deal of knowledge is transmitted informally between colleagues and others who we come into contact with during our work. Often we learn as much at social events or in discussions that take place over a drink after a formal presentation has been given than we do at the presentation itself. This occurs because the situation is more intimate and relaxed and because specific questions can be asked and requests for elaboration made much more easily than in a formal setting. Information exchange is also two-way or three-way, rather than one-way, so all parties benefit and this makes people more inclined to share their ideas and experiences.

Recently I was asked to travel to China for a week to teach a group of students about HRM in the UK. I had never been to China before and had little idea about what to expect or about what I should do preparation-wise in order to help ensure that I was able to provide the best possible learning experience for the students. A number of formal meetings were held ahead of the trip at which the teaching team discussed the content of the courses and the teaching methods that we would use. These were useful, but not nearly as useful from a learning point of view as a conversation I struck up with a colleague who I did not know very well at another colleague's retirement party. I learned much more about what to expect, how to prepare and how to plan the trip from this encounter over a glass or two of wine than I gained from several formal meetings. Had I not happened to go to that party and met this person, the quality of my teaching in China would have been a great deal less satisfactory.

HR managers cannot force people to share tacit knowledge of this kind, but they should recognise its significance for the organisation and take steps to provide opportunities for knowledge-sharing of this kind. Not everyone will take advantage, but some will, and the organisation ultimately benefits as a result. Opportunities to create and share knowledge are provided by job rotation schemes, for example, and by secondments to other divisions in an organisation. The effect is to stimulate employees, to broaden their experience and to facilitate new thinking about familiar issues. Much knowledge is also gained and shared through interdisciplinary teamworking, through mentoring and attendance at training events which include participants from different branches of the business.

We also pick up valuable tacit knowledge alongside explicit knowledge at conferences and external training events. Here too it is through socialising, networking and participating in recreational activities outside the formal proceedings of the event that we pick up the most useful knowledge. Often it may just be a nugget or the germ of an idea that subsequently develops in our heads and grows into something much more substantial. There is thus much to be gained from encouraging employees to engage with their professions outside the organisation and a good case too for funding such activities. Moreover, particularly when it is quite costly (eg attending an overseas event), it makes sense to ask the employee to brief colleagues both formally and informally about what they have learned on their return.

A perennial problem that many organisations face when trying to encourage sharing of knowledge among colleagues is a tendency for people to resist and to hoard their knowledge by keeping it to themselves. This is a widely recognised phenomenon which researchers in the knowledge management field have written a great deal about. It happens quite naturally simply because 'knowledge is power' in many organisational settings, meaning that we tend to perceive that our position and influence will be diminished if we share our precious knowledge too widely among our colleagues. This is particularly true of longer-serving and highly experienced staff who fear that they may be eclipsed by newer, but less experienced, colleagues if they are too generous in sharing their knowledge.

There is no easy solution to this problem, not least because while we all know it happens, it is difficult to prove and pin down. While it may be damaging to the organisation, we can hardly label knowledge-hoarding as some kind of disciplinary offence. The long-term response of the HR manager seeking to encourage knowledge-sharing must thus be to try to encourage the creation of a high-trust culture, for example by maximising job security and ensuring that people perceive that they have a stake in the organisation's success. Shorter-term initiatives can include making specific reference to the sharing of knowledge and experience during formal appraisals. Colleagues can be asked about what they have learned from each other and the tendency to share can then be acknowledged and rewarded.

CONTINGENCY-BASED APPROACHES TO KNOWLEDGE MANAGEMENT

The following article was published in *People Management* on 17 February 2000. You can download it from the CIPD website.

'Insight track' by Nancy Dixon

This article is now more than ten years old but its key messages are very relevant for organisations today. It is notable for including an example of an organisation in which knowledge management initiatives have failed as well as another – Ford – which has enjoyed greater success. Nancy Dixon explores why this was the case and

makes some very sound points in the process.

Questions

1 What do you think would have happened if the company Nancy Dixon calls FastTech had adopted the approach to knowledge management used in Ford?

2 What about Ford using the approaches used by FastTech?

3 What could your organisation learn from the framework that Nancy Dixon develops at the end of her article?

LEARNING ORGANISATIONS

The term *learning* differs from *knowledge* in that it implies understanding and interpretation as well as merely knowing things. It is through learning that we give meaning to our knowledge. This is important because it allows us to make better decisions and also to avoid making the same past mistakes when faced with a similar set of conditions.

In recent years a great deal has been written about 'organisational learning', much of which is highly theoretical in nature and beyond the scope of this book (see Jashapara 2011 for an excellent critical summary). Central to this body of literature is the contention that organisations can 'learn' and that they can benefit in important ways from doing so. As was the case above in our discussion of communities of practice and of knowledge held at the organisational level, many argue that it is entirely plausible to think about learning as being collective in nature, existing beyond the level of the individual. People come and go from organisations, bringing learning with them which they contribute and taking it away with them when they leave. But there remains a body of learning which resides collectively in an organisation, and which builds up over time, irrespective of which particular individuals are employed at any one time. Just as organisations can be said to have identifiable cultures which survive and evolve over time, so they can be said to hold a body of learning which informs decision-making and can sometimes explain an organisation's response to developments in its environment.

A related and very useful concept is that of *organisational memory*, which refers to the stock of stories and understandings about past experiences that tend to be built up and shared across an organisation. Over time we tend to build up a collective understanding of what happened in the past and why, even though as individuals we were not necessarily present at the right place or right time to have shared in the experience. The more striking organisational memories are about specific episodes or people. They may be good or bad; what matters is that we are able to draw on them and learn their lessons to improve decision-making today.

Argyris and Schon (1978) developed a theory of 'single loop', 'double loop' and 'triple loop' learning which has considerable relevance for learning at the organisational level. They defined single loop learning as learning about how to do things better. We learn from our experiences, but stick with the same objectives, trying to improve on what we did before. Double loop learning, by contrast, involves rethinking the objectives in response to past experience and trying to achieve the same things differently. Finally, triple loop learning involves questioning our original objectives. These latter two approaches to learning are more easily achieved by a group than by an individual because they involve challenging preconceptions and thinking about new ways of doing things. We achieve this by questioning, debating and arguing. According to many, the more diverse a group is in terms of its make-up, the more likely it is that an organisation will engage in meaningful double and triple loop learning.

A recent development in this field is the idea that an organisation can improve its operation over the long term if it becomes *a learning organisation*. This term is widely used by HR managers and consultants and has been developed somewhat in the academic literature. However, like employer branding and total reward (see Chapter 8), it is an under-researched idea and one which is still in its infancy as an HR management tool. In short, there is no extensive body of research into whether or not learning organisations achieve more than others, or indeed about whether many learning organisations yet exist at all. Yet the idea has considerable attractions for managers who aim to increase their organisation's capacity for effective learning.

For practical purposes, the idea of a learning organisation is probably best seen as a rather vague aspiration. The term is too woolly and inexactly defined to allow us to label any organisation as having successfully achieved the status of a learning organisation, but that does not mean to say that in knowledge-intensive organisations, in particular, moving in this direction will not bring considerable benefits.

The first use of the term *learning organisation* is generally attributed to the American academic Peter Senge (1990: 3), who tried to define it in his influential book *The fifth discipline*. His definition was as follows:

> *Organisations where people continually expand their capacity to create the results they truly desire, where new and expansive patterns of thinking are nurtured, where collective aspiration is set free, and where people are continually learning to see the whole together.*

Senge (1990) went on to elaborate on his rather evangelical definition by setting out in more detail some of the features that he associates with learning organisations. These include a capacity for 'team learning' driven by discussion and dialogue, 'systems thinking' involving an acceptance of complexity and the need to avoid simplistic frameworks of understanding, and 'shared vision' in respect of the organisation's future direction.

A rather more grounded and practically worded definition was advanced by Pedler et al (1991: 1):

> It can only happen as a result of learning at the whole organisation level. A learning company is an organisation that facilitates the learning of all its members and continuously transforms itself.

Their framework contains 11 specific characteristics that are shared by learning organisations. These include:

- an approach to strategy-making which makes use of learning processes
- participative policy-making involving 'all organisational members'
- the use of IT to disseminate information widely and 'tolerance' on the part of managers as to how it is interpreted and used
- constant, open dialogue between employees
- structures which provide opportunities for development at all levels and reward people for learning
- openness and receptivity to ideas from outside the organisation.

All of this is quite idealistic in its tone. These authors are advocating an approach to management which is very open and participative indeed, in which information about the organisation is shared among everyone and in which managers are very relaxed about having their visions and decisions questioned by other staff. The use of the term *organisation member* instead of *employee* or *staff member* itself suggests a type of organisation which lacks hierarchy and has little by way of any power structures. The literature on learning organisations can thus be criticised for being unrealistic in its assumptions about what is achievable, describing an ideal state in which decision-making is democratic and in which all are fully engaged and working together to improve the organisation's performance through collective learning.

This idealistic and somewhat unreal side to thinking about learning organisations is easy to criticise, but that does not mean that the vision has nothing to teach us or that the underpinning ideas do not have considerable merit. This is particularly true of organisations which are seriously knowledge-intensive and which are staffed by highly qualified people who are doing work which they enjoy and are genuinely committed to. I also think that the idea has much to offer departmental/divisional managers who are responsible for teams of knowledge workers. In such situations democratic styles of management which encourage collective self-criticism alongside experimental thinking and debate about future strategies and decisions will often be highly productive. The reason is simple. If you have assembled together a team of people who are all well qualified to contribute to decision-making, it makes sense to involve them actively. Managers who deny their teams a role in deciding what happens next on the basis of their expertise and experience not only tend to make ill-informed decisions, but also often demotivate their people in the process.

There has for some time now been a thriving debate among HR managers, consultants and researchers about the extent to which an employee who is engaged in knowledge-intensive types of work should be managed differently from what we might call 'traditional employees'. In part, this debate is an extension of the one I referred to above about whether or not pretty well all jobs can now be said to involve 'knowledge work'. People who take the view that they do and who thus define 'knowledge work' broadly naturally tend to disagree with the idea that there is an elite group of people whose work is so distinct that they require a different style of management in order to be effective.

It is easy to be side-tracked into debates of this kind which are primarily about definitions. From a practical management perspective, it is clear that there is no clearly defined boundary which separates knowledge workers from non-knowledge workers. The truth is that there is a range. It is also true that many jobs which are neither particularly well paid nor filled only by graduates require a reasonably high degree of knowledge to perform well. That does not, however, preclude the idea that there is at one end of the continuum a substantial and growing category of employees whose work is very knowledge-intensive and who for various compelling reasons are best managed differently from other groups. We are talking here about people whose roles require them to have serious expertise in a particular field and who do more than simply apply received knowledge. They also create new knowledge, interpret it in different ways, are required to explain it to others and also often have to operate in conditions of uncertainty or ambiguity. Swart (2007: 452) provides the following, succinct definition:

> Knowledge workers can be defined as employees who apply their valuable knowledge and skills (developed through experience) to complex, novel and abstract problems in environments that provide rich collective knowledge and relational resources.

Moynagh and Worsley (2005: 29) extend this approach slightly by making specific reference to the growth of the 'aesthetic economy' in which a capacity for creativity in addition to specialised knowledge is central.

So we are talking here about traditional professions (lawyers, doctors, architects, scientists, teachers, engineers, etc) as well as members of newer professions (management consultants, software engineers, PR specialists – even HR people), people engaged in creative work (in TV, film and design) and managers working in these industries. All of these groups can properly be described as carrying out knowledge-intensive work for most of their working weeks, particularly at more senior levels.

WHAT MAKES KNOWLEDGE WORKERS DIFFERENT?

From an HR perspective, the most important way in which many knowledge workers differ from others is their relatively strong labour market position. Knowledge workers tend to have specialised skills which are in short supply. When combined with experience, these skills make them attractive to employers. Their skills are often also very valuable to employers, being central to their ability to meet their objectives and to be successful. Moreover, it is often the case that knowledge workers bring with them to their jobs established relationships with other parties (customers, suppliers, opinion-formers, regulators, etc), which make them more attractive still from an employer's perspective. We can sum this up by stating that knowledge workers bring with them to their employment a good deal of human capital.

The net result is that knowledge workers tend to be harder to recruit and harder to retain. They have choices about who they work for and are thus able to demand high rates of pay and attractive terms and conditions of employment. Great care has to be taken to manage them effectively and sensitively.

Secondly, knowledge workers tend to have a particular need to keep their knowledge and skills up to date. A failure to do this makes them a good deal less employable. This means that they require developmental opportunities from their own employers. It also means that they are usually active members of professional groups and networks outside the organisation (ie communities of practice) which they rely on in order to keep their know-how current. Many see themselves first and foremost as members of a profession and only after that as employees of a particular organisation. Loyalties are thus split and it is inevitably harder for managers to exercise control over them. Knowledge workers have many places to turn for advice and are also quite capable of articulating alternative views to those which are orthodox at management level in an organisation.

Finally, knowledge workers tend to choose their professions because they are genuinely and passionately interested in their work. They are intrinsically motivated, keen to develop further and likely to thrive when given challenging tasks to perform. They typically work long hours and want to do their jobs well. Indeed, some researchers have noted a trend for knowledge workers to be keener on quality enhancement than their managers are, creating tension over standards of work that run in a different direction than is usually the case. Being pushed by managers into cutting corners and producing work which is 'sub-perfect' can also be a major source of dissatisfaction (Kusnet 2008).

HRM AND KNOWLEDGE WORK

The first point to make here is that managing knowledge workers is harder than managing typical employees because they are both more able and more willing to resist management actions when they disagree with them. They also tend to have knowledge of their industries greater than or at least equal to that of their managers. They will thus be sceptical, if not hostile, towards managers who seem to them to be basing decisions on an inaccurate or insufficient understanding. In short, managers have to earn their respect and can quickly lose it if they make avoidable mistakes.

There is thus an overwhelming need to adopt a management style which is democratic, consultative and participative. Failing to do so with teams of knowledge workers leads to cynicism, disrespect and a lack of co-operation. Involving knowledge workers in decision-making, particularly when the decisions affect their own areas of work, is thus essential. Moreover, the involvement must be genuine. Too often managers think they can get away with pseudo-consultation involving going through the motions but, ultimately, doing so with no intention of adjusting the original plan. This breeds further cynicism and is counterproductive. Indeed, in many situations the less management to which knowledge workers are subjected, the more effectively they will perform.

The second key point to make is that sophisticated HR practices and processes need to be in place if an organisation is to be successful at recruiting, retaining and engaging knowledge workers. Use of what have been described as 'asinine' approaches to performance management (ie only carrots and sticks) are unlikely to work well. Knowledge workers like and expect to be managed as individuals. Each will have his or her own motivations and ambitions, and so general assumptions about these should be avoided. This is particularly true when it comes to developmental matters. Managers need to avoid standardising what they provide. Each knowledge worker will have his or her own current priorities and these need to be satisfied as far as is possible.

When it comes to selection, it is important to consider what personality attributes make someone a productive knowledge worker in addition to the obvious need to have the required knowledge in the first place. Just as it is often argued that the possession of a good bedside manner is as important for doctors as their medical know-how, it is true generally that some kinds of knowledge work are best performed by people who have an open, collaborative attitude. As I explained above, the biggest problem facing organisations seeking to 'manage knowledge' and enhance collective learning is the tendency for people to hoard their knowledge rather than to share it. Hansen et al (1999: 107) in a highly influential article suggested that two strategies are available to managers seeking to promote knowledge-sharing. The first is labelled *codification* and it involves requiring or encouraging staff to store knowledge for future use by others using databases of various kinds. The other, which they call *personalisation*, involves encouraging sharing of knowledge directly with colleagues. When an organisation wishes to pursue this second approach, it is important that it employs personable people who are generous in nature and happy to share their thinking and expertise with colleagues.

The final point to make about managing knowledge workers brings us back to our original discussions about human capital and knowledge management and builds on this last point. It is in the interests of the organisation to create an environment in which knowledge workers are both willing and able to co-operate and, importantly, to share their knowledge with one another. Not only does this serve to increase the stock of organisational knowledge, but it also facilitates the creation of new knowledge and of new interpretations that can be of immense long-term value. It follows that teamworking is highly appropriate, projects being entrusted to groups of employees who are left to get on with the job without too much supervision, and certainly not unnecessary supervision.

Newell et al (2009) have developed a general set of points about the management of knowledge workers which involves managers promoting what they call 'an enabling context'. By this they mean organisational structures, cultures and HR practices which promote knowledge-sharing, creation and integration. They make a good case for the use of a wide range of enablers, summarised as follows:

> *Organisational culture, time, diversity, autonomy, shared identity, shared perspectives, trust, social networking, boundary spanning, boundary objects are all crucial enablers.*

Some of these require no explanation as they are so obvious, such as giving people time to share knowledge or building up shared perspectives. The term *boundary spanning* refers to situations in which we share knowledge across barriers that tend to exist in organisations between work groups, departments or teams based in different locations. Newell et al (2009) identify the key role played by 'boundary spanners' – people who actively try to develop relationships across these boundaries. Such behaviours can be encouraged by managers using performance appraisal and reward systems, as well as through HRD interventions. 'Boundary objects' are barriers that tend to exist between social groups in organisations which serve to prevent collaboration. They often operate subtly and are only apparent to people working within the groups. The use of shared language and jargon, for example, can act as an effective 'boundary object' which gets in the way of knowledge transfer around an organisation. The manager's role is to spot these and to reduce their impact, while at the same time ensuring that productive teams of colleagues remain intact.

KEY ARTICLE

FRIENDSHIP AT WORK

The following article was published in *People Management* on 30 March 2011. You can download it from the CIPD website.

'Organisational learning: the social network' by Alexander Fliaster

In this article the author argues in favour of a shift in emphasis from facilitating individual development as a means of fostering creativity in organisations to fostering the development of friendships between colleagues. This is the most effective way, according to his research, of encouraging people to come up with new ideas, to share their thinking and to give one another advice.

Questions

1 How convincing do you find the central argument made in the article that relationships are more important than individuals when it comes to creating and exploiting knowledge?

2 Why is friendship the most effective way of overcoming the 'structural holes' that Fliaster identifies?

3 To what extent would your organisation (or department) benefit from more out-of-work activity aimed at fostering friendships and why?

- The idea of 'human capital' has been one of the most influential and significant to emerge and be developed in HRM in recent years.

- There are strong arguments in favour of the proposition that HR managers should perceive themselves as being stewards of human capital.

- As the number of knowledge-intensive organisations has grown, so has the priority given to formal and informal knowledge management initiatives.

- It is important to grasp the distinction between 'explicit' and 'tacit' knowledge when considering how to encourage the creation and sharing of knowledge in an organisation.

- The field of organisational learning has grown and deepened greatly in recent years. While controversial, the ideal of 'learning organisations' has an important contribution to make to HR work.

- There is a good case in favour of the proposition that people whose work is especially knowledge-intensive should be managed in a subtler and more participative way if their organisations are to compete effectively over the long term.

EXPLORE FURTHER

Mark and Cynthia Lengnick-Hall's (2003) book on human capital is a good, readable introduction that deals with the practical as well as the theoretical issues most effectively.

Lengnick-Hall, M. and Lengnick-Hall, C. (2003) *Human resource management in the knowledge economy: new challenges, new roles new capabilities*. San Francisco: Berrett-Koehler.

Two good, general introductions to knowledge management are provided in the books by Alvesson (2004) and Dalkir (2005).

Dalkir, K. (2005) *Knowledge management in theory and practice*. Burlington, MA: Elsevier.

Alvesson, M. (2004) *Knowledge work and knowledge intensive firms*. Oxford: Oxford University Press.

REFERENCES

Argyris, C. and Schon, D. (1978) *Organisational learning*. Reading: Addison-Wesley.

Brinkley, I. and Lee, N. (2006) The knowledge economy in Europe. London: The Work Foundation.

Burton-Jones, A. and Spender, J.-C. (2011) Introduction. In A. Burton-Jones and J.-C. Spender (eds) *The Oxford handbook of human capital.* Oxford: Oxford University Press.

Department for Children, Schools and Families (2009) *14–19 briefing: making change happen.* www.dcsf.gov.uk/14-19.

Dixon, N. (2000) Insight track. *People Management.* 17 February.

Drucker, P.F. (1995) *Managing in a time of great change.* New York: Truman Talley Books/Dutton.

Fliaster, A. (2011) Organisational learning: the social network. *People Management.* 30 March.

Foss, N. (2011) Human capital and transaction cost economics. In A. Burton-Jones and J.-C. Spender (eds) *The Oxford handbook of human capital.* Oxford: Oxford University Press.

Frappaolo, C. (2006) *Knowledge management.* Chichester: Capstone Publishing.

Grant, K., Hackney, R. and Edgar, D. (2010) *Strategic information systems management.* Andover: Cengage.

Griffeths, A. and Wall, S. (2008) *Economics for business and management.* 2nd edition. London: FT/Prentice Hall.

Hansen, M., Nohria, N. and Tierney, T. (1999) What's your strategy for managing knowledge? *Harvard Business Review.* Vol 77, No 2. pp106–117.

Hislop, D. (2009) *Knowledge management in organisations.* 2nd edition. Oxford: Oxford University Press.

Holbeche, L. (1999) *Aligning human resources and business strategy.* London: Butterworth-Heinemann.

Jashapara, A. (2011) *Knowledge management: an integrated approach.* London: FT/Prentice Hall.

Kusnet, D. (2008) *Love the work, hate the job.* Hoboken, NJ: Wiley.

Laudon, K. and Starbuck, W. (1997) Organizational information and knowledge. In A. Sorge and M. Warner (eds) *The IEBM handbook of organizational behaviour.* London: Thomson Learning.

Leitch, S. (2006) *Prosperity for all in the global economy – world class skills. Final report. The Leitch review of skills.* London: HM Treasury.

Lengnick-Hall, M. and Lengnick-Hall, C. (2003) *Human resource management in the knowledge economy: new challenges, new roles new capabilities.* San Francisco: Berrett-Koehler.

Lepak, D. and Snell, S. (1999) The human resource architecture: toward a theory of human capital allocation and development. *Academy of Management Review.* Vol 24. pp31–48.

Loasby, B. (2011) Human capital, entrepreneurship and the theory of the firm. In A. Burton-Jones and J.-C. Spender (eds) *The Oxford handbook of human capital*. Oxford: Oxford University Press.

Micklethwait, J. and Wooldridge, A. (1996) *The witch doctors*. London: Heinemann

Morris, S., Snell, S. and Lepak, D. (2005) An architectural approach to managing knowledge stocks and flows. In R.J. Burke and C. Cooper (eds) *Reinventing HRM: challenges and new directions*. London: Routledge.

Moynagh, M. and Worsley, R. (2005) *Working in the twenty-first century*. Leeds: ESRC/The Tomorrow Project.

Newell, S., Robertson, M., Scarbrough, H. and Swan, J. (2009) *Managing knowledge work and innovation*. 2nd edition. Basingstoke: Palgrave.

Ng, K.-Y., Tan, M.L. and Ang, S. (2011) Global culture capital and cosmopolitan human capital: the effects of the global mindset and organisational routines on cultural intelligence and international experience. In A. Burton Jones and J.-C. Spender (eds) *The Oxford handbook of human capital*. Oxford: Oxford University Press.

Nonaka, I. and Takeuchi, H. (1995) *The knowledge creating company*. New York: Oxford University Press.

Pedler, M., Burgoyne, J. and Boydell, T. (1991) *The learning company: a strategy for sustainable development*. London: McGraw-Hill.

Senge, P. (1990) *The fifth discipline: the art and practice of the learning organization*. New York: Doubleday Currency.

Stewart, T. (1997) *Intellectual capital: the new wealth of organisations*. London: Nicholas Brealey.

Storey, J. and Quintas, P. (2001) Knowledge management and HRM. In J. Storey (ed.) *Human resource management: a critical text*. 2nd edition. London: Thomson Learning.

Swart, J. (2007) HRM and knowledge workers. In P. Boxall, J. Purcell and P. Wright (eds) *The Oxford handbook of human resource management*. Oxford: Oxford University Press.

Thompson, J.B. (2010) *Merchants of culture*. Cambridge: Polity Press.

CHAPTER 11

Managing an international workforce

Introduction

In Chapter 2 I explained how the globalisation of markets for goods and services has played a major role in increasing the extent of the competition which organisations face. This development, of course, also has other significant management implications. One of the most important is the presence of many more international organisations than used to be the case. Most multinational corporations remain firmly based in and controlled from one country, but they grow by spreading their activities into new regions, most often by acquiring businesses and assimilating them into their global groups. The result is a situation in which more and more British employees are either working for organisations that are based overseas (either directly or for subsidiaries) or are working in British-based companies which operate and employ people overseas.

According to the Office for National Statistics (ONS) (www.statistics.gov.uk), we have seen very significant increases over the past two decades in both the number of mergers and acquisitions taking place in the UK which involve overseas companies as well as their total value. In 2007, before economic activity decelerated with the onset of recession, the ONS reported that 269 mergers or takeovers had occurred involving UK-based companies and overseas corporations in deals worth a combined sum of £82.1 billion. Ten years earlier, in 1997, the equivalent figure was only £15.1 billion and the number of deals 193. In 1987, just 61 deals were recorded with a total value of only £2.7 billion.

The same trend is apparent from the statistics on UK companies engaging in merger and acquisition activities overseas. In 1987, UK companies were involved in 431 such transactions to a total value of £12 billion, 1997 seeing 464 transactions worth £19 billion. The following decade then saw substantial increases in the size of the deals, so that by 2007 the 441 mergers or acquisitions involving UK companies overseas that were recorded were worth £57.8 billion.

These developments pose two major challenges for HR managers. Firstly, they mean that expatriate staff have to be employed to work for extended periods of time overseas, often in demanding, senior roles which have real significance for an organisation's performance. Secondly, it means that reporting structures along with policies and practices have to evolve that suit the diverse international contexts in which the organisation operates.

In addition to the rise of multinationals, as we established in Chapter 3, recent decades have seen substantial increases in the number of people from overseas who have settled in the UK for the long term. It is now estimated that at least 11% of the total UK population is made up of people who were born in another country, but because the vast majority of these people are of working age, the proportion of our labour force which originated overseas is estimated at 13% or more (Coleman 2010). There is also huge regional variation. London accounts for 10% of all jobs in the UK, but for almost 40% of jobs occupied by people who have come from overseas. By contrast, in Scotland, where a similar proportion of the UK-born population is employed, the proportion of overseas-born workers is just 5%. There are also types of workplace (such as hospitals and restaurants) in which the proportion of employees who have come from other countries is vastly higher than the national average. Here it is now the norm for teams of staff to be very diverse in terms of their national origin. A second issue of increasing significance from an HR point of view is thus the effective management of culturally diverse teams.

In this chapter we will review the practical HRM consequences arising from these two major trends. We will start by explaining why it is necessary to understand and to take account of cultural differences when employing people overseas and when employing overseas-born staff in the UK. We will go on to explore the ways in which institutional differences between countries also need to be appreciated when an organisation aspires to operate internationally. We then discuss some practical issues relating to expatriation and to the employment of overseas workers in the UK, before ending by briefly highlighting one or two other salient issues relating to HRM in international organisations.

LEARNING OUTCOMES

The objectives of this chapter are to:

- debate how far approaches to HRM are converging or diverging internationally
- introduce the major research on the mapping of workplace cultures
- show how institutional variations can explain why HR practices vary so much from country to country
- discuss why expatriate assignments often fail to meet their objectives
- explain why it is important to take great care when managing expatriation and repatriation processes
- discuss the challenges that face managers who are responsible for culturally diverse teams of staff
- set out the strengths and weaknesses of the major alternative structural arrangements that international organisations can adopt.

CONVERGENCE AND DIVERGENCE

One of the most interesting and fundamental debates that has exercised many researchers who specialise in international HRM concerns the extent to which over time we are witnessing either a convergence of approaches across different countries and regions, or a divergence. It is not an easy question to answer because it is so multidimensional. There are hundreds of countries, thousands of different industries and millions of employers around the world. How is it possible to establish with any confidence whether or not they are moving in broadly the same direction in terms of the way they manage people? Inevitably, with such a big and difficult question, people have different views.

It is fair to argue that with the growth of globalisation and, in particular, with the growth of multinational corporations, we might expect to see greater convergence across borders. Surely if an approach can be shown to work well in one place, managers elsewhere (encouraged by governments) will adopt it in a bid to improve their competitiveness? The answer is 'not necessarily'. Just because a type of HR initiative has been most effective in one part of the world, it does not always follow that it will work equally effectively elsewhere. Indeed, it may be wholly inappropriate, counterproductive and potentially economically dangerous for managers in one place to imitate the practices used by managers on the other side of the world.

For this reason it can be argued that responses to increased global competition as far as HRM is concerned not only should be, but are, properly very different in different places.

The debate between those who argue for convergence and those that believe in ongoing divergence becomes even more polarised when looking to the future. Is it true that over time some form of 'best practice HRM' will become the norm across the world, or are we likely to continue to observe a multiplicity of different approaches in use?

It is difficult to reach anything but an equivocal conclusion. It is undoubtedly the case that approaches to people management that are associated with strong economic performance have proved influential globally. For example, during the 1970s and 1980s there was very considerable interest in Western countries in Japanese approaches to management, born out of the terrific success the Japanese economy had during this period. These have had a significant influence on contemporary approaches to HRM in the UK and continue to do so. Japan is the source of much thinking, for example, on partnership approaches to the management of employment relations with their single-union arrangements and heavy emphasis on involving employees in decision-making. In more recent years, there is no question that the US model of 'best practice' HRM has had a significant influence on practice elsewhere in the world. This has certainly been true in the UK, and to a significant if rather less an extent elsewhere in western Europe. It is also true to state that there is a huge thirst for information about Western approaches to HRM in China and elsewhere in south-east Asia, as well as in eastern Europe.

However, aside from general influences of this type, it is hard to conclude that a strong degree of convergence is actually occurring in the way that people are managed on a day-to-day basis. Numerous research studies attest to the continuation of different approaches in different countries, even within the operations of the same multinational corporations. Local people management traditions appear stubbornly resistant to change. All that can be said with any confidence is that a degree of 'soft convergence' has occurred in recent years (see Björkman and Budhwar 2007) as managers have absorbed ideas from elsewhere in the world. There is much less evidence of 'hard convergence' in the form of actual implementation. It is more common for international thinking to be adapted to meet local needs and established local traditions.

The big question that follows is: why? Why is it that employers and employees appear so keen to stick with their established approaches and are hesitant, even quite resistant, towards adopting alternatives that can be shown to have worked well when introduced elsewhere in the world?

The answer lies in the continued presence, in spite of the globalisation of so much economic activity, of major cultural and institutional differences between countries. The same is true of language. More and more people around the world are becoming proficient English speakers. But this does not mean that English is replacing other local languages. A fair number of English words have found their way into commonly spoken Hindi, French and Japanese, but that is as far as it goes. English remains the second language of most of its speakers. The same appears to be true of HRM practices. International approaches are increasingly used, but they are not dislodging the established local approaches.

As to the future, as long as these differences persist, we can expect to see only limited and slow progress towards convergence around any single vision of effective HRM. The practical implications are highly significant and it is on these that the remainder of the chapter is going to focus.

CRITICAL REFLECTION

Over the past few decades, despite the globalisation of so much human activity, there is only limited and patchy evidence to suggest that HR practices have converged internationally. The way that organisations manage people still tends to vary substantially from one country to another. Established national approaches appear resistant to influence from overseas.

How far do you think this will remain the case in the future? Looking forward 20 or 30 years, can we expect to observe greater international convergence? Set out the arguments for and against this proposition.

CULTURAL DIFFERENCES

One of the more controversial streams of research in HRM in recent years has been the attempt made by a number of research teams systematically to 'map' workplace cultures around the world. The main reason for the controversy is the apparent tendency of these exercises to oversimplify the reality of the situation by categorising countries according to rather crude labels which leave little room for diversity *within* national borders, focusing entirely on differences between countries in terms of the way that people tend to be managed. This is a fair criticism to make, and we must acknowledge that there is a good deal of variation in the cultures that are prevalent across workplaces in the same town or even within the same company, let alone the same country. Nonetheless, even though it inevitably involves simplification, mapping exercises of this kind are still helpful. First of all, they draw our attention to the fact that cultures do vary between countries in highly significant ways. The experience of working in Germany or China is genuinely very different from that of working in the USA or South Africa. Secondly, from a more practical perspective, these maps can help us to understand why colleagues who come from different countries have different expectations from those we do.

Over recent years several large-scale, international studies have been carried out involving thousands of employees based in dozens of countries which aim to establish in what major ways workplace cultures vary across the globe. The most widely quoted examples are the following:

- Kluckhohn (1954)
- Strodtbeck (1961)
- Hofstede (1980, 1991)
- Hall and Hall (1990)

- Trompenaars (1993)
- Lewis (1996)
- House et al (2004).

Of these there is no question that the most widely read and debated studies are those that have been carried out by the Dutch academic and consultant Geert Hofstede, one of the most influential and widely quoted management writers in the world.

Hofstede's work is ongoing. He and his son continue to refine their findings and publish the results of new studies. You can download their most up-to-date data from their website (www.geert-hofstede.com). Hofstede's core ideas, however, have remained much the same since they were first published more than 30 years ago. Much of Hofstede's work has been carried out with the IT company IBM. His approach has involved issuing detailed questionnaires to their staff in various different global locations. Thousands of staff have taken part in this survey over the years; there having been sufficient numbers of participants from 70 different countries to enable statistically significant analysis of the data to be carried out.

The results are striking, the key finding being that there is a much greater degree of cultural divergence between countries than there is between different workplaces within the same country. In other words, according to Hofstede, it makes sense to think about the workplaces based in each country as having a definable culture. The experience of working in the UK varies across organisations, but it is a great deal more similar to working in Hong Kong or the USA.

The resulting cultural map that Hofstede produced and continues to refine measures each country's prevalent workplace culture in terms of four distinct dimensions:

INDIVIDUALISM/COLLECTIVISM

Individualism is defined as the extent to which people in a country are primarily focused on providing for themselves and their immediate families. Collectivism, by contrast, relates to the extent to which people look to a wider community or social group for support and protection. In collectivist cultures, community leaders emerge who are highly influential and often powerful. In individualist cultures, such people have very limited influence, if they exist at all.

POWER DISTANCE

This is the extent to which the less powerful members of a society (including workplaces) accept an unequal distribution of power. Where power distance is high, senior managers are very powerful authority figures whose judgement is not questioned. When the boss says jump, people jump. By contrast, managers in countries characterised as having low power distance cultures are managed more democratically. Leaders actively involve subordinates in decision-making, delegate much authority and expect that their thinking will be challenged.

UNCERTAINTY AVOIDANCE

This dimension is all about how comfortable people are with risk-taking. Where uncertainty avoidance is low, people tend to be entrepreneurial and quite relaxed about taking risks in the hope/expectation that they will gain a good return from doing so. By contrast, where uncertainty avoidance is high, people tend to be much more cautious and limit the extent of the risks that they take.

MASCULINITY/FEMININITY

Hofstede can be accused of sexual stereotyping here in choosing to ascribe to certain sets of values the labels *masculine* and *feminine*. Masculinity, in terms of workplace culture, refers to how assertive people are and how focused they are on money-making and visible achievement. Feminine-dominated cultures, by contrast, tend to value consensus and relationship-building, work–life balance and caring for others to a rather greater extent.

Having developed these four key dimensions, Hofstede went on to score each country according to how 'high' or 'low' their dominant workplace cultures are against each. In his more recent work, as a result of undertaking research in more south-east Asian countries, he has developed a further dimension, which is labelled *long-term orientation*. It is in some ways an extention of uncertainty avoidance because it involves prevailing attitudes towards risk. But it is different in that it focuses on the extent to which people have either longer- or shorter-term outlooks. Workplace cultures in countries which score highly on 'long-term orientation', such as China and Japan, differ from those which score low (ie Western countries) in having a preference for longer-term planning and evolutionary rather than revolutionary approaches to the management of change.

Other studies have undertaken similar kinds of exercise using differently defined dimensions of cultural difference. The GLOBE project (House et al 2004) added 'performance orientation', 'future orientation' and 'assertiveness' to Hofstede's original four, also distinguishing between 'institutional' and 'in group' forms of collectivism. Hall (1981) focused on rather different dimensions, which are labelled *context*, *space* and *time*. However, while the labels differ somewhat along with the definitions, the key underlying ideas and findings of the different research projects have been broadly similar. They show that the dominant culture in workplaces varies from country to country in important ways, notably in terms of power distribution, individualism, attitudes to risk and the extent to which people seek to control their environment.

According to Hofstede's studies, the predominant culture in UK workforces is characterised as follows:

- low power distance
- high individualism
- high masculinity

- low uncertainty avoidance
- low long-term orientation.

The findings from other countries with predominantly Anglo-Saxon roots, such as the USA, Canada, Australia and New Zealand, are very similar. But things are different in most EU countries. France, for example, only shares high scores on individualism with the UK. In other respects its business culture is very different, being characterised by high power distance, higher uncertainty avoidance and rather lower masculinity than is the case in the UK. In Sweden and the other Scandinavian countries, as well as in the Netherlands, high levels of individualism are combined with very low scores for power distance and especially for masculinity. By contrast, in the eastern European countries, power distance tends to be much higher, reflecting more autocratic leadership styles, while uncertainty avoidance also scores highly. The same is true in the Arab world, but here individualism scores much lower than it does in eastern Europe. In south-east Asia, aside from having very high scores on 'long-term orientation', the defining characteristics are relatively high scores both for masculinity and power distance and relatively low scores for individualism. It is in west Africa, however, that things differ most from those which Hofstede found to be prevalent in the UK. Here high power distance and uncertainty avoidance combine with relatively low levels of masculinity and individualism to create dominant workplace cultures which are the polar opposite to those which are the norm in the UK.

Hofstede's analysis of the practical impact of his findings places particular stress on uncertainty avoidance and power distance because of the role these two dimensions play in determining leadership styles in organisations. This led him to develop the idea that there are four major types of business culture in the world:

- pyramid of people (high power distance, high uncertainty avoidance)
- well-oiled machine (low power distance, high uncertainty avoidance)
- village market (low power distance, low uncertainty avoidance)
- family (high power distance, low uncertainty avoidance).

In countries which fit the 'well-oiled machine' category, such as Germany and Israel, democratic cultures are restrained by bureaucracy and rules which reduce risk. By contrast, where 'pyramids of people' are the norm (eg southern Europe and South America), a hierarchical but paternalistic management style is usual. In 'village markets' such as the UK, the USA, Ireland and the Netherlands, managers tend to be pragmatic and delegate a lot, while in 'family' cultures (eg Africa and south-east Asia) delegation is rare. Here people look to the boss for leadership and work in cultures which are much less rule-bound than is the case in Europe.

Studies of cultural difference are of very significant practical significance, notwithstanding the inevitable simplifications that they accept. They provide a useful basis for any manager seeking to understand why colleagues who originate in other countries have different expectations from their workplaces, act differently in some types of situation, carry different sets of assumptions to work with them and, most importantly, tend to lead others in different ways.

Understanding culture clash is the first step to handling it, and it is only by looking in detail at studies of the kind I have summarised here that we can thus begin to address the inevitable tensions that exist within teams that are made up of people with different cultural backgrounds.

INSTITUTIONAL DIFFERENCES

It has become fashionable among some academic writers to downplay the significance of culture as an explanation for the ways in which HRM practices tend to vary from country to country. Instead, some strongly argue that institutional differences play a much more significant role (see Whitley 1999, Edwards and Rees 2006, Wright and Van de Voorde 2009). The case that is made by institutionalists is based in part on research undertaken in multinational companies which have strong corporate cultures and a desire to harmonise HR practices across their global operations. They appear, in some cases at least, to overcome the restraints placed on them by cultural differences, but nonetheless find it necessary to vary the approach they take to the management of people due to the presence of insurmountable institutional restraints in different countries.

Institutional differences are partly legal in nature. Despite the attempts of the European Union and, to a lesser extent, of the International Labour Organization (ILO) to define a set of minimum employment rights which member states must observe, employment law regimes continue to operate very differently from country to country.

Interestingly and importantly, this is true of countries which are similar culturally. A good example is the operation of dismissal law in the UK, the USA and the Netherlands. These three countries are culturally very similar in terms of their workplaces. All three fall into the 'village market' category developed by Hofstede, and yet HR practices vary considerably. In part this is due to the very different approaches that each takes as far as dismissal law is concerned.

The USA, famously, adheres to the principle of 'employment at will' and has no unfair dismissal regulations. One or two states have introduced some very limited rights, but for the vast majority of American workers there is no legal comeback when they are dismissed, however long their length of service with their employer. A Tennessee judge once stated that in America employers were free to dismiss staff 'for good reason, bad reason or no reason at all' and that remains the case today. The result is that work in the USA is necessarily more insecure than is the case in most EU countries and this inevitably means that people are obliged to work harder at impressing their bosses. Interestingly, however, the lack of general legal protection from dismissal has also served to make American workers more litigious. They are keener than European workers need be about the negotiation of terms and conditions when they start a new employment, because it is through contractual rights rather than statutory rights that they attain some job security. Moreover, because levels of compensation ordered by US courts are higher than is the case in Europe, there is a greater incentive for employees to sue their former employers and, conversely, a greater incentive for employers to ensure that they do not dismiss in such a way as to breach someone's contract.

Things could not be more different in the Netherlands, where the unfair dismissal regime is as restrictive from an employer's point of view as it is anywhere in the world. Here the rule is that employees cannot be dismissed until their employer has first secured the approval of their local labour inspectorate – officers who are employed by local authorities to supervise workplace standards. The process of getting approval takes six to eight weeks, during which time the dismissed employee can appeal. Employers are able to suspend staff legally provided they follow a correct procedure and have a genuine business reason for doing so, but they then need to ask permission if they want to dismiss. There is no possibility of negotiating compromise agreements or paying staff off in order to avoid the requirements of the law. The inevitable result is a situation in which employees have considerable job security and know that they can only be dismissed if they really deserve to be. The extent to which employers exercise easy power over staff is thus much more restricted than in the case of the USA.

In the UK we have a position that falls somewhere in between the Dutch and American systems. It can be unlawful to dismiss for no good reason or to do so in an unreasonable fashion, but only once someone has completed a year's service as an employee (likely to rise to two years soon). Moreover, because the remedies are limited in terms of compensation, it is often not worth the while of an unfairly dismissed person to take his or her employer to court. In any event, it is the norm for employers to pay people off by settling disputes over dismissal ahead of any tribunal hearing with the payment of a compensatory sum.

We can see from this example how very significant the law itself is, as well as the manner in which it is enforced, in explaining different approaches to HRM in different countries. As long as these differences remain, genuine convergence across the world is not going to happen.

Institutional differences go well beyond the world of employment law. Researchers working in the area of comparative HRM have stressed the importance of all manner of other examples too, such as:

- government and local government policies
- collective bargaining structures
- labour market institutions
- national training systems
- pension arrangements
- social security systems.

The role played by trade unions, for example, varies considerably as does their preferred method of operation. In Germany, for example, the presence of employee (and often trade union) representation on works councils means that a consensual, consultative approach to the management of employment relations is the norm. Both sides have to agree things before they are implemented. As a result industrial action is relatively rare and high-trust employment relationships prevail. Things are very different in France. Here trade union membership levels are among the lowest in Europe, but the unions are highly active and do not baulk at the idea of taking strike action. Industrial relations thus has a tendency to be confrontational.

All over Europe and America it is the case that collective agreements are legally enforceable. Once agreed between unions and management there are major risks for both sides associated with breaching any agreement. As a result, the terms are drawn up with great care using precise language so that everyone knows where they stand and little room is left for interpretation. Agreements stick. By contrast, in the UK collective agreements are 'binding in honour only', meaning that in 99% of cases there is no possibility of one side suing another when an agreement is broken or even gaining an injunction to prevent a breach from occurring in the first place. There are advantages and disadvantages, one of the main advantages being that collective agreements can be made quite easily in negotiations between management and staff representatives without the need to involve lawyers at all. The terms of collective agreements in the UK are often vague and open to interpretation, leading many to assert that negotiating them is 'more of an art than a science'.

Ultimately it seems to me that it is pretty futile to debate how far differences in HR practice are culturally determined and how far they are institutionally determined. Both are clearly significant and, what is more, impact hugely on one another. At least in democratic countries, culture clearly helps to determine the nature of the institutional arrangements that evolve, while by the same token, institutions clearly play a major role in determining workplace cultures. What matters from a practical management point of view is that both are given full account when deciding what approach to HRM will be adopted. Both help to ensure that it is not possible for international corporations to harmonise HR perfectly across their global operations. Different approaches have to be used in different countries. It is fruitful and generally necessary to devise broad HR strategies that operate internationally, but how these are interpreted must be allowed to vary from country to country. The often quoted mantra 'think global, act local' (see Torrington 1994) must thus be adhered to if the chances that international operations will succeed are to be maximised.

KEY ARTICLE

CULTURE, INSTITUTIONS AND INTERNATIONAL DIVERSITY

The following article was published in *People Management* on 15 November 2007. You can download it from the CIPD website.

'A world difference' by Philip Stiles

This article describes the findings of a substantial research project carried out at the Judge Institute in Cambridge. The researchers looked in detail at the HR practices in use across the world in a group of international organisations. They were keen to establish how far such organisations were able to develop genuinely global approaches to HRM and how far they had to adapt them to suit local needs. A particular aim of the research was to discover how far local adaptations were due to cultural differences and how far to institutional differences.

Questions

1 What evidence do these researchers find of organisations 'thinking globally but acting locally' in their approaches to HRM practice?

2 What is their view of Hofstede's work?

3 What conclusions did the study reach about the relative significance of cultural and institutional difference in explaining local adaptation of international HR practices?

EXPATRIATES

The particular issues which arise when organisations employ expatriate staff to work on their behalf overseas have long interested researchers specialising in international HRM. For the most part studies have focused on traditional expatriate assignments in which a home-based employee, typically working at a reasonably senior level, is 'posted' overseas for a period of two to five years in an overseas operation or foreign subsidiary. With the growth of multinational organisations both in the private and public sectors, expatriate assignments of this kind have become increasingly common. It is also fair to state that with increasing competition, the significance of ensuring that expatriation arrangements are effective is also becoming greater.

Before we look in detail at how to help ensure effectiveness, it is important to point out that the traditional model of expatriation is by no means the only form of international employment. Suutari and Brewster (2009), for example, draw our attention to the existence of some other increasingly common types:

- migrant workers who move overseas for prolonged periods in order to take up a permanent job or to look for one

- global careerists who move from country to country, and often from employer to employer, to take up assignments of varying length

- self-initiates who take up job opportunities overseas for a temporary period in order to gain international experience

- international commuters who work in a country that is near to their home country, travelling back and forth each week and returning home at the weekends

- short-term assignees who work on projects overseas for a period of a few weeks' or months' duration before returning to their home-based jobs

- frequent flyers who are based in their home countries but who regularly undertake business trips overseas

- virtual internationalists who remain at home, but who work closely with colleagues based overseas as part of an international team which communicate using video-conferencing and e-communications.

In the case of each of these groups, significant HR issues arise which differ in terms of their nature and complexity from those that relate to typical, home-based employees. It is important that these issues are not underestimated if the management of international employment episodes is to be successful. Particular attention needs to be given to selection, training and reward matters, as well as to the management of repatriation at the end of a spell spent working overseas.

EXPATRIATE FAILURE

The research literature on expatriate working has long stressed how hard it is for organisations to ensure that the expatriation of staff works well from the point of view of both employer and employee. In fact, failure of some sort is very common as are situations in which expatriation episodes fail fully to meet expectations. Black and Gregerson (1999) looked at the experience of American managers undertaking expatriate assignments. They found that:

- 10–20% return before scheduled to do so

- 30% completed the assignment but failed to meet their supervisors' performance expectations

- 25% left soon after returning to their jobs in the USA.

When the costs associated with expatriation are considered, there is clearly a very strong business case for taking great care in selecting and preparing people for these kinds of assignment. It should not be assumed, as it often is, that anyone who really wants to will cope well, nor is it right to take the view that anyone who has senior management potential is suitable to send on an expatriate assignment. Moreover, however urgent the need sometimes can be to fill an overseas posting rapidly, it always makes sense to take enough time to select the right person and prepare him or her properly. Finally, all the research evidence demonstrates that repatriation also has to be managed carefully. It is wholly wrong to assume that people will adjust easily when they return home after having worked overseas for some years.

SELECTING EXPATS

In many multinational organisations it is considered necessary for would-be senior managers to spend periods of time overseas as they build up the experience they will later require in a top corporate post. People who are ambitious and who have senior management potential are aware of the career boost that having extensive international experience can give them and so are often keen to put themselves forward for expatriate roles. The result is a tendency in many organisations either to select people for the wrong reasons (ie without fully considering if they are likely to do a good job) or without giving sufficient attention to their suitability. Ng et al (2009) complain that despite the increasing frequency and complexity of expatriate assignments, selection decisions 'typically rely on informal and low-utility selection criteria'. It is very common, for example, when an organisation is looking to select someone to undertake a senior role overseas, for it to stipulate that candidates must have previous international management experience. Alternatively, decisions about who to send are based entirely on technical knowledge and ability or are based on a more general desire to develop an individual's career for succession planning purposes. Superficially this all makes sense, but in practice it tends to lead to high rates of failure.

The attribute that is needed most of all from a would-be expatriate manager is the ability to adapt quickly and effectively to foreign surroundings. This requires what Ng et al (2009) refer to as 'cultural intelligence', a concept which encompasses both sensitivity to cultural difference and the ability to learn how to adjust working methods accordingly. Others stress the importance of language skills and more generally of resilience in the face of difficult challenges. A further factor to take into account is someone's family circumstances. It has become 'politically incorrect' in recent years to pay attention to factors such as this for fear that accusations of unfair discrimination will be made, but such are the costs and financial risks associated with expatriation that it must be taken account of by any thoughtful selection panel. The blunt truth is that some people's personal circumstances make it difficult for them to spend time overseas and perform effectively while doing so. This means that when selecting people for these kinds of job there is a clear need – in a way that there is not when selecting people for regular home-based posts – to give consideration to partners and their circumstances. What is great for a husband's career may bring significant drawbacks for his wife's, or vice versa. Similarly, issues such as children's education have to be discussed and taken account of. Expatriation is often highly disruptive to family life and such factors may in effect amount either to insurmountable barriers or risks in individual cases.

PREPARING FOR EXPATRIATION

Partners and families also have to be included in formal preparation programmes designed to maximise the likelihood of an effective expatriate episode that lasts as long as it is planned to. A variety of developmental interventions are appropriate here from one-to-one coaching, courses of formal education, informal discussions with experienced expats and short visits to the country before the full assignment begins. Caligiuri et al (2005) usefully suggest that three distinct forms of preparatory training are useful:

- language training
- diversity training
- cross-cultural training.

Diversity training is concerned in a general sense with helping people to work effectively (or perhaps more effectively) in diverse teams. It is particularly important for people who have supervisory responsibilities to gain a full understanding of the different ways that team members react and behave depending on their backgrounds.

Cross-cultural training goes further. This is culture-specific and is concerned with equipping expatriates in very practical ways to learn the behaviours that will be expected of them once they are overseas, and to develop appropriate expectations about work as well as living generally in a foreign place. When the location of the assignment is very distant geographically (eg a European going to Australia) and when the nature of the culture shock that the expat experiences is likely to be sizeable (eg a European in Africa, an African in Europe) there is a further need for the cross-cultural training to include sessions on personal coping strategies.

REWARD MANAGEMENT

Expatriate reward is a specialised and quite complex area of HR practice, but it is an area which organisations have to take great care about getting right. If too little is paid, there will be problems recruiting expats and subsequently in persuading them to remain in post for its full planned duration. On the other hand, paying too much, aside from being a waste of money, can lead to problems in the locality to which the expatriate is being sent. Senior managers in the host country are not going to take kindly to the arrival of people from overseas to work in subordinate positions who are able to afford a far better lifestyle than they are. It can also make repatriation difficult.

Traditionally, multinational organisations have paid expatriate incentives to encourage staff to put themselves forward for overseas assignments. This has become less common in recent years as the gaining of international experience has become more and more significant in determining who gets the top jobs in international corporations. The career development opportunities presented from expatriation are considered to be incentive enough. The ending of routine payments of this kind has not, however, hugely reduced the costs of expatriation. This is because so much else has to be paid out in the form of relocation expenses (at the start and end of an assignment), housing costs, costs relating to children's education, the costs of flights home from time to time and, often, some form of compensation to cover the loss of a partner's career opportunities during a period overseas. On top of that, organisations also incur the training and development costs referred to above.

Because living standards vary greatly in different economies and because taxation arrangements for expats differ so much, it is not always at all straightforward to calculate an appropriate final salary figure. For this reason organisations frequently employ the services of specialist consultants to advise them on what they should pay. This is particularly helpful when managers have insufficient knowledge or experience of market rates in particular regions to enable them to make informed decisions.

REPATRIATION

One very clear message emerges from nearly all research into expatriation and that is the immense importance of handling repatriation effectively. From an HR management perspective this should be seen as a high-risk activity. A good proportion of returning expatriates find it necessary to find a new job soon after they get 'home', finding it impossible to settle back into the lives they had before departing.

Linehan and Mayrhofer (2005) explain that the emotional and practical stresses associated with a return to one's home country and one's old workplace after three or four years spent living abroad are just as stressful as those associated with the move overseas. In fact, for many people the experience of repatriation is more stressful because it is not accompanied by the inevitable feelings of excitement that people experience when moving overseas. However, this is not something that organisations tend to appreciate. An assumption is made that repatriation requires little intervention from the employer on the grounds that employees require little practical assistance.

While it is true that people don't have problems with language or understanding the culture they are returning to, adjustment can still be difficult. Moving back home after a few years away involves pulling up roots and putting them down again. Particularly when families are involved and when there is a need to find suitable new accommodation, this tends to be a stressful and unsettling process. The nub of the problem is often financial. When people work overseas they tend to enjoy what is often known as 'an expatriate lifestyle', which can be a great deal more pleasurable than the one they left behind. Living standards, if not the actual salary, thus tend to reduce on repatriation. Managers posted to work in overseas subsidiaries also tend to find that they enjoy greater seniority and freedom to make decisions when overseas. The return home can thus be accompanied by losses of status and power, which are never easy to adjust to. There is a need to feel one's way back into the hierarchy and to adjust to a changed political environment.

Another observation made by Linehan and Mayrhofer (2005) is that there tends to be a mismatch between the expectations of the repatriate and those of the employer. People returning from a period spent working overseas are naturally keen to put their international experience to use and find it hard to understand why they are not able to do so immediately. Organisations are rarely ready to make any use of the expertise gained abroad, resulting in disappointment.

The upshot is that there is a good, strong business case in support of the proposition that HR departments should take as much interest in the effective management of repatriation as they do in expatriation. The needs are different – less practical and more psychological in nature – but they are needs nonetheless. The keys are firstly to treat each case individually on its own merits and, secondly, to prepare the ground well in advance. Expectations can be managed to ensure that hopes are not built up and then dashed, finances can be sorted out, and people can be warned about some of the difficulties they may well face when returning, steps being taken to minimise the extent of any 'reverse culture shock'.

CRITICAL REFLECTION

Expatriate reward

Assume that your organisation has recently established a presence for the first time in a developing country where living standards are low, taxation is very low and crime rates are high. You are asked if you would consider working for the new subsidiary, based in the capital of this developing country. The assignment will last for three years, after which you will return to your present job. It is strongly hinted to you that your long-term career prospects with your organisation will be enhanced if you agree to take up this opportunity.

What would you require in terms of a reward package to persuade you to take up this opportunity? What sum would you ask for at the start of negotiations with your boss about the compensation package? What might you be prepared to settle for and why?

CULTURALLY DIVERSE TEAMS

A great deal more research has been carried out about expatriates who are sent to work on overseas assignments than about the effective management of teams based in UK organisations who are diverse in terms of their national origin. Managers with responsibility for overseeing culturally diverse teams of staff can nonetheless learn a great deal from the literature on expatriation, particularly as regards cultural sensitivity and the different expectations this brings about the experience of work.

Steers et al (2010) set out what they describe as three 'coping strategies' to use and develop when managing culturally diverse teams:

- Avoid cultural stereotypes (ie don't make assumptions about people based on a crude and limited understanding of their national cultures).

- See cultural differences in neutral terms (ie be fully aware of both the advantages and disadvantages that can come from the employment of diverse teams).

- Prepare for the unexpected (ie be aware of your own biases and cultural perspectives so that you can adapt quickly when dealing with those of others).

These are not always easy to achieve because they require us to go against what may be our natural tendencies. But it is important that managers seeking to get the most out of their teams successfully meet these challenges if the team is to thrive.

Laroche and Rutherford (2007) have written an excellent book which is focused on getting the best out of staff who are working in Canadian companies having migrated to Canada from overseas. They focus on the basic HR processes of recruitment, selection, induction, teamworking, communication and staff retention. In each case they draw both on their own experience as specialist consultants working in this area and on the literature on cultural difference to give sound, well-informed, practical advice. At base it is all about being aware of cultural differences, understanding their origins and taking care to take them into account when managing teams on a day-to-day basis. Here are three examples which illustrate their main message:

1 As we saw in our discussion of Hofstede's work, Anglo-Saxon countries such as the UK and Canada have relatively low scores for 'power distance'. This means that managers, by comparison with those in most countries, are more democratic in their styles of management, consulting before making decisions, preferring to have open and friendly relationships with their subordinates and even encouraging colleagues to scrutinise their thinking critically. Management hierarchies are very much a feature of Anglo-Saxon workplaces, but these can be quite loose and flexible. A great deal of decision-making is delegated, people at low levels not only being invited to contribute ideas, but being expected to.

   This is very different from the experiences that people who originate in many other countries will be used to. Where power distance is high, consultation and delegation are rare and people do not ever question their bosses' decisions. People expect to be told what to do and to be held accountable for achieving their objectives. Being asked to contribute to the setting of one's own performance objectives or to participate in a 360-degree appraisal exercise does not come at all naturally.

2 Selection of new staff, as well as promotion, in Anglo-Saxon business cultures is usually underpinned by a formal assessment of someone's skills and experience. We tend to work from job descriptions and think in terms of selecting the most qualified person to do that particular job. This too is an approach that seems alien to many who have worked in other countries. This is particularly true of people from the Middle East and from India and Pakistan, where things are done differently. Skill-matching plays much less of a role in selection decision-making than other more general factors such as whether you have a degree and which schools you studied at. Educational qualifications matter much more than they generally do in the UK. Managers need to know this because they might otherwise be put off, for example by a CV submitted by someone from India which puts all the stress on educational attainment. This may be the best person for the job, so it is unwise to reject their CV simply because it is framed with a different set of expectations in mind.

3 Anglo-Saxon business cultures often seem very cold and impersonal to people who arrive having worked in other countries. People in the UK, for example, generally like to maintain a very clear divide between their home and work lives. Colleagues will treat each other differently, with total naturalness when they meet socially from the more aloof way that they treat each other when at work. When at work we like to maintain quite a substantial 'personal space' around our bodies. We shake hands and just occasionally pat one another on the back, but beyond that not a lot of touching goes on. It is rare, for example, for colleagues at work to hug or kiss. Yet such types of behaviour are entirely commonplace and expected in many other cultures. More generally, Anglo-Saxons tend to be quite buttoned up emotionally, particularly when at work. We make rational decisions with our heads (or at least pretend to), keeping

emotions and the feelings of the heart out of the way. This too can seem very alien to people whose expectations originate in their experience of working overseas.

STRUCTURAL ISSUES

A final issue of underlying significance for HR managers in international organisations concerns internal structures and reporting lines. While these are complex issues at the best of times for large organisations, they are made a great deal more involved when geographically diverse workforces are included. The problem is best illustrated with a fictional example – a catering conglomerate that operates only within the UK and runs a chain of restaurants and a chain of hotels. How should it structure itself? One option is for the two product groups to be managed separately, with two managerial hierarchies, each with its own maintenance, marketing, finance and personnel functions, and both reporting at the very senior level to corporate directors. Alternatively, the whole group could be managed functionally, all the chefs (from both hotels and restaurants) reporting to regional food and beverage managers, and the housekeepers, accountants, maintenance, finance, marketing and personnel people doing likewise. The third option is to organise the whole company into separate regional divisions so that there are managers with responsibility for both restaurants and hotels operating in the south-east, the Midlands, Scotland, etc. All three are plausible approaches. Because one language is spoken and one broad organisation culture shared, and because operations are confined to a reasonably small geographic area, any inherent tensions can be resolved relatively easily. Hence, if the organisation is structured regionally, it is still very easy for maintenance staff based in different locations to communicate, share their expertise and equipment, and come together to take part in project work. The same goes for general managers of hotels in different regions and wine-buyers within the restaurant chain. In other words, it is possible for each member of staff to have a single line manager who appoints and appraises them, but it is also possible to work to or with others on a regional or functional basis.

The larger and more complex an organisation becomes, the harder it is to resolve the tensions described in the example given above. Once international divisions are established, a further tension emerges in the form of the need for the organisation to have a common strategic focus while simultaneously taking account of local cultural norms and organisational traditions. Hence, to take the catering example further, there is a need in an international hotel chain for all units to adhere to the same basic standards, so that they can be marketed as a group, while at the same time they will be managed very differently depending on the country in which they are based. So to whom should the sales manager at the Hong Kong unit report? Should it be the hotel's general manager, a worldwide director of sales or a manager with responsibility for sales and marketing activity within south-east Asia? In practice, the answer will vary, depending on the established traditions in the company, the political strength of particular managers and the costs and benefits associated with each option.

A further option is for organisations to develop matrix structures, whereby there is no single reporting line, so that employees may be accountable to a number of different individuals at the same time. In the above example, that might mean that an aspiring sales manager for the Hong Kong hotel would be interviewed by all three potential bosses but would report to each about different areas of work. Day-to-day supervision might come from the local general manager, but this would not prevent the regional sales and marketing managers overseeing much of the individual's work. In addition, he or she might be involved in some international project work, which would require work to be undertaken for the international director. Ideally this would maximise the individual's contribution while ensuring that responsibilities at organisational, regional and unit level were all met. Such matrix structures are becoming increasingly common in international companies because they permit cost-effective achievement of organisational objectives, but in different ways depending on local conditions. Further information on different approaches to such forms, together with a number of examples in the international field, are provided by Sparrow and Hiltrop (1994: 288–298) and Jackson (2002).

Linked to the question of the overall structure is the issue of who should manage plants or other units located in countries other than that of the corporate headquarters (HQ). In a truly global organisation, where the original location of the corporate HQ is irrelevant to staffing policy, and perhaps where ownership is no longer concentrated in one country, the nationality of each unit manager is less of an issue. The corporate culture supersedes separate national cultures, and it becomes possible simply to promote people to new positions across different countries on the basis of individual merit. Hence a Dutch person can be appointed to manage a Polish factory owned by a US-based corporation. It is also more common for people based in subsidiaries to spend time working at the corporate HQ as much as the other way round. However, as has already been pointed out, this kind of global organisation remains relatively rare at present, with most multinationals dominated by a strong nationally based HQ which keeps a tight rein on its overseas subsidiary units. In such situations, the choice in the above example would more typically be between a local Polish manager and an expatriate American one. The advantage of the former is local knowledge and language skills. By contrast the advantage of the latter is knowledge of organisational culture and strategy, together with expertise in the international aspects of the operation. Again, as in the case of matrix organisation structures, the usual solution is to try to achieve the best of both worlds by employing local and home country nationals to work together – perhaps one acting as deputy to the other. Hall (2005) has made a particular study of how the HR function is best organised in multinational organisations. He suggests that where functions are global in nature (typically, pay strategy, succession planning, management development), the reporting structures should operate at a global level. By contrast, where the functions carried out are more local (recruitment and selection, for example), reporting lines should be to local managers. In other cases there will be a need for a matrix structure.

KEY ARTICLE

RECRUITMENT AND SELECTION WORK IN INTERNATIONAL ORGANISATIONS

The following article was published in *People Management* on 25 October 2006. You can download it from the CIPD website.

'Foreign policies' by Paul Sparrow

In this article Professor Paul Sparrow (now of Lancaster University) discusses research he has undertaken in international companies looking in particular at their recruitment and selection practices. He found that there was a desire to harmonise the way that recruitment and selection was carried out across a company's global operations, but that there were limits to how far this was possible. He goes on to argue that employer branding initiatives of the kind we discussed in Chapter 7

have the potential to offer a great deal to multinational organisations.

Questions

1 Why are international organisations so keen to establish universal, global policies and practices in areas such as recruitment and selection?

2 Why can this be difficult to achieve in practice?

3 To what extent do you agree that employer branding has a lot to offer organisations seeking to harmonise recruitment and selection across its global operations? Why?

KEY LEARNING POINTS

- Increased levels of migration from one country to another and the growth of multinational organisations are creating new challenges for many managers who are faced with the need to motivate culturally diverse teams of staff.

- Several influential studies have sought to map international cultural differences as far as the workplace is concerned. These have found that differences between countries are much greater than differences within countries.

- The persistence over time of substantial differences in the way that people are managed from one country to another can in part be explained by significant institutional diversity.

- There is a strong business case for taking considerable care when selecting and preparing people for expatriate assignments. The case for taking such care when managing repatriation is also very strong.

- Cultural sensitivity and understanding are necessary competences for managers of culturally diverse teams to gain.

- Very considerable HR management challenges are associated with the design of international organisation structures.

EXPLORE FURTHER

International HRM is a very well-researched subject which is discussed in many books and articles. On the specific issue of cultural differences and their consequences for managers, a good general introduction is provided by Richard Steers and his colleagues in *Management across cultures: challenges and strategies* (2010).

Steers, R., Sanchez-Runde, C. and Nardon, L. (2010) *Management across cultures: challenges and strategies*. Cambridge: Cambridge University Press.

Laroche and Rutherford (2007) provide a good discussion and also advice on how to manage teams of staff with diverse cultural backgrounds. Torrington (1994), meanwhile, provides an excellent introduction to the world of expatriate management in particular.

Laroche, L. and Rutherford, D. (2007) *Recruiting, retaining and promoting culturally different employees*. London: Elsevier.

Torrington, D. (1994) *International human resource management: think globally, act locally*. London: Prentice Hall.

REFERENCES

Björkman, I. and Budhwar, P. (2007) When in Rome? Human resource management and the performance of foreign firms operating in India. *Employee Relations*. Vol 29, No 6. pp595–610.

Black, J. and Gregerson, H. (1999) The right way to manage expats. *Harvard Business Review*. Vol 77, No 2. pp52–60.

Caligiuri, P., Lazarova, M. and Tarique, I. (2005) Training, learning and development in multinational organisations. In H. Scullion and M. Linehan (eds) *International human resource management: a critical text*. Basingstoke: Palgrave.

Coleman, J. (2010) *Employment of foreign workers: 2007–2009*. London: Office for National Statistics.

Edwards, T. and Rees, C. (2006) *International human resource management: globalisation, national systems and multinational companies*. London: FT/Prentice Hall.

Hall, E. (1981) *The silent language*. New York: Anchor Books.

Hall, E. and Hall, M. (1990) *Understanding cultural differences*. Yarmouth: Intercultural Press.

Hall, K. (2005) Global division. *People Management*. 24 March. pp44–45.

Hofstede, G. (1980) *Culture's consequences: international differences in work-related values*. Beverly Hills, CA: Sage Publications.

Hofstede, G. (1991) *Cultures and organizations: software of the mind.* London: McGraw-Hill.

House, R., Hanges, P., Javidan, M., Dorfman, P. and Gupta, V. (2004) *Culture, leadership and organisations: the GLOBE study of 62 societies.* Thousand Oaks, CA: Sage.

Jackson, T. (2002) *International HRM: a cross-cultural approach.* London: Sage.

Kluckhohn, C. (1954) *Culture and behaviour.* New York: Free Press.

Laroche, L. and Rutherford, D. (2007) *Recruiting, retaining and promoting culturally different employees.* London: Elsevier.

Lewis, R.D. (1996) *When cultures collide: managing successfully across cultures.* London: Nicholas Brealey.

Linehan, M. and Mayrhofer, W. (2005) International careers and repatriation. In H. Scullion and M. Linehan (eds) *International human resource management: a critical text.* Basingstoke: Palgrave.

Ng, K.-Y., Van Dyne, L. and Ang, S. (2009) Beyond international experience: the strategic role of cultural intelligence for executive selection in IHRM. In P. Sparrow (ed.) *Handbook of international human resource management.* Chichester: Wiley.

Sparrow, P. (2006) Foreign policies. *People Management.* 25 October.

Sparrow, P. and Hiltrop, J.M. (1994) *European human resource management in transition.* London: Prentice Hall.

Steers, R., Sanchez-Runde, C. and Nardon, L. (2010) *Management across cultures: challenges and strategies.* Cambridge: Cambridge University Press.

Stiles, P. (2007) A world difference. *People Management.* 15 November.

Strodtbeck, K. (1961) *Variations in value orientations.* Westport, CT: Greenwood.

Suutari, V. and Brewster, C. (2009) Beyond expatriation: different forms of international employment. In P. Sparrow (ed.) *Handbook of international human resource management: integrating people, process and context.* Chichester: John Wiley & Sons Ltd.

Torrington, D. (1994) *International human resource management: think globally, act locally.* London: Prentice Hall.

Trompenaars, F. (1993) *Riding the waves of culture: understanding cultural diversity in global business.* London: McGraw-Hill.

Whitley, R. (1999) *Divergent capitalisms: the social structuring and change of national business systems.* Oxford: Oxford University Press.

Wright, P. and Van de Voorde, K. (2009) Multilevel issues in IHRM: mean differences, explained variance and moderated relationships. In P. Sparrow (ed.) *Handbook of international human resource management.* Chichester: Wiley.

CHAPTER 12

Managing ethically

Introduction

In the first part of the book I put forward the following propositions when analysing long-term trends in the HRM business environment:

1 There is clear, if limited, evidence of increased ethical awareness on the part of consumers, investors and among some groups of job-seekers in recent years. A growing proportion of people act on their ethical beliefs when making decisions about what to buy, who to buy it from, where to invest their money and where to work.

2 There are good grounds for anticipating a tightening of many labour markets in future years as demand for knowledge workers with specific qualifications and experience outpaces supply. For workers in these groups there will be greater choice available about where to work.

3 Increasing competitive intensity among organisations is developing alongside the growth of global markets for goods and services, and networking technologies which allow negative messages about corporations to be spread very rapidly using new media which are not, at least in practice, subject to the same regulations as traditional forms of media.

If these propositions are accurate, it follows that organisations are going to have greater incentives in the future than they have had in the past both to act ethically in their dealings and to be seen to do so. Gaining a reputation as an unethical organisation has never been as easy as it is now, while turning such a reputation around is increasingly costly and difficult to achieve. For corporations which need to foster the reputation of strong brands in order to maintain their competitive position, the consequences of this evolving environment are far-reaching, as this quotation from Terry Leahy (former CEO of Tesco) makes clear:

Trust will matter more and more. As the world shrinks but people's lives become more complicated, so people will turn to brands and products they know and trust. Furthermore, perceptions of trust will be shaped not just by price and service, but also by issues like the environment, health, labour conditions and animal welfare.

Consumers are more interested in these issues than ever and they have access to huge amounts of information at the click of a mouse. The role of the media and the internet also makes campaigning easier and far more effective, so in the battle for trust ethical considerations will increasingly weigh in the scales alongside economic ones. Here is something of a paradox. The bigger a brand becomes, the more sensitive it has to be to what its customers want. Its very size and fame make it more susceptible to consumer pressure. The knowledge that one slip can destroy a reputation that has been carefully nurtured over many years helps keep consumers in the driving seat. Those who think that the bigger and better-known a company becomes, the more it can afford to ignore its customers, have got the wrong end of the stick. (Leahy 2005)

The HR function potentially plays two distinct roles in efforts aimed at enhancing an organisation's ethical reputation. The first is a general contribution achieved by encouraging the adoption of ethical awareness and behaviour across the workforce as a whole. The HR role is to help promote ethical action by recruiting and retaining people who are inclined to think and behave ethically, through ethically oriented training and reward systems, and by building in ethical considerations when deciding who to promote and how severely to discipline people who fall short of ethical expectations. It is increasingly common for HR specialists to take a leading role in the promotion of ethical behaviours in organisations, for example by drawing up and subsequently enforcing written codes of conduct which are designed to achieve this purpose.

The second role played by the HR function in helping to build an ethical reputation is more direct. It involves acting ethically itself in the way that it carries out its own activities. As is demonstrated by Provis (2010), pretty well all HR activities commonly carried out in organisations have some kind of ethical angle to them. Wherever an HR manager turns, almost on a day-to-day basis, be it in setting policies or in handling day-to-day casework, he or she can expect to come face to face with tricky ethical dilemmas. This is inevitable given the human significance of the decisions which are taken, be they about who to appoint, who to make redundant, whether to dismiss, how to reorganise teams or, particularly, about how much different people should be paid. There are nearly always winners and losers, the losers reacting much more negatively if they perceive their treatment to have been unethical in some way.

It is a paradox, given the centrality of ethics to so much HR activity, that our function has generally sought, at least in recent years, to distance itself from perceptions that it plays a significant ethical role (see Winstanley and Woodall 2000: 5, Pinnington et al 2007: 1). Since the 1980s the emphasis has been on shedding our image as a management function concerned with employee welfare or even one which seeks to represent the interests of employees. Such a role has been seen as outdated and likely to detract from our credibility in the eyes of other managers.

Instead, a very deliberate attempt has been made to craft a vision of HRM as being 100% business-focused, delivering key strategic objectives on behalf of the organisation and adding financial value. In the future it is likely that there will be some reversal of this established trend. For the reasons stated above, HR managers will have to rediscover an interest in ethics, actively promote ethical behaviour across the organisation and take care that they apply ethical approaches towards the management of people themselves. While there is a strong business case there to deploy in favour of such an approach, it is one based on long-term reputation-building and will not always resonate with line managers struggling to meet shorter-term financial objectives in increasingly competitive business conditions. Achieving higher ethical standards while also maintaining the HR function's hard-won credibility in the wider management community is thus not going to be at all easy to achieve in practice.

There is one area of HR practice which stands out as an exception to the rule as far as the active promotion of an ethical position is concerned. This is the area of equality management, where HR managers have often been in the vanguard of promoting a positive approach. It is a field which has attracted much debate about all manner of issues and it remains controversial in some organisations. Indeed many would argue that it is inappropriate to describe it as an ethical issue. There are, after all, as we explained in Chapter 4, plenty of legal obligations in this area, and many passionately argue a business case in favour of active equal opportunities policies. For others it is essentially a question of politics rather than ethics. Nonetheless, a case can be made for improved equality management being a proper ethical objective for organisations to aim for. Moreover, because many organisations have made considerable progress in recent years, it is reasonable to include a brief overview of the key debates in this chapter alongside broader ethical questions.

LEARNING OUTCOMES

The objectives of this chapter are to:

- introduce the major theories relating to ethics and the management of people

- discuss how an HR professional can act ethically in practice

- distinguish between ethical and lawful practices in HRM

- set out the contribution made by HR professionals to corporate social responsibility initiatives

- explain why ethical matters are likely to move up the HR agenda in the future

- discuss key debates and developments in the field of equality management.

ETHICAL DECISION-MAKING IN HRM – THEORY

In recent years interest in corporate ethics has grown, largely in response to high-profile scandals such as the collapses of Enron, Lehman Brothers and the Maxwell Group of companies. These have all received extensive coverage in the media, leading people to question the ethical orientation of those who led them to disaster. Interest in HR aspects of corporate ethics has been fuelled by stories about MPs 'fiddling' expenses, apparently unjustified pay inflation among senior executives and instances of macho management being practised during the 2008–10 recession and in its aftermath.

A great deal of the published research on HRM and ethics is theoretical in nature, authors debating how far long-held philosophical positions about ethics can be applied to the realm of twenty-first-century management. The perspectives generated as a result of this type of analysis are fascinating, but they are only of limited help from a practical point of view because debates about ethics tend to be very involved and because philosophers differ profoundly when asked to debate questions such as 'what is right?', 'what is good?' and 'what is moral?'

Some analyses have attempted to generate ideas about what contemporary HR managers should seek to do in their day-to-day work from a study of ethical theories, but in truth the prescriptions advanced are quite broad in nature. Mick Fryer (2009: 76), for example, in a well-argued paper, comes out in favour of 'intersubjectivist theory' as being 'the magnetic pole towards which HRM practitioners might orientate their ethical compasses'. His argument is rooted in a reading of Aristotle's writings on virtue and its role in the ancient Greek democratic system. While there may be no general agreement about what constitutes ethical conduct across the world, Fryer argues, there is generally a fair degree of agreement within individual communities. In Aristotle's view, moral legitimacy in the field of government decision-making is conferred through a direct system of democracy in which the citizens who are to be subject to a law are able to participate in the making of that law. It can be described as being 'ethical' because it is ethically acceptable to the community in which it applies.

Translated to a modern workplace, this means giving employees a voice in the making of decisions that will affect them. Doing so helps ensure that management decisions do not offend against the ethical beliefs of the people employed in the relevant workplaces. This is a useful observation, but it only provides guidance of quite a general nature to an organisation seeking to act ethically and to be seen to be doing so.

Walsh (2007) also provides some most interesting general guidance for HR managers derived from a reading of philosophical theories in the field of ethics. He is primarily concerned with the maintenance of human dignity in the workplace and the avoidance of 'moral hazards', which he defines as situations in which shareholder and worker interests diverge. Walsh argues that there are three distinct ways of approaching management in a competitive commercial environment.

Firstly there is what he calls 'lucrepathic actions', which involve managers taking account only of the need to maximise profit when making decisions. Secondly, there are 'accumulative actions', where the pursuit of profit is moderated in some shape or form by ethical constraints. Finally, there are 'stipendiary actions' in which the objective served by a decision is not to make profit, but where the need to do so acts as a constraint on the nature of those decisions.

The conclusion, as far as practical guidance for HR managers is concerned, is that 'lucrepathic actions' should be avoided. In other words, a decision can only be said to have ethical legitimacy when it is either taken primarily in the interests of employees (albeit restricted in its extent or impact by the need to maintain profitability) or when the impact on employees is taken into consideration and allowed to moderate the decision in some way. Ignoring employee interests altogether and taking a decision that operates purely in the interests of shareholders is inherently 'unethical' because it is lucrepathic (ie serves only to help one group to exploit another in order to gain more 'filthy lucre' for itself).

Exactly the opposite conclusion was reached by the economist Milton Friedman (1970) in his writing on business ethics and corporate social responsibility. In an article entitled 'The social responsibility of business is to increase its profits', Friedman argues strongly against businesses being tempted into taking any decision which is contrary to the interests of the business's owners, which is generally 'to make as much money as possible while conforming to the basic rules of the society, both those embodied in law and those embodied in ethical custom'. According to this argument 'lucrepathic activity' on the part of commercial organisations is not only ethical, but is the only course of action which *is* ethical. This is so, according to Friedman, due to the way that in a market economy profit maximisation ultimately serves everyone's interests because it maximises the wealth that is created by society. It is then the job of democratically elected governments to regulate businesses and to ensure that the wealth they create is properly redistributed through taxation and public spending. When organisations veer from the path of profit maximisation, they are effectively 'spending someone else's money' because they are reducing society's wealth. It may make managers feel good to 'declaim that business is not concerned merely with profit', but ultimately they are harming the interests of those they believe they are helping.

Friedman's contribution to the debate about corporate ethics has been by far the most controversial of recent years. Many have sought to pick his arguments apart and put an alternative case in favour of the view that businesses can and should actively seek to improve society through actions which have a positive impact on human lives, even if profits are somewhat reduced in the process. Melé (2008), for example, makes the point that 'economic performance is not the whole public good' and that some profit-maximising activities have socially damaging effects (eg exploiting workers unreasonably, depleting natural resources, polluting, etc). Salazar and Husted (2008: 142) remind us that many successful businesses were not set up as profit maximisers in the first place, having other more socially desirable aims. The Body Shop and Ben and Jerry's are given as examples.

The other major argument put against Friedman concerns his contention that ethical and profit maximisation are incompatible and that an organisation which gives too much attention to ethical endeavours loses money it would otherwise have made in profit. Mulligan (1986) challenges the basic premise of Friedman's position by arguing that an organisation can easily act in a socially responsible way without damaging its profitability at all. Indeed, it may find that acting ethically increases shareholder value.

We thus have a position in which there is no agreement whatever between leading writers on business ethics about what in practical terms constitutes an ethical approach to the management of people. This reflects debates in the wider field of ethics where we find distinct traditions which are incompatible with one another. Some philosophers have taken what is known as a 'consequentialist' view, judging whether an act is ethical by assessing its practical impact on people. The most common form of consequentialist thinking is utilitarianism, whose protagonists argue in favour of choosing the path which generates the greatest happiness to the greatest number of people. According to such a view, when faced with an ethical problem, a manager should resolve it by choosing the course of action which will bring most benefit to most people. The major alternative perspective is non-consequentialist or 'deontological' in nature. Derived from the philosophy of figures such as Immanuel Kant, deontologists argue that some courses of action represent 'the right thing to do' even if they do not serve the interests of the greatest number. In other words, it is possible to identify enduring ethical values for which it is right to pursue in all circumstances. Some writers characterise this as being a 'human rights perspective' and associate it with enduring concepts such as justice, fairness and equality which, it is argued, are ethical in themselves and should be supported even if the consequence is not to bring greatest benefit to the greatest number.

We can see the presence of these two distinct philosophical traditions reflected in the arguments that people put forward in support of different positions. An example from HR might be a decision about whether to give everyone a modest pay rise irrespective of performance or whether to focus available resources on rewarding relatively few people whose performance has been outstanding during the past year. A utilitarian argument can be put in favour of the first course of action (greatest benefit to the greatest number) while a deontological argument supports the second (it is right to reward people for superior effort/performance).

Shultz and Brender-Ilan (2004) set out to establish which, if either, of these two perspectives is more attractive as the basis for HR decision-making in organisations according to employees. They found that opinion was divided, there being two clearly identifiable clusters of opinion broadly reflecting a utilitarian–deontological divide. Women tended to prefer deontological approaches and men the utilitarian, but there were differences of view across as well as between the genders.

So it is not just philosophers and academic writers who are divided about the question of what path to follow in order to give ethical legitimacy to management decisions; employees are too.

KEY ARTICLE

CITIGROUP

The following article was published in *People Management* on 27 July 2005. You can download it from the CIPD website.

'Recovery plan' by Sarah Butcher

The article describes how senior managers at Citigroup set about embedding a commitment to high ethical standards across all parts of its operation. The central role played by the HR function is discussed at length.

Questions

1 How is the company using its training, performance management and reward management systems to enhance its ethical credentials?

2 How has the company used ideas with an ethical underpinning to enhance its corporate culture?

3 What other motives underpin the initiatives discussed in this article?

ETHICAL DECISION-MAKING IN HRM – PRACTICE

The fact that there is no clear, unambiguous answer to the question 'what is ethical?' when it comes to choosing how to manage people at work does not mean that the issue can be ignored. Just because people disagree or are unsure about the ethicality of particular courses of action does not mean that 'being ethical and being seen to be ethical' is any less important if an HR function is to maximise its capacity to recruit, retain and motivate a workforce.

What it does mean, however, is that there are no easy answers and that subtle thinking and communication is necessary if an ethical reputation is to be gained and maintained. Winstanley and Woodall (2000: 5) in their seminal article on this subject are thus right to argue that while people will often disagree about what constitutes an ethical path in HRM, there is nonetheless 'a strong case for the ethical rearmament of HR professionals' so that 'ethical sensitivity and awareness might become a legitimate reference point alongside the prevalent recourse to arguments justifying 'the business case', 'strategic fit' and 'best practice'.

I would argue for the adoption of an even more pragmatic position. It seems to me that the ethics of HRM, just as is true of ethics in the wider political field, are generally impossible to resolve satisfactorily.

Most contested courses of action in HR can be both justified ethically and also criticised using different ethical arguments. This is true even in quite extreme cases, such as a decision to pay a chief executive more by way of an annual bonus or pay rise than members of an organisation's workforce get paid for several years' work. The ethical case in favour of the pay rise may well be a lot weaker from most people's perspective than the case in favour, but that does not mean that there is not an ethical argument to be deployed. On the one hand, you can argue that the pay rise is unethical in that it distributes pay in a wholly unfair manner. On the other hand, you could argue that in order to retain an excellent CEO, more money has to be paid and that if the result is a more successful organisation, everyone, including lower-paid employees, stands to benefit in the long run.

The political philosopher Isaiah Berlin (1969) famously observed that conflicts between competing sets of values are 'an intrinsic, irremovable element in human life', arguing in effect that no resolution is ever going to be possible. In accepting this Berlin took issue with many of the most influential figures in his field, including Plato, Marx and Hegel. His conclusion was, quite simply, that:

> the notion of a final harmony in which all riddles are solved, all contradictions reconciled, is a piece of crude empiricism, abdication before brute facts, intolerable bankruptcy of reason before things as they are, failure to explain and to justify, to reduce everything to a system, which 'reason' indignantly rejects.

It follows that we should not try to figure out whether or not there are any clear general principles on which to base ethical HR practice. Doing so will always end up being unsatisfactory because what seems or feels ethical to one person will jar against the ethics of another. It is important to consider these matters and to be guided by the thinking of Walsh, Friedman, Kant and the utilitarians, but ultimately when faced with the messy, practical reality of organisational life, the HR manager must act pragmatically.

What does this mean in practice? In my view, it means two things:

Firstly, it is necessary to accept that day-to-day HRM is carried out in organisations in which different groups of stakeholders have different interests and, importantly, in which some are more powerful than others. It may be deeply unfair and regrettable that an over-promoted, blinkered and semi-competent senior manager wields huge power over everyone else in an organisation, but that is a fact of organisational life in many workplaces. Those of us who work in the public sector may despair at the way that blunt, ill-thought-through and sometimes damaging policies are imposed on our organisations by government. In the private sector, by contrast, the overriding need to meet short-term financial targets is deeply frustrating to HR managers who are looking to meet longer-term objectives. These are all facts of organisational life. Complaining about them is understandable, but usually of no more use in terms of bringing about change than complaining about the weather.

We therefore have to accept that we are obliged to work within an ethically compromised organisational structure and a wider business environment that operates according to economic principles more than it does to ethical ones. This inevitably prevents us from being able to act with total integrity or to make decisions which are as just as we might like in an ideal world. Instead, the best we can aim for is to act as ethically as we can given the many restrictions that the reality of contemporary organisational life places upon us. As Wyburd (1998: 140) observed in his book on these matters, it is a question of 'striking a balance' between remaining competitive and acting ethically:

> They should certainly strive to be winners, but not at any cost.

Secondly, Isaiah Berlin's principle teaches us that we need to use our own judgement when deciding what the most ethical course of action to take is in any given situation. There is no neat set of principles from which an answer to any dilemma can easily be derived.

A pragmatic approach is therefore necessary. Cases must be decided on their own merits, ethical arguments of different kinds being carefully considered alongside one another.

But what kind of ethical arguments? In most organisations an HR manager who made reference to the ideas of Aristotle, Kant or even Milton Friedman when debating what course of action to take would be treated as if he or she were the village idiot. In order to be taken seriously and have a positive impact ethics-wise it is thus necessary to make use of some more readily understood ways of thinking.

DO AS YOU WOULD BE DONE TO

This very simple Biblical instruction should inform thinking about the making of practical decisions when an ethical defence is needed. It can also form the basis of powerful arguments in favour of taking a more ethical course when consideration is being given to others which are less ethical.

FAIR DEALING

J.S. Adams (1963), in his writing on management, argued in favour of 'equity theory'. The premise was that people do not expect to be treated equally in a workplace. Some, for example, deserve to earn more than others because they put in greater effort or carry greater responsibility. But there is an expectation of 'fair dealing' in a broader sense. What matters in terms of maximising trust, commitment and ultimately effort is not what managers think or intend, but how their actions are perceived by the workforce.

The same argument can be harnessed from an ethical perspective. Organisational effectiveness will decline if people generally perceive that they are not being dealt with fairly. HR decisions thus need to be made with an eye on what is considered to be ethical by employees. If your staff are comfortable with the ethics of your HR policies and practices, there is no major problem. If, on the other hand, they perceive that you are acting unethically, you have a problem.

THE RULE OF LAW

An interesting dilemma in all organisations as far as HR matters are concerned is the extent to which 'a rule of law' should apply. This is a long-held principle in political philosophy, often cited as being a fundamental governing principle of good, enlightened, democratic government. A state in which the rule of law applies is one in which there is one set of laws and regulations for everyone. There are no exceptions, however powerful someone is or however powerful their friends and relatives may be. The millionaire peer is in the same position as someone who is unemployed.

It is very difficult always to adhere to the same approach in the management of organisations. Imperative business needs inevitably mean that sometimes a policy of 'one rule for some, another for the rest' is sometimes followed. Effective, high-performing and long-serving staff tend to get a better deal, for example, than new starters who are yet to prove their worth. Someone who is considered indispensable tends to be held on rather a looser lead and perhaps given the benefit of the doubt more than those who are not.

Bending rules somewhat to suit the interests of a high-performer is unlikely to be seen by most as unethical. Such is not the case, however, where it is powerful people who are indulged in the same way, or people who are favoured by the powerful for other reasons.

THE NEWSPAPER TEST

This is another useful barometer to bear in mind when considering the ethics of a decision. You simply ask whether you would be comfortable defending your course of action if its results were to be splashed across the pages of a newspaper. In the political world a more extreme version of this test supposes that it is the front page of a tabloid newspaper, with all that implies about the one-sided and salacious nature of the reporting.

In the case of some major decisions that HR people take, this is by no means a theoretical question. Newspapers frequently report the proceedings of employment tribunal cases, for example, rarely explaining every nuance. When dismissing someone it is wise therefore to think not just about whether it could be justified legally in a court of law, but also ethically in the wider court of public opinion as represented by newspaper coverage.

It is likely in the future that we will increasingly consider other media when applying this test. The growing power of social networking groups in particular should cause us to pause for thought when making decisions that could be perceived as being unethical.

ETHICS AND EMPLOYMENT LAW

It is often tempting when working in HRM to avoid questions of ethics by making reference to employment law and health and safety regulations. The view is taken that 'the rules of the game' are set by lawmakers in the EU, Parliament and the courts and that this means we do not have to ask ourselves questions about the ethics of our actions. Provided we are acting within the limitations imposed by the law, we assume that we are acting in an acceptable manner as far as our ethics are concerned. Employment law thus acts as a kind of proxy for any other would-be ethical code.

This would be a reasonable position to take up were it the case that employment law adequately represented a proxy for ethical HRM. In practice, this is far from being the case. While employment law intends to protect people from unethical actions on the part of employers and to deter managers from taking unethical actions in the first place, it only achieves this in a very patchy and unsatisfactory way.

First of all, of course, and rather paradoxically, employment law itself does not require employers to apply the principle of 'the rule of law' when managing their own organisations. The rights derived from employment statutes are far from universal in their application. Some rights such as equal pay and other discrimination measures apply universally to anyone who works under any kind of contract, sometimes including self-employed people, but other rights do not. Major groups such as agency workers and casual staff typically have no rights at all under unfair dismissal law, however long they have worked for the same employer – basic dismissal rights also being denied to people who work under contracts of employment until they have completed at least a year (soon possibly to be two years) in their roles.

The right not to be required to work for more than 48 hours a week is effectively compromised by regulations that do not just permit workers to 'opt out' of their rights in this area, but also permit employers to make signing an 'opt-out clause' a condition of making an offer of employment. In any event it remains possible to require people to work excessive hours for periods of time because the 48 hours can be averaged over a four-month period. It is only unlawful if someone is required to work for more than 48 hours a week on average in any one 17-week period.

Even the National Minimum Wage is by no means a universal right for everyone, as is often thought. Aside from the presence of lower youth and training rates, anyone who works under a piece-work or commission-based contract can easily find themselves being paid at a rate that is lower than the set national minimum quite lawfully. Moreover, there are some groups such as au pairs, barristers' pupils and interns who appear to fall wholly outside the protection of this law and are not entitled to be paid the National Minimum Wage.

Similar points can be made about the detail of the law and the way that employment tribunals apply it. Of particular concern to many commentators is the way that employers are able to justify summary dismissals on grounds of misconduct even when in most people's eyes their decision to dismiss would be considered unacceptably harsh and probably unethical. The courts are increasingly reluctant to second-guess an employer's decisions in these areas by ruling that a warning would have been a more appropriate sanction than dismissal. Nowadays they seem only interested in whether or not a dismissal was carried out correctly in terms of procedure. Provided some kind of business-related argument can be deployed in support of its 'reasonableness', it will now generally be ruled to have been fair in law.

More than ever now it is therefore unconvincing to argue that acting within the strictures of employment law constitutes managing HR matters in an ethical way.

CORPORATE SOCIAL RESPONSIBILITY

The term *corporate social responsibility* (CSR) encompasses within its meaning a commitment to ethical decision-making, but it is a rather wider concept. Precise definitions vary, but the underlying idea behind all of them is that organisations which commit to CSR are seeking to involve themselves in initiatives which will have a positive impact on society and the environment. The idea is neatly summed up by Cohen (2010: 15):

> A way of doing business that is based on ethical principles and structured management controls, and that takes into account social and environmental considerations alongside economic considerations when making business decisions, and attempts to create positive impacts on all stakeholders. CSR is a voluntary approach going beyond compliance with laws and regulations.

Contrary to many people's perception, neither the term 'CSR' nor the ideas that underpin it are at all recent. They have their origins in the late nineteenth and early twentieth centuries when some large corporations decided that they had a great deal to gain by acting philanthropically and by treating their staff rather better than most employers did. By the 1940s, according to Carroll (2008: 23–24), the vast majority of business leaders when polled agreed that their organisations had social obligations to fulfil and thought that a majority acted on these principles in practice.

However, it has only been in the last two decades that CSR and its rhetoric have been adopted publicly by the majority of larger, international corporations. This has led, according to Carroll (2008: 42), to 'the institutionalization of CSR' by managers across the world. Companies now routinely develop codes of ethics, appoint specialist managers to bring forward CSR initiatives and develop CSR strategies.

Kotler and Lee (2005) provide a useful summary of the major types of CSR initiatives that organisations involve themselves with:

- cause promotion (ie helping to publicise important social causes)
- cause-related marketing (ie donating a portion of income derived from a sales initiative to a good cause)
- corporate social marketing (ie helping to influence changes in behaviour that will have social benefits)
- corporate philanthropy (ie direct donations to good causes)
- community volunteering (ie employees giving up their time and deploying their skills to support good causes)
- socially responsible business practices (ie managing organisations with an eye to business ethics).

We can see from this list that a key feature of CSR is corporations actively engaging with the wider community and associating themselves with 'good causes' of one kind or another. Often this simply involves traditional fundraising activities, as happens when an organisation raises money for an established charity. However, it may also involve sponsorship of artistic and educational activities or collaboration with government to help advance public policy objectives such as healthy eating, awareness of domestic violence or global warming.

The HR function has a major role to play in co-ordinating some of these activities, in promoting them across a workforce and, more generally, in encouraging and facilitating initiatives that originate among groups of employees.

Another common way of defining CSR is to stress its focus on helping to meet the needs of a range of stakeholder groups. The starting point here is to establish who are the major stakeholders, meaning people and organisations who have an economic stake of one kind or another in a business's success. Typically stakeholders will include a business's owners, its managers, its employees, its suppliers, its customers and the wider community from which it draws its resources.

The idea is that all groups have a legitimate interest in the activities of an organisation and that there is a need to balance these interests when making decisions.

Here too HR inevitably plays an important role. Because employees are stakeholders it follows that a right and proper role for HR managers is to advocate and to champion employee interests. But there is also a wider role to play associated with selecting, promoting and developing staff so as to help ensure that a stakeholder-based philosophy pervades decision-making across the organisation.

CSR is often derided for being a cynical exercise which organisations only do in order to benefit themselves. Corporations sponsor ballet companies, associate themselves with environmental causes and involve themselves in charitable activities not because they aim to be ethical, but because it helps to bring them positive publicity. A response to this criticism is to say 'yes, of course – but so what?' Handled well, CSR is a win–win type of activity. Corporations benefit alongside good causes of one kind or another.

CRITICAL REFLECTION

Codes of ethics

Many leading UK-based corporations now draw up codes of ethics for their staff which they publicise on their websites. By being transparent in this way, greater pressure is placed on all staff to adhere to the code and act ethically than would be the case if the codes were kept private.

Here are the web addresses of some major examples from different industries.

1 Banking group, Santander
   www.santander.com/csgs/StaticBS?blobcol=urldata&blobheader=application%2Fpdf&blobkey
   =id&blobtable=MungoBlobs&blobwhere=1265274770273&cachecontrol=immediate&ssbinary
   =true&maxage=3600

2 Defence group, BAE systems
   www.baesystems.com/BAEProd/groups/public/documents/bae_publication/bae_
   pdf_7590f003_001.pdf

3 InterContinental Hotels
   www.ihgplc.com/index.asp?pageid=244

4 Oil giant, BP
   www.bp.com/liveassets/bp_internet/globalbp/STAGING/global_assets/downloads/C/coc_en_
   full_document.pdf

Read through these codes in order to establish what they have in common and in what respects they differ.

What do they tell us about the perspective of contemporary managers on the issue of business ethics?

What do they tell us about the roles that the HR function can potentially take in promoting high standards of ethical conduct in organisations?

CONCLUDING THOUGHTS ON HR AND ETHICS

There is every reason to anticipate that CSR and corporate ethics more generally will move up organisational agendas in the future, not least because consumers, investors and would-be employees want to see that happen. Moreover, there are good business reasons related to enhancing corporate reputation and improving brand image, for taking the issue more seriously than has tended to be the case.

For HR managers in many organisations there is probably going to have to be a change of gear in this area. In recent years we have spent too much time and effort trying to distance the HR function from its roots as a promoter of employee welfare and an advocate of employee interests. This has been done in order to improve the credibility of HR work in the eyes of managers from other functions and hence to gain greater influence. But too often it has resulted in an overly harsh, macho management type of approach to people management, which serves no one's long-term interests.

In truth the two aims are not incompatible. It is perfectly possible, and indeed right, that the HR team in an organisation should promote and advocate both employer *and* employee interests, not least to one another. Clear management messages need to be communicated and justified to staff, but a good HR function also sees its role as being to communicate staff concerns and suggestions back up to managers.

When it comes to decision-making about HR issues there is probably little to be gained from trying to seek out any comprehensive, universally applicable set of ethical principles to apply. Instead, judgement must be exercised on a case-by-case basis, the ultimate test of a decision being whether it can genuinely be justified both ethically and commercially.

EQUALITY AND DIVERSITY

Many of the themes and ideas we discussed above also play a part in debates about the promotion of equality and diversity in organisations. This is by no means an issue which can be characterised purely in ethical terms – there are important business, political and legal dimensions – but there is an ethical angle and for many organisations decisions about whether and how far to develop their equality agenda is as much an ethical judgement as it is a business one. In practice there are a wide mix of motives, as was demonstrated by the CIPD in an extensive research project carried out in 2007 (see Table 12.1). Their data (collected from HR managers across all sectors in the UK) showed clearly that notions of social justice, corporate social responsibility and morality are significant drivers behind the promotion of equality in many organisations.

It is generally agreed that considerable progress has been made towards greater fairness in organisations as far as under-represented groups are concerned. Women and members of ethnic minorities are sometimes characterised as being 'the big winners' in the world of work over the past 20 years. But as the following statistics from research by Walby et al (2008) and Longhi and Platt (2008) show, there is still a very long way to go before true equality is reached, or anything like it:

- 20% of white people live in low-income households; the figure for black people is 41%.

- Men's average gross hourly pay is £12.90; the figure for women is £10.10. Women's average pay is 78% of men's.

- 81% of able-bodied people have jobs; the figure for disabled people is only 60%

- On average, men aged 60–64 earn 24% less than men aged 40–44.

Table 12.1 Drivers of equality and diversity measures

Drivers	Most important	Some importance
Legal pressures	32%	68%
To recruit and retain the best talent	13%	64%
Corporate social responsibility	13%	63%
To be an employer of choice	15%	61%
Because it makes business sense	17%	60%
Because it's morally right	13%	60%
To improve business performance	6%	48%
To address recruitment problems	8%	46%
Belief in social justice	9%	46%
Desire to improve customer relations	5%	43%
To improve products and services	10%	44%
To improve creativity and innovation	6%	43%
To reach diverse markets	6%	39%
To improve corporate branding	5%	37%
To enhance decision-making	3%	35%
Trade union activities	3%	32%
To respond to competition in the market	6%	32%
To respond to the global market	6%	30%

- 24% of able-bodied people are educated to degree level or above; the figure for disabled people is only 13%.
- 19% of men are employed in senior, managerial jobs; the figure for women is only 11%.
- 13.5% of black people perceive that they have personally suffered from discrimination at work; the figure for white people is 0.5%.

The reasons for persistent inequality based on characteristics such as gender, sexuality and race are many and complex. In part it is due to stereotyping whereby society expects women, for example, to head into caring, nurturing careers which tend to be less well paid than the more masculine managerial and physical roles. Raw prejudice also plays its part, often unconsciously, resulting in society having lower regard for the abilities of some racial groups and of disabled people. These and other factors come together to shape our expectations of ourselves and others, perpetuating deep-seated and wholly unjustified inequality at work. The unconscious or semi-conscious nature of these thoughts and assumptions leads organisations to be described as 'institutionally sexist' or 'institutionally racist'.

There is a business case that can be advanced for tackling inequality in the workplace very directly. It is based on a number of sound propositions which echo a number of the points made elsewhere in this book. In 2007, the CIPD published a position paper (CIPD 2007) which clearly set out the case with seven distinct propositions, each backed up with some supporting evidence:

- Staff are impressed when their employer commits to an agenda which is seen as being fair to everyone; the result is lower staff turnover and higher levels of engagement.

- An organisation which treats people fairly will gain a positive reputation as an employer and be better able to attract high-performers to come to work for it.

- A more diverse range of people are likely to apply for vacancies when an employer commits to improved equality. This widens the potential candidate selection pool.

- An organisation which reflects in its make-up the diversity of its customer base is better able to provide a high standard of service to its clients and hence attract and retain their business more effectively than competitors.

- Public sector organisations such as local authorities often take account of the extent and nature of equality initiatives pursued by employing organisations when awarding contracts in competitive tendering exercises.

- Decision-making is often better when the senior cadres in organisations include people who reflect the full diversity of the community from which business opportunities arise.

- Equality initiatives can help an organisation to create a strong socially responsible image which also serves to attract customers and investors as well as employees.

These are all good, fair arguments, but many question their real strength. They suggest that organisations will do better if they commit, conspicuously, to an equality agenda, but by how much? Only a little bit in all probability for most organisations, and over a longish period of time. The business case is thus sound but not especially compelling in raw financial terms. The real business case, it seems to me, lies in the risks associated with being labelled 'racist', 'sexist' or 'homophobic' through lack of action. Poor publicity can then accrue, resulting in serious amounts of lost business and potential business.

A legal case can also be put in favour of a broad equal opportunities agenda. But this rests only on the dangers associated with failing to comply with very basic requirements. No law really requires employers to act positively to reduce inequality beyond some limited requirements in the public sector. Overwhelmingly its purpose is to deter employers from acting negatively by causing someone a detriment on grounds of a range of quite limited 'protected characteristics'.

Ultimately, therefore, an ethical case underpinning equality management initiatives is necessary if real progress is to be made. But what kind of case should that be? The answer, according to many, involves making equality an issue which is relevant for all and from which everyone in an organisation can benefit. It needs to cease to be seen as a minority issue of relevance to 'the few' and should be made into an issue in which 'the many' perceive themselves as having a stake. This is very much the thinking behind the shift in approach we have seen in recent years as initiatives designed to improve 'equality of opportunity' have given way to those aimed at 'promoting diversity'.

The CIPD (2007) neatly sums up the distinction as follows:

> *Managing diversity is about ensuring that all employees have the opportunity to maximise their potential and enhance their self-development and their contribution to the organisation. It's not about positive or affirmative action for select groups to create a level playing field for all. By doing this we're automatically (unconsciously) not indulging in stereotyping, inaccurate perceptions and practising discrimination, but accepting that* all *employees can have a positive input into the processes and objectives of the organisation.*

Equality management is thus recast as fair dealing for all. But this a lot easier to say than to do. In order to make it a reality, senior managers must commit and do so loudly and conspicuously. They also have to re-commit continually so that initiatives are not simply seen as fads which will soon be replaced by others. Diversity then has to be embedded across all the organisation's policies and practices, and particularly in those that fall within the HR manager's realm of responsibility. It needs to feature prominently in management development programmes, for example in performance appraisal systems, in recruitment literature and in company mission statements.

At all times we need to remember that management perceptions of the commitment to diversity are much less important than employee and customer perceptions – hence the need for regular reinforcement and for new initiatives to be introduced periodically.

 CRITICAL REFLECTION

1 What potential lessons can managers with an interest in promoting a wider ethical and corporate social responsibility agenda in their organisations learn from the experience of the promotion of equality at work in recent years?

2 Are there any particular lessons that can be learned from the apparent success of a 'managing diversity' approach to equality management?

3 To what extent is it sound to label the promotion of 'equal opportunities' as comprising a broadly Kantian or deontological approach, and 'managing diversity' as being more utilitarian in its thinking?

KEY LEARNING POINTS

- Increased interest in ethics on the part of consumers, investors and would-be employees means that organisations are wise to try to ensure that they gain a positive ethical reputation.

- The HR function has an important role to play in promoting ethical conduct across organisations and also in making ethical decisions about people management issues.

- It is very difficult indeed to establish any general set of ethical principles that can or should govern HR activity in organisations, so there is a good case for using judgement on a case-by-case basis and acting pragmatically when seeking to make ethical HR decisions.

- HR managers have a key role to play when an organisation seeks to act in a socially responsible manner.

- A significant field of organisational ethics in which much progress has been made is equality management, although there remains much further progress to be made.

- Lessons can potentially be learned across the wider field of ethics from the recent trend towards a 'managing diversity' approach to the promotion of equality in the workplace.

EXPLORE FURTHER

HR ethics are well covered from a variety of angles in the book of articles edited by Ashly Pinnington and his colleagues (2007). A bigger book, containing contributions from a variety of scholars, covering CSR generally is the *Oxford handbook* edited by Andrew Crane and colleagues (2008).

Pinnington, A., Macklin, R. and Campbell, T. (2007) *Human resource management: ethics and employment*. Oxford: Oxford University Press.

Crane, A., McWilliams, A., Matten, D., Moon, J. and Siegel, D. (eds) (2008) *The Oxford handbook of corporate social responsibility*. Oxford: Oxford University Press.

The best single book on equality management and all its surrounding debates is by Gill Kirton and Anne-Marie Greene (2010).

Kirton, G. and Greene, A.-M. (2010) *The dynamics of managing diversity: a critical approach*. London: Butterworth-Heinemann.

REFERENCES

Adams, J.S. (1963) Toward an understanding of inequity. *Journal of Abnormal and Social Psychology*. Vol 67. pp422–436.

Berlin, I. (1969) Two concepts of liberty. In I. Berlin (ed.) *Liberty*. Oxford: Oxford University Press.

Carroll, A. (2008) A history of corporate social responsibility. In A. Crane, A. McWilliams, D. Matten, J. Moon and D. Siegel (eds) *The Oxford handbook of corporate social responsibility*. Oxford: Oxford University Press.

CIPD (2007) *Managing diversity: people make the difference at work, but everyone is different*. London: Chartered Institute of Personnel and Development.

Cohen, E. (2010) *CSR for HR: a necessary partnership for advancing responsible business practices*. Sheffield: Greenleaf Publishing.

Friedman, M. (1970) The social responsibility of business is to increase its profits. *New York Times Magazine*. 13 September.

Fryer, M. (2009) HRM: an ethical perspective. In G. Wood and D. Collings (eds) *Human resource management: a critical approach*. Abingdon: Routledge.

Kotler, P. and Lee, N. (2005) *Corporate social responsibility: doing the most good for your company and your cause*. Hoboken, NJ: Wiley.

Leahy, T. (2005) Britain: a picture of people power. *The Economist*. 18 November.

Longhi, S. and Platt, L. (2008) *Pay gaps across equality groups*. Manchester: Equality and Human Rights Commission.

Melé, D. (2008) Corporate social responsibility theories. In A. Crane, A. McWilliams, D. Matten, J. Moon and D.S. Siegel (eds) *The Oxford handbook of corporate social responsibility*. Oxford: Oxford University Press.

Mulligan, T. (1986) A critique of Milton Friedman's essay 'The social responsibility of business is to increase its profits'. *Journal of Business Ethics*. Vol 5, No 4. pp265–269.

Pinnington, A., Macklin, R. and Campbell, T. (2007) Introduction. In A. Pinnington, R. Macklin and T. Campbell (eds) *Human resource management: ethics and employment*. Oxford: Oxford University Press.

Provis, C. (2010) Ethics and HRM. In A. Wilkinson, N. Bacon, T. Redman and S. Snell (eds) *The Sage handbook of human resource management*. London: Sage.

Salazar, J. and Husted, B.W. (2008) Principals and agents: further thoughts on the Friedmanite critique of corporate social responsibility. In A. Crane, A. McWilliams, D. Matten, J. Moon and D.S. Siegel (eds) *The Oxford handbook of corporate social responsibility*. Oxford: Oxford University Press.

Shultz, T. and Brender-Ilan, Y. (2004) Beyond justice: introducing personal moral philosophies to ethical evaluations of human resource practices. *Business Ethics: A European Review*. Vol 13, No 4. pp302–316.

Walby, S., Armstrong, J. and Humphries, L. (2008) *Review of equality statistics*. Manchester: Equality and Human Rights Commission.

Walsh, A. (2007) HRM and the ethics of commodified work in a market economy. In A. Pinnington, R. Macklin and T. Campbell (eds) *Human resource management: ethics and employment*. Oxford: Oxford University Press.

Winstanley, D. and Woodall, J. (2000) The ethical dimension of human resource management. *Human Resource Management Journal*. Vol 10, No 2. pp5–20.

Wyburd, G. (1998) *Competitive and ethical? How business can strike a balance*. London: Kogan Page.

CHAPTER 13

Developing HR strategies

Introduction

In Chapter 1 I explained that one of the key defining features of HRM, as opposed to its predecessor 'personnel management', is the presence of a prominent strategic ingredient in the approach that organisations take to the management of people. There is no question that the move away from a predominantly reactive approach to one which is essentially strategic in nature is one of the most significant contemporary HR trends. Since the 1980s, as trade union influence has declined and collective agreements have been downplayed or abandoned, HR managers have been presented with the opportunity to take control of people management policy and practice and to shape it to suit the needs of their organisations. A consequence has been a great deal of research activity and the publication of numerous books and articles aimed at different audiences developing ideas about 'strategic HRM' and how to go about practising it.

Partly because of the sheer volume of material written about it, this remains, however, a somewhat bewildering field. Different people have different ideas about exactly what a 'strategic approach' to HR involves. Theories abound but in many respects thinking about strategy has run ahead of practice, resulting in a situation in which the nature of strategic HRM is much debated, while practical implementation has been rather patchy. Senior HR people deploy strategic rhetoric all the time, but the reality often fails to match aspirations.

There is thus a great deal more progress to make in this area and it is likely that organisations will refine their approaches in the coming years, moving the strategic HR agenda forward in new directions. There is every reason to expect this to be the case as labour markets for skilled staff tighten and the need to recruit, retain and engage people effectively becomes more important in increasingly competitive and volatile market conditions.

Interestingly, one of the principal ways in which a strategic approach to HRM has often been taken in the past has been in decline at the same time that rhetoric about the importance of strategy has been increasing. Manpower planning formed a significant element of personnel practice in the 1960s and 1970s, since when its use has declined rapidly. It is now more commonly labelled *workforce planning* or *human resource planning* (HRP) and is very much a minority pursuit as far as contemporary organisations are concerned. There are now signs that interest in a modernised approach to HRP is starting to grow again as organisations look for ways of operationalising some of their more general strategic thinking about people management.

In this chapter my purpose is to introduce readers to some of the research on these subjects with a view to bringing some clarity to what can be quite a confusing field. We will start by summarising the major alternative approaches to HR strategy-making, none of which is mutually exclusive, before going on to outline some of the key recent contributions to thinking in these areas. After this we will reflect on the likely future evolution of human resource planning and associated activities.

LEARNING OUTCOMES

The objectives of this chapter are to:

● introduce the major alternative conceptions of 'strategic HRM'

● illustrate the principles of strategic alignment using some well-known contingency models

● discuss some criticisms that have been made of contingency thinking in HRM

● introduce tools to help managers position themselves in their labour markets as employers

● explain how HR planning and succession planning can and should be reconceived for twenty-first-century business conditions.

ALTERNATIVE CONCEPTIONS OF HR STRATEGY

The first point to make when summarising thinking on HR strategy is that there are a number of quite different ways that it can be conceptualised. These are different, but not at all exclusive. It is helpful to see them as different ways of thinking about HR strategy or of approaching the development of an HR strategy.

1 TAKING A MILITARY-TYPE APPROACH

One straightforward way of conceptualising strategic HRM is to view it quite broadly as an organisation responding in a strategic fashion to the people management challenges that it faces. It is useful here to use a military metaphor and to think in terms of taking a strategic approach to the fighting of a battle. This enables us to contrast strategy with tactics.

A strategic approach to HRM under this definition involves taking a long-term, helicopter-type view, planning responses ahead of time, preparing to meet a number of possible contingencies and acting proactively rather than reactively. Seen this way the HR director in an organisation is like a military commander planning an operation. Long-term objectives are set and each intervention planned in advance with some care.

It is fair to state that this first approach represents a kind of 'layman's view' of what HR strategy involves and many who have not studied the subject in any depth naturally come to think about it in this way. While such an approach can characterise the entire HR operation in an organisation, the military-type definition can also be usefully applied to specific projects. Hence we can take a broadly strategic approach to the management of the people aspects of a merger, a redundancy programme or an expansion involving hiring large numbers of new staff. Indeed, any change management programme, structural or cultural, can be thought of usefully in these terms.

2 STRATEGIC ALIGNMENT

Much academic research in strategic HRM over recent decades has taken this second approach. Here the idea of 'strategic HRM' is conceived far more narrowly and precisely as a set of HR policy and practices which are aligned with and which aim to support the achievement of wider organisational objectives. In other words, HRM is seen as having a strategic character when its activities and priorities are derived from and are designed to reinforce the achievement of the organisation's strategy.

The starting point involves gaining a clear understanding of organisational strategic objectives. The HR strategy is then developed directly from these, its aim being to ensure as far as possible that people management activities are appropriate and contribute to the successful achievement of those objectives.

Hence if an organisation's declared strategic objectives include a commitment to downsize and improve productivity by 10% in the coming year, the strategic HR response is to put in place policies which ensure that aim is delivered. By contrast, if an organisation's aim is to improve the quality of its products so as to reposition itself in the market, a strategically focused HR function will respond by adjusting its selection and development practices accordingly.

This conception of HR strategy is very much associated with the idea of strategic integration. The HR strategy will only help to deliver the organisation's strategy if it is both vertically integrated (ie HR objectives directly support organisational objectives) and horizontally integrated (ie different areas of HR practice mutually reinforce one another and are all fully aligned with the strategy).

During the 1990s in particular, academics and consultants took this idea of strategic alignment and developed a variety of 'contingency models' which link organisational strategy with HR strategy. A number were then tested empirically, the aim being to establish how far organisations which had aligned their HR strategies with their business strategies enjoyed greater success than competitors who had failed to do so. We will return later in this chapter to look at some of these models.

3 ENVIRONMENTAL SCANNING

A third alternative way of thinking about HR strategy is focused on developments in the wider business environment. To a considerable extent this is the approach that I have taken in this book, starting in the first chapters with an analysis of the key contemporary environmental trends that are affecting HR, before going on to assess what responses are evolving and are likely to evolve further in the future. Thinking of this kind appears also to be underpinning much of the research work that the CIPD is now embarking upon and was also very influential in determining the type of research carried out in recent years under the auspices of the Economic and Social Research Council (ESRC) 'Future of Work' programme.

The core idea here is to focus on how an organisation is likely to evolve over a five- to ten-year period. What will its future needs be as far as human resources are concerned? How will its skills needs change? What will be the key challenges it has to face as far as people management is concerned? From this analysis, initiatives are developed which aim to help ensure that it is well placed to 'meet the future' when it arrives. It is about ensuring that an organisation has robust plans in place to develop the HR capabilities it is going to require in the foreseeable future.

The approach requires that a periodic, formal review takes place which focuses on key trends in an organisation's industry and in its competitive environment. What are the key opportunities and threats that it faces? What are the HR implications? The analysis then needs to take account of key trends that are outside the organisation's immediate control (ie wider social, demographic, technological, legal, economic and political trends) before going on to think about the best way of responding.

4 FOCUSING ON THE LABOUR MARKET

Another way of thinking about HR strategy is narrower, but offers a great deal to organisations which are faced with skills shortages or are obliged to compete with other organisations to secure high-performing staff in relatively tight labour market conditions. It also has relevance for all organisations which are concerned about their capacity, either now or in the future, to recruit and retain a high-quality workforce.

This fourth approach involves thinking specifically about an organisation's reputation as an employer, the aim being to take control of that reputation and to position itself in the labour market appropriately *vis-à-vis* its major competitors. Just as the marketing function seeks to position product ranges in consumer markets so as to maximise profitability, so the HR function can position the organisation competitively in the labour market so as to attract and retain the best-quality people that it can afford to employ.

It is astonishing how underdeveloped thinking about this area of HR activity has been, even in the 2003–08 period when labour markets tightened and skills shortages became a major preoccupation for many employers. Much was written about the 'war for talent' and the need to become 'an employer of choice', but with the exception of some fledgling research on employer branding (see Chapter 7), remarkably little detailed research has been carried out specifically on labour market reputation and strategic positioning of organisations' employment offerings. I am sure that a great deal more research effort will be focused in this direction in the future.

5 RESOURCE-BASED APPROACHES

A fifth and final major alternative way of thinking about HR strategy-making draws on some of the ideas I have set out above when introducing the first four, but does so from a very different perspective. Whereas their starting point is the external environment, resource-based thinking starts with an analysis of internal resources. In terms of HR this means existing human resources.

The resource-based view (RBV) of the firm has attained substantial influence in HR circles in recent years. It can perhaps be seen very much as today's fashion, certainly among academic researchers, and as a result this is where a great deal of cutting-edge research into strategic HR is now being focused. At base is the notion that competitive advantage in the evolving business environment now tends to accrue to those organisations which are best able to adapt to change and to seize and develop new business opportunities more effectively and faster than their competitors are able to. The capacity to innovate is central, as is organisational agility. The key point is that new developments, often of a game-changing kind, come along much more frequently than they used to. Highly competitive, global market conditions mean that organisations do not any longer have the luxury of time, as once they did, to plan a response, buy in new people and build up new business capabilities. By the time this has happened, competitors will already be established players. It follows that the organisation needs to be 'oven ready' ahead of time and that requires the development over a long period of its internal resources and capabilities. Of particular importance is the need to be at the forefront of contemporary scientific and technological developments, shaping the future of an industry as far as possible, rather than responding to developments as they come along.

A resource-based HR strategy therefore starts by establishing what human resources an organisation has which give it a competitive edge now, and more importantly which have the capacity to do so in the future. On one level we are talking here about skills and the capacity to further enhance skills. But increasingly we need to think rather more broadly in terms of knowledge and our capacity to manage that knowledge creatively and effectively (see Chapter 10).

It is also necessary to establish what makes an organisation's human resource base effective in more general terms, so we need to focus on culture and levels of employee engagement too. Having carried out this kind of analysis, resource-based thinking requires that ways are found of protecting, enhancing and reinforcing the people-oriented attributes the organisation has at its disposal.

Barney (1991) suggested that the focus should be on understanding which human resources are:

- valuable

- rare

- inimitable (ie hard for competitors to replicate)

- non-substitutable.

These can then provide the basis of a human resource strategy which seeks to sustain and strengthen existing competitive advantage enjoyed on the people management front.

KEY ARTICLE

Read the article entitled 'Self-service' by Mark Easterby-Smith and Manuel Graça, featured in *People Management* (12 February 2004). This can be downloaded from the *People Management* archive on the CIPD website (www.cipd.co.uk).

In this article the authors describe and assess two excellent examples of resource-based HR thinking to positive effect.

Questions

1 In what ways did the two companies described in this article make use of their existing capabilities to enhance their competitive capacity?

2 What evidence more generally do the case studies provide of managers taking a strategic approach to the management of people?

3 What are the barriers that many organisations would have to overcome before they could achieve 'dynamic capabilities' of the kind discussed in this article?

CONTINGENCY MODELS

The idea that organisations should have a coherent strategy for the management of people emerged in the 1960s, in part as a result of the highly influential work carried out by Joan Woodward of Imperial College in London and her colleagues. They carried out one of the first major government-funded studies of UK industrial relations practices, looking in great depth at the way workers were managed in 100 manufacturing firms, all of which were based in a small part of Essex (many were food manufacturing concerns). More than 90% of the firms in this area were visited, lengthy interviews being conducted with staff at all levels. Joan Woodward found that some firms were much more tightly controlled than others. In some employees were allowed plenty of discretion over how they did their work and permitted flexible working practices of various kinds. Others were tightly supervised – even skilled people – continual pressure being placed on staff to work faster and increase productivity.

What was interesting about her findings was that the larger and smaller firms tended to take a light-touch approach to managing people, whereas the medium-sized firms preferred a tougher approach. The explanation was the greater financial pressure faced by the medium-sized firms. They were competing with the larger firms, but did not have the advantage of economies of scale, so they had to intensify work. The smaller firms were serving niche markets prepared to pay a premium for quality products and so were under less financial pressure.

More interesting still, and very important in the subsequent evolution of HR theory, was the finding that the most financially successful firms were those which conformed to type. In other words, medium-sized firms which took a relaxed approach were less successful than medium-sized firms which took a tough approach, but the reverse was true of the largest and smallest organisations.

Woodward's conclusion was thus in favour of contingency theory. As far as the management of people is concerned, there is no single right way to go. It all depends on the circumstances of the firm. What is right for one set of conditions is not necessarily right for another.

Later researchers have developed Woodward's theories and integrated them with theories about the gaining and maintaining of competitive advantage. The result has been a steady stream of contingency models and typologies which identify different types of business situation or strategy and argue that a different approach to the management of people is appropriate in each case. Research identifying and testing the validity of these models has formed a major academic contribution to thinking about strategic HRM in recent years, particularly to thinking about strategic alignment and vertical and horizontal integration. The approach is best illustrated with some examples of the genre:

THE BOSTON CONSULTING GROUP MODEL

This very well-known model was developed in the 1970s as a means of helping large corporations classify different businesses with a view to building up a balanced portfolio of types. It has, however, been adapted for use by HR strategists as a contingency model (see Purcell 1989). It is often used as a lifecycle model, the idea being that businesses start out as wildcats, grow into stars, become cash cows and then degenerate into dogs. Here, as with all contingency models, the proposition is that different HR strategies are appropriate for each of the four business types. Figure 13.1 illustrates the model, the four segments being differentiated by their share of the market and whether or not the market is growing or declining.

Wildcats are in the early stages of development. Their major strategic aim is to grow market share, a purpose for which excess cash needs to be generated. In HR terms this requires a no-frills, flexible approach. Bureaucracy is minimised and people are paid at or slightly below market rates. There is an emphasis on teamworking, but little formal employee development. HR needs to be ad hoc and opportunist, but must be fair and positive. By contrast, stars are large, established, successful organisations. They can afford to develop sophisticated HR policies and will aim to be seen as 'employers of choice'. There is plenty of investment in training, strongly delineated career ladders, extensive 'good practice' policy, good pay and benefits, and an emphasis on improving morale and motivation.

Figure 13.1 Boston Consulting Group model

STAR Rising market	High market share **CASH COW**
WILDCAT Low market share	Falling market **DOG**

Cash cows are established, large organisations but with few growth opportunities. If part of a group of companies, their role is to generate the cash needed to grow other areas of the business. Otherwise their only goal is protecting an existing market share. In HR terms they are run efficiently, but not especially humanely. Bureaucracy is established, costs are kept under control and training opportunities limited. Employee relations tend to be a priority because cash cows are more likely than the other types to have active unions. Dogs are struggling businesses. Survival is the major priority leading to below-market wages, few development opportunities and management by 'stick' rather than 'carrot'.

PORTER'S GENERIC STRATEGIES

Michael Porter argued that there are three generic business strategies – cost leadership, differentiation and focus. In practice, focus is really just a refined version of the other two, but two distinct types of differentiation strategy are identified – quality enhancement and innovation. So there are three principal alternative approaches that can be adopted. A number of HR strategists (eg Schuler and Jackson 1987) have used Porter's thinking to develop contingency models based on the idea that HR strategy should vary depending on whether the organisation's prime competitive strategy relates to cost-cutting, innovation or quality enhancement.

Cost leadership requires a financial focus, great attention being paid to the achievement of budget targets. Pay is kept low and cheap approaches to HR are followed. There is likely to be a fair amount of bureaucracy, but there is no need for sophisticated HR policies aimed at encouraging motivation and career development. By contrast, innovation requires a staffing focus because here the effective recruitment and retention of people with specialised skills is central. HR policies will thus seek high levels of commitment and engagement. Risk-taking and creativity will be rewarded, and there will be a great deal of emphasis placed on knowledge-sharing. Finally, quality enhancement strategies require a motivation focus, the business strategy being dependent on the continual achievement of high levels of quality (ie high levels of individual performance and high levels of customer service). So there is plenty of training and development, good pay, a commitment to employee involvement and a consultative management style.

MILES AND SNOW

This is another well-known and influential model (Miles and Snow 1978). Here, too, as in Porter's model, three basic types of business strategy are identified, but a different strategic dimension is the focus. The three types are described as defenders, prospectors and analysers. Defenders compete by deepening their penetration in their existing markets. They thus operate in one industry and seek to grow their market share by competing with others in the same industry. Their appeal to potential employees is their relative stability and their capacity for developing people internally. Pay tends to be good. They thus invest in their people, but are bureaucratically structured and have established procedures to follow, so that administrative costs are minimised.

Prospectors, by contrast, grow by seeking out alternative business opportunities. They are smaller and more flexible than defenders, opportunistic in outlook. Flexibility of all sorts is central to their HR needs, so there is a lot of variable pay, plenty of movement around the organisation, decentralised management and a tendency to employ subcontractors, casual staff and temporary workers. Finally, analysers combine both of the above approaches. They seek to compete by growing existing markets, but also seek out new opportunities and enter other new markets when there is an opportunity. They are often 'second to market', allowing a prospector to establish a market, before joining them. In HR terms the key is to develop people and then to redeploy them as required. So flexibility is mixed with the provision of long-term career prospects. HR planning is important as is training and development.

OTHER MODELS

Numerous other contingency models of this kind have been published over the years, some of which have gained greater influence than others. Examples include the Lengnick-Hall model (1988), which is based on growth expectations (high or low) and readiness to adapt to change (high and low). Another is the Devanna model (1984), which suggests that HR strategy needs to vary according to the structure of the business (single product, holding companies, diversified products, international, etc). James Walker's model (1992) was prominent for a while. His four categories of organisational strategy are 'flexible', 'entrepreneurial', 'institutional' and 'niche'. These are heavily influenced by Henry Mintzberg's thinking about models based around complexity and the rate of change. Walker essentially takes Mintzberg's categories and suggests that different HR strategies are appropriate for each.

CRITICISMS OF CONTINGENCY APPROACHES

Criticism of the contingency models of HR strategy has come from two very different directions. The first essentially argues that they are overly complex, the second that they are overly simple. The best known critiques have come from advocates of best practice approaches to HRM, such as Jeffrey Pfeffer (1994) and Mark Huselid (1995), who argue that HR strategy should not be contingent on business strategy at all. Their research has led them to conclude that the same set of 'good practice' HR policies and practices will help all organisations to achieve competitive advantage whatever the business strategy being pursued.

They advocate high pay, sophisticated selection programmes, positive approaches to performance management, employee involvement, training and development opportunities and active promotion of equality of opportunity. These always lead to superior performance and lower turnover and thus always enhance an organisation's competitive position.

An alternative criticism argues that there is nothing at all wrong with contingency approaches *per se*, but that the contingency models oversimplify the situation by focusing wholly on product markets and what organisations are doing to compete in them. In the real world HRM also requires organisations to take account of the labour market conditions and of the different regulatory regimes around the world. And these may, in practice, act as a barrier preventing HR managers from simply aligning their strategy with that of the organisation in the manner suggested by the above models. HR strategies in the real world are necessarily more sophisticated, taking account of a wider range of environmental variables.

POSITIONING AN ORGANISATION IN THE LABOUR MARKET

It is at least arguable that labour market conditions, in particular, matter and should determine an organisation's HR strategy as much as product market conditions. Expensive, sophisticated HR practices are wasteful when labour markets are loose, because you can achieve HR objectives just as well at lower cost. By contrast, when labour markets are tight, low-cost, low-performance-type HR strategies are useless however tight the financial situation, because you won't be able to recruit and retain the people you need. It can thus be argued that contingency models which are based on labour market conditions are as useful, if not more useful, as the basis for determining HR strategy.

Higgs (2004) provides a rare example of this kind of thinking. He suggests that employers have much to gain from 'segmenting' their employment markets and positioning themselves strategically in accordance with such an analysis (see Figure 13.2).

Figure 13.2 The Higgs model

High rewards   High rewards
Low culture   High culture

EMPLOYER OF CASH	EMPLOYER OF CHOICE
EMPLOYER OF CHURN	EMPLOYER OF VALUES

Low rewards   Low rewards
Low culture   High culture

He presents a model which suggests four potential basic strategic choices with two variables. One is the amount of money the employer is willing or able to pay. The other is not fully explained, but is labelled 'culture', and appears to refer to the extent to which employees are treated in a professional or ethical manner.

One strategic choice is therefore to be 'an employer of cash', whereby employees are treated quite harshly, perhaps autocratically or by being expected to work excessive hours, but are nonetheless rewarded well. Such a strategy involves attracting good recruits with large pay packets and then retaining them by ensuring that they will have to take a pay cut if they opt to work elsewhere. The aim is to allow the employer to buy acceptance from its employees of a range of 'low-commitment/high-control' HR practices.

The opposite strategy involves paying poorly, perhaps rather less than the going market rate, but to compensate by treating staff conspicuously better than would-be competitors do. Higgs labels this 'the employer of values' strategy. Such approaches have traditionally been associated with work in the public and voluntary sectors, where pay has tended to be relatively low, but the work remains attractive because it is perceived as meaningful and rewarding by employees who also enjoy a superior level of job security.

The top right quartile in the Higgs model is labelled 'employer of choice', a term which is increasingly commonly used to describe an organisation which sets out to achieve an excellent labour market reputation by both paying well and treating people well. Examples of such organisations, many of which operate in the professional and financial services sectors, are found in the annual *Sunday Times* survey of the best 100 companies to work for in the UK. Finally, in the bottom left-hand corner is the box labelled 'employer of churn'. In such organisations pay is lousy as is the way that employees are treated. The result is high staff turnover. In a tight labour market, where people have choice about where they work, such organisations find it hard to recruit and keep good staff. In recent years they have tended to rely on workers recruited overseas as well as on people who have very low skills and are thus incapable of finding alternative jobs.

Within the 'employer of choice' category, it is possible to identify further divisions, the idea here being that there are distinctly different ways of achieving 'employer of choice' status. Which a particular organisation chooses will in large part be determined on the type of labour market conditions it faces. A potentially useful approach therefore involves simply classifying organisations according to the relative strengths of their internal and external labour markets, the rationale being that different approaches to HR in general, and people resourcing activities in particular, are appropriate in each case. Figure 13.3 is a suggested approach which makes use of the familiar four-quadrant choice type of model.

Figure 13.3 External and internal labour market model

tight market/career opportunities **EMPLOYEE DEVELOPMENT FOCUS**	tight market/few career opportunities **REWARD MANAGEMENT FOCUS**
loose market/career opportunities **EMPLOYEE RESOURCING FOCUS**	loose market/few career opportunities **EMPLOYEE RELATIONS FOCUS**

Where an organisation can offer people little by way of internal career progression because it is small or has a flat hierarchy it must either pursue HR policies which are relations-focused or reward-focused. If labour markets are tight it must focus on rewarding people if it is to recruit and retain the people it needs. If labour markets are loose this is not a problem, but the organisation is more likely to be unionised because the only way terms and conditions will improve is through collective action, hence the focus on the management of employee relations. By contrast, where there are internal career opportunities available, pay and conditions will be less significant from an HR point of view. If the labour market is tight, people can be attracted and subsequently retained with a heavy focus on personal development. On the other hand, where the market is loose, the problem will be the number of job applications the organisation faces. Retention will not be a problem, so the central aim of the HR function will be to recruit and select good people, hence the resourcing focus.

CONTEMPORARY APPROACHES TO HUMAN RESOURCE PLANNING

Until quite recently it was usual for larger organisations in the UK to carry out systematic workforce planning. This involved forecasting the likely demand for labour over coming years (numbers of people required in which types of job, etc) and putting plans in place to ensure that this demand could in fact be met. In the case of public sector organisations, ten-year plans were common. It was also the norm for organisations to engage in formal succession planning activities, plotting the development of high-flying recruits from early on in their careers so that they were in a position to assume key leadership roles in middle age.

It is often stated that a key distinction between 'old' personnel management approaches and 'new' human resource management is the presence in the latter of a strategic element which is absent in the case of the former. In fact this is a simplification which is highly misleading unless a very narrow definition of the term *strategy* is adopted. In carrying out systematic workforce planning, personnel departments were very much acting in a strategic fashion, thinking long term about their personnel needs and taking steps to ensure that these would be met in practice. What has happened, paradoxically, is that with the advent of HRM since the 1980s, this traditional type of strategic HR activity has become a good deal less pervasive. Workforce planning is still carried out in the NHS and in some larger corporations, but on a far lesser scale than was the case 30 years ago. In this respect HRM can be said to be less strategic in its approach than personnel management used to be.

The reasons for the decline in formal workforce planning (now more often labelled human resource planning) are the subject of some debate. Undoubtedly, however, a key reason has been the evolution of a far less predictable business environment which has rendered the traditional approach (drawing up five-year and ten-year plans) less and less useful. Organisations simply do not know, as they typically did in the 1960s and 1970s, what their future demand for labour is going to be in five or ten years' time. Increased competitive pressures, radical technological advances and more extensive merger and acquisition activity have made the business environment too unpredictable to make meaningful HRP of the traditional kind worth carrying out. As soon as plans were drawn up, they would have to be changed. Indeed a good case can be made in favour of the argument that HRP *should* no longer be carried out. Henry Mintzberg is particularly associated with this view. In his influential book *The rise and fall of strategic planning* (1994), he argued that this kind of established business practice no longer had relevance due to the turbulence of markets and the regular occurrence of what he called 'discontinuities' or game-changing episodes. Not only, in his view, is strategic planning now a waste of resources, he also believes that it serves to stifle the creativity and innovative thinking which are now far more likely to be the source of competitive advantage.

There is no question that long-term workforce planning as traditionally carried out is now pretty much dead as far as most organisations are concerned. It really only remains relevant in sectors which are characterised by relatively predictable environments and in which long lead times are necessary in order to train and develop the next generation of key employees. The NHS is a good example. It takes ten years or more to develop senior doctors and it is also quite possible to predict future health needs with some accuracy, so HRP is practicable, necessary and cost-effective. But this is not the case elsewhere in the economy.

However, this does not mean that HR managers should not be thinking strategically and systematically about their organisations' future human resource needs and putting in place plans to help ensure that these will in fact be met. The case for doing this is in many respects made stronger rather than weaker by the declining predictability of our business environment. Just as choppier seas do not lead sailors to abandon attempts at navigation, greater turbulence in the competitive environment means that HR managers should be more rather than less inclined to plan ahead with some care. What is needed, and what is increasingly happening in forward-thinking HR departments, is a fresh approach to HR planning which is appropriate to today's conditions.

The same is true of succession planning. It still has very great relevance for organisations. Senior managers still retire or leave suddenly and need to be replaced with experienced, able successors. But here too there is a need to modernise traditional approaches which have tended to be rather elitist and secretive in nature.

TWENTY-FIRST-CENTURY HRP

In order to be relevant and to contribute value for an organisation, human resource planning needs to be reinvented for the contemporary and evolving business environment. In my view, a number of different adjustments can be made in order to achieve this.

First, HRP needs to broaden its scope. Traditionally it has very much been about numbers of people and jobs, there being an assumption that job content is not going to change to any great degree over time and that the organisation's structure will also remain broadly unchanged. Another assumption embedded in traditional HRP is that the organisation will source the human resources it needs by providing permanent employment opportunities. All of these assumptions can now be seen as unsafe. Job content changes all the time as organisations alter their activities in response to changing business opportunities. Similarly, organisations regularly restructure, if they are not pretty well permanently doing so. Moreover, as we saw in Chapter 6, flexible working of various kinds is now the norm and is likely to become even more common in the future as organisations seek to become more agile. It follows that HRP needs to focus more widely on its future demand for and supply of skills. The question asked should not be 'how many people will we need in job X in three years' time?' but 'what skills are we going to need to source in three years' time?'

Refocusing HRP from jobs to skills also has the advantage of drawing the attention of managers specifically towards skills that are likely to be in short supply. HR plans are thus heavily weighted towards the tighter labour markets where greater effort and expense needs to be focused if good, experienced staff are to be recruited and developed.

The second major way in which traditional HRP can and should be reinvented is by including 'soft' issues alongside the traditional 'hard' ones. By this I mean that when we look forward with a view to preparing the organisation to meet future HR challenges we should do more than just think about sourcing skills and people. We also need to think about how we are going to manage them, taking into consideration cultural as well as structural HR matters. This involves taking full account of key social trends such as those we discussed in Chapter 5. In particular managers need to develop a clear view about the ways in which employee expectations are likely to change as members of the Baby Boom generation move into retirement and are replaced by members of 'generation me'. There is a good deal of evidence available now that suggests a qualitatively different type of leadership will be needed if organisations are to engage, attract and retain younger people. Managers in the future are going to have to be more emotionally intelligent, more prepared to involve staff in decisions and more flexible in their thinking. These are not qualities that either 'grow on trees' or which can be developed overnight. Management development programmes need to be preparing leaders now for the challenges they will face in three or five years' time.

Thirdly, HRP needs to be quite radically re-mastered to make it fit for purpose in a business world which is inherently less predictable than the one in which it was traditionally practised. This requires a fundamental switch in objectives. Instead of aiming to produce a single plan which we then adjust over time in the light of evolving circumstances, twenty-first-century HR planning has to involve the production of several plans. In other words, a contingency approach needs to be taken. The aim should not be simply to forecast the one most likely future scenario and prepare for that, but to plan for multiple possible future scenarios. Plans then need to be put in place which give the organisation the capability to cope effectively with any of the possible futures it may in fact meet.

SUCCESSION PLANNING

Developing future organisational leaders is as important now as it ever was. But traditional approaches to succession planning no longer fit well with employee expectations or perceptions of fairness. As Hirsh (2000) argues very effectively, there is a need to modernise this area of HR activity to make it much fairer and more inclusive. It is no longer appropriate or sensible for senior managers simply to pick successors in their own mould and to give these chosen few accelerated career development opportunities. Fast-track programmes are needed, but they should be open to all, places being filled using transparent and fair selection criteria. Moreover, when doing this, managers need to think very carefully about the kinds of competency that future leaders of their organisations are going to need, as these may be rather different from those associated with today's most effective leaders.

KEY ARTICLE

Read the article entitled 'Workforce planning: a force for good' by Hashi Syedain, featured in *People Management* (3 June 2010). This can be downloaded from the *People Management* archive on the CIPD website (www.cipd.co.uk).

In this article the case is put for reviving workforce planning (ie human resource planning) following its years 'in the doldrums'. A number of ideas are advanced for making it more relevant to contemporary HR practice and thinking.

Questions

1 Why, according to the article, is HR planning enjoying something of a resurgence in today's HR departments?

2 What does the article suggest should be done to make HRP more relevant for organisations?

3 What benefits is it suggested follow when effective HRP is introduced by organisations?

KEY LEARNING POINTS

- There are a number of distinct approaches that can be taken when developing an HR strategy: taking a military approach, aligning HR activity with business objectives, environmental scanning, formulating a competitive labour market strategy; and taking a resource-based approach. These are not mutually exclusive.

- A good number of contingency models have been published in recent decades which can be used by HR managers as tools to improve the extent to which their activities are in alignment with organisational strategies.

- Contingency thinking can also be usefully employed when positioning an organisation as an employer in a competitive labour market. To date there has been little research published in this field.

- Traditional approaches to workforce planning and succession planning are less and less used. However, these activities remain significant and thus need to be reinvented to suit HR strategy-making in the contemporary business environment.

EXPLORE FURTHER

The best single book on contemporary debates about HR strategy is *Strategy and human resource management* by Peter Boxall and John Purcell, now in its 3rd edition.

Boxall, P. and Purcell, J. (2011) *Strategy and human resource management*. 3rd edition. Basingstoke: Palgrave.

I would also recommend the seminal research papers written in this field by Jay Barney (1991) and Mark Huselid (1995).

Barney, J. (1991) Firm resources and sustained competitive advantage. *Journal of Management*. Vol 17, No 1. pp99–120.

Huselid, M. (1995) The impact of human resource practices on turnover, productivity and corporate financial performance. *Academy of Management Journal*. Vol 38, No 3. pp635–672.

REFERENCES

Barney, J. (1991) Firm resources and sustained competitive advantage. *Journal of Management.* Vol 17, No 1. pp99–120.

Devanna, M., Fombrun, C. and Tichy, N. (1984) A framework for strategic human resource management. In C. Fombrun, N. Tichy and M. Devanna (eds) *Strategic human resource management.* New York: Wiley.

Easterby-Smith, M. and Graça, M. (2004) Self-service. *People Management.* 12 February.

Higgs, M. (2004) Future trends in HRM. In D. Rees and R. McBain (eds) *People management: challenges and opportunities.* Basingstoke: Palgrave Macmillan.

Hirsh, W. (2000) *Succession planning demystified.* IES Report 372. Brighton: Institute for Employment Studies.

Huselid, M. (1995) The impact of human resource practices on turnover, productivity and corporate financial performance. *Academy of Management Journal.* Vol 38, No 3. pp635–672.

Lengnick-Hall, C. and Lengnick-Hall, M. (1988) Strategic human resource management: a review of the literature and a proposed typology. *Academy of Management Review.* Vol 13, No 3. pp454–470.

Miles, R.E. and Snow, C.C. (1978) *Organization strategy, structure and process.* New York: McGraw-Hill.

Mintzberg, H. (1994) *The rise and fall of strategic planning.* New York: Prentice Hall.

Pfeffer, J. (1994) *Competitive advantage through people.* Boston: Harvard University Press.

Purcell, J. (1989) The impact of corporate strategy on human resource management. In J. Storey (ed.) *New perspectives on human resource management.* London: Routledge.

Schuler, R. and Jackson, S. (1987) Linking competitive strategies with human resource management. *Academy of Management Executive.* Vol 1, No 3. pp207–219.

Syedain, H. (2010) Workforce planning: a force for good. *People Management.* 3 June.

Walker, J. (1992) *Human resource strategy.* New York: McGraw-Hill.

CHAPTER 14

Managing the HR function

Introduction

In the first few chapters of this book I explained how a variety of environmental developments are combining to make HR work both more important to organisations and also rather harder to carry out effectively. I also explained how in the future we can expect to see added pressure placed on the HR function in organisations to achieve more with comparatively fewer resources. In short, the trend over time is towards a situation in which corporations require their HR functions to both add value and provide better value for money. Greater efficiency is thus required alongside enhanced effectiveness and a capacity for demonstrating that these objectives are being achieved.

In this chapter we will explore some contemporary and likely future trends in the way that the HR function organises itself. After a short introductory section discussing what exactly 'adding value' means in a practical sense, we will go on to focus on two key topics. First we will look at current debates about how the HR function should best be organised in order to maximise its effectiveness and efficiency. We will then go on in the second half of the chapter to look at the major alternative methods used to evaluate HR activities in financial terms.

LEARNING OUTCOMES

The objectives of this chapter are to:

- set out the major ways in which the HR function can and should add value in organisations
- explore the case for outsourcing HR activities to external providers
- describe and evaluate the models of effective and efficient HR service delivery proposed by Dave Ulrich and his colleagues
- explain why formal evaluation of HR interventions is central to demonstrating how an HR function adds value
- set out the major alternative criteria used by HR managers to evaluate their activities
- explore some of the evaluation methods that can be used to demonstrate added value.

ADDING VALUE

It is helpful before we start thinking about the methods that can be used to deliver 'added value' to summarise briefly what are the major ways in which the HR function in an organisation can or should add value. By 'adding value' I mean creating more by way of wealth for the organisation than the function costs to operate. Where an HR function adds value, the organisation it serves would be worse off in financial terms over the long term were it not to be there. A value-adding HR function is thus not simply a costly necessity or an overhead that has to be financed out of income. Its presence enhances the capacity of the organisation to succeed financially.

There are four major ways in which this can be achieved in practice, although demonstrating clearly in financial terms, as we will see later, is not at all easy.

1 RECRUITMENT AND RETENTION

An HR function can add value by helping to ensure that the organisation is able to recruit and retain more able and experienced staff than its competitors are able to. This is achieved by making sound choices about where and how to advertise vacancies, ensuring that pay and terms and conditions are appropriate and by developing leaders whose styles of management serve to attract rather than to repel would-be employees. Key is the building-up over time of a positive labour market reputation. This involves understanding the dynamics of the labour markets in which your organisation competes and becoming seen as 'an employer of choice'. The tighter the labour market, the more significant recruitment and retention becomes as a value-adding activity.

2 PERFORMANCE

The HR function should also add value by helping to ensure that an organisation's staff perform to a higher standard than competitors are able to match. Central here is the need to treat people in such a way as to stimulate discretionary effort on the part of employees. Superior organisational performance can only be maintained if you secure superior and properly directed individual performance. This is achieved when people happily work beyond contract, going further in the service of their employers than they are strictly required to do in order to meet basic contractual obligations. Sustained and genuine employee engagement is thus essential as is the need to have in place incentives in the form of pay, career development opportunities and other intangible rewards which help to elicit discretionary effort. Here too the significance of effective line management cannot be overstated. Essential too is the maintenance of a high-trust employment relations environment bolstered by employee involvement and positive psychological contracts.

3 CHANGE

Studies that have focused on the ways in which HR functions add value demonstrate that the impact is greatest at times of major change. In ensuring that the people management side of change is given proper attention by an organisation, HR functions make a crucial contribution to ensuring its success. It is sometimes a question of contributing effectively towards planned, discrete change management episodes such as downsizing, reorganisations or mergers with other organisations – all increasingly common. But there is also a wider role that HR plays in ongoing, long-term evolutionary change through organisational development activities. Here the focus is increasingly on helping an organisation to enhance its agility and its capacity to be both flexible and opportunist. We also need to remember the important role that HR functions often play in minimising and managing the inevitable conflict that arises in the wake of significant organisational change.

4 ADMINISTRATION

In recent decades HR managers have tended to wish to downplay the administrative side of their work in order to boost the function's image as strategic, business-focused and proactive in its orientation. This is understandable but wrong. The truth is that HR functions can add value through their administrative activities and should aim, proudly, for the achievement of administrative excellence. All organisations need, whether they like it or not, to finance a certain amount of HR activity that is administrative in nature. Letters have to be sent to job applicants, payrolls have to be compiled, contracts issued, absence recorded and dismissals sanctioned from time to time. There are always health and safety obligations, along with a need to maintain training records and the requirement to maintain policy documentation. Given that these things are necessary, if not glamorous, it follows that doing them more effectively and with greater cost-efficiency than competitors can manage constitutes a very significant way in which a well-run HR function adds real value for an organisation.

OUTSOURCING

In recent years it has become more common for organisations to outsource to subcontractors activities that either have been or could be carried out in-house (see Colling 2005: 93–95 and Kersley et al 2006: 105–6). There is nothing new about this, but the tendency to move in this direction has accelerated recently. On the whole functions that are outsourced are those which an organisation considers to be peripheral or 'non-core' to their principal activity. Support services of various kinds are the most common examples of organisational activities that have been outsourced:

- cleaning
- maintenance

- security

- catering.

These are necessary activities that do not add value. The aim is therefore to pay an external provider to carry them out for whom they do represent the core business. The purpose is generally to secure a better level of service provision at a lower cost. In addition, of course, the complexities associated with managing a peripheral activity about which managers have little specialist knowledge can be handed over to experienced, expert providers. Moreover, if the contractor proves unsatisfactory, a threat can readily be made to terminate the contract when it is due for renewal. This can lead to service improvements which the contracting organisation need not bring about itself.

Another reason that is given for outsourcing is the ability it gives an organisation to access specialist expertise that it does not have and could not afford to have in-house. Smaller organisations in particular benefit from this type of arrangement. As a result it has become the norm for organisations to outsource legal services, IT maintenance and market research.

HRM is an area of organisational activity that lends itself to outsourcing in some, but not all, respects. Some HR activities are very commonly outsourced, particularly by smaller companies. These include payroll administration, pension provision, training, employee counselling, outplacement, child care and employment law advisory services. By doing this, unnecessary overheads are avoided while high-quality specialised services are accessed at a good price. In recent years, however, much more HR activity has been outsourced, comprising in some cases a large chunk of work that has traditionally been carried out by HR staff who are directly employed by the organisation. This has comprised what is often referred to as 'transactional HR activities', by which is meant basic office-based tasks of the kind discussed above under the heading 'administration'. In many cases this includes the task of answering enquiries about terms and conditions and HR policies from line managers, staff and job applicants. Such activities can be carried out very efficiently from a call-centre-type operation run by a specialist provider of HR services. Recent developments in information technologies have made such arrangements more attractive and cost-efficient, and there are now a number of well-resourced providers in the market who have signed up some big corporations. Well-known examples are Accenture, Ceridian and NorthgateArinso, all of which provide both a core administrative service and extensive specialist advisory services in areas such as employment law, succession planning and training. Ceridian sum up the business case for outsourcing neatly as follows on their website:

> HRO (Human Resources Outsourcing) is a way of removing the burden of administration and shifting focus back to people strategies. More and more, HRO is being seen not just as a way of saving costs, but as a way of adding value to the business, and proving its value with a return on investment that goes straight to the bottom line.

Companies such as these claim to provide tailored services which are bespoke to meet the needs of each client, but in practice inevitably a standard package of services form the core of their offering. This is how economies of scale are achieved resulting in a higher-quality, lower-cost service than their client organisations would be able to develop in-house.

Ten to fifteen years ago it was common to read articles in the HR press predicting that HR outsourcing on a large scale would become the norm among larger UK corporations in the future. In practice this has not turned out to be the case, and there is thus good reason to be cautious about how far this approach will grow further in the future. Scott-Jackson et al (2005) carried out an extensive survey for the CIPD and found that while 29% of their survey respondents outsourced some HR activities (payroll, pensions, etc), only a small minority (4%) had outsourced HR administration in its entirety to a specialist provider. Moreover, only 11% saw any possibility of this occurring in the near future. The big majority had kept HR administration in-house and had every intention of continuing to do so.

One reason may be that the experience of outsourcing HR has not always proved satisfactory to those organisations that experimented with it when the option started to become available in the 1990s. We have recently seen some high-profile examples of organisations bringing HR administrative services back in-house again once the contract with their outsourcer has come to an end (Pickard 2007). These arrangements often seem to disappoint in practice, anticipated cost savings failing to be achieved or promised service levels not materialising.

ULRICH'S MODELS

Over recent years the American academic and consultant Dave Ulrich, working with a number of colleagues, has proposed a variety of ways in which contemporary HR functions can organise their activities so as to maximise their effectiveness and their efficiency. These 'Ulrich models' have achieved great prominence internationally and have been put into practice either in whole or in part by a number of larger UK organisations.

The best known and best established Ulrich model for HR is often referred to as the 'three-legged stool approach', originally proposed in 1997. Here Ulrich suggested that there were three core types of HR role and that each should be carried out by distinct teams working in different ways in order to ensure that quality and efficiency were maximised. In other words, he argued against the retention by organisations of a traditional generalist HR function in which a single team carries out all roles. The three were as follows:

1 CENTRES OF EXPERTISE

HR staff located centrally in an organisation structure who provide specialist knowledge-based services and develop HR policy for the rest of the organisation. Diversity specialists, employment lawyers and pensions teams are examples of the kinds of common activities that are carried out by these people.

2 SHARED SERVICE CENTRES

The more standardised, transactional HR tasks should be centralised and performed by a team of administrators operating in a call-centre type of environment. This will include processing recruitment documentation, maintaining training, absence and holiday records, payroll administration and the whole range of other more basic activities that are carried out by HR administration teams on behalf of an organisation.

3 BUSINESS PARTNERS

HR managers who are based in business units working closely with line managers on the people management aspects of delivering their strategic objectives.

In fact, Ulrich also proposed a fourth role in his original book, which is less often referred to and sits on top of the three legs. This is the HR leader role, based at the corporate centre with the task of overseeing and co-ordinating the activities of the three legs.

More recently Ulrich has refined his own model in response to issues raised in the many organisations which have sought to implement it (see Ulrich et al 2009). The service centres, corporate HR leaders and centres of expertise are still there, but the HR business partner role has been reconceived somewhat. Two distinct types of business partnering activity are now identified:

- 'embedded HR' – generalist staff who work with line managers on strategic issues, leading change and evaluating the impact of HR interventions
- 'operational executors' who carry out case work (selection interviews, disciplinary matters, performance reviews) and also implement initiatives on behalf of the central corporate HR function.

Ulrich's ideas have been hugely influential in recent years and have been widely adopted in some larger organisations, at least in part. However, they have also been the subject of some criticism. The main point that is made in opposition relates to what is inevitably lost when the HR function is split up or 'balkanised' in the manner that Ulrich proposes. These are neatly summed up by Reilly et al (2007) as follows:

> …remote experts delivering gold-plated but business-illiterate policies and business partners becoming the opposite – too embedded within their business units to see the importance of the organisation overall.

There have also been doubts cast on the claims that introducing shared service centres really brings about any meaningful cost savings and simplifies systems to any great extent. In fact, many organisations appear to have found that when adopted, the Ulrich model can increase costs and overcomplicate administrative activities which were previously handled quickly and simply by locally based teams of HR generalists.

An extensive CIPD survey in which nearly 800 UK-based HR departments took part was carried out in 2007 at a time when interest in the original Ulrich model was at its peak. Eighty-one per cent of the respondents stated that their organisations had reorganised their HR function in the previous three years and that more than half (57%) had adopted some form of the three-legged stool model, although only 29% had established clearly distinct shared services centres. As we would expect, the proportions of larger organisations that have moved in the Ulrich direction is much higher than is the case among smaller ones. This is because the economies of scale that can be gained by organisations employing several thousand are far greater than is the case where a few hundred staff are employed. Smaller organisations have thus tended to retain a more traditional approach in which a single HR team provides a range of different services either to the whole organisation or to each of a number of larger divisions (Reilly et al 2007).

In the future it is logical to anticipate that HR functions will increasingly reorganise themselves along the kind of lines proposed by Ulrich and his colleagues, although we can also expect to see varied permutations developing. While this approach will always have less to offer small and medium-sized businesses, adopting the Ulrich model will make complete sense for larger organisations under pressure both to reduce management costs and to increase the sophistication with which they manage their people. Ulrich argues strongly for an HR function which sees itself as being 'a business within a business', adding value by providing a high level of service at as low a cost as is achievable. At the very least, his model provides a road map for organisations seeking to move in that direction.

KEY ARTICLE

SHARED SERVICE CENTRES

Read the article by Peter Reilly entitled 'The links effect' featured in *People Management* (16 July 2009). This can be downloaded from the *People Management* archive on the CIPD website (www.cipd.co.uk).

In this article Peter Reilly draws on his CIPD research to discuss the trend towards greater use of shared service centres in larger organisations to deliver HR services as well as others too. He notes the pressures on public sector organisations to save money by sharing shared services and for international organisations to move towards a single shared services hub serving workplaces based across the globe.

Questions

1 What points are made in this article which support the proposition that shared service centres will become increasingly widely used in HRM?

2 What potential sources of resistance to shared services does Reilly identify?

3 What is suggested needs to happen in order to overcome such resistance and ensure the introduction of a successful shared services approach?

EVALUATING THE HR CONTRIBUTION

Accurately evaluating the HRM contribution to organisational performance in financial terms has always been problematic. This is because so many of the outcomes are intangible and not readily measured. They are also complex and difficult to isolate in terms of their impact from other initiatives. How, for example, is it possible to measure meaningfully the value gained by an organisation of sponsoring an aspiring HR professional through courses in order to gain a professional CIPD qualification? The cost in terms of fees, materials and time off for study runs to several thousand pounds, but what is the payback for the organisation and over what timescale is the investment recouped? The truth is that it is impossible to calculate in monetary terms with any degree of accuracy, and in any case the answer will vary from individual to individual, organisation to organisation, and will depend on the type of circumstances which arise.

However, the fact that evaluation cannot be perfect cannot stop us from formally reviewing our activities in terms of their contribution, from tracking progress over time, comparing performance with other organisations and from seeking wherever possible to quantify the value that is added.

HUMAN CAPITAL REPORTING

In recent years a great deal of interest has been developing in the idea that public companies should be required by law to report annually on their human capital as well as giving the detailed financial information that is currently included in their annual reports. In other words, in addition to reporting publicly each year on the value of physical assets and their profit and loss for the financial year, specific types of information about their people should also be included so as to allow shareholders and potential investors to make judgements about how effectively the organisation is managed. The case was summed up by the CIPD's former Director General, Geoff Armstrong, as follows:

> We have seen huge corporate failures where rigorously measured, audited and apparently conscientiously managed firms have gone bust because they have focused too narrowly on their drivers of value. Although it is well known that by far the highest proportion of stock market capitalisation is in intangible assets – mainly people and brands – companies have sleepwalked to disaster by using only traditional accounting measures. The impact that human capital can have on markets is huge. In advanced economies the only distinctive asset that cannot be imitated easily is the skills, talent and know-how of people. Now is the time to move beyond the rhetoric of 'people are our most important asset' and start developing processes that effectively measure and report on the contribution of that asset. (Armstrong 2003)

While this idea is easily expressed and the arguments for its adoption compelling, there remain problems with putting it into practice. How exactly can 'human capital' be accurately measured and reported on in any kind of standard format to permit inter-company comparisons?

Possible answers to this question were provided by two important reports published a few years ago. The first, published in 2003, was that of the Accounting for People Taskforce chaired by Denise Kingsmill. Here it was argued that it was impractical to require organisations to publish the same types of 'indicators or metrics' about their human capital, but that a measure of consistency could nonetheless be achieved if directors were required to set out in annual reports details of their approach to human capital measurement and their understanding of links between this and their business's performance. The second report put flesh on these bones. This was published by the CIPD's own human capital taskforce in 2003, and included within it a 'human capital external reporting framework'. While accepting the need to avoid rigid requirements about what data to disclose, the taskforce suggested four headings under which relevant information could be provided:

- acquisition and retention of people

- learning and development

- human capital management (refers principally to general HR policies and strategies)

- performance.

In each case, it was argued, directors should give a narrative statement explaining how the company approaches these areas of activity and suggests several statistical indicators that could be used to back up the points made in these statements.

For some time it looked as if the government would be legislating to require disclosure of human capital measurements of this kind, at least for the larger companies listed on the London Stock Exchange. The Kingsmill Taskforce report was welcomed by the then Secretary of State for Trade and Industry and many commentators assumed that in a few years' time human capital reporting would become standard practice. However, it now appears that the hopes of the proponents of forced disclosure have been dashed. Company annual reports published since January 2006 have had to contain a mandatory Operating Financial Review (OFR), which is intended to give an overview of the company's position, including information about its objectives, its strategy, its past performance and its future prospects, including information on brands, research and development activity, market position and relationships with stakeholders such as customers, suppliers and employees. However, OFRs fall well short of requiring any detailed disclosure of human capital measurements as were recommended by the Accounting for People Taskforce. In order to comply in practice, companies are able to make quite bland statements about people being important to them and setting out their total headcount.

There remains, however, a strong case for developing and publishing clearer measures of HR outcomes. This is particularly the case in organisations which are knowledge-intensive and which rely very heavily on effective employee performance to achieve competitive advantage. In such industries, according to Becker et al (2001: 8–9), investment decisions, and hence the value of the company's shares, are increasingly made using non-financial information. Analysts advising investors are interested in the relative ability of organisations to attract and retain talented individuals, to manage change effectively, to develop professional management systems and to innovate effectively. There is thus a good case for formally evaluating organisational performance against such indicators, for expressing the results in a readily understood manner and for disseminating them widely.

Non-financial indicators of organisation performance can play a direct role in public sector organisations too, especially where they are competing for contracts with private sector counterparts. Local authorities and government departments, for example, will look at an organisation's HR policies and practices when deciding to which organisations (private or public) they are going to award contracts. Ministers and local politicians do not want to be found to have paid large sums of public money to organisations which turn out to be providing low-cost services on the back of unprofessional people management practices. They are thus interested in recruitment and selection policy, will look for evidence of effective human resource planning and have a preference for organisations which maintain accurate personnel records. They also want to be assured that their suppliers are acting lawfully, so human resource expertise is also *in itself* a substantial asset for organisations operating in these areas of activity.

KEY ARTICLE

JAMIE'S KITCHEN

Read the article by Harry Scarbrough entitled 'Recipe for success' featured in *People Management* (23 January 2003: 32–35). This can be downloaded from the *People Management* archive on the CIPD website (www.cipd.co.uk).

This article uses the example of the TV programme *Jamie's Kitchen* to illustrate the way that human capital is developed. It goes on to report on research which suggests that human capital measurement is more significant to some organisations than others and takes very different forms in different industries.

Questions

1 Why has the idea of human capital taken so long to become established? Why is it still resisted or disregarded by so many managers?

2 Why do some firms focus their human capital measurement processes on all employees, while others focus in on specific groups such as managers or people of unusually high talent?

3 To what extent do you agree with Harry Scarbrough's conclusion that elaborate measurement systems are 'of little use' to organisations which rely very heavily on individual skills and to those whose competitive advantage derives principally from their tangible assets?

EVALUATION CRITERIA

The first step in setting up formal systems of evaluation is to determine against what criteria we are going to evaluate the performance of HR interventions. Several different approaches are available, none of which are mutually exclusive. At root the evaluation of most core HR activities involves answering three basic questions:

- Are we doing what we are doing as effectively as possible?
- Are we doing it as efficiently as possible?
- Are we doing it as fairly as possible?

The first question concerns the fulfilment of organisational objectives. It involves asking how far in practice an intervention, activity, policy or practice achieves what it sets out to achieve. It also leads to consideration of possible alternative methods which might achieve the same set of objectives more effectively. The second question recognises that effectiveness cannot be the only measure used to evaluate HR activity and that value-for-money considerations also need to be taken into account. It is often the case that the most effective approach is a great deal more expensive than viable alternatives. A Rolls-Royce may be a very reliable, comfortable and attractive car, but there are far more economic means of getting from one place to another without losing too much by way of effectiveness.

In most areas of organisational activity, effectiveness/efficiency trade-offs are all that managers have to consider when carrying out formal evaluations. However, in the HR field, a third criterion – fairness – can be of equal importance. This is because effectiveness and efficiency can readily be undermined where people perceive a practice to operate unfairly. Fairness needs to be considered an evaluation criterion partly because it plays an important role in meeting legal obligations and partly, as was argued in Chapter 8, because of the central role it plays in maximising employee motivation and commitment. The surest way to raise staff turnover, reduce job satisfaction, increase absence, lower productivity and engender low-trust relationships at work is to pursue policies which are inequitable. Management perspectives on the relative fairness or unfairness of a practice are unimportant here. All that matters are employee perceptions. There is thus a need for practices not just to be fair in their operation, but also to be seen to be fair.

FORWARD- AND BACKWARD-LOOKING CRITERIA

A criticism that is often made of traditional financial measures of organisational activity, such as annual reports to shareholders and sets of accounts, is that they reflect past performance rather than future potential. It is possible to use reports of past performance to make assumptions about future performance, but more information is needed in addition for any kind of realistic assessment to be made. Becker et al (2001) use the terms *lagging* and *leading* indicators to describe the distinction between two approaches to evaluation of organisational performance, arguing that many HR measures are effective 'leading indicators', providing information about likely future performance.

In practice, proper evaluation of an organisation's HR performance makes use of both forward- and backward-looking criteria. Data on past performance needs to be collected and reported regularly, allowing progress to be tracked, problem areas to be identified and action plans formulated. In this way past evaluation data thus becomes the platform for improved future performance. By contrast, future-oriented evaluation usually takes the form of a cost–benefit analysis. Past data, together with management judgement, is used to establish the likely outcomes of particular interventions such as a new supervisors' training course, the introduction of psychometric tests or an attendance incentive scheme. Wherever possible these outcomes are then expressed in financial terms and the total compared with the costs of carrying them out.

QUANTITATIVE EVALUATION CRITERIA

As a means of demonstrating added value, progress over time and for making comparisons with other organisations, the favoured approach is the use of quantitative criteria, sometimes referred to as HR metrics (see Burkholder 2007). These are readily understood, clear and unambiguous measures of performance on a range of HRM indicators. Some, but not all, are also readily and meaningfully expressed in financial terms of cost. The following are some of the most widely used examples:

- voluntary staff turnover rates
- absence rates
- accident rates
- average speed with which vacancies are filled
- candidate acceptance rate
- proportion of recruits from ethnic minorities
- proportion of staff who have been formally appraised in the past 12 months
- number of tribunal cases fought/settled
- overtime worked in the past year
- number of formal grievance/disciplinary hearings.

A second category comprises measures which use this and other classes of data to create ratios of the kind used by accountants to evaluate financial performance. Examples such as the following can be expressed in terms of cost. The standard approach is to use a measure of 'full-time equivalents' rather than the crude number of employees working under part-time and full-time contracts:

- profit generated per employee in the past year
- sales per employee in the past year
- recruitment cost per new recruit

- labour costs as a proportion of total costs
- absence costs as a proportion of staff costs
- voluntary turnover costs as a proportion of staff costs
- HR department costs as a proportion of total costs.

A third category comprises quantitative data which is not usually collected as a matter of course in organisations, so it requires the development of evaluative tools such as questionnaires. These can either ask for opinions or test knowledge. Examples are as follows:

- proportion of employees who are satisfied with their work
- proportion of employees who are satisfied with their supervision/management
- proportion of employees who consider the employer to act ethically/equitably
- proportion of employees who are clear about organisational goals/objectives
- proportion of employees who are clear about their own objectives/goals.

The final category of measures relates to the HR function itself and how effectively it is rated by users in the organisation. Examples are as follows:

- proportion of employees who are aware of the content of HR policies on recruitment, diversity, absence, etc
- satisfaction rates among managers of the services and advice provided by the HR function
- knowledge among managers of key HR policies and objectives.

QUALITATIVE EVALUATION CRITERIA

Qualitative evaluation is less helpful than the quantitative variety when it comes to demonstrating in a very clear, crisp way that objectives are being met and value being added. It is nevertheless useful to carry out for a number of reasons. Its major advantage is that it helps to provide explanations of why objectives are not being fully met and thus can form the basis of future improvements. Quantitative evaluation might, for example, show that 75% of employees are uncertain of their personal objectives for the current year. Such a statistic would be a matter of concern for HR managers in an organisation which practised objective-based performance appraisal, but as a raw figure it can do no more than cause concern. It is only through qualitative evaluation, undertaken through questionnaires or focus groups, that a clear, objective view can be formed about *why* the appraisal system is working poorly and about what could be done to improve it in the future. Secondly, qualitative evaluation, in providing more detail, helps an organisation to gain a far richer understanding of processes and perceptions than is possible using basic quantitative measures. It is only through the use of qualitative approaches that the real reasons for high or low employee absence rates in different departments can be understood. The reasons may be complex, hard to articulate, mixed together or changing over time. Quantitative evaluation rarely provides such information, so it needs to be backed up with qualitative approaches.

Thirdly, it is possible to argue that the results of qualitative evaluation can themselves be used effectively as part of the process by which the performance of the HR function is formally reported. Qualitative evaluation may not allow ready comparison of different units within an organisation, or with external competitors (as is the case with quantitative data), but it is nonetheless a useful tool to use to back up key messages and to add background colour to the numbers-based data.

EVALUATING RECRUITMENT PROCESSES

Using the criteria set out above, the following example describes how an organisation might go about formally evaluating its recruitment processes. We start with three evaluation questions:

1 Do our recruitment practices yield sufficient numbers of suitable candidates to enable us to select sufficient numbers of high-calibre employees?

2 Could a sufficient pool of suitable candidates be attracted using less expensive methods?

3 Are the recruitment methods used fulfilling the organisation's equal opportunities responsibilities?

The first question focuses on the effectiveness of recruitment practices. Asking it will lead to consideration of whether too few sufficiently qualified candidates are applying for jobs. It may be the case that those of the very highest calibre are not being caught in the recruiters' net. The second question focuses on efficiency. It leads to consideration of the relative merits of different recruitment methods in terms of their cost. It is also possible that too many applications are being received, leading to unnecessary expenditure in terms of the time spent on administration. The third question considers the fairness of recruitment processes. Subsequent questions might focus on the extent to which applicant pools are, or are not, representative of all sections of the community.

Answering these questions is a good deal harder than asking them. However, it is possible to move some way to finding answers by using quantitative and qualitative approaches.

Quantitative approaches involve comparing various recruitment methods with each other in terms of their results. We might, for example, choose to compare the effectiveness of using a recruitment advertisement designed by an advertising agency with a similar but less elaborate version set by the newspaper. Which one brought in the greater number of applications? Which one yielded the highest-quality applications? Is there a difference between them in terms of the subsequent performance or turnover rates among selected employees? The same kind of analysis can be undertaken to compare the results of national newspaper advertising with local newspapers, or simply comparing formal with informal recruitment methods. The larger the organisation, the more meaningful the analysis will be. However, it is important to be careful not to read too much into a relatively small sample of cases – plenty of other factors aside from the recruitment method might explain any differences discovered.

Quantitative evaluations of recruitment methods are routinely carried out by many large employing organisations. The main vehicle used is the job reference number, which employees are asked to quote when they respond to advertisements in newspapers, job centres, careers centres, etc. Employers wishing to compare the different methods include a different reference number in each advertisement and then undertake quantitative comparisons like those described above.

By contrast, qualitative evaluation methods try to locate potential problems with recruitment practices in terms of the three criteria identified above and consider possible missed opportunities. The aim is to think constructively about ways in which improvements can be made. While a number of approaches are possible, the most common involve asking both successful and unsuccessful candidates to evaluate their experiences during the recruitment process and to compare them with those they have encountered in the past. Reaching successful candidates is straightforward – it is less easy to gather meaningful information from those who have not been offered jobs. One way of doing so is to offer all candidates feedback on their performance at the selection stage. Such activity is often seen as being solely for the benefit of candidates, but this is not the case: it also provides a good opportunity for employers to gain constructive qualitative feedback on their own recruitment processes from the candidates' perspective.

Other forms of qualitative evaluation might involve investigating the length of time the organisation took to respond to enquiries and formal applications, or evaluating how effectively telephonists and receptionists respond to enquiries about actual or possible vacancies. It may be that good candidates are put off applying because of a lack of courtesy on the part of the employer. Another common form of qualitative evaluation focuses on investigating ways of reducing the number of words in an advertisement without diminishing its effectiveness.

EVALUATION METHODS

Having described the different criteria that can be used in carrying out formal evaluations of HR activities, we now need to turn in more detail to the evaluation processes themselves. There are a number of alternatives here, but they are not mutually exclusive and can be used in combination with one another.

BENCHMARKING

Bramham (1997: 1) defines benchmarking very succinctly as follows:

> *Benchmarking is simply the systematic process of comparing your business with others, or parts of your own with one another, to test how you stand and to see whether change is needed. Usually you will identify examples of superior performance, and when you do you should set out to emulate and even better them.*

Internal benchmarking is the most common form and the easiest to set up and run. This occurs in larger organisations where several units or departments carry out similar types of activity and operate in the same kinds of labour market. The major examples are 'chain operations' such as supermarkets, hotels or hospitals where a single organisation owns and operates several workplaces in different locations. It is just as feasible, however, to carry out internal benchmarking between different departments within the same workplace or in organisations which simply wish to compare the relative importance of two business units. All that is required is the collection of data such as that identified above on the same basis across the organisation. Comparisons can then be made and efforts made to establish the reasons for differential performance. Ideally, over time, the performance of the whole organisation improves.

External benchmarking is less common and more problematic. First, of course, there is likely to be a reluctance on the part of organisations that either compete or believe that they will compete in the future to share information with one another. Even where they do so, it is not in the interests of the better-performing organisations to assist the poorer performers by sharing more than raw benchmarking data. Where this kind of constructive outcome is sought it is necessary to find partners who run similar operations but do not compete directly. The best examples are service organisations which operate entirely in different geographical areas. Sharing quite detailed information is useful to both parties in these kinds of relationship. Alternative approaches are less satisfactory, but are nonetheless often worth pursuing. Examples are as follows:

- Simply sharing raw data and no more. This enables organisations to know where they stand in terms of key indicators such as employee turnover, absence, sales per employee, cost per recruit, size of HR department, etc, but does not allow them further information to establish why they stand where they do. An employer that finds itself doing relatively well in such exercises or sees an improvement over time can use this information as an effective means of demonstrating added value.

- Informal benchmarking. This involves steering clear of systematic, formal schemes, but nonetheless using information which comes your way to establish how you are performing on key indices *vis-à-vis* competitors. The main sources of information are stories in newspapers and trade journals and knowledge that is brought by new staff who have been hired from a competitor.

- Using published data. Quite a lot of HR benchmarking data is published and freely available in libraries and on websites. It is possible to use this in order to compare your own organisation's performance with that of similar organisations. The surveys included regularly in publications such as *IDS Study* and CIPD research reports are examples of sources of such information.

- A number of consultants specialise in setting up and running detailed benchmarking exercises, while similar activities also form a part of what employers' associations have to offer their members. Aside from participating, there is usually an additional fee to pay to gain access to the full data, but the result is information which is robust because all participating organisations have completed the same questionnaires with the same sets of explanatory notes.

HUMAN RESOURCE AUDITING

The audit approach, like benchmarking, involves an organisation comparing its own performance against that of others, but here the comparison is made with standards which are generally acknowledged to constitute 'good practice' or the best attainable results. The approach is thus, by its nature, most appropriate for organisations which are seeking as a matter of policy to be 'employers of choice' or leaders in their field.

The starting point is the results of large-scale research exercises which link certain HR practices to positive business outcomes across a range of different industries. The best known such studies have been carried out by Mark Huselid and his colleagues (see Huselid et al 1997), but a wide range of others, including a number carried out in the UK, are reviewed by Boselie et al (2005). These kinds of study, as well as those which focus on the approach to HRM adopted in the fastest-growing organisations, consistently find a correlation between the presence of particular practices and superior business performance. These tend to be the more sophisticated and costly approaches to the management of people, so they are not going to be an option in organisations which are heavily constrained by cost. However, where it is practicable to employ them, and where an organisation actively seeks to be recognised as an excellent employer, it follows that these are the standards to which it should aspire.

The aim is then to audit the organisation's performance against that of 'good practice' as defined by these research findings. One method used is to develop an audit tool (or detailed questionnaire) which mirrors the questions asked by the researchers responsible for these studies. Examples of the kind of questions that could be included are as follows:

1 What proportion of new employees in the past year were selected using psychometric tests?

   a) 100%
   b) 75–100%
   c) 50–75%
   d) 25–50%
   e) less than 25%

2 To what extent is the following statement a true reflection of practice in the organisation?

   'Employees are actively encouraged to participate in decision-making at the operational level.'

   a) Always true
   b) Sometimes true
   c) Occasionally true
   d) Usually untrue
   e) Always untrue

3 How many people are employed in the organisation for each HR specialist?

   a) fewer than 150
   b) 150–200
   c) 200–250
   d) 250–300
   e) more than 300

In the case of each question in the audit tool a score can be given (eg a=40, b=20, c=10, d=5, e=0) and a total figure calculated. This will show how the organisation compares with the 'best practice employers', but it also allows comparisons to be made between different units and improvements to be tracked over time. HR auditing tools also provide a means by which the areas that need most attention can be readily identified.

SURVEY-BASED EVALUATION

A third way of evaluating the contribution made by the HR function involves surveying opinion within the organisation – best seen as taking the form of a customer satisfaction survey. Ideally such surveys should be carried out annually, using the same sets of questions so that progress can be tracked over time. Surveys can be divided into two main types: those which focus on management opinion of the HR function and those which gather information about employee attitudes and knowledge.

Management surveys are straightforward to compile in a questionnaire format and can often be distributed and returned electronically. Typically they consist of multi-choice questions with five possible answers (eg very satisfied, satisfied, neither satisfied nor dissatisfied, dissatisfied, very dissatisfied) about each of the key services offered by the HR function or each of its major objectives. Most management surveys will also include space for extensive qualitative feedback to be given.

Surveys of employees are rather different, but equally useful as part of a wider evaluation exercise. The most common approaches involve surveying employee attitudes and surveying employee knowledge. The latter is principally of relevance to employee development processes. The former is concerned with discovering how people feel about their work, how far they are satisfied in their jobs, how fairly they perceive that they are treated and how committed they believe themselves to be.

GOAL-BASED EVALUATION

A fourth commonly used evaluation method is in many ways the most straightforward: the HR function's equivalent of an individual performance appraisal exercise. It also the method that is best used for determining how effectively specific strategic objectives are being met. At base the approach simply involves an HR function setting itself objectives for the months ahead, ideally choosing goals which fit the requirements of the 'SMART' acronym (ie specific, measurable, achievable, realistic and time-bound). The more directly related to organisational strategic objectives, the more appropriate the objectives are to set. Evaluation can subsequently be made depending on how far in practice objectives have been met for a particular year, half-yearly or quarterly period.

A danger with goal-based evaluation systems, as with individual performance appraisals run along similar principles, is that the context can easily change, leaving you chasing targets which no longer comprise priorities for the organisation. Objectives must thus be flexible and able to be reviewed, removed or added to at any time. It is also important not to set too many separate objectives for any one time period. What matters is that those which are really essential and genuinely contribute to organisation performance are achieved fully.

These are what Ulrich (see Becker et al 2001: 80) has referred to as the 'doables' and 'deliverables' which 'really make a difference'. Where there is a written organisational strategy with clear operational goals, the priorities for the HR function should derive directly from these documents.

CUTTING-EDGE APPROACHES TO EVALUATION

In recent years larger corporations and specialist consultants have begun to develop approaches to the evaluation of HR programmes which are a great deal more sophisticated and complex than those described so far in this chapter. Many features of the newer approaches are problematic and it will take some years before they become widely accepted. It is beyond the scope of this book to describe these approaches in great detail, but it is useful to know about their development and to consider how far they may become standard in years to come. A good introduction to some of the approaches, with exercises to complete, is provided by Cascio and Boudreau (2010).

Different terms are used to describe the cutting-edge approaches. Some use the term *balanced scorecard* and have developed this attractive idea, while others use the language of accounting specialists by thinking in terms of *return on investment* or *human asset accounting*. Whatever terminology is used, the core principles are the same. The evolving methods all involve measuring the impact of HRM activities on organisation performance *in financial terms*. Because this is not easily done, it is necessary to make various assumptions about cause and effect and to employ techniques which are akin to standard accounting conventions. In the financial world, however, there are Generally Accepted Accounting Practices (GAAPs) which everyone understands and accepts. It will take some time for such standardisation to occur in the HR field, if it ever does, so for the time being there are on offer several different systems mainly developed by different firms of consultants. Many of the approaches described above are used in combination in these kinds of exercise.

An often quoted example is the exercise carried out by the Sears Group in the USA. It serves to illustrate very well what results these activities are intended to bring. At Sears over a period of some years a great deal of data was collected by taskforces concerning employee development and teamworking, customer needs and satisfaction, and revenue growth, sales per square foot and other financial measures. Central was the way that the company sought to capture 'soft issues' such as staff satisfaction using hard measurements. This was done through the use of questionnaire surveys. Correlations were then made between changes in the HR indicators and improvements in the financial performance of different business units (ie benchmarking). The analysis allowed the company to make the following statement:

> A 5 point improvement in employee attitudes will drive a 1.3 point improvement in customer satisfaction which in turn will lead to a 0.5 per cent improvement in revenue growth.

The key process which makes this kind of analysis possible is the isolation of the effects of a particular HR intervention. Among the 'ten strategies' for achieving this aim, Phillips et al (2001) suggest the following, the other seven being variations on these three:

- The use of control groups. Here a workforce is divided into two groups as if taking part in a scientific experiment. In practice two separate business units would be used. One is subjected to the new HR intervention while practices for the other group remain untouched. Differences are then measured over time.

- The use of trend line analyses. Here organisational performance (eg sales levels, production costs, customer satisfaction ratings) is tracked before and after the implementation of an HR intervention and the extent to which improvements occur in excess of expected projections measured.

- Participant estimates. Employees and managers are asked to give a reasoned estimate of the extent to which any performance improvements derive directly from an HR intervention. Standard questionnaires are used to enable ready collation of the data.

The next stage involves calculating an estimate of the value added in monetary terms. In the case of sales or output increases, this is straightforward; calculating the monetary value of improved customer satisfaction, reduced employee turnover or improved product quality is a good deal harder. However, many organisations have developed methods that enable them to do so. Most involve tapping into the expertise of experienced staff. For example, a sales manager with long experience will be able to estimate how great a difference in terms of repeat sales is typical as between a satisfied and a dissatisfied customer. Similarly, a head receptionist will be able to work out how great a cost is sustained in terms of management and staff time as a direct result of a new, inexperienced employee replacing an established receptionist on their team. Product quality can be measured in terms of customer satisfaction, but also using defect rates, the cost of replacing faulty products, or waste generated because of mistakes, all of which are readily expressed in financial terms. Which method is used will depend on the specific activities of the organisation concerned.

Once the impact of HR activities has been measured in financial terms, it becomes possible to calculate a figure for 'return on investment'. This is simply done by working out the cost of the HR intervention in terms of staff time, consultants' fees, equipment and overheads. The following formula is then applied:

$$\text{return on investment} = (\text{benefits less cost} / \text{cost}) \times 100$$

A simple example might be the introduction of assessment centres as a method of selecting sales staff in a computer company. Such an intervention is reasonably straightforward to cost. The results could be expected to include the following:

- improved levels of new business (eg £400,000 of new business per year generated as opposed to £300,000 before the introduction of assessment centres)

- improved repeat sales levels

- enhanced customer satisfaction ratings

- lower turnover among new graduates (eg down from 50% over two years to 25%)

- higher levels of employee satisfaction.

Using the methods outlined above these benefits are converted into monetary values. Finally, a calculation is made of return on investment, possibly as follows:

total programme costs: £250,000
estimated total benefits: £750,000

$$\frac{(750,000 - 250,000)}{(250,000)} = 2$$

$2 \times 100 = 200$
ROI = 200%

KEY ARTICLE

HUMAN ASSET WORTH

Read the article by Andrew Mayo entitled 'A thorough evaluation' featured in *People Management* (4 April 2002: 36–39). This can be downloaded from the *People Management* archive on the CIPD website (www.cipd.co.uk).

This article starts by setting out some of the problems associated with some of the most commonly used approaches to human asset accounting, such as the balanced scorecard. It goes on to argue that organisations stand to gain a great deal if they try to measure the 'total asset worth' of individual employees, focusing on the measurement both of financial and non-financial 'value added'. A method of achieving this is briefly described.

Questions

1   What is Mayo referring to when he writes about the 'non-financial added value' created by individual staff?

2   For what practical purposes could managers use data collected about each employee's 'human asset worth'?

3   What problems can you identify with the approach to evaluating employee contribution outlined by Andrew Mayo?

- Formal evaluation of HR programmes enhances the credibility of the function within organisations and provides a basis for successful bids for future investment. HR-oriented outcomes are also increasingly taken into account by investment analysts.

- Core HR activities are best evaluated in terms of their effectiveness, efficiency and fairness. Evaluation can be forward-looking, backward-looking or can be a combination of both.

- Evaluation can be either quantitative or qualitative in nature. Which approach is used depends on the type of evaluation exercise and the way that results are going to be reported.

- The major methods of evaluation used are benchmarking, audit-based, survey-based and goal-based. Each has a role to play and all can be used in combination.

- In recent years cutting-edge approaches to evaluation have been developed. These involve expressing the impact of HR interventions in monetary terms.

EXPLORE FURTHER

A good introduction to current approaches to the organisation of HR work is provided in the CIPD report *The changing HR function: transforming HR?* by Peter Reilly and colleagues from the Institute for Employment Studies.

Reilly, P., Tamkin, P. and Broughton, A. (2007) *The changing HR function: transforming HR?* London: CIPD.

It is also instructive to read the book written by Dave Ulrich in 1997 about possible new ways of organising HR work as 'a business within a business.' It is called *Human resource champions: the next agenda for adding value and delivering results* and is probably the most influential single book in HRM of the past 20 years.

Ulrich, D. (1997) *Human resource champions: the next agenda for adding value and delivering results*. Boston: Harvard Business Press.

On evaluating HR work in terms of its impact on the bottom line, the best starting point is *Investing in people: financial impact of human resource initiatives* by Wayne Cascio and John Boudreau (2010), now in its 2nd edition.

Cascio, W. and Boudreau, J. (2010) *Investing in people: financial impact of human resource initiatives*. 2nd edition. New York: Prentice Hall/Financial Times.

REFERENCES

Armstrong, G. (2003) Just how intangible is this asset? *People Management*. 12 June. p23.

Becker, B., Huselid, M. and Ulrich, D. (2001) *The HR scorecard: linking people, strategy and performance*. Cambridge, MA: Harvard Business School Press.

Boselie, P., Dietz, G. and Boon, C. (2005) Commonalities and contradictions in research on human resource management and performance. *Human Resource Management Journal*. Vol 15, No 3. pp67–94.

Bramham, J. (1997) *Benchmarking for people managers: a competency approach.* London: Chartered Institute of Personnel and Development.

Burkholder, N. (2007) *Ultimate performance: measuring human resources at work.* Hoboken, NJ: Wiley.

Cascio, W. and Boudreau, J. (2010) *Investing in people: financial impact of human resource initiatives.* 2nd edition. New York: Prentice Hall/Financial Times.

CIPD (2003) *Human capital measurement: external reporting framework.* London: Chartered Institute of Personnel and Development.

Colling, T. (2005) Managing human resources in the networked organisation. In S. Bach (ed.) *Managing human resources: personnel management in transition.* 4th edition. Oxford: Blackwell.

Huselid, M. (1995) The impact of human resource practices on turnover, productivity and corporate financial performance. *Academy of Management Journal.* Vol 38, No 3. pp635–672.

Huselid, M., Jackson, S.E. and Randall, R.S. (1997) Technical and strategic human resource management effectiveness as determinants of firm performance. *Academy of Management Journal.* Vol 40, No 1. pp171–188.

Kersley, B., Alpin, C., Forth, J., Bryson, A., Bewley, H., Dix, G. and Oxenbridge, S. (2006) *Inside the workplace: findings from the 2004 workplace employment relations survey.* Abingdon: Routledge.

Kingsmill, D. (2003) *Accounting for people.* London: Department for Business, Innovation and Skills.

Mayo, A. (2002) A thorough evaluation. *People Management.* 4 April.

Phillips, J., Stone, R. and Pulliam Phillips, P. (2001) *The human resources scorecard: measuring the return on investment.* Boston, MA: Butterworth-Heinemann.

Pickard, J. (2007) Spring in its step. *People Management Guide to HR Outsourcing.* February.

Reilly, P. (2009) The links effect. *People Management.* 16 July.

Reilly, P., Tamkin, P. and Broughton, A. (2007) *The changing HR function: transforming HR?* London: Chartered Institute of Personnel and Development.

Scarborough, H. (2003) Recipe for success. *People Management.* 23 January.

Scott-Jackson, W., Newham, T. and Gurney, M. (2005) *HR outsourcing: the key decisions.* Executive briefing. London: Chartered Institute of Personnel and Development.

Ulrich, D. (1997) *Human resource champions: the next agenda for adding value and delivering results.* Boston, MA:. Harvard Business School Press.

Ulrich, D., Younger, J. and Brockbank, W. (2009) The next evolution of the HR organization. In J. Storey, P. Wright and D. Ulrich (eds) *The Routledge companion to strategic human resource management.* London: Routledge.

Index

Administration
HR function, 292
Affluence
generally, 81–86
social impact, 88–92
Atkinson's model
change management, 129–131

Baby Boom generation
supply of people, 37–39
Benchmarking
evaluation of HR contribution, 304–305
Benefits
see **Reward management**
Branding
see **Employer branding**
Business partners
HR roles, 295–296

Case-based reasoning (CBR)
knowledge management, 216–217
Centres of expertise
HR roles, 294
Change management
case study, 117–118
conclusions, 133–134
consequences of change
conflict, 124–125
generally, 124
stress, 125–127
expectations, 175
flexible working
flexible firm, 129–131
generally, 127
intelligent flexibility, 132–133
mutual flexibility, 131–132
types, 128–129
HR function, 292
ineffective management, 114–117
introduction, 112–114
planning change, 118–121
politics, 121–124
types, 114
Collective bargaining arrangements
regulation, 61
Collectivism
cultural differences, 234

Competition
competitive intensity
consumerism, 26
criticisms, 25–26
generally, 16–17
globalisation, 17–19
government action, 21–25
impact, 29
technology, 19–21
financialisation, 27–29
introduction, 15
Conduct
expectations, 175
Conflict
change management, 124–125
Conjoint analysis
labour market segmentation, 154–155
Consumerism
competition, 26
ethical awareness, 103–104
Contingency models
Boston Consulting Group model, 279–280
criticisms, 282
generally, 278–279, 281–282
Miles and Snow, 281
Porter's generic strategies, 280–281
Convergence
international workforce, 231–233
Corporate social responsibility
ethics, 263–265
Cultural differences
international workforce, 233–237
Cultural diversity
international workforce, 245–247

Differentiating models
knowledge management, 210–212
Diffusion of innovation model
planning change, 120
Discretionary effort
expectations, 160
Discussion forums
knowledge management, 217
Divergence
international workforce, 231–233
Diversity
ethics, 266–269

Employee engagement
   criticisms, 193–195
   definitions, 182–184
   employee benefits, 186–188
   employer benefits, 188–190
   improvement, 191–192
   introduction, 181–182
   line management
      generally, 195–197
      golden rules, 198–200
      policies, 200
      standards, 197–198
   statistics, 190
   trends, 184–186
Employee expectations
   see **Expectations**
Employees
   see **People**
Employer branding
   communication, 149–151
   frameworks, 148–149
   generally, 147–148
Employer expectations
   see **Expectations**
Employment law
   see also **Regulation**
   ethics, 262–263
Engagement
   see **Employee engagement**
Equality
   affluence
      case study, 87
      generally, 85–86
   ethics, 266–269
Equity theory
   expectations, 166–167
Ethics
   awareness
      case study, 107
      consumerism, 103–104
      generally, 102–103
      impact on HRM, 106–107
      investment, 105
   conclusion, 265–266
   corporate social responsibility, 263–265
   employment law, 262–263
   equality and diversity, 266–269
   fair dealing, 260–261
   introduction, 252–254
   newspaper test, 261–262
   practice, 258–260

   rule of law, 261
   theory, 255–258
European Union
   regulation, 60–61
Expatriates
   failure, 241
   generally, 240–241
   preparation, 242–243
   repatriation, 244
   reward management, 243
   selection, 241–242
Expectations
   change management, 175
   change, 176–177
   conclusion, 163–164
   conduct, 175
   equity theory, 166–167
   expectancy theory, 164–166
   induction, 174
   introduction, 159–161
   job satisfaction, 161–163
   performance management, 174–175
   psychological contracts
      breaches, 169–170
      generally, 168–169
      management, 170–172
   recruitment and selection, 173–174
Expert listings
   knowledge management, 217
Explicit knowledge
   knowledge management, 215

Fair dealing
   ethics, 260–261
Female participation
   supply of people, 36–37
Femininity
   cultural differences, 235
Financialisation
   competition, 27–29
Flexible benefits
   reward management, 144–147
Flexible working
   flexible firm, 129–131
   generally, 127
   intelligent flexibility, 132–133
   mutual flexibility, 131–132
   types, 128–129
Following the market
   reward management, 139–140
Force field analysis

planning change, 119
Forums
knowledge management, 217

Globalisation
see also **International workforce**
competition, 17–19
Goal-based evaluation
evaluation of HR contribution, 307–308
Government action
competition, 21–25
Green initiatives
public policy, 75–77

Hourglass metaphor
skills, 52–53
HR function
activities
administration, 292
change, 292
performance, 291
recruitment and retention, 291
evaluation
cutting-edge approaches, 308–310
generally, 297
human capital reporting, 297–299
evaluation criteria
forward- and backward-looking criteria,
300–301
generally, 300
qualitative evaluation, 302–303
quantitative evaluation, 301–302
recruitment processes, 303–304
evaluation methods
benchmarking, 304–305
generally, 304
goal-based evaluation, 307–308
human resource auditing, 305–307
survey-based evaluation, 307
introduction, 290
outsourcing, 292–294
Ulrich's models
business partners, 295–296
centres of expertise, 294
generally, 294
shared service centres, 295, 296
value, 291
Human capital
differentiating models, 210–212
generally, 205–208
investment, 212–213

knowledge economy, 208–210
reporting, 297–299
Human resource auditing
evaluation of HR contribution, 305–307
Human resource management (general)
future agendas
case study, 13
generally, 10–12
introduction, 1–2
new HRM, 5–8
resource dependency theory, 8–10
trends, 3–5
Human resource planning
generally, 284–286
succession planning, 287
twenty-first-century HRP, 286–287

Immigration
supply of people, 39–45
Individualism
cultural differences, 234
generally, 92–96
impact on HRM, 96–98
solo living, 98–102
Induction
expectations, 174
Ineffective management
change management, 114–117
Inequality
case study, 87
ethics, 266–269
generally, 85–86
**Information and communication
technologies (ICTs)**
globalisation, 19–21
Institutional differences
international workforce, 237–239
Intellectual capital
knowledge management, 206–207
Intelligent flexibility
flexible working, 132–133
International workforce
convergence, 231–233
cultural differences, 233–237
cultural diversity, 245–247
divergence, 231–233
expatriates
failure, 241
generally, 240–241
preparation, 242–243
repatriation, 244

reward management, 243
selection, 241–242
institutional differences, 237–239
introduction, 229–230
structural issues, 247–248
Investment
ethical awareness, 105

Job satisfaction
expectations, 161–163
statistics, 190

Knowledge management
formal initiatives
case-based reasoning (CBR), 216–217
discussion forums, 217
expert listings, 217
generally, 216
knowledge repositories, 216
human capital
differentiating models, 210–212
generally, 205–208
investment, 212–213
knowledge economy, 208–210
reporting, 297–299
informal initiatives, 217–218
intellectual capital, 206–207
introduction, 203–204, 213–215
knowledge workers
generally, 222–223
management, 223–225
learning organisations, 219–222
types of knowledge, 215–216

Labour market positioning
strategic HRM, 282–284
Labour market segmentation
conjoint analysis, 154–155
generally, 152–154
Law
see also **Regulation**
ethics, 262–263
Leading the market
reward management, 137–138
Learning
see **Knowledge management**
Line management
generally, 195–197
golden rules, 198–200
policies, 200
standards, 197–198

Masculinity
cultural differences, 235
Mutual flexibility
flexible working, 131–132

New HRM
generally, 5–8
Newspaper test
ethics, 261–262

Onboarding
expectations, 174
Outsourcing
HR function, 292–294

Pay
see **Reward management**
Pension reform
public policy, 71–72
People
case study, 33–34
demand, 34–35
introduction, 32–33
shortages, 44
skills
case study, 48
demand, 45–48
hourglass metaphor, 52–53
shortages, 51–52
supply, 49–51
supply
Baby Boom generation, 37–39
case study, 39–40
female participation, 36–37
generally, 36
immigration, 39–45
Performance management
expectations, 174–175
HR function, 291
Planning change
change management, 118–121
Politics
change management, 121–124
Power distance
cultural differences, 234
Productivity
reward management, 139
Psychological contracts
breaches, 169–170
generally, 168–169
management, 170–172

Public policy
case study, 74
green initiatives, 75–77
objective, 71
pension reform, 71–72
up-skilling, 72–74
welfare to work, 74–75

Qualitative evaluation
evaluation of HR contribution, 302–303
Quantitative evaluation
evaluation of HR contribution, 301–302

Recruitment and selection
expectations, 173–174
HR function, 291
Regulation
benefits, 62
case study, 68
collective bargaining arrangements, 61
debates, 63–68
ethics, 262–263
European Union, 60–61
future developments, 68–71
history, 58–60
introduction, 57–58
motives, 62–63
public policy
case study, 74
green initiatives, 75–77
objective, 71
pension reform, 71–72
up-skilling, 72–74
welfare to work, 74–75
trade unions, 61
Repatriation
expatriates, 244
Resource dependency theory
generally, 8–10
Reward management
case study, 144
employer branding
communication, 149–151
frameworks, 148–149
generally, 147–148
expatriates, 243
flexible benefits, 144–147
following the market, 139–140
introduction, 136–137
labour market segmentation
conjoint analysis, 154–155

generally, 152–154
leading the market, 137–138
productivity, 139
total reward, 140–143
Rule of law
ethics, 261

Shared service centres
HR roles, 295, 296
Skills
case study, 48
demand, 45–48
hourglass metaphor, 52–53
introduction, 32–33
shortages, 51–52
supply, 49–51
Social trends
affluence
generally, 81–86
social impact, 88–92
ethical awareness
case study, 107
consumerism, 103–104
generally, 102–103
impact on HRM, 106–107
investment, 105
individualism
generally, 92–96
impact on HRM, 96–98
solo living, 98–102
inequality
case study, 87
generally, 85–86
introduction, 79
Socially responsible investment
ethical awareness, 105
Solo living
social trends, 98–102
Staff
see **People**
Strategic HRM
approaches
environmental scanning, 276
generally, 274
labour market focus, 276–277
military-type approach, 274–275
resource-based approach, 277–278
strategic alignment, 275–276
contingency models
Boston Consulting Group model,
279–280

criticisms, 282
generally, 278–279, 281–282
Miles and Snow, 281
Porter's generic strategies, 280–281
human resource planning
generally, 284–286
succession planning, 287
twenty-first-century HRP, 286–287
introduction, 273–274
labour market positioning, 282–284
Stress
change management, 125–127
Succession planning
strategic HRM, 287
Survey-based evaluation
evaluation of HR contribution, 307

Tacit knowledge
knowledge management, 215–216
Technology
competition, 19–21
Total reward

reward management, 140–143
Trade unions
regulation, 61

Ulrich's models
business partners, 295–296
centres of expertise, 294
generally, 294
shared service centres, 295, 296
Uncertainty avoidance
cultural differences, 235
Up-skilling
public policy, 72–74

Welfare to work
public policy, 74–75
Women
supply of people, 36–37
Work satisfaction
expectations, 161–163
statistics, 190

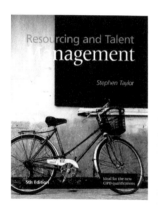

Also from CIPD Publishing...

Critical Issues in Human Resource Management

Edited by Ian Roper, Rea Prouska and Uracha Chatrakul Na Ayudhya

This is a substantial and authoritative multi-author textbook for HRM modules that take a critical approach. It problematises core HRM topics, encouraging sophisticated thinking about HR interventions.

The textbook:
- draws out the importance of state/corporate governance of the workplace and the politics of workplace relations
- integrates students' prior understanding of the key operational aspects of HRM with the wider institutional and social contexts in which they occur
- expands students' knowledge of HR-related theory with wider social and business theory, enabling them to apply critical approaches to HR problems.

'The depth and breadth of this book is unparalleled. It is unique in its coverage of global topics and new and emerging fields such as ICT and the future of work organisations. The text is critical and research-based but written in an accessible and engaging way.'
Celia Stanworth, Senior Lecturer, University of Greenwich Business School.

Order your copy now online at cipd.co.uk/bookstore or call us on 0844 800 3366

- **Ian Roper** is Principal Lecturer in Employment Relations and Director of Programmes for HRM at Middlesex University Business School.
- **Rea Prouska** is a Senior Lecturer in Human Resource Management and programme leader for the BA Human Resource Management degree at Middlesex University Business School.
- **Uracha Chatrakul Na Ayudhya** is a Lecturer in Human Resource Management at Middlesex University Business School.

| Published Nov 2010 | ISBN: 978 1 84398 242 5 | Paperback | 470 pages |

The Chartered Institute of Personnel and Development is the leading publisher of books and reports for HR and L&D professionals, students and all those concerned with the effective management and development of people at work.